Student Solutions Manual

for

Statistics for Management and Economics

EIGHTH EDITION

Prepared by

Gerald Keller

Wilfrid Laurier University

SOUTH-WESTERN
CENGAGE Learning

Australia • Brazil • Japan • Korea • Mexico • Singapore • Spain • United Kingdom • United States

SOUTH-WESTERN
CENGAGE Learning™

Statistics For Management and Economics, 8e
Gerald Keller

VP/Editorial Director: Jack W. Calhoun

VP/Editor-in-Chief: Alex von Rosenberg

Acquisitions Editor: Charles McCormick,

Jr. Developmental Editor: Elizabeth Lowry

Editorial Assistant: Bryn Lathrop

Sr. Marketing Communications Manager:

Larry Qualls

Marketing Communications Manager:

Libby Shipp

Senior Marketing Coordinator:

Angela Glassmeyer

Content Project Manager:

Jacquelyn K Featherly

Technology Project Manager: John Rich

Senior Manufacturing Coordinator:

Diane Gibbons

Production House/Compositor:

ICC McMillan

Printer: RR Donnelley

Willard Manufacturing Division

Art Director: Stacy Jenkins Shirley

Cover/Internal Designer: Ke Design,

Mason OH

Cover Image: Getty Images

Photography Manager: Deanna Ettinger

Photo Researcher: Terri Miller

For product information and technology assistance, contact us at
Cengage Learning Academic Resource Center, 1-800-423-0563

For permission to use material from this text or product,
submit all requests online at **www.cengage.com/permissions**
Further permissions questions can be emailed to
permissionrequest@cengage.com

ExamView® and ExamView Pro® are registered trademarks of FSCreations, Inc. Windows is a registered trademark of the Microsoft Corporation used herein under license. Macintosh and Power Macintosh are registered trademarks of Apple Computer, Inc. used herein under license.

© 2009 Cengage Learning. All Rights Reserved.

Cengage Learning WebTutor™ is a trademark of Cengage Learning.

Student Edition Package 13: 978-0-324-56949-0

Student Edition Package 10: 0-324-56949-1

Student Edition ISBN 13: 978-0-324-56953-7

Student Edition ISBN 10: 0-324-56953-X

Instructor's Edition Package ISBN 13: 978-0-324-56959-9

Instructor's Edition Package ISBN 10: 0-324-56959-9

Instructor's Edition ISBN 13: 978-0-324-56958-2

Instructor's Edition ISBN 10: 0-324-56958-0

South-Western Cengage Learning
5191 Natorp Boulevard
Mason, OH 45040
USA

Cengage Learning products are represented in Canada by

Nelson Education, Ltd.

For your course and learning solutions, visit **academic.cengage.com**

Purchase any of our products at your local college store or at our preferred online store **www.ichapters.com**

Printed in Canada
1 2 3 4 5 6 7 11 10 09 08 07

TABLE OF CONTENTS

How the Solutions Were Produced

All answers have been-double-checked for accuracy. However, we cannot be absolutely certain that there are no errors. When and if we discover mistakes we will post corrected answers on our web page. (See page 8 in the textbook for the address.) If you find any errors, please email the author (address on web page). We will be happy to acknowledge you with the discovery.

Chapter 2

Excel was employed to draw the histograms, bar charts, pie charts, line charts, and scatter diagrams.

Chapter 4

Excel was used to draw box plots and compute the descriptive statistics for exercises with data sets.

Chapters 6 through 9

Probabilities were computed manually. Probability trees were used where possible.

Chapters 10 through 19 and 21

Calculations for exercises that provided statistics either in the exercise itself or in Appendix A were completed manually. The solutions to exercises requiring the use of a computer were produced using Excel. Confidence interval estimates used critical values obtained from the tables in Appendix B. In some cases we were required to use approximations. As a consequence some confidence interval estimates will differ slightly from those produced by computer. In tests of hypothesis where the sampling distribution is normal, p-values were computed manually using Table 3. Excel was employed to calculate the p-value for all other tests.

Chapters 13, and Appendixes 13 to 17, and 19

We employed the F-test of two variances at the 5% significance level to decide which one of the equal-variances or unequal-variances t-test and estimator of the difference between two means to use to solve the problem. Additionally, for exercises that compare two populations and are accompanied by data files, our answers were derived by defining the sample from population 1 as the data stored in the first column (often column A in Excel

1

and column 1 in Minitab). The data stored in the second column represent the sample from population 2. Paired differences were defined as the difference between the variable in the first column minus the variable in the second column.

Chapter 19 and Appendix 19

In the exercises whose datasets contained interval data we used a nonparametric technique after examining the relevant histograms and subjectively judging the variable to be "extremely nonnormal."

Chapters 17 and 18

Excel produced all the solutions to these exercises.

Chapter 20

Most solutions were produced manually. Excel solved the more time-consuming exercises.

Chapter 21

All control charts were produced by Excel.

Chapter 22

Solutions to these exercises were completed manually.

Chapter 1

1.2   Descriptive statistics summarizes a set of data. Inferential statistics makes inferences about populations from samples.

1.4   a.   The complete production run

            b.   1000 chips

            c.   Proportion of the production run that is defective

            d.   Proportion of sample chips that are defective (7.5%)

            e.   Parameter

            f.   Statistic

            g.   Because the sample proportion is less than 10%, we can conclude that the claim is true.

1.6   a.   Flip the coin 100 times and count the number of heads and tails

            b.   Outcomes of flips

            c.   Outcomes of the 100 flips

            d.   Proportion of heads

            e.   Proportion of heads in the 100 flips

1.8   a.   The population consists of the fuel mileage of all the taxis in the fleet.

            b.   The owner would like to know the mean mileage.

            c.   The sample consists of the 50 observations.

            d.   The statistic the owner would use is the mean of the 50 observations.

            e.   The statistic would be used to estimate the parameter from which the owner can calculate total costs.

We computed the sample mean to be 19.8 mpg.

Chapter 2

2.2   a.   Interval

           b.   Interval

           c.   Nominal

           d.   Ordinal

2.4   a.   Nominal

           b.   Interval

           c.   Nominal

           d.   Interval

           e.   Ordinal

2.6   a.   Interval

           b.   Interval

           c.   Nominal

           d.   Ordinal

           e.   Interval

2.8   a.   Interval

           b.   Ordinal

           c.   Nominal

           d.   Ordinal

2.10   a.   Ordinal

           b.   Ordinal

           c.   Ordinal

2.12

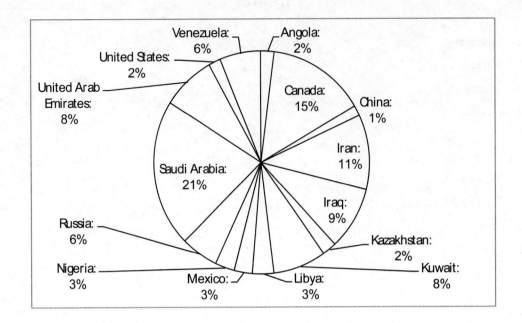

2.14

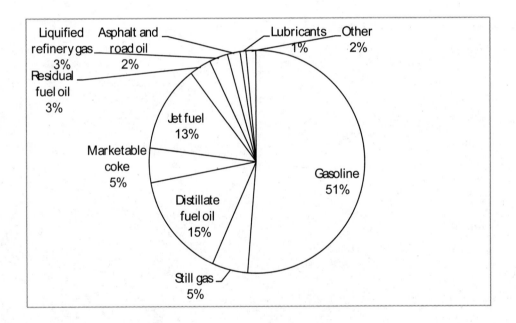

2.16

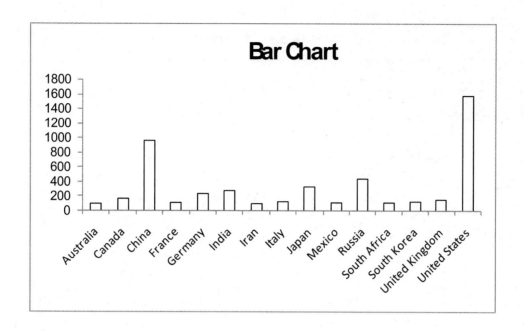

2.18

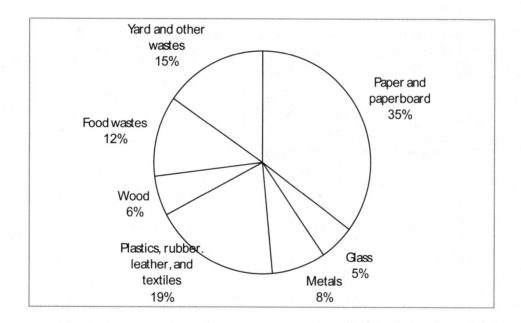

2.20   a.

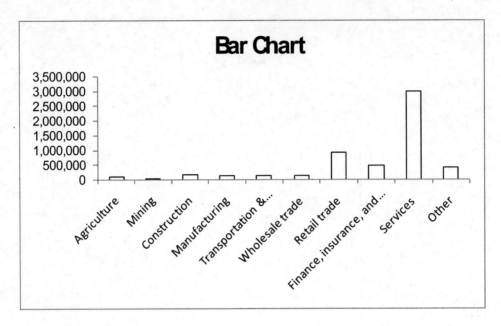

b.

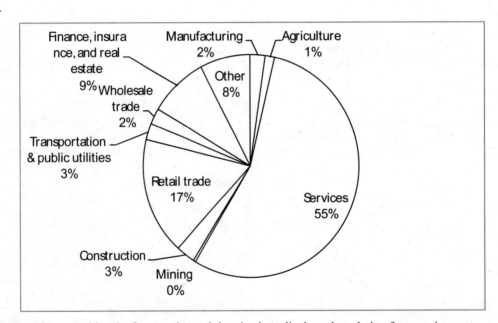

The bar chart provides the frequencies and the pie chart displays the relative frequencies.

2.22

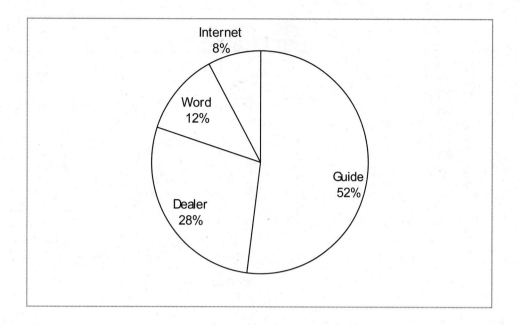

2.24 a.

Newspaper	Frequency	Relative Frequency
Daily News	141	.39
Post	128	.36
Times	32	.09
WSJ	59	.16

b.

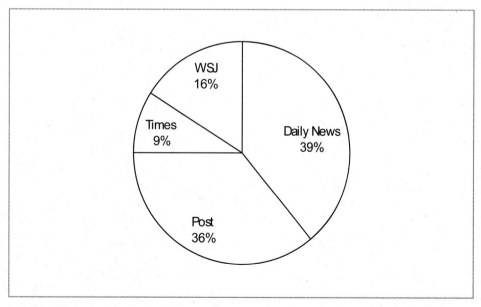

The Daily News and the Post dominate the market

2.26

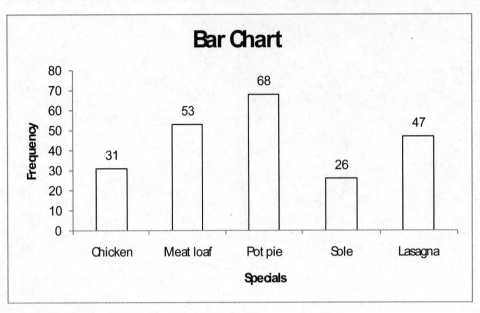

The two most popular specials are turkey pot pie and meat loaf.

2.28   a.

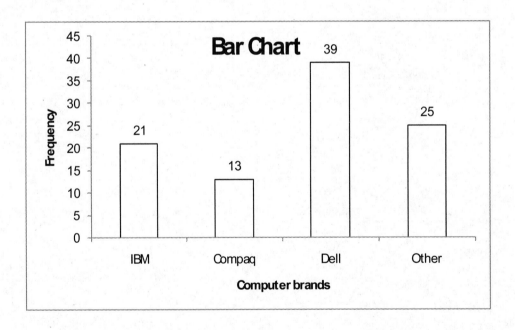

b.

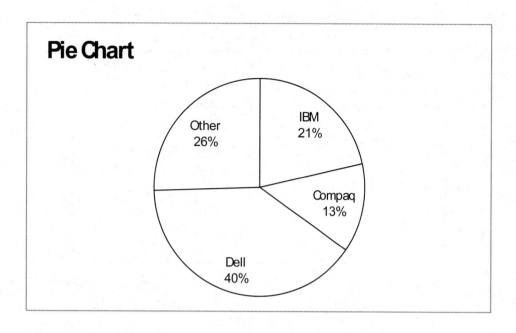

Pie Chart

Other 26%

IBM 21%

Compaq 13%

Dell 40%

c.   Dell is most popular with 40% proportion, followed by other, 26%, IBM, 21% and Compaq, 13%.

2.30

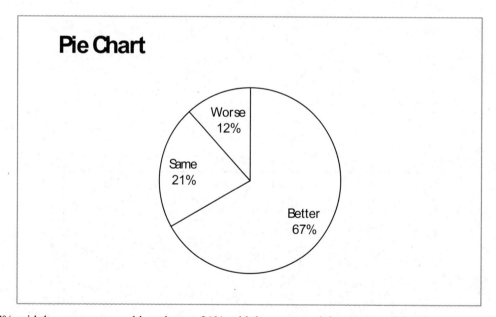

Pie Chart

Worse 12%

Same 21%

Better 67%

67% said the economy would get better, 21% said the same, and the rest stated that the economy would worsen.

2.32   10 or 11

2.34   a.   7 to 9

        b.   Interval width $\approx \dfrac{6.1 - 5.2}{7} = .13$ (rounded to .15); upper limits: 5.25, 5.40, 5.55, 5.70, 5.85, 6.00, 6.15

2.36   a.

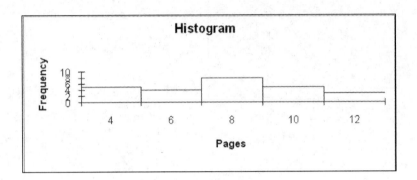

        b.

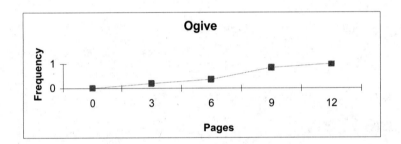

        c.   The number of pages is bimodal and slightly positively skewed.

2.38

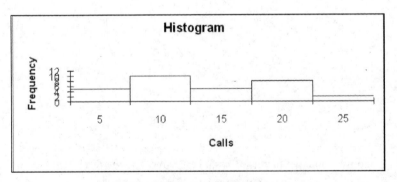

        The histogram is bimodal.

2.40   a.

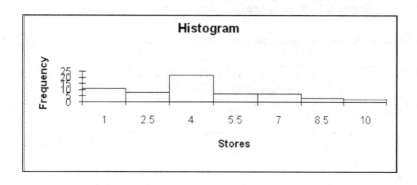

   b.

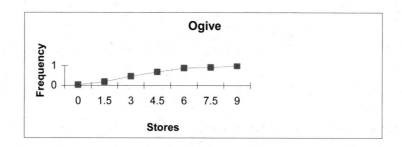

   c.   The number of stores is bimodal and positively skewed.

2.42   a.

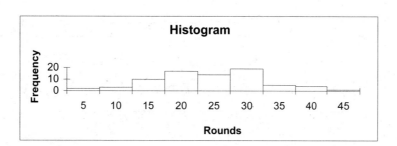

b.

Stem & Leaf Display				
Stems	Leaves			
0	->359			
1	->00233344455566677888888899			
2	->0000122333444445556666788888999		
3	->00000112556668			
4	->2			

c.

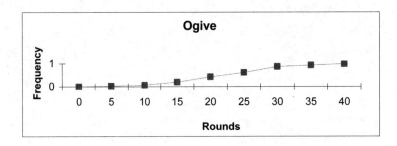

d.   The histogram is symmetric (approximately) and bimodal.

2.44   a.

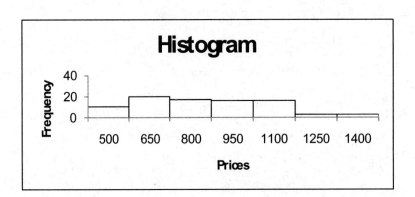

14

b.

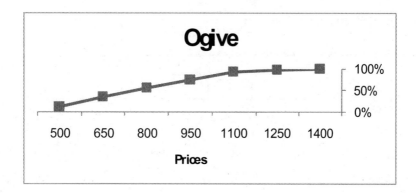

c.

	A	B	C
1	**Stem & Leaf Display**		
2			
3	**Stems**	**Leaves**	
4	4	->2445677789	
5	5	->0122224668899	
6	6	->0001244555667	
7	7	->00022237889	
8	8	->01333445667	
9	9	->012246667788	
10	10	->00233788	
11	11	->015	
12	12	->18	
13	13	->23	

d. The histogram is slightly positively skewed, unimodal, and not bell-shaped.

2.46 a. The histogram should contain 9 or 10 bins. We chose 10.

b.

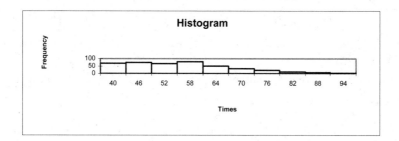

c. The histogram is positively skewed.

d. The histogram is not bell-shaped.

2.48

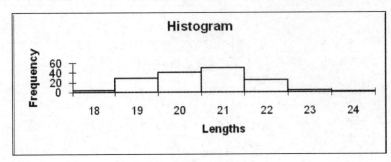

The histogram is unimodal, bell-shaped and roughly symmetric. Most of the heights lie between 18 and 23 inches.

2.50

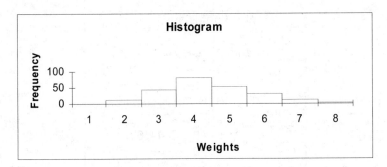

The histogram is unimodal, symmetric and bell-shaped. Most tomatoes weigh between 2 and 7 ounces with a small fraction weighing less than 2 ounces or more than 7 ounces.

2.52

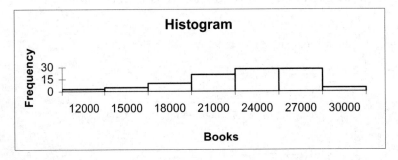

The histogram of the number of books shipped daily is negatively skewed. It appears that there is a maximum number that the company can ship.

2.54   a.

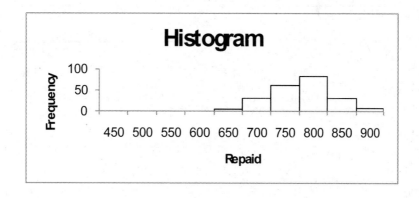

b.

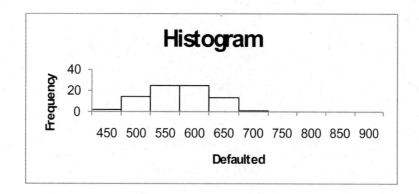

c.   and d. This scorecard is a much better predictor.

2.56

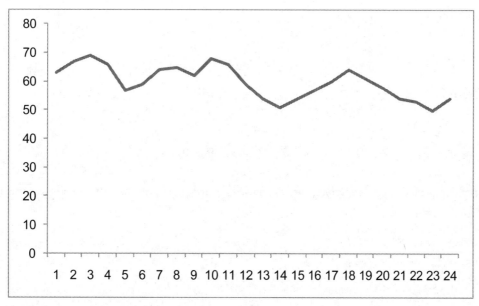

There appears to be a small downward trend.

2.58

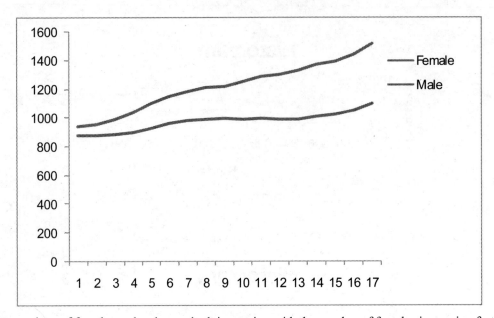

The numbers of females and males are both increasing with the number of females increasing faster.

2.60

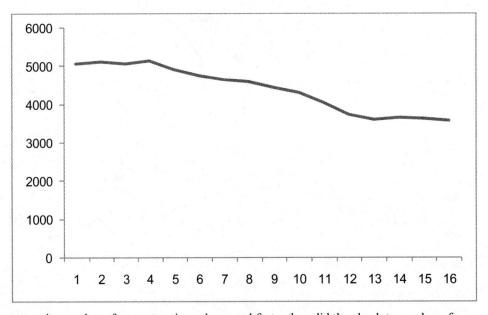

The per capita number of property crimes decreased faster than did the absolute number of property crimes.

2.62

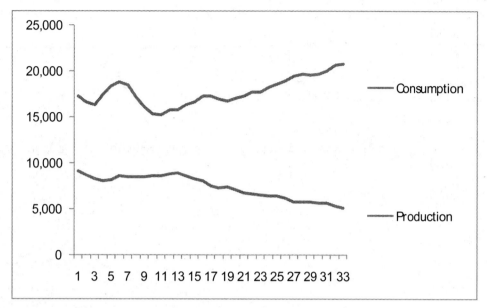

Consumption is increasing and production is falling.

2.64   a.

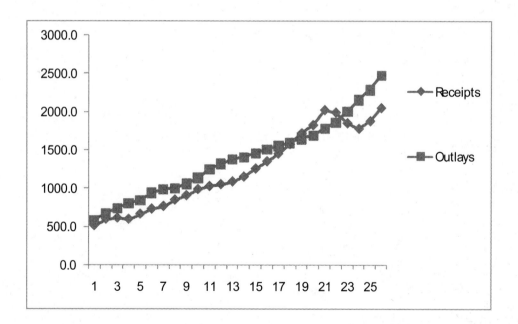

19

b.

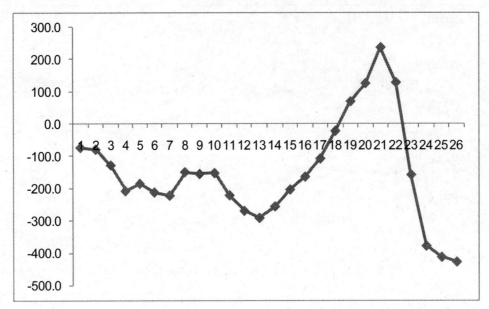

c. Over the last 25 years both receipts and outlays increased rapidly. There was a five-year period where receipts were higher than outlays

2.66

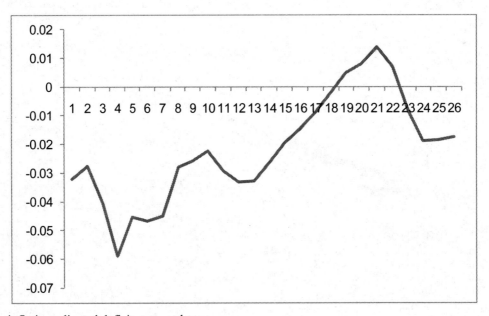

The inflation adjusted deficits are not large.

2.68   Exports to Canada

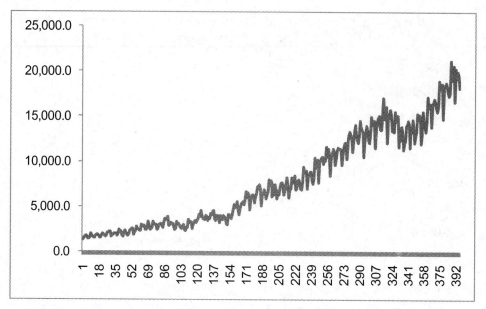

Imports from Canada

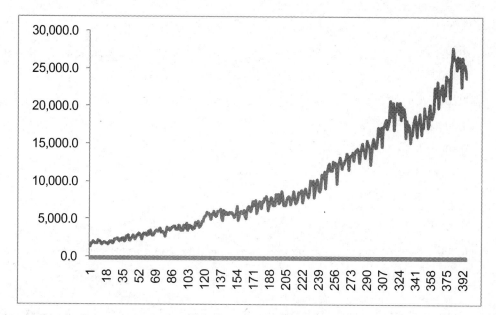

Balance of trade: Exports to Canada – Imports from Canada

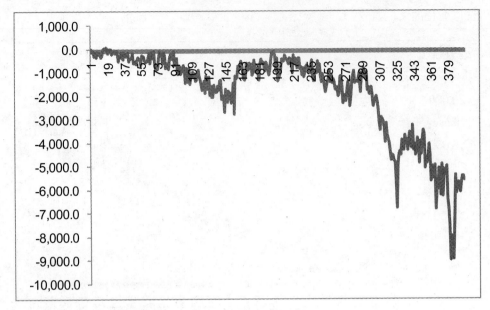

Imports from Canada has greatly exceeded exports to Canada.

2.70

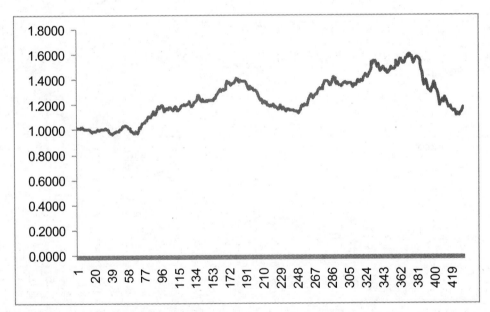

In the early seventies the Canadian dollar was worth more than the U.S. dollar. By the late seventies the Canadian lost ground but has recently recovered.

2.72

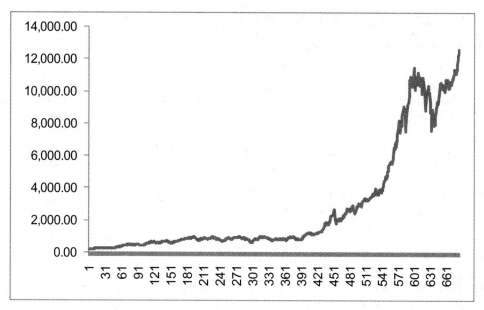

The index grew slowly until month 400 and then grew quickly until month 600. It then fell sharply and recently recovered.

2.74

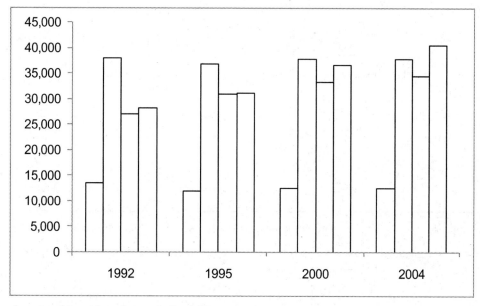

The educational level has changed since 1992.

2.76

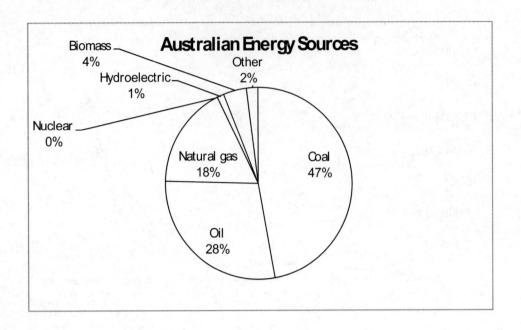

Australian Energy Sources

Biomass 4%
Other 2%
Hydroelectric 1%
Nuclear 0%
Natural gas 18%
Coal 47%
Oil 28%

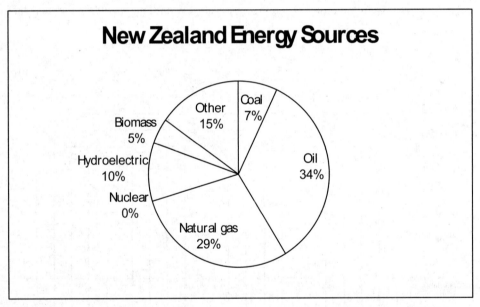

New Zealand Energy Sources

Other 15%
Coal 7%
Biomass 5%
Hydroelectric 10%
Oil 34%
Nuclear 0%
Natural gas 29%

There appears to be differences between female and male students in their choice of light beer.

2.78

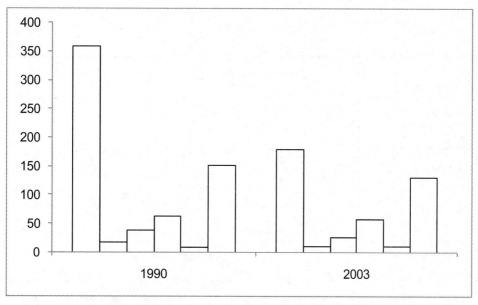

The distribution of crimes has not changed.

2.80

	A	B	C	D	E	F
2						
3	Count of Owner	Last				
4	Second-last	1	2	3	4	Grand Total
5	1	39	36	51	23	149
6	2	36	32	46	20	134
7	3	54	46	65	29	194
8	4	24	20	28	10	82
9	Grand Total	153	134	190	82	559

	A	B	C	D	E	F
2						
3	Count of Owner	Last				
4	Second-last	1	2	3	4	Grand Total
5	1	0.25	0.27	0.27	0.28	0.27
6	2	0.24	0.24	0.24	0.24	0.24
7	3	0.35	0.34	0.34	0.35	0.35
8	4	0.16	0.15	0.15	0.12	0.15
9	Grand Total	1.00	1.00	1.00	1.00	1.00

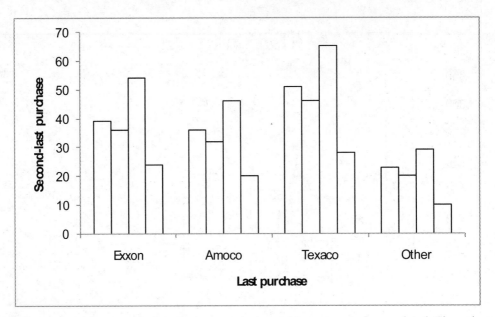

The column proportions are similar; the two nominal variables appear to be unrelated. There does not appear to be any brand loyalty.

2.82

	A	B	C
1		Men	Women
2	Lost job	364	257
3	Left job	64	68
4	Reentrant	149	216
5	New entrant	49	55

	A	B	C
1		Men	Women
2	Lost job	0.581	0.431
3	Left job	0.102	0.114
4	Reentrant	0.238	0.362
5	New entrant	0.078	0.092

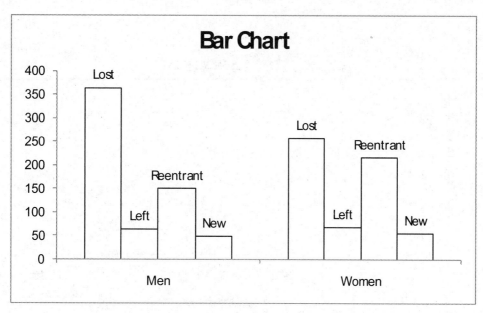

Bar Chart

The row proportions are different but the patterns are similar. There are some differences between men and women in terms of the reason for unemployment.

2.84

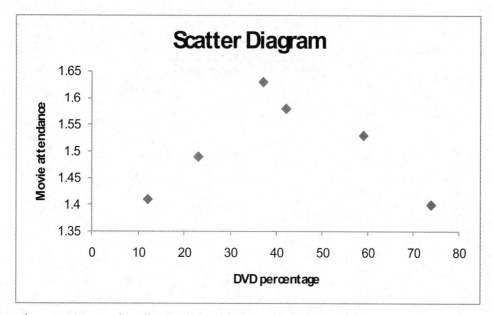

Scatter Diagram

There does not appear to be a linear relationship between the two variables.

2.86   a.

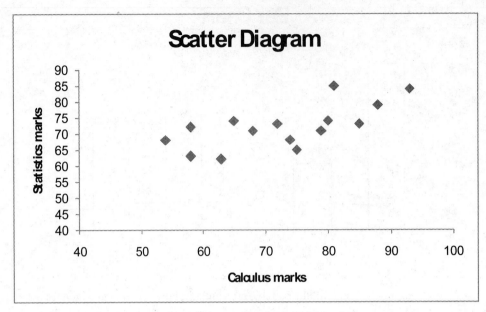

b.   There is a positive linear relationship between calculus and statistics marks.

2.88   a.

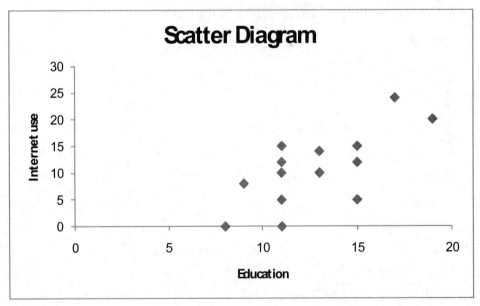

b.   There is a moderately strong positive linear relationship. In general those with more education use the Internet more frequently.

2.90   a.

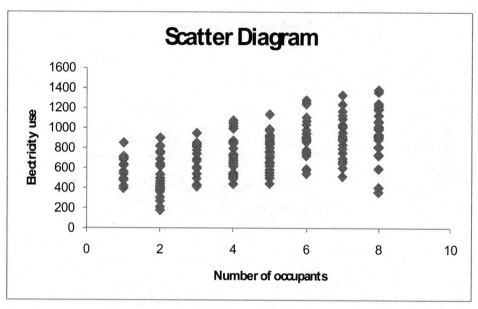

b.   There is a moderately strong positive linear relationship.

2.92   a.

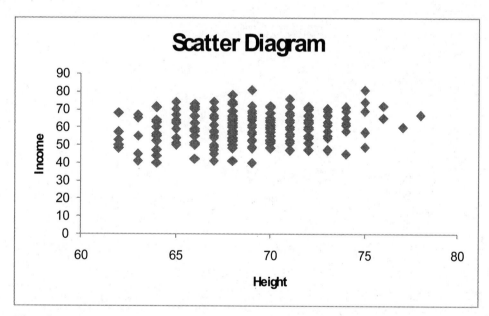

b.   There is a very weak positive linear relationship.

2.94

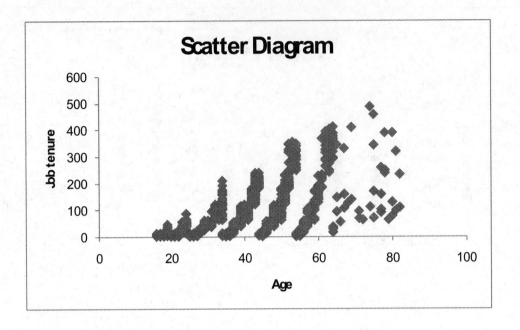

There is a moderately strong positive linear relationship.

2.96

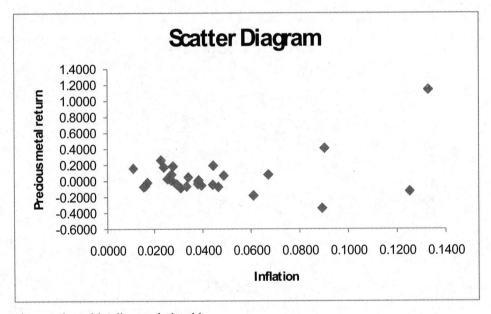

There is a weak positive linear relationship.

2.98

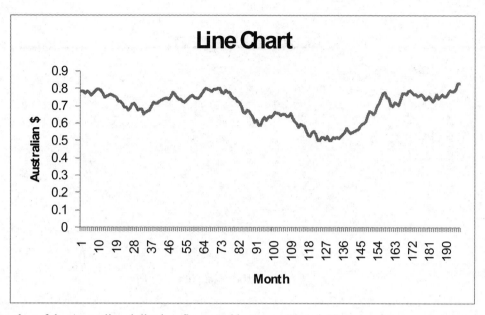

The value of the Australian dollar has fluctuated between .50 and .80.

2.100

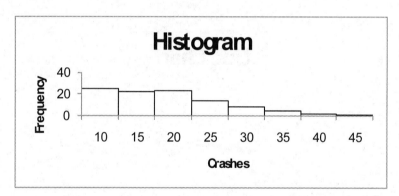

The histogram of the number of crashes is positively skewed.

2.102

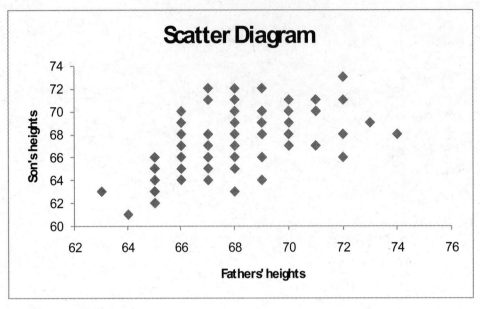

b.   The slope is positive

c.   There is a moderately strong linear relationship.

2.104

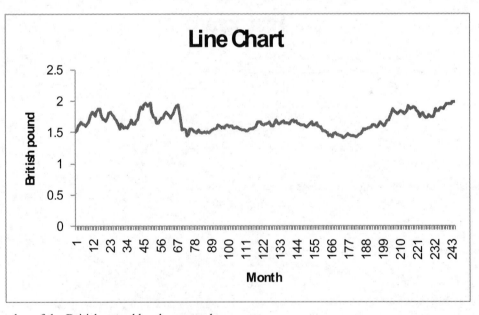

The value of the British pound has been steady.

2.106

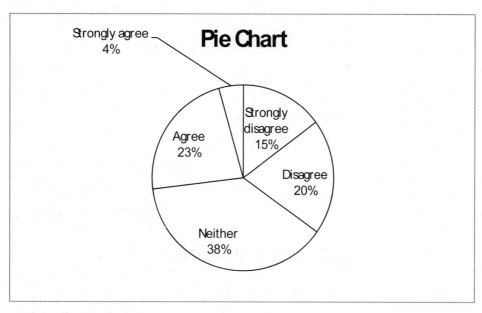

More students disagree than agree.

2.108

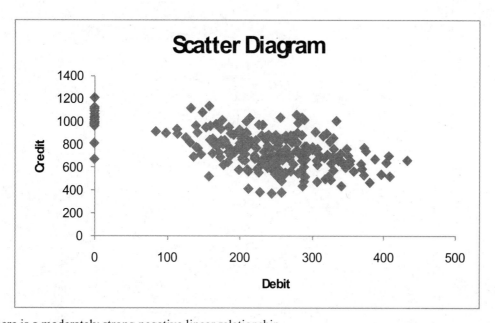

There is a moderately strong negative linear relationship.

2.110

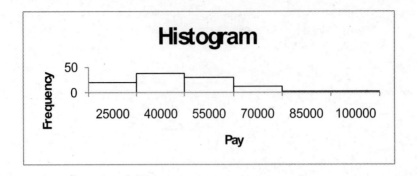

2.112

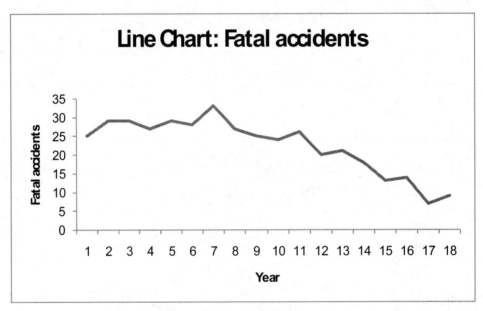

The number of fatal accidents and the number of deaths have been decreasing.

2.114

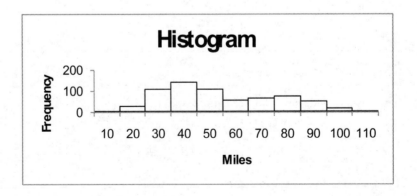

2.116   Business Statistics course (Example 2.6)

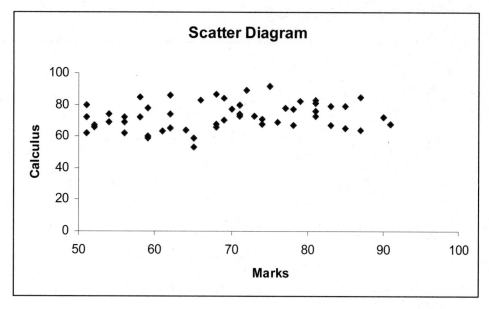

Mathematical Statistics course (Example 2.7)

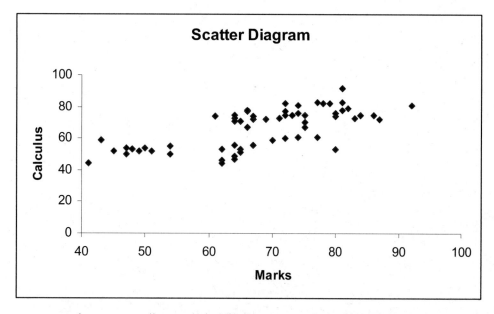

There appears to be a stronger linear relationship between marks in the mathematical statistics course and calculus than the relationship between the marks in the business statistics course and the marks in calculus.

Chapter 3

3.2.1   We can draw a bar chart showing number of returns and the average paid by taxpayers for each of the five taxable income categories for all five years.

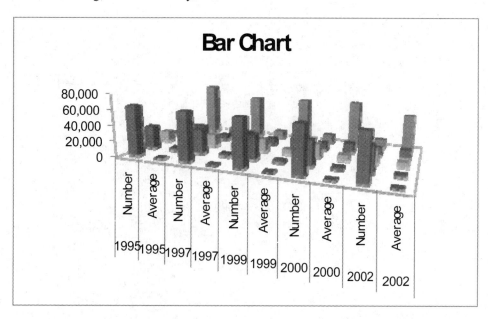

However the problem of the difficulty of interpretation remains. Here is another way of representing the numbers. The table below converts the number of taxpayers in each category to the proportion of the total number of taxpayers. It also converts the average tax in each category to the proportion of the total amount of income tax.

	A	B	C	D	E	F	G	H	I	J	K
1		1995	1995	1997	1997	1999	1999	2000	2000	2002	2002
2	Taxable Inc	Prop	Prop	Prop	Prop	Prop	Prop	Prop	Prop	Prop	Prop
3	< 25,000	0.546	0.067	0.513	0.064	0.483	0.044	0.468	0.048	0.457	0.046
4	25,000-49,999	0.248	0.148	0.252	0.146	0.248	0.114	0.250	0.107	0.255	0.112
5	50,000-74,999	0.116	0.157	0.124	0.148	0.132	0.128	0.132	0.116	0.134	0.125
6	75,000-00,000	0.045	0.120	0.053	0.107	0.061	0.104	0.066	0.099	0.071	0.113
7	Over 100,000	0.045	0.508	0.059	0.534	0.075	0.611	0.084	0.630	0.083	0.603

The graph that follows depicts these numbers.

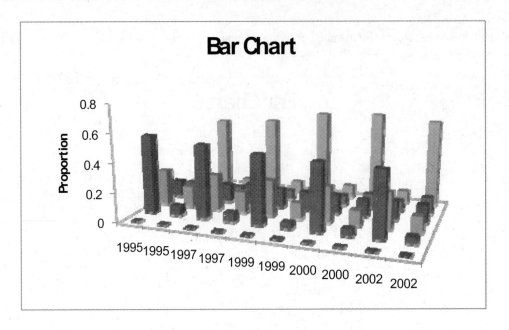

3.4   Region: Sales last year

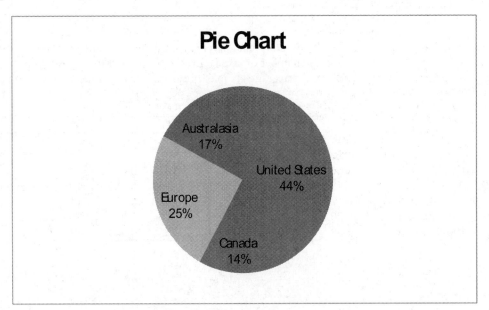

Region: Sales previous year

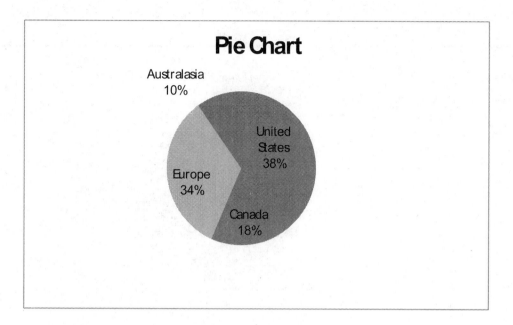

The pie charts were drawn so that the area in each pie is proportion to the total sales in each year. For example to draw the first pie chart we solved for the radius as follows.
$\Pi r^2 = 152.3$
Solving for r we find
 r = 6.96

For the second pie chart we find r = 5.78.
We draw the pie charts for the divisions in each year in the same way.

Division: Sales last year

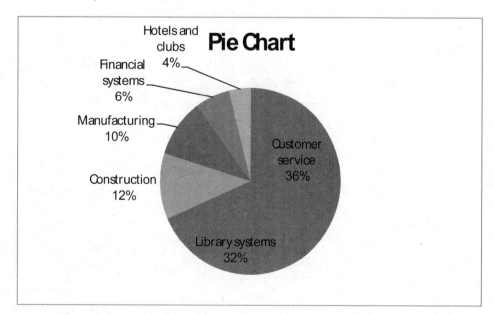

Division: Sales previous year

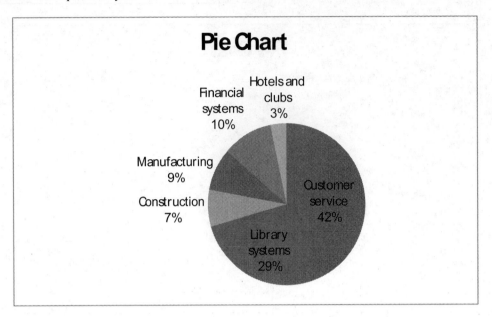

3.6.1 We divided the number of crimes by the population and multiplied by 1,000. The result is the number of crimes per thousand of population.

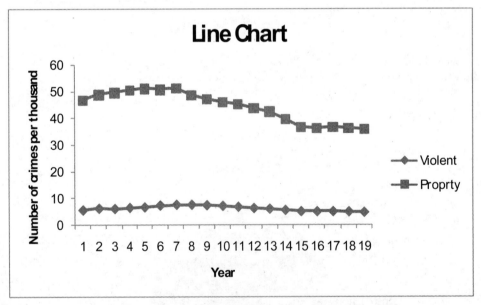

We can see that there has been a decrease in the number of crimes per thousand of population
Another possible chart is a scatter diagram of the number of crimes and population.

Violent crimes

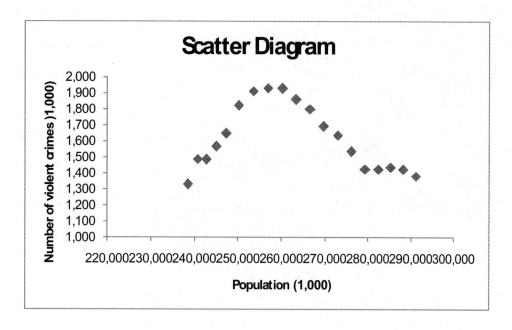

Property crimes

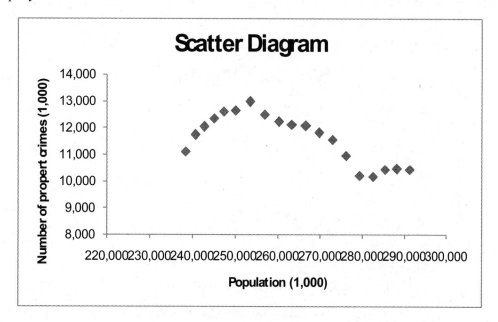

The unusual shapes of the scatter diagram are difficult to explain. Both charts are quadratic rather than linear. They suggest that when the population was less than 255 million the population and the number of crimes were positively linear related, whereas when the population was more than 255 million the relationship was negative.

3.8

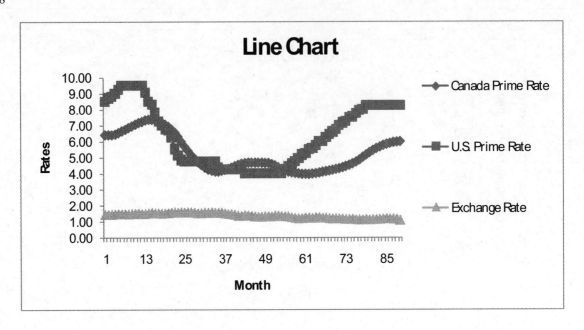

There does not appear to be a relationship between the exchange rate and either prime rate. The scatter diagram below was created by computing the difference between prime rates (Canadian prime rate minus American prime rate).

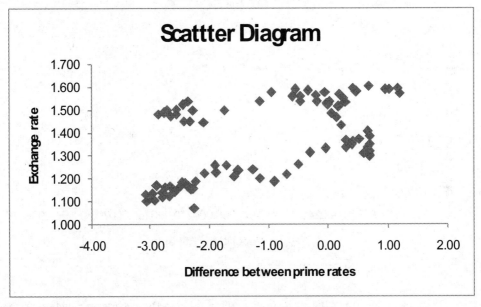

There is a weak positive linear relationship between the two variables.

3.10

	A	B	C
1	Age group	Injury rate (per 100 accidents)	Fatal injury rate (per accident)
2	20 or less	0.0042	0.0041
3	21-24	0.0042	0.0048
4	25-34	0.0040	0.0041
5	35-44	0.0040	0.0051
6	45-54	0.0041	0.0048
7	55-64	0.0041	0.0052
8	65-74	0.0042	0.0070
9	75-84	0.0044	0.0120
10	85 or more	0.0044	0.0236

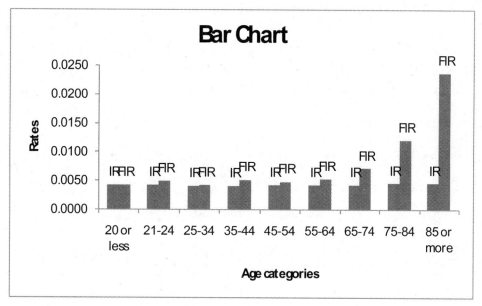

c. Older drivers who are in accidents are more likely to be killed or injured.

d. Exercise 3.9 addressed the issue of accident rates, whereas in this exercise we consider the severity of the accidents.

3.12   a.

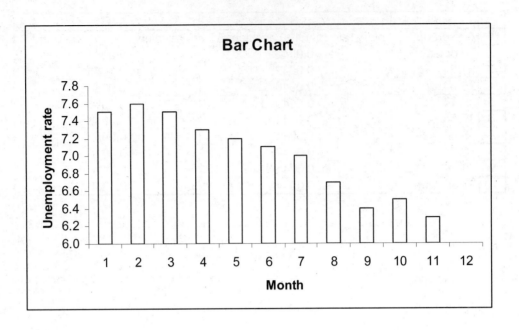

b.

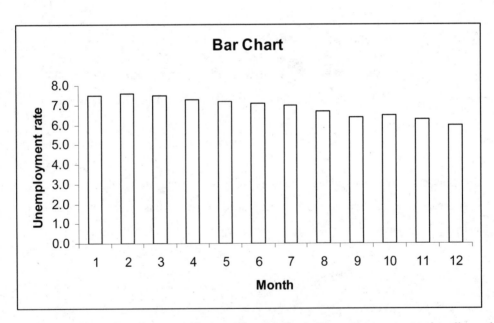

c.   Caption a: Unemployment rate falling rapidly. Caption b: Unemployment rate virtually unchanged.

d.   The chart in a is more honest.

3.14   a.

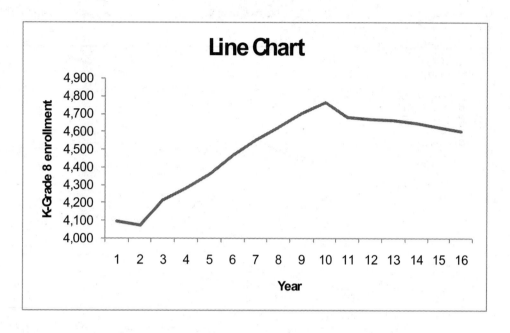

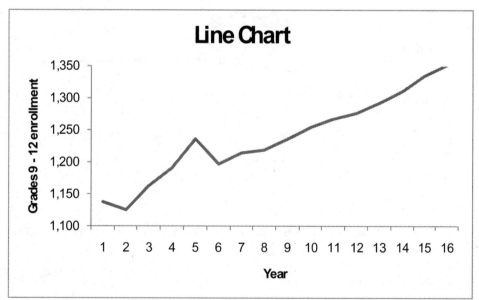

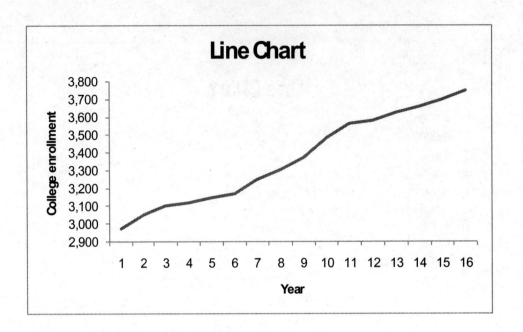

b.

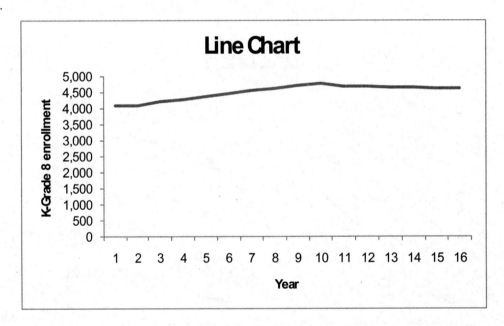

46

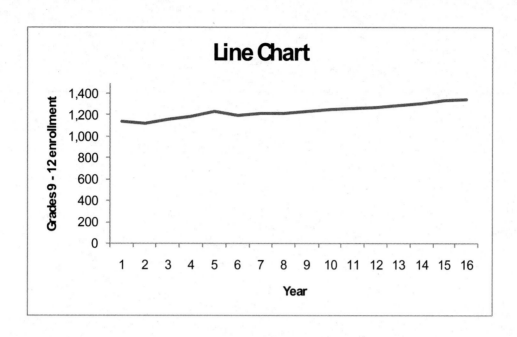

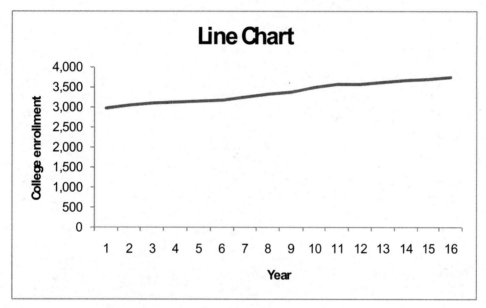

Chapter 4

4.2 $\bar{x} = \dfrac{\sum x_i}{n} = \dfrac{5+7+0+3+15+6+5+9+3+8+10+5+2+0+12}{15} = \dfrac{90}{15} = 6.0$

Ordered data: 0, 0, 2, 3, 3, 5, 5, 5, 6, 7, 8, 9, 10, 12, 15; Median = 5

Mode = 5

4.4   a. $\bar{x} = \dfrac{\sum x_i}{n} = \dfrac{33+29+45+60+42+19+52+38+36}{9} = \dfrac{354}{9} = 39.3$

       Ordered data: 19, 29, 33, 36, 38, 42, 45, 52, 60; Median = 38

       Mode: all

   b.   The mean amount of time is 39.3 minutes. Half the group took less than 38 minutes.

4.6 $R_g = \sqrt[3]{(1+R_1)(1+R_2)(1+R_3)} - 1 = \sqrt[3]{(1+.25)(1-.10)(1+.50)} - 1 = .19$

4.8   a. $\bar{x} = \dfrac{\sum x_i}{n} = \dfrac{.10+.22+.06-.05+.20}{5} = \dfrac{.53}{5} = .106$

       Ordered data: −.05, .06, .10, .20, .22; Median = .10

   b. $R_g = \sqrt[5]{(1+R_1)(1+R_2)(1+R_3)(1+R_4)(1+R_5)} - 1 = \sqrt[5]{(1+.10)(1+.22)(1+.06)(1-.05)(1+.20)} - 1 =$

       .102

   c.   The geometric mean is best.

4.10   a.   Year 1 rate of return = $\dfrac{1200-1000}{1000} = .20$

       Year 2 rate of return = $\dfrac{1200-1200}{1200} = 0$

       Year 3 rate of return = $\dfrac{1500-1200}{1200} = .25$

       Year 4 rate of return = $\dfrac{2000-1500}{1500} = .33$

   b. $\bar{x} = \dfrac{\sum x_i}{n} = \dfrac{.20+0+.25+.33}{4} = \dfrac{.78}{4} = .195$

       Ordered data: 0, .20, .25, .33; Median = .225

   c. $R_g = \sqrt[4]{(1+R_1)(1+R_2)(1+R_3)(1+R_4)} - 1 = \sqrt[4]{(1+.20)(1+0)(1+.25)(1+.33)} - 1 = .188$

   d.   The geometric mean is best because $1000(1.188)^4 = 2000$.

4.12　a.　$\bar{x} = 24{,}329$; median = 24,461

　　　b.　The mean starting salary is \$24,329. Half the sample earned less than \$24,461.

4.14　a.　$\bar{x} = 128.07$; median = 136.00

　　　b.　The mean expenditure is \$128.07 and half the sample spent less than \$136.00.

4.16　a.　$\bar{x} = 30.53$; median = 31

　　　b.　The mean training time is 30.53. Half the sample trained for less than 31 hours.

4.18　a.　$\bar{x} = 519.20$; median = 523.00

　　　b.　The mean expenditure is \$519.20. Half the sample spent less than \$523.00

4.20
$$\bar{x} = \frac{\sum x_i}{n} = \frac{4+5+3+6+5+6+5+6}{8} = \frac{40}{8} = 5$$

$$s^2 = \frac{\sum (x_i - \bar{x})^2}{n-1} = \frac{[(4-5)^2 + (5-5)^2 + ... + (6-5)^2]}{8-1} = \frac{8}{7} = 1.14$$

4.22
$$\bar{x} = \frac{\sum x_i}{n} = \frac{0+(-5)+(-3)+6+4+(-4)+1+(-5)+0+3}{10} = \frac{-3}{10} = -.30$$

$$s^2 = \frac{\sum (x_i - \bar{x})^2}{n-1} = \frac{[(0-(-.3))^2 + ((-5)-(-.3))^2 + ... + (3-(-.3))^2]}{10-1} = \frac{136.1}{9} = 15.12$$

$$s = \sqrt{s^2} = \sqrt{15.12} = 3.89$$

4.24　a:　$s^2 = 51.5$

　　　b:　$s^2 = 6.5$

　　　c:　$s^2 = 174.5$

4.26　6, 6, 6, 6, 6

4.28　a.　From the empirical rule we know that approximately 68% of the observations fall between 46 and 54. Thus 16% are less than 46 (the other 16% are above 54).

　　　b.　Approximately 95% of the observations are between 42 and 58. Thus, only 2.5% are above 58 and all the rest, 97.5% are below 58.

　　　c.　See (a) above; 16% are above 54.

4.30   a.   Nothing

       b.   At least 75% lie between 60 and 180.

       c.   At least 88.9% lie between 30 and 210.

4.32 $s^2 = 40.73$ mph^2 and $s = 6.38$ mph; at least 75% of the speeds lie within 12.76 mph of the mean; at least 88.9% of the speeds lie within 19.14 mph of the mean

4.34 $s^2 = .0858$ cm^2, and $s = .2929$cm; at least 75% of the lengths lie within .5858 of the mean; at least 88.9% of the rods will lie within .8787 cm of the mean.

4.36   a. $s = 15.01$

       b.   In approximately 68% of the days the number of arrivals falls within 15.01 of the mean; in approximately 95% of the hours the number of arrivals falls within 30.02 of the mean; in approximately 99.7% of the hours the number of arrivals falls within 45.03 of the mean

4.38   30th percentile: $L_{30} = (10+1)\dfrac{30}{100} = (11)(.30) = 3.3$; the 30th percentile is 22.3.

       80th percentile: $L_{80} = (10+1)\dfrac{80}{100} = (11)(.80) = 8.8$; the 80th percentile 30.8.

4.40   First quartile: $L_{25} = (13+1)\dfrac{25}{100} = (14)(.25) = 3.5$; the first quartile is 13.05.

       Second quartile: $L_{50} = (13+1)\dfrac{50}{100} = (14)(.5) = 7$; the second quartile is 14.7.

       Third quartile: $L_{75} = (13+1)\dfrac{75}{100} = (14)(.75) = 10.5$; the third quartile is 15.6.

4.42   Interquartile range = 15.6 − 13.05 = 2.55

4.44   First quartile = 5.75, third quartile = 15; interquartile range = 15 − 5.75 = 9.25

4.46

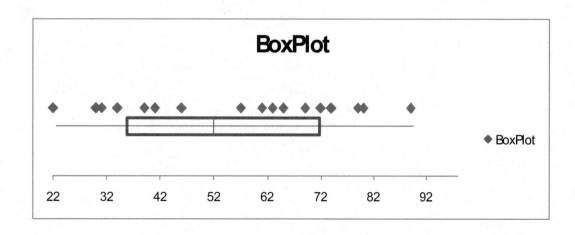

4.48   Dogs

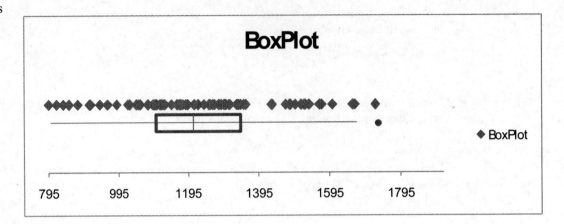

Cats

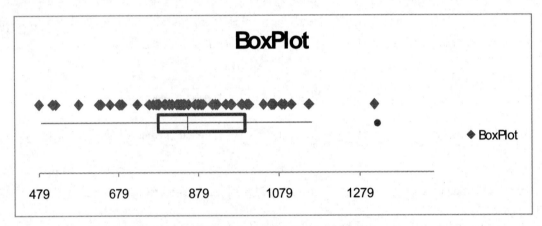

Dogs cost more money than cats. Both sets of expenses are positively skewed.

4.50   BA

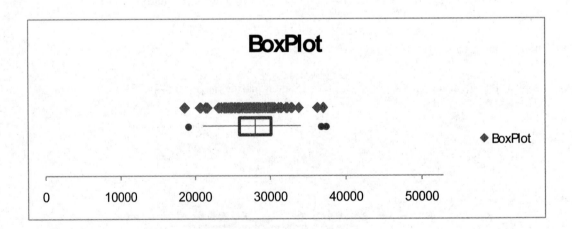

BSc

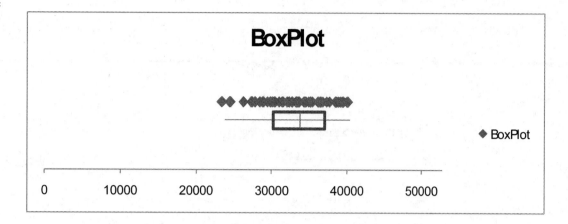

BBA

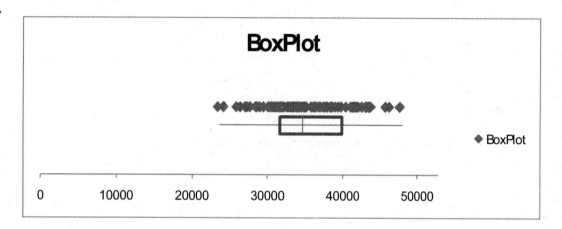

Other

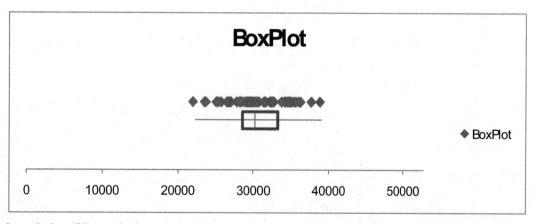

The starting salaries of BA and other are the lowest and least variable. Starting salaries for BBA and BSc are higher.

53

4.52   a.

Private course:

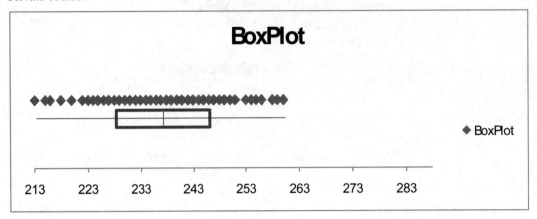

Public course:

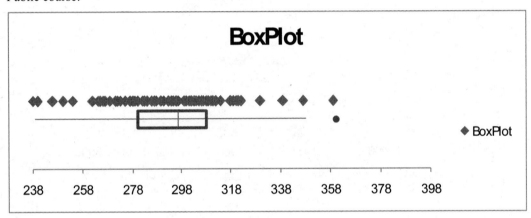

b.   The amount of time taken to complete rounds on the public course are larger and more variable than those played on private courses.

4.54   The quartiles are 697.19, 804.90, and 909.38. One-quarter of mortgage payments are less than $607.19 and one quarter exceed $909.38.

4.56   a. $r = \dfrac{s_{xy}}{s_x s_y} = \dfrac{-150}{(16)(12)} = -.7813$

There is a moderately strong negative linear relationship.

b. $R = r^2 = (-.7813)^2 = .6104$

61.04% of the variation in y is explained by the variation in x.

4.58

x_i	y_i	x_i^2	y_i^2	$x_i y_i$
40	77	1,600	5,929	3,080
42	63	1,764	3,969	2,646
37	79	1,369	6,241	2,923
47	86	2,209	7,396	4,041
25	51	625	2,601	1,276
44	78	1,936	6,084	3,432
41	83	1,681	6,889	3,403
48	90	2,304	8,100	4,320
35	65	1,225	4,225	2,275
28	47	784	2,209	1,316
Total 387	719	15,497	53,643	28,712

$$\sum_{i=1}^{n} x_i = 387 \qquad \sum_{i=1}^{n} y_i = 719 \qquad \sum_{i=1}^{n} x_i^2 = 15,497 \quad \sum_{i=1}^{n} y_i^2 = 53,643 \quad \sum_{i=1}^{n} x_i y_i = 28,712$$

a. $$s_{xy} = \frac{1}{n-1}\left[\sum_{i=1}^{n} x_i y_i - \frac{\sum_{i=1}^{n} x_i \sum_{i=1}^{n} y_i}{n}\right] = \frac{1}{10-1}\left[28,712 - \frac{(387)(719)}{10}\right] = 98.52$$

$$s_x^2 = \frac{1}{n-1}\left[\sum_{i=1}^{n} x_i^2 - \frac{\left(\sum_{i=1}^{n} x_i\right)^2}{n}\right] = \frac{1}{10-1}\left[15,497 - \frac{(387)^2}{10}\right] = 57.79$$

$$s_y^2 = \frac{1}{n-1}\left[\sum_{i=1}^{n} y_i^2 - \frac{\left(\sum_{i=1}^{n} y_i\right)^2}{n}\right] = \frac{1}{10-1}\left[53,643 - \frac{(719)^2}{10}\right] = 216.32$$

b. $$r = \frac{s_{xy}}{s_x s_y} = \frac{98.52}{\sqrt{(57.79)(216.32)}} = .8811$$

c. $R^2 = r^2 = .8811^2 = .7763$

d. $b_1 = \dfrac{s_{xy}}{s_x^2} = \dfrac{98.52}{57.79} = 1.705$

$\bar{x} = \dfrac{\sum x_i}{n} = \dfrac{387}{10} = 38.7$

$\bar{y} = \dfrac{\sum y_i}{n} = \dfrac{719}{10} = 71.9$

$b_0 = \bar{y} - b_1\bar{x} = 71.9 - (1.705)(38.7) = 5.917$

The least squares line is

$\hat{y} = 5.917 + 1.705x$

e. There is a strong positive linear relationship between marks and study time. For each additional hour of study time marks increased on average by 1.705.

4.60

	A	B	C
1		*Unemployment Rate*	*Employment Rate*
2	Unemployment Rate	1	
3	Employment Rate	-0.6332	1

$R^2 = r^2 = (-.6332)^2 = .4009$; 40.09% of the variation in the employment rate is explained by the variation in the unemployment rate.

4.62

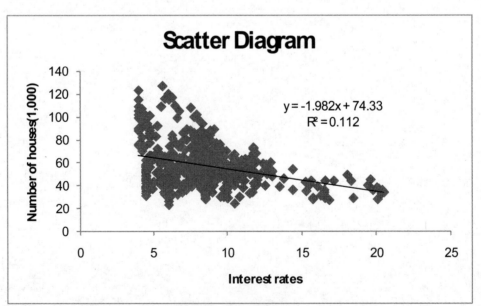

The coefficient of determination is .112. Only 11.2% of the variation in the number of houses sold is explained by the variation in interest rates.

4.64

	A	B	C
1		*Unemployment rate*	*Help wanted index*
2	Unemployment rate	1	
3	Help wanted index	0.0830	1

There is a positive relationship between the two variables.
$R^2 = r^2 = (.0830)^2 = .0069$. The relationship is very week.

4.66

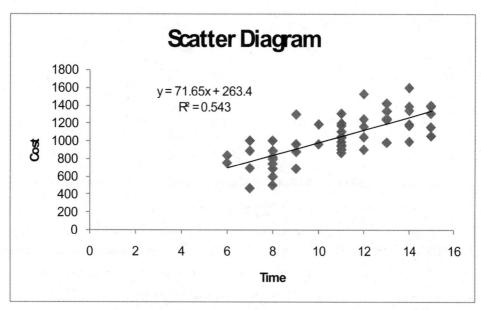

$\hat{y} = 263.4 + 71.65x$; Estimated fixed costs = \$263.40, estimated variable costs = \$71.65

4.68   a.

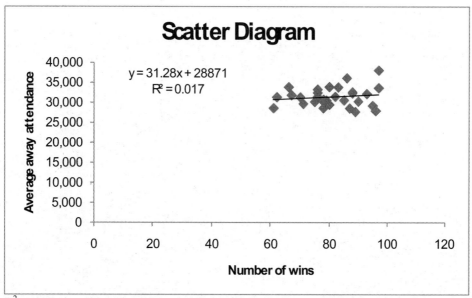

$R^2 = .017$; there is a very week relationship between the two variables.

b.　The slope coefficient is 31.28; away attendance increases on average by 31.28 for each win. However, the relationship is very weak.

4.70

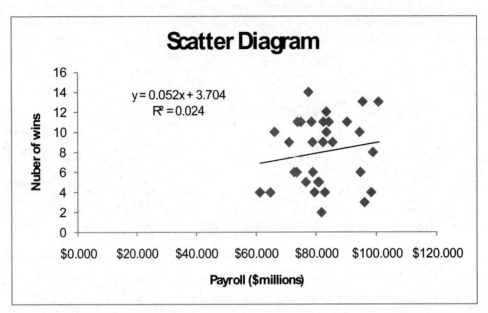

a.　The slope coefficient is .052; for each million dollars in payroll the number of wins increases on average by .052. Thus, to cost of winning one addition game is $1/.052$ million = $19.231 million.

b.　The coefficient of determination = .024, which reveals that the linear relationship is very weak.

4.72

Barrick Gold	.574	.086
Bell Canada Enterprises	.414	.103
Bank of Montreal	.447	.151
MDS Laboratories	.882	.173
Petro-Can	.535	.093
Research in Motion	2.698	.302

4.74   a.

	A	B	C	D	E
1	*Repaid*			*Defaulted*	
2					
3	Mean	752.45		Mean	545.73
4	Standard Error	3.53		Standard Error	6.07
5	Median	757		Median	549.5
6	Mode	759		Mode	552
7	Standard Deviation	52.35		Standard Deviation	54.25
8	Sample Variance	2740.61		Sample Variance	2943.49
9	Kurtosis	-0.23		Kurtosis	-0.67
10	Skewness	-0.11		Skewness	-0.09
11	Range	252		Range	237
12	Minimum	616		Minimum	419
13	Maximum	868		Maximum	656
14	Sum	165539		Sum	43658
15	Count	220		Count	80

b.   We can see that among those who repaid the mean score is larger than that of those who did not and the standard deviation is smaller. This information is similar but more precise than that obtained in Exercise 2.54.

4.76

	A	B	C
1		*Calculus*	*Statistics*
2	Calculus	1	
3	Statistics	0.6784	1

$R^2 = .6784^2 = .4603$; 46.03% of the variation in statistics marks is explained by the variation in calculus marks. The coefficient of determination provides a more precise indication of the strength of the linear relationship.

4.78

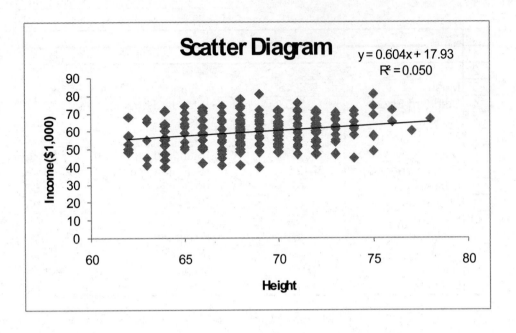

a. $\hat{y} = 17.93 + .6045x$

b.   The coefficient of determination is .050, which indicates that only 5% of the variation in incomes is explained by the variation in heights.

4.80   a.

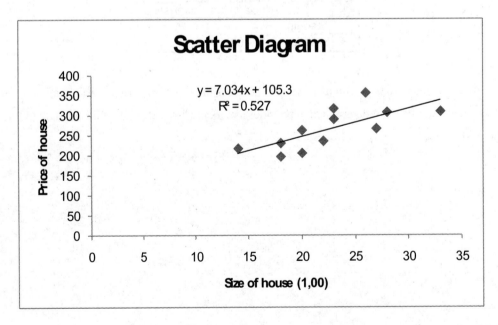

b. The slope coefficient is 7.034; For each additional 100 square feet the price increases on average by $7.034 thousand. More simply for each additional square foot the price increases on average by $70.34.

c. From the least squares line we can more precisely measure the relationship between the two variables.

4.82

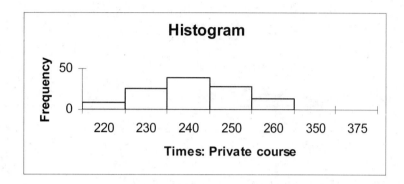

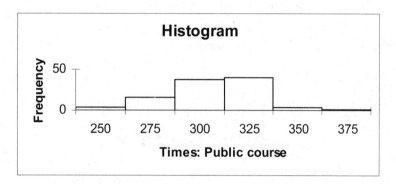

The information obtained here is more detailed than the information provided by the box plots.

4.84

	A	B
1	*Coffees*	
2		
3	Mean	29,913
4	Standard Error	1,722
5	Median	30,660
6	Mode	#N/A
7	Standard Deviation	12,174
8	Sample Variance	148,213,791
9	Kurtosis	0.12
10	Skewness	0.22
11	Range	59,082
12	Minimum	3,647
13	Maximum	62,729
14	Sum	1,495,639
15	Count	50

a. $\bar{x} = 29,913$, median $= 30,660$

b. $s^2 = 148,213,791$; s = 12,174

c.

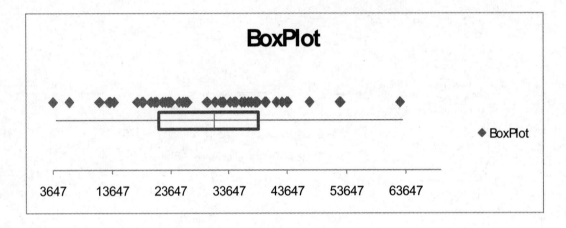

d. The number of coffees sold varies considerably.

4.86 a & b

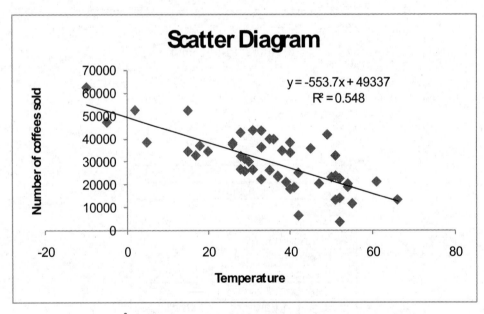

$R^2 = .548$ and the least squares line is $\hat{y} = 49,337 - 553.7x$

c. 54.8% of the variation in the number of coffees sold is explained by the variation in temperature. For each additional degree of temperature the number of coffees sold decreases on average by 554 cups. Alternatively for each 1-degree drop in temperature the number of coffees increases on average, by 553.7 cups.

d. We can measure the strength of the linear relationship accurately and the slope coefficient gives information about how temperature and the number of coffees sold are related.

4.88

	A	B
1	*Internet*	
2		
3	Mean	26.32
4	Standard Error	0.60
5	Median	26
6	Mode	21
7	Standard Deviation	9.41
8	Sample Variance	88.57
9	Kurtosis	-0.071
10	Skewness	0.15
11	Range	52
12	Minimum	2
13	Maximum	54
14	Sum	6579
15	Count	250

a. $\bar{x} = 26.32$ and median = 26

b. $s^2 = 88.57$, $s = 9.41$

c.

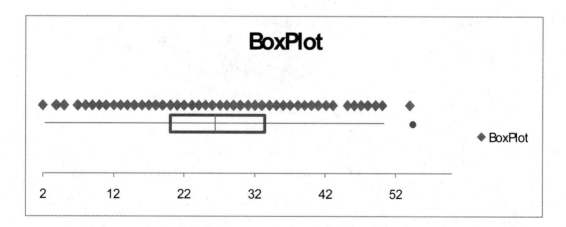

d. The times are positively skewed. Half the times are above 26 hours.

4.90   a & b

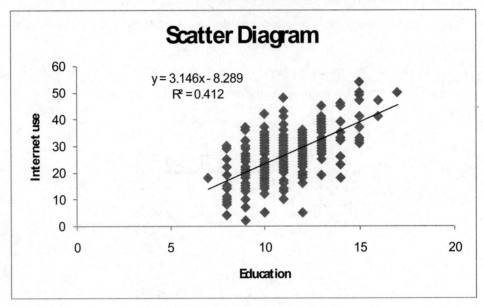

$R^2 = .412$ and the least squares line is $\hat{y} = -8.289 + 3.146x$

c.   41.2% of the variation in Internet use is explained by the variation in education. For each additional year of education Internet use increases on average by 3.146 hours.

d.   We can measure the strength of the linear relationship accurately and the slope coefficient gives information about how education and Internet use are related.

4.92

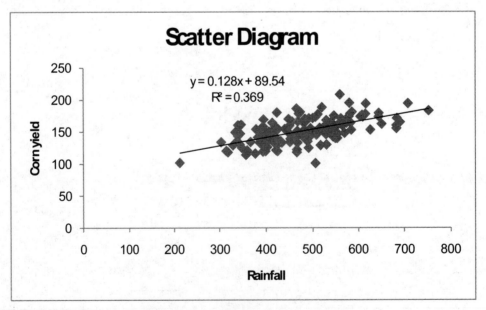

$R^2 = .369$ and the least squares line is $\hat{y} = 89.54 + .128$ Rainfall

c.   36.9% of the variation in yield is explained by the variation in rainfall. For each additional inch of rainfall yield increases on average by .128 bushels.

d.   We can measure the strength of the linear relationship accurately and the slope coefficient gives information about how rainfall and crop yield are related.

4.94   a.

	A	B
1	*Debts*	
2		
3	Mean	12,067
4	Standard Error	179.9
5	Median	12,047
6	Mode	11,621
7	Standard Deviation	2,632
8	Sample Variance	6,929,745
9	Kurtosis	-0.41325
10	Skewness	-0.2096
11	Range	12,499
12	Minimum	4,626
13	Maximum	17,125
14	Sum	2,582,254
15	Count	214

b.   The mean debt is $12,067. Half the sample incurred debts below $12,047 and half incurred debts above. The mode is $11,621.

Chapter 5

5.2 a. The study is observational. The statistics practitioner did not randomly assign stores to buy cans or bottles.

b. Randomly assign some stores to receive only cans and others to receive only bottles.

5.4 a. A survey can be conducted by means of a personal interview, a telephone interview, or a self-administered questionnaire.

b. A personal interview has a high response rate relative to other survey methods, but is expensive because of the need to hire well-trained interviewers and possibly pay travel-related costs if the survey is conducted over a large geographical area. A personal interview also will likely result in fewer incorrect responses that arise when respondents misunderstand some questions. A telephone interview is less expensive, but will likely result in a lower response rate. A self-administered questionnaire is least expensive, but suffers from lower response rates and accuracy than interviews.

5.6 a. The sampled population will exclude those who avoid large department stores in favor or smaller shops, as well as those who consider their time too valuable to spend participating in a survey. The sampled population will therefore differ from the target population of all customers who regularly shop at the mall.

b. The sampled population will contain a disproportionate number of thick books, because of the manner in which the sample is selected.

c. The sampled population consists of those eligible voters who are at home in the afternoon, thereby excluding most of those with full-time jobs (or at school).

5.8 a. A self-selected sample is a sample formed primarily on the basis of voluntary inclusion, with little control by the designer of the survey.

b. Choose any recent radio or television poll based on responses of listeners who phone in on a volunteer basis.

c. Self-selected samples are usually biased, because those who participate are more interested in the issue than those who don't, and therefore probably have a different opinion.

5.10 No, because the sampled population consists of the responses about the professor's course. We cannot make draw inferences about all courses.

5.12   We used Excel to generate 30 six-digit random numbers. Because we will ignore any duplicate numbers
        generated, we generated 30 six-digit random numbers and will use the first 20 unique
        random numbers to select our sample. The 30 numbers generated are shown below.

169,470	744,530	22,554	918,730	320,262	503,129
318,858	698,203	822,383	938,262	800,806	56,643
836,116	123,936	80,539	154,211	391,278	940,154
110,630	856,380	222,145	692,313	949,828	561,511
909,269	811,274	288,553	749,627	858,944	39,308

5.14   A stratified random sampling plan accomplishes the president's goals. The strata are the four areas enabling
        the statistics practitioner to learn about the entire population but also compare the four areas.

5.16   Use cluster sampling, letting each city block represent a cluster.

5.18   Three types of nonsampling errors:
        (1)   Error due to incorrect responses
        (2)   Nonresponse error, which refers to error introduced when responses are not obtained from some
        members of the sample. This may result in the sample being unrepresentative of the target population.
        (3)   Error due to selection bias, which arises when the sampling plan is such that some members of the
        target population cannot possibly be selected for inclusion in the sample.

Chapter 6

6.2 a. Subjective approach

   b. If all the teams in major league baseball have exactly the same players the New York Yankees will win 25% of all World Series.

6.4 a. Subjective approach

   b. The Dow Jones Industrial Index will increase on 60% of the days if economic conditions remain unchanged.

6.6 {Adams wins. Brown wins, Collins wins, Dalton wins}

6.8 a. {0, 1, 2, 3, 4, 5}

   b. {4, 5}

   c. $P(5) = .10$

   d. $P(2, 3, \text{ or } 4) = P(2) + P(3) + P(4) = .26 + .21 + .18 = .65$

   e. $P(6) = 0$

6.10 P(Contractor 1 wins) = 2/6, P(Contractor 2 wins) = 3/6, P(Contractor 3 wins) = 1/6

6.12 a. P(shopper does not use credit card) = P(shopper pays cash) + P(shopper pays by debit card)

     = .30 + .10 = .40

   b. P(shopper pays cash or uses a credit card) = P(shopper pays cash) + P(shopper pays by credit card)

     = .30 + .60 = .90

6.14 a. $P(\text{single}) = .15$, $P(\text{married}) = .50$, $P(\text{divorced}) = .25$, $P(\text{widowed}) = .10$

   b. Relative frequency approach

6.16 $P(A_1) = .1 + .2 = .3$, $P(A_2) = .3 + .1 = .4$, $P(A_3) = .2 + .1 = .3$.
   $P(B_1) = .1 + .3 + .2 = .6$, $P(B_2) = .2 + .1 + .1 = .4$.

6.18 a. $P(A_1 \mid B_1) = \dfrac{P(A_1 \text{ and } B_1)}{P(B_1)} = \dfrac{.4}{.7} = .57$

   b. $P(A_2 \mid B_1) = \dfrac{P(A_2 \text{ and } B_1)}{P(B_1)} = \dfrac{.3}{.7} = .43$

   c. Yes. It is not a coincidence. Given B_1 the events A_1 and A_2 constitute the entire sample space.

6.20   The events are not independent because $P(A_1 \mid B_2) \neq P(A_1)$.

6.22 $P(A_1 \mid B_1) = \dfrac{P(A_1 \text{ and } B_1)}{P(B_1)} = \dfrac{.20}{.20+.60} = .25$; $P(A_1) = .20 + .05 = .25$; the events are independent.

6.24 $P(A_1) = .15 + .25 = .40$, $P(A_2) = .20 + .25 = .45$, $P(A_3) = .10 + .05 = .15$.
        $P(B_1) = .15 + 20 + .10 = .45$, $P(B_2) = .25 + .25 + .05 = .55$.

6.26   a. $P(A_1 \text{ or } A_2) = P(A_1) + P(A_2) = .40 + .45 = .85$

        b. $P(A_2 \text{ or } B_2) = P(A_2) + P(B_2) - P(A_2 \text{ and } B_2) = .45 + .55 - .25 = .75$

        c. $P(A_3 \text{ or } B_1) = P(A_3) + P(B_1) - P(A_3 \text{ and } B_1) = .15 + .45 - .10 = .50$

6.28   a.   P(debit card) = .04 + .18 + .14 = .36

        b.   P(over \$100 | credit card) = $\dfrac{P(\text{credit card and over \$100})}{P(\text{credit card})} = \dfrac{.23}{.03+.21+.23} = .49$

        c.   P(credit card or debit card) = P(credit card) + P(debit card) = .47 + .36 = .83

6.30   a.   P(He is a smoker) = .12 + .19 = .31

        b.   P(He does not have lung disease) = .19 + .66 = .85

        c.   P(He has lung disease | he is a smoker) = $\dfrac{P(\text{he has lung disease and he is a smoker})}{P(\text{he is a smoker})} = \dfrac{.12}{.31} = .387$

        d.   P(He has lung disease | he does not smoke) =
              $\dfrac{P(\text{he has lung disease and he does not smoke})}{P(\text{he does not smoke})} = \dfrac{.03}{.69} = .044$

6.32   a.   P(manual | math-stats) = $\dfrac{P(\text{manual and math}-\text{stats})}{P(\text{math}-\text{stats})} = \dfrac{.23}{.23+.36} = .390$

        b.   P(computer) = .36 + .30 = .66

        c.   No, because P(manual) = .23 + .11 = .34, which is not equal to P(manual | math-stats).

6.34   a.   P(ulcer) = .01 + .03 + .03 + .04 = .11

        b.   P(ulcer | none) = $\dfrac{P(\text{ulcer and none})}{P(\text{none})} = \dfrac{.01}{.01+.22} = \dfrac{.01}{.23} = .043$

        c.   P(none | ulcer) = $\dfrac{P(\text{ulcer and none})}{P(\text{ulcer})} = \dfrac{.01}{.01+.03+.03+.04} = \dfrac{.01}{.11} = .091$

        d.   P(One, two, or more than two | no ulcer) = $1 - \dfrac{P(\text{ulcer and none})}{P(\text{ulcer})} = 1 - .091 = .909$

6.36   a.   P(remember) = .15 + .18 = .33

b. $P(\text{remember} \mid \text{violent}) = \dfrac{P(\text{remember and violent})}{P(\text{violent})} = \dfrac{.15}{.15+.35} = \dfrac{.15}{.50} = .30$

c.   Yes, the events are dependent.

6.38   a.   P(uses a spreadsheet) = .311 + .312 = .623

b. $P(\text{uses a spreadsheet} \mid \text{male}) = \dfrac{P(\text{uses a spreadsheet and male})}{P(\text{male})} = \dfrac{.312}{.312+.168} = \dfrac{.312}{.480} = .650$

c. $P(\text{uses a spreadsheet} \mid \text{female}) = \dfrac{P(\text{uses a spreadsheet and female})}{P(\text{female})} = \dfrac{.311}{.311+.209} = \dfrac{.311}{.520} = .598$

6.40   a.   P(provided by employer) = .166 + .195 + .230 = .591

b.   P(provided by employer | professional/technical) =

$\dfrac{P(\text{provided by employer and professional / technical})}{P(\text{professional / technical})} = \dfrac{.166}{.166+.094} = \dfrac{.166}{.260} = .638$

c. $\dfrac{P(\text{provided by employer and blue}-\text{collar / services})}{P(\text{blue}-\text{collar / services})} = \dfrac{.230}{.230+.180} = \dfrac{.230}{.410} = .561$

6.42   a.   P(under 20) = .2307 + .0993 + .5009 = .8309

b.   P(retail) = .5009 + .0876 + .0113 = .5998

c. $P(20 \text{ to } 99 \mid \text{construction}) = \dfrac{P(20 \text{ to } 99 \text{ and construction})}{P(\text{construction})} = \dfrac{.0189}{.2307+.0189+.0019} = \dfrac{.0189}{.2515} = .0751$

6.44 $P(\text{purchase} \mid \text{see ad}) = \dfrac{P(\text{purchase and see ad})}{P(\text{see ad})} = \dfrac{.18}{.18+.42} = \dfrac{.18}{.60} = .30$; P(purchase) = .18 + .12 = .30. The events are independent and thus the ads are not effective.

6.46   a.   P(bachelor's degree | west)

$= \dfrac{P(\text{bachelor's deg ree and west})}{P(\text{west})} = \dfrac{.0418}{.0359+.0608+.0456+.0181+.0418+.0180} = \dfrac{.0418}{.2202} = .1898$

b.   P(northwest | high school graduate)

$= \dfrac{P(\text{northwest and high school graduate})}{P(\text{high school graduate})} = \dfrac{.0711}{.0711+.0843+.1174+.0608} = \dfrac{.0711}{.3336} = .2131$

c.   P(south) = .0683 + .1174 + .0605 + .0248 + .0559 + .0269 = .3538

d.   P(not south) = 1 – P(south) = 1 – .3538 = .6462

6.48

		Joint events	Probabilities
A 0.8	B|A 0.4	A and B	$(0.8)(0.4) = 0.32$
	$B^c\|A$ 0.6	A and B^c	$(0.8)(0.6) = 0.48$
A^c 0.2	B|A^c 0.7	A^c and B	$(0.2)(0.7) = 0.14$
	$B^c\|A^c$ 0.3	A^c and B^c	$(0.2)(0.3) = 0.06$

6.50

		Joint events	Probabilities
A 0.8	B|A 0.3	A and B	$(0.8)(0.3) = 0.24$
	$B^c\|A$ 0.7	A and B^c	$(0.8)(0.7) = 0.56$
A^c 0.2	B|A^c 0.3	A^c and B	$(0.2)(0.3) = 0.06$
	$B^c\|A^c$ 0.7	A^c and B^c	$(0.2)(0.7) = 0.14$

6.52

		Joint events	Probabilities
R 0.9	R 0.9	R and R	$(0.9)(0.9) = 0.81$
	L 0.1	R and L	$(0.9)(0.1) = 0.09$
L 0.1	R 0.9	L and R	$(0.1)(0.9) = 0.09$
	L 0.1	L and L	$(0.1)(0.1) = 0.01$

a. P(R and R) = .81

b. P(L and L) = .01

c. P(R and L) + P(L and R) = .09 + .09 = .18

d. P(Rand L) + P(L and R) + P(R and R) = .09 + .09 + .81 = .99

6.54   a.

			Joint events	Probabilities
		R|R 89/99	R R	$(90/100)(89/99) = 0.8091$
	R 90/100			
		L|R 10/99	R L	$(90/100)(10/99) = 0.0909$
		R|L 90/99	L R	$(10/100)(90/99) = 0.0909$
	L 10/100			
		L|L 9/99	L L	$(10/100)(9/99) = 0.0091$

b.   P(RR) = .8091

c.   P(LL) = .0091

d.   P(RL) + P(LR) = .0909 + .0909 = .1818

e.   P(RL) + P(LR) + P(RR) = .0909 + .0909 + .8091 = .9909

6.56

First contract	Second contract	Joint events	Probabilities
	win|win 0.7	win and win	$(0.4)(0.7) = 0.28$
win 0.4			
	lose|win 0.3	win and lose	$(0.4)(0.3) = 0.12$
	win|lose 0.5	lose and win	$(0.6)(0.5) = 0.3$
lose 0.6			
	lose|lose 0.5	lose and lose	$(0.6)(0.5) = 0.3$

a.   P(win both) = .28

b.   P(lose both) = .30

c.   P(win only one) = .12 + .30 = .42

6.58

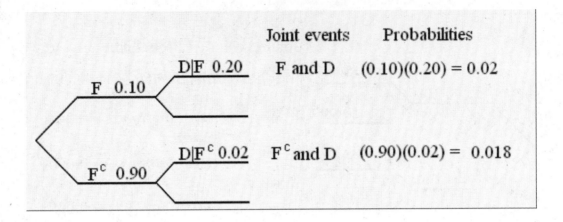

$P(D) = .02 + .018 = .038$

6.60

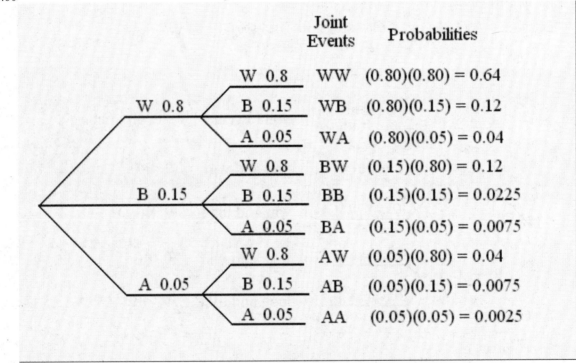

Diversity index = .12 + .04 + .12 + .0075 + .04 + .0075 = .335

74

6.62

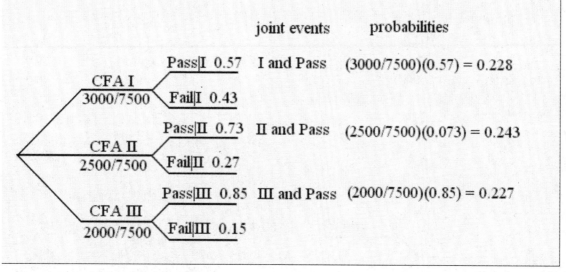

P(pass) = .228 + .243 + .227 = .698

6.64

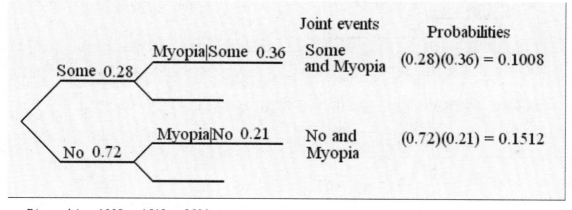

P(myopic) = .1008 + .1512 = .2520

6.66   Let A = mutual fund outperforms the market in the first year
      B = mutual outperforms the market in the second year

P(A and B) = P(A)P(B | A) = (.15)(.22) = .033

75

6.68   Define the events:
       M: The main control will fail.
       B_1: The first backup will fail.
       B_2: The second backup will fail

       The probability that the plane will crash is
       $P(M \text{ and } B_1 \text{ and } B_2) = [P(M)][P(B_1)][P(B_2)]$
       $= (.0001)(.01)(.01)$
       $= .00000001$
       We have assumed that the 3 systems will fail independently of one another.

6.70

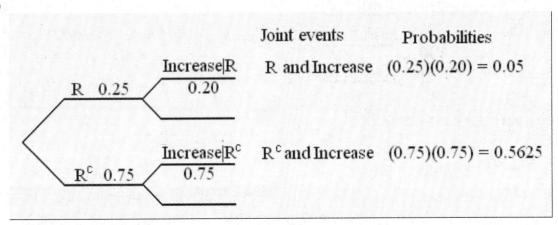

       P(Increase) = .05 + .5625 = .6125

6.72   P(A and B) = .32, P(A^C and B) = .14, P(B) = .46, P(B^C) = .54

       a. $P(A \mid B) = \dfrac{P(A \text{ and } B)}{P(B)} = \dfrac{.32}{.46} = .696$

       b. $P(A^C \mid B) = \dfrac{P(A^C \text{ and } B)}{P(B)} = \dfrac{.14}{.46} = .304$

       c. $P(A \text{ and } B^C) = .48; \; P(A \mid B^C) = \dfrac{P(A \text{ and } B^C)}{P(B^C)} = \dfrac{.48}{.54} = .889$

       d. $P(A^C \text{ and } B^C) = .06; \; P(A^C \mid B^C) = \dfrac{P(A^C \text{ and } B^C)}{P(B^C)} = \dfrac{.06}{.54} = .111$

6.74 $P(F \mid D) = \dfrac{P(F \text{ and } D)}{P(D)} = \dfrac{.020}{.038} = .526$

6.76 $P(\text{CFA I} \mid \text{passed}) = \dfrac{P(\text{CFA I and passed})}{P(\text{passed})} = \dfrac{.228}{.698} = .327$

6.78 $P(A) = .40$, $P(B \mid A) = .85$, $P(B \mid A^C) = .29$

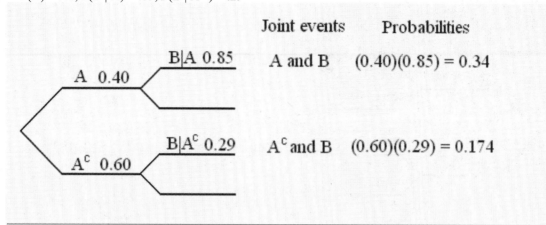

Joint events	Probabilities
A and B	$(0.40)(0.85) = 0.34$
A^c and B	$(0.60)(0.29) = 0.174$

$P(B) = .34 + .174 = .514$

$$P(A \mid B) = \frac{P(A \text{ and } B)}{P(B)} = \frac{.34}{.514} = .661$$

6.80   Define events: A, B, C = airlines A, B, and C, D = on time
$P(A) = .50$, $P(B) = .30$, $P(C) = .20$, $P(D \mid A) = .80$, $P(D \mid B) = .65$, $P(D \mid C) = .40$

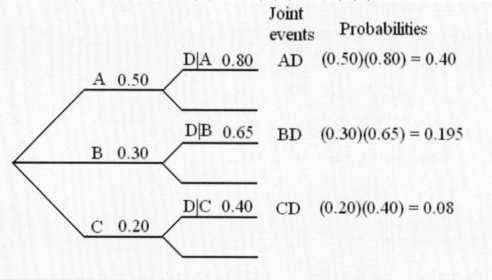

Joint events	Probabilities
AD	$(0.50)(0.80) = 0.40$
BD	$(0.30)(0.65) = 0.195$
CD	$(0.20)(0.40) = 0.08$

$P(D) = .40 + .195 + .08 = .675$

$$P(A \mid D) = \frac{P(A \text{ and } D)}{P(D)} = \frac{.40}{.675} = .593$$

6.82

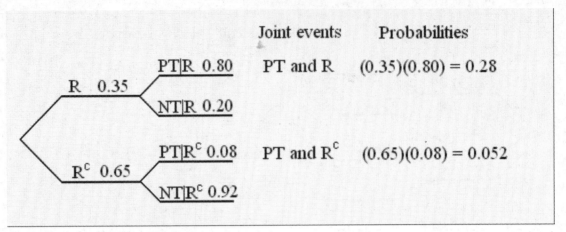

$P(PT) = .28 + .052 = .332$

$P(R \mid PT) = \dfrac{P(R \text{ and } PT)}{P(PT)} = \dfrac{.28}{.332} = .843$

6.84   Sensitivity $= P(PT \mid H) = .920$

Specificity $= P(NT \mid H^C) = .973$

Positive predictive value $= P(H \mid PT) = .1460$

Negative predictive value $= P(H^C \mid NT) = \dfrac{P(H^C \text{ and } NT)}{P(NT)} = \dfrac{.9681}{.0004 + .9681} = \dfrac{.9681}{.9685} = .9996$

6.86   a. $P(\text{Marketing A}) = .053 + .237 = .290$

b. $P(\text{Marketing A} \mid \text{Statistics not A}) = \dfrac{P(\text{Marketing A and Statistics not A})}{P(\text{Statistics not A})} = \dfrac{.23}{.237 + .580} 7 = \dfrac{.237}{.817} = .290$

c.   Yes, the probabilities in Parts a and b are the same.

6.88   a. $P(\text{second}) = .05 + .14 = .19$

b. $P(\text{successful} \mid -8 \text{ or less}) = \dfrac{P(\text{successful and} -8 \text{ or less})}{P(-8 \text{ or less})} = \dfrac{.15}{.15 + .14} = \dfrac{.15}{.29} = .517$

c.   No, because $P(\text{successful}) = .66 + .15 = .81$, which is not equal to $P(\text{successful} \mid -8 \text{ or less})$.

6.90 $P(A^C \mid B) = \dfrac{P(A^C \text{ and } B)}{P(B)} = \dfrac{.221}{.749} = .295$

6.92

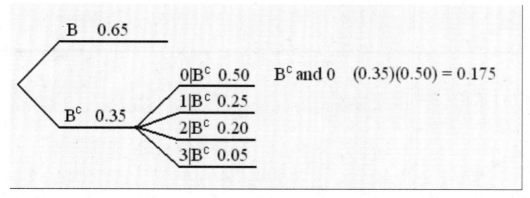

P(no sale) = .65 + .175 = .825

6.94

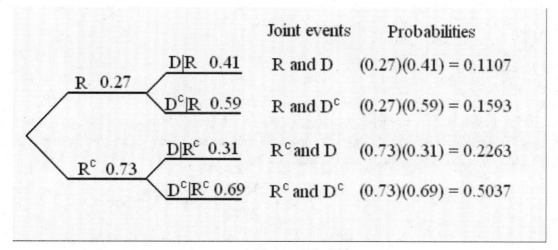

a. P(D) = P(R and D) + P(R^C and D) = .1107 + .2263 = .3370

$$P(R \mid D) = \frac{P(R \text{ and } D)}{P(D)} = \frac{.1107}{.3370} = .3285$$

b. P(D^C) = P(R and D^C) + P(R^C and D^C) = .1593 + .5037 = .6630

$$P(R \mid D^C) = \frac{P(R \text{ and } D^C)}{P(D^C)} = \frac{.1593}{.6630} = .2403$$

6.96

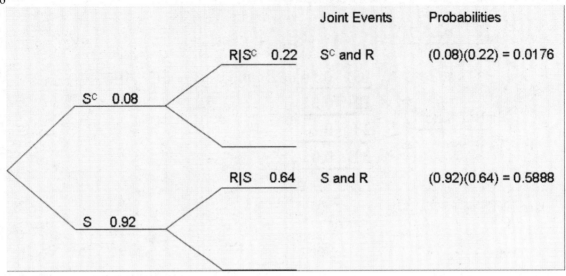

	Joint Events	Probabilities
R|S^c 0.22	S^c and R	(0.08)(0.22) = 0.0176
R|S 0.64	S and R	(0.92)(0.64) = 0.5888

$P(R) = .0176 + .5888 = .6064$

$P(S \mid R) = \dfrac{P(S \text{ and } R)}{P(R)} = \dfrac{.5888}{.6064} = .9710$

6.98   Define the events: A_1 = envelope containing two Maui brochures is selected, A_2 = envelope containing two Oahu brochures is selected, A_3 = envelope containing one Maui and one Oahu brochures is selected. B = a Maui brochure is removed from the selected envelope.

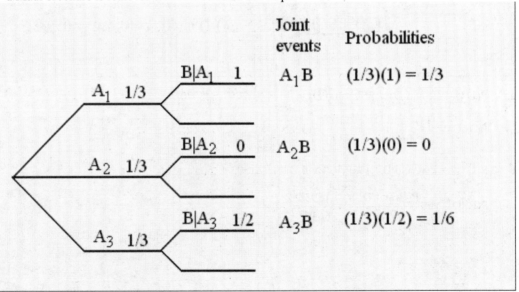

	Joint events	Probabilities
B|A$_1$ 1	A$_1$B	(1/3)(1) = 1/3
B|A$_2$ 0	A$_2$B	(1/3)(0) = 0
B|A$_3$ 1/2	A$_3$B	(1/3)(1/2) = 1/6

$P(B) = 1/3 + 0 + 1/6 = 1/2$

$P(A_1 \mid B) = \dfrac{P(A_1 \text{ and } B)}{P(B)} = \dfrac{1/3}{1/2} = 2/3$

80

6.100   Define events: A = company fail, B = predict bankruptcy
         $P(A) = .08$, $P(B \mid A) = .85$, $P(B^C \mid A^C) = .74$

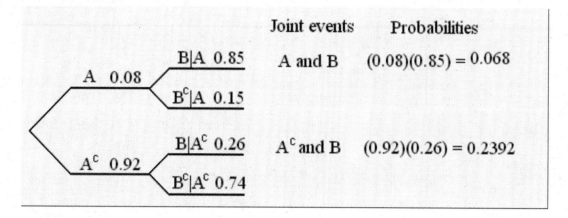

         $P(B) = .068 + .2392 = .3072$

         $P(A \mid B) = \dfrac{P(A \text{ and } B)}{P(B)} = \dfrac{.068}{.3072} = .2214$

6.102   Probabilities of outcomes: $P(HH) = .25$, $P(HT) = .25$, $P(TH) = .25$, $P(TT)$ .25
         $P(TT \mid HH \text{ is not possible}) = .25/(.25 + .25 + .25) = .333$

Chapter 7

7.2   a.   any value between 0 and several hundred miles

         b.   No, because we cannot identify the second value or any other value larger than 0.

         c.   No, uncountable means infinite.

         d.   The variable is continuous.

7.4   a.   0, 1, 2, …, 100

         b.   Yes.

         c.   Yes, there are 101 values.

         d.   The variable is discrete because it is countable.

7.6 $P(x) = 1/6$ for $x = 1, 2, 3, 4, 5,$ and 6

7.8   a. $P(2 \leq X \leq 5) = P(2) + P(3) + P(4) + P(5) = .310 + .340 + .220 + .080 = .950$

               $P(X > 5) = P(6) + P(7) = .019 + .001 = .020$

               $P(X < 4) = P(0) + P(1) + P(2) + P(3) = .005 + .025 + .310 + .340 = .680$

         b. $E(X) = \sum xP(x) = 0(.005) + 1(.025) + 2(.310) + 4(.340) + 5(.080) + 6(.019) + 7(.001) = 3.066$

         c. $\sigma^2 = V(X) = \sum (x - \mu)^2 P(x) = (0-3.066)^2(.005) + (1-3.066)^2(.025) + (2-3.066)^2(.310)$

               $+ (3-3.066)^2(.340) + (4-3.066)^2(.220) + (5-3.066)^2(.080) + (6-3.066)^2(.019)$

               $+ (7-3.066)^2(.001) = 1.178$

               $\sigma = \sqrt{\sigma^2} = \sqrt{1.178} = 1.085$

7.10   a. $P(X > 0) = P(2) + P(6) + P(8) = .3 + .4 + .1 = .8$

          b. $P(X \geq 1) = P(2) + P(6) + P(8) = .3 + .4 + .1 = .8$

          c. $P(X \geq 2) = P(2) + P(6) + P(8) = .3 + .4 + .1 = .8$

          d. $P(2 \leq X \leq 5) = P(2) = .3$

7.12 $P(\text{Losing 6 in a row}) = .5^6 = .0156$

7.14

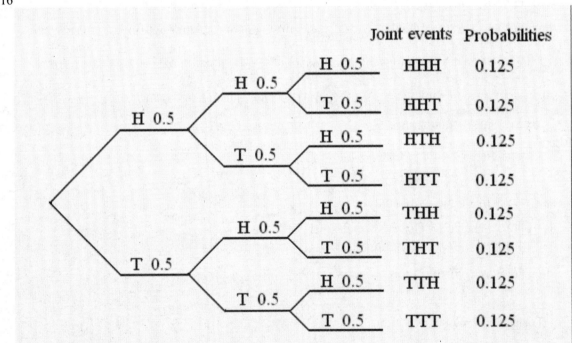

a. P(HH) = .25

b. P(HT) = .25

c. P(TH) = .25

d. P(TT) = .25

7.16

7.18 a. $\mu = E(X) = \sum xP(x) = -2(.59) + 5(.15) + 7(.25) + 8(.01) = 1.40$

$\sigma^2 = V(X) = \sum (x-\mu)^2 P(x) = (-2-1.4)^2 (.59) + (5-1.4)^2 (.15) + (7-1.4)^2 (.25) + (8-1.4)^2 (.01)$

$= 17.04$

b.

x	–2	5	7	8
y	–10	25	35	40
P(y)	← .59	.15	.25	.01

c. $E(Y) = \sum yP(y) = -10(.59) + 25(.15) + 35(.25) + 40(.01) = 7.00$

   $V(Y) = \sum (y - \mu)^2 P(y) = (-10-7.00)^2 (.59) + (25-7.00)^2 (.15) + (35-7.00)^2 (.25)$

   $+ (40-7.00)^2 (.01) = 426.00$

d. $E(Y) = E(5X) = 5E(X) = 5(1.4) = 7.00$

   $V(Y) = V(5X) = 5^2 V(X) = 25(17.04) = 426.00.$

7.20   a. $P(X \geq 2) = P(2) + P(3) = .4 + .2 = .6$

   b. $\mu = E(X) = \sum xP(x) = 0(.1) + 1(.3) + 2(.4) + 3(.2) = 1.7$

   $\sigma^2 = V(X) = \sum (x - \mu)^2 P(x) = (0-1.7)^2 (.1) + (1-1.7)^2 (.3) + (2-1.7)^2 (.4) + (3-1.7)^2 (.2) = .81$

7.22   a. $P(X > 4) = P(5) + P(6) + P(7) = .20 + .10 + .10 = .40$

   b. $P(X \geq 2) = 1 - P(X \leq 1) = 1 - P(1) = 1 - .05 = .95$

7.24 $Y = .25X; E(Y) = .25E(X) = .25(4.1) = 1.025$
   $V(Y) = V(.25X) = (.25)^2 (2.69) = .168$

7.26   a. $P(4) = .06$

   b. $P(8) = 0$

   c. $P(0) = .35$

   d. $P(X \geq 1) = 1 - P(0) = 1 - .35 = .65$

7.28   a. $P(X = 3) = P(3) = .21$

   b. $P(X \geq 5) = P(5) + P(6) + P(7) + P(8) = .12 + .08 + .06 + .05 = .31$

   c. $P(5 \leq X \leq 7) = P(5) + P(6) + P(7) = .12 + .08 + .06 = .26$

7.30 $\mu = E(X) = \sum xP(x) = 0(.04) + 1(.19) + 2(.22) + 3(.28) + 4(.12) + 5(.09) + 6(.06) = 2.76$
   $\sigma^2 = V(X) = \sum (x - \mu)^2 P(x) = (1-2.76)^2 (.04) + (2-2.76)^2 (.19) + (3-2.76)^2 (.28)$
   $+ (4-2.76)^2 (.12) + (5-2.76)^2 (.09) + (6-2.76)^2 (.06) = 2.302$
   $\sigma = \sqrt{\sigma^2} = \sqrt{2.302} = 1.517$

7.32 $\mu = E(X) = \sum xP(x) = 1(.24) + 2(.18) + 3(.13) + 4(.10) + 5(.07) + 6(.04) + 7(.04) + 8(.20) = 3.86$

$\sigma^2 = V(X) = \sum (x-\mu)^2 P(x) = (1-3.86)^2 (.24) + (2-3.86)^2 (.18) + (3-3.86)^2 (.13) + (4-3.86)^2 (.10)$

$+ (5-3.86)^2 (.07) + (6-3.86)^2 (.04) + (7-3.86)^2 (.04) + (8-3.86)^2 (.20) = 6.78$

$\sigma = \sqrt{\sigma^2} = \sqrt{6.78} = 2.60$

7.34 E(Value of coin) = 400(.40) + 900(.30) + 100(.30) = 460. Take the $500.

7.36 E(damage costs) = .01(400) + .02(200) + .10(100) + .87(0) = 18. The owner should pay up to $18 for the device.

7.38 $\mu = E(X) = \sum xP(x) = 1(.05) + 2(.12) + 3(.20) + 4(.30) + 5(.15) + 6(.10) + 7(.08) = 4.00$

$\sigma^2 = V(X) = \sum (x-\mu)^2 P(x) = (1-4.0)^2 (.05) + (2-4.0)^2 (.12) + (3-4.0)^2 (.20) + (4-4.0)^2 (.30)$

$+ (5-4.0)^2 (.15) + (6-4.0)^2 (.10) + (7-4.0)^2 (.08) = 2.40$

7.40 $\mu = E(X) = \sum xP(x) = 0(.10) + 1(.25) + 2(.40) + 3(.20) + 4(.05) = 1.85$

7.42 Breakeven point = 15,000/(7.40 – 3.00) = 3,409

7.44 a. $\displaystyle\sum_{\text{all } x} \sum_{\text{all } y} xyP(x, y) = (1)(1)(.5) + (1)(2)(.1) + (2)(1)(.1) + (2)(2)(.3) = 2.1$

$\displaystyle COV(X, Y) = \sum_{\text{all } x} \sum_{\text{all } y} xyP(x, y) - \mu_x \mu_y = 2.1 - (1.4)(1.4) = .14$

$\sigma_x = \sqrt{\sigma_x^2} = \sqrt{.24} = .49, \ \sigma_y = \sqrt{\sigma_y^2} = \sqrt{.24} = .49$

$\rho = \dfrac{COV(X, Y)}{\sigma_x \sigma_y} = \dfrac{.14}{(.49)(.49)} = .58$

7.46 a.

x + y	P(x + y)
2	.5
3	.2
4	.3

b. $\mu_{x+y} = E(X+Y) = \sum (x+y)P(x+y) = 2(.5) + 3(.2) + 4(.3) = 2.8$

$\sigma_{x+y}^2 = V(X+Y) = \sum [(x+y) - \mu_{x+y}]^2 P(x+y) = (2-2.8)^2 (.5) + (3-2.8)^2 (.2) + (4-2.8)^2 (.3) = .76$

c. Yes

7.48   a. $\displaystyle\sum_{\text{all } x}\sum_{\text{all } y} xyP(x,y) = (1)(1)(.28) + (1)(2)(.12) + (2)(1)(.42) + (2)(2)(.18) = 2.08$

$\displaystyle COV(X,Y) = \sum_{\text{all } x}\sum_{\text{all } y} xyP(x,y) - \mu_x\mu_y = 2.08 - (1.6)(1.3) = 0$

$\sigma_x = \sqrt{\sigma_x^2} = \sqrt{.24} = .49,\ \sigma_y = \sqrt{\sigma_y^2} = \sqrt{.21} = .46$

$\rho = \dfrac{COV(X,Y)}{\sigma_x\sigma_y} = \dfrac{0}{(.49)(.46)} = 0$

7.50   a.

x + y	P(x + y)
2	.28
3	.54
4	.18

b. $\mu_{x+y} = E(X+Y) = \displaystyle\sum (x+y)P(x+y) = 2(.28) + 3(.54) + 4(.18) = 2.9$

$\sigma_{x+y}^2 = V(X+Y) = \displaystyle\sum [(x+y) - \mu_{x+y}]^2 P(x+y) = (2-2.9)^2(.28) + (3-2.9)^2(.54) + (4-2.9)^2(.18) =$ .45

c.   Yes

7.52   x

y	0	1	2
1	.42	.21	.07
2	.18	.09	.03

7.54   a.   Refrigerators,

x	P(x)
0	.22
1	.49
2	.29

b.   Stoves,

y	P(y)
0	.34
1	.39
2	.27

c. $\mu_x = E(X) = \sum xP(x) = 0(.22) + 1(.49) + 2(.29) = 1.07$

     $\sigma^2 = V(X) = \sum (x-\mu)^2 P(x) = (0-1.07)^2 (.22) + (1-1.07)^2 (.49) + (2-1.07)^2 (.29) = .505$

d. $\mu_y = E(Y) = \sum yP(y) = 0(.34) + 1(.39) + 2(.27) = .93$

     $\sigma^2 = V(Y) = \sum (y-\mu)^2 P(y) = (0-.93)^2 (.34) + (1-.93)^2 (.39) + (2-.93)^2 (.27) = .605$

e. $\sum\limits_{all\ x} \sum\limits_{all\ y} xyP(x, y) = (0)(0)(.08) + (0)(1)(.09) + (0)(2)(.05) + (1)(0)(.14) + (1)(1)(.17)$

     $+ (1)(2)(.18) + (2)(0)(.12) + (2)(1)(.13) + (2)(2)(.04) = .95$

     $COV(X, Y) = \sum\limits_{all\ x} \sum\limits_{all\ y} xyP(x, y) - \mu_x\mu_y = .95 - (1.07)(.93) = -.045$

     $\sigma_x = \sqrt{\sigma_x^2} = \sqrt{.505} = .711, \ \sigma_y = \sqrt{\sigma_y^2} = \sqrt{.605} = .778$

     $\rho = \dfrac{COV(X, Y)}{\sigma_x \sigma_y} = \dfrac{-.045}{(.711)(.778)} = -.081$

7.56   a. $P(X = 1 \mid Y = 0) = P(X =1 \text{ and } Y = 0)/P(Y = 0) = .14/.34 = .412$

     b. $P(Y = 0 \mid X = 1) = P(X =1 \text{ and } Y = 0)/P(X = 1) = .14/.49 = .286$

     c. $P(X = 2 \mid Y = 2) = P(X =2 \text{ and } Y = 2)/P(Y = 2) = .04/.27 = .148$

7.58 $E\left(\sum X_i\right) = \sum E(X_i) = 35 + 20 + 20 + 50 + 20 = 145$

     $V\left(\sum X_i\right) = \sum V(X_i) = 8 + 5 + 4 + 12 + 2 = 31$

     $\sigma = \sqrt{31} = 5.57$

7.60 $E\left(\sum X_i\right) = \sum E(X_i) = 10 + 3 + 30 + 5 + 100 + 20 = 168$

     $V\left(\sum X_i\right) = \sum V(X_i) = 9 + 0 + 100 + 1 + 400 + 64 = 574$

     $\sigma = \sqrt{574} = 24.0$

7.62 $E(R_p) = w_1 E(R_1) + w_2 E(R_2) = (.30)(.12) + (.70)(.25) = .2110$

     a. $V(R_p) = w_1^2 \sigma_1^2 + w_2^2 \sigma_2^2 + 2 w_1 w_2 \rho \sigma_1 \sigma_2$

       $= (.30)^2(.02)^2 + (.70)^2(.15^2) + 2(.30)(.70)(.5)(.02)(.15) = .0117$

       $\sigma_{R_p} = \sqrt{.0117} = .1081$

b. $V(R_p) = w_1^2\,\sigma_1^2 + w_2^2\,\sigma_2^2 + 2\,w_1\,w_2\,\rho\,\sigma_1\,\sigma_2$

$= (.30)^2(.02)^2 + (.70)^2(.15^2) + 2(.30)(.70)(.2)(.02)(.15) = .0113$

$\sigma_{R_p} = \sqrt{.0113} = .1064$

c. $V(R_p) = w_1^2\,\sigma_1^2 + w_2^2\,\sigma_2^2 + 2\,w_1\,w_2\,\rho\,\sigma_1\,\sigma_2$

$= (.30)^2(.02)^2 + (.70)^2(.15^2) + 2(.30)(.70)(0)(.02)(.15) = .0111$

$\sigma_{R_p} = \sqrt{.0111} = .1052$

7.64 $E(R_p) = w_1 E(R_1) + w_2 E(R_2) = (.60)(.09) + (.40)(.13) = .1060$

$V(R_p) = w_1^2\,\sigma_1^2 + w_2^2\,\sigma_2^2 + 2\,w_1\,w_2\,\rho\,\sigma_1\,\sigma_2$

$= (.60)^2(.15)^2 + (.40)^2(.21^2) + 2(.60)(.40)(.4)(.15)(.21) = .0212$

$\sigma_{R_p} = \sqrt{.0212} = .1456$

The statistics used in Exercises 7.66 to 7.78 were computed by Excel. The variances were taken from the variance-covariance matrix. As a result they are the population parameters. To convert to statistics multiply the variance of the portfolio returns by n/(n–1).

7.66   a.

Stock	Mean	Variance
Coca-Cola	−.00022	.00261
Genentech	.01658	.01533
General Electric	.00031	.00354
General Motors	.00234	.01117
McDonalds	.00791	.00549
Motorola	.00800	.01042

	A	B	C	D	E	F	G
1		*Coca Cola*	*Genentech*	*GE*	*GM*	*McDonalds*	*Motorola*
2	Coca Cola	0.00257					
3	Genentech	0.00199	0.01511				
4	GE	0.00014	0.00150	0.00349			
5	GM	0.00133	0.00018	0.00108	0.01102		
6	McDonalds	0.00145	0.00129	0.00153	0.00199	0.00541	
7	Motorola	0.00165	0.00201	0.00093	0.00413	0.00251	0.01028

b.

7.68 The stocks with the smallest variances are Coca-Cola (.00261) and General Electric (.00354).

	A	B	C	D
1	**Portfolio of 2 Stocks**			
2			**Coca Cola**	**GE**
3	**Variance-Covariance Matrix**	**Coca Cola**	0.00257	
4		**GE**	0.00014	0.00349
5				
6	**Expected Returns**		-0.00022	0.00031
7				
8	**Weights**		0.50000	0.50000
9				
10	**Portfolio Return**			
11	**Expected Value**	**0.00005**		
12	**Variance**	**0.00158**		
13	**Standard Deviation**	**0.03981**		

The expected value is .00005 and the standard deviation is .03981.

7.70

	A	B	C	D	E
1	**Portfolio of 3 Stocks**				
2			**Coca Cola**	**Genentech**	**GE**
3	**Variance-Covariance Matrix**	**Coca Cola**	0.0026		
4		**Genentech**	0.0020	0.0151	
5		**GE**	0.0001	0.0015	0.0035
6					
7	**Expected Returns**		-0.0002	0.0166	0.0003
8					
9	**Weights**		0.3333	0.3333	0.3333
10					
11	**Portfolio Return**				
12	**Expected Value**	**0.0056**			
13	**Variance**	**0.0032**			
14	**Standard Deviation**	**0.0562**			

The expected value is .0056 and the standard deviation is .0562.

90

7.72

	A	B	C	D	E	F
1	Portfolio of 4 Stocks					
2			GE	GM	McDonalds	Motorola
3	Variance-Covariance Matrix	GE	0.0035			
4		GM	0.0011	0.0110		
5		McDonalds	0.0015	0.0020	0.0054	
6		Motorola	0.0009	0.0041	0.0025	0.0103
7						
8	Expected Returns		0.0003	0.0023	0.0079	0.0080
9						
10	Weights		0.3000	0.1000	0.4000	0.2000
11						
12	Portfolio Return					
13	Expected Value	0.0051				
14	Variance	0.0030				
15	Standard Deviation	0.0545				

The expected value is .0051 and the standard deviation is .0545.

7.74   The stocks with the largest means are Petro-Canada (.01533) and Research in Motion (.03113).

	A	B	C	D
1	Portfolio of 2 Stocks			
2			Petro-Can	RIM
3	Variance-Covariance Matrix	Petro-Can	0.00465	
4		RIM	0.00135	0.03643
5				
6	Expected Returns		0.01533	0.03113
7				
8	Weights		0.50000	0.50000
9				
10	Portfolio Return			
11	Expected Value	0.02323		
12	Variance	0.01095		
13	Standard Deviation	0.10462		

The expected value is .02323 and the standard deviation is .10462.

7.76   The two-stock portfolio with the largest expected value is composed of Petro-Canada and Research in Motion, the two stocks with the highest means. Its expected value is .02323 and its standard deviation is 10462. The two-stock portfolio with the smallest variance is composed of Bell Canada Enterprises and Bank of Montreal, the two stocks with the smallest variances. The expect value is .00355 and the standard deviation is .03398.

7.78

	A	B	C	D	E	F
1	**Portfolio of 4 Stocks**					
2			**BMO**	**MDS**	**Petro-Can**	**RIM**
3	**Variance-Covariance Matrix**	**BMO**	0.00199			
4		**MDS**	0.00040	0.00679		
5		**Petro-Can**	-0.00027	0.00153	0.00465	
6		**RIM**	0.00075	0.00221	0.00135	0.03643
7						
8	**Expected Returns**		0.01027	0.00319	0.01553	0.03113
9						
10	**Weights**		0.20000	0.30000	0.30000	0.20000
11						
12	**Portfolio Return**					
13	**Expected Value**	**0.01390**				
14	**Variance**	**0.00334**				
15	**Standard Deviation**	**0.05783**				

The expected value is .01390 and the standard deviation is .05783.

7.80 a.

Stock	Mean	Variance
Amgen	.00358	.00557
Ballard Power Systems	−.01510	.03427
Cisco Systems	.00412	.01701
Intel	.00313	.01575
Microsoft	.00994	.00752
Research in Motion	.03538	.03855

b. Stocks, Research in Motion, Microsoft, Cisco Systems, and Amgen have the largest means.

c. Stocks Amgen, Microsoft, Intel, and Cisco Systems have the smallest variances.

7.84 $P(X = x) = \dfrac{n!}{x!(n-x)!} \, p^{x}(1-p)^{n-x}$

a. $P(X = 3) = \dfrac{10!}{3!(10-3)!} \, (.3)^{3}(1-.3)^{10-3} = .2668$

b. $P(X = 5) = \dfrac{10!}{5!(10-5)!} \, (.3)^{5}(1-.3)^{10-5} = .1029$

c. $P(X = 8) = \dfrac{10!}{8!(10-8)!} \, (.3)^{8}(1-.3)^{10-8} = .0014$

7.86 a. .26683

b. .10292

c. .00145

7.88   a. $P(X = 2) = P(X \leq 2) - P(X \leq 1) = .9011 - .6554 = .2457$

b. $P(X = 3) = P(X \leq 3) - P(X \leq 2) = .9830 - .9011 = .0819$

c. $P(X = 5) = P(X \leq 5) - P(X \leq 4) = .9999 - 9984 = .0015$

7.90   a. $P(X = 18) = P(X \leq 18) - P(X \leq 17) = .6593 - .4882 = .1711$

b. $P(X = 15) = P(X \leq 15) - P(X \leq 14) = .1894 - .0978 = .0916$

c. $P(X \leq 20) = .9095$

d. $P(X \geq 16) = 1 - P(X \leq 15) = 1 - .1894 = .8106$

7.92   Binomial distribution with p = .25

a. $P(X = 1) = \dfrac{4!}{1!(4-1)!} (.25)^1 (1 - .25)^{4-1} = .4219$

b.   Table 1 with n = 8: $p(2) = P(X \leq 2) - P(X \leq 1) = .6785 - .3671 = .3114$

c.   Excel: $p(3) = .25810$

7.94   Table 1 with n = 25 and p = .90

a. $P(X = 20) = P(X \leq 20) - P(X \leq 19) = .0980 - .0334 = .0646$

b. $P(X \geq 20) = 1 - P(X \leq 19) = 1 - .0334 = .9666$

c. $P(X \leq 24) = .9282$

d. $E(X) = np = 25(.90) = 22.5$

7.96 $P(X = 0) = \dfrac{4!}{01!(4-0)!} (.7)^0 (1 - .7)^{4-0} = .0081$

7.98 $P(X = 0) = \dfrac{25!}{0!(25-0)!} (.08)^0 (1 - .08)^{25-0} = .1244$

7.100 $P(X = 20) = \dfrac{20!}{20!(20-20)!} (.75)^{20} (1 - .75)^{20-20} = .00317$

7.102   a. $P(X = 2) = \dfrac{5!}{2!(5-2)!} (.45)^2 (1 - .45)^{5-2} = .3369$

b.   Excel with n = 25 and p = .45: $P(X \geq 10) = 1 - P(X \leq 9) = 1 - .24237 = .75763$

7.104   a. $P(X = 2) = \dfrac{5!}{2!(5-2)!} (.52)^2 (1 - .52)^{5-2} = .2990$

b.   Excel with n = 25 and p = .52: $P(X \geq 10) = 1 - P(X \leq 9) = 1 - .08033 = .91967$

7.106 a. Excel with n = 100 and p = .52: $P(X \geq 50) = 1 - P(X \leq 49) = 1 - .30815 = .69185$

b. Excel with n = 100 and p = .36: $P(X \leq 30) = .12519$

c. Excel with n = 100 and p = .06: $P(X \leq 5) = .44069$

7.108 a. Excel with n = 10 and p = .23: $P(X \geq 5) = 1 - P(X \leq 4) = 1 - .94308 = .05692$

b. Excel with n = 25 and p = .23: $P(X \leq 5) = .47015$

7.110 a. $P(X = 0) = \dfrac{e^{-\mu}\mu^{x}}{x!} = \dfrac{e^{-2}2^{0}}{0!} = .1353$

b. $P(X = 3) = \dfrac{e^{-\mu}\mu^{x}}{x!} = \dfrac{e^{-2}2^{3}}{3!} = .1804$

c. $P(X = 5) = \dfrac{e^{-\mu}\mu^{x}}{x!} = \dfrac{e^{-2}2^{5}}{5!} = .0361$

7.112 a. Table 2 with $\mu = 3.5$: $P(X = 0) = P(X \leq 0) = .0302$

b. Table 2 with $\mu = 3.5$: $P(X \geq 5) = 1 - P(X \leq 4) = 1 - .7254 = .2746$

c. Table 2 with $\mu = 3.5/7$: $P(X = 1) = P(X \leq 1) - P(X \leq 0) = .9098 - .6065 = .3033$

7.114 a. $P(X = 0$ with $\mu = 2) = \dfrac{e^{-\mu}\mu^{x}}{x!} = \dfrac{e^{-2}(2)^{0}}{0!} = .1353$

b. $P(X = 10$ with $\mu = 14) = \dfrac{e^{-\mu}\mu^{x}}{x!} = \dfrac{e^{-14}(14)^{10}}{10!} = .0663$

7.116 a. Excel with $\mu = 30$: $P(X \geq 35) = 1 - P(X \leq 34) = 1 - .79731 = .20269$

b. Excel with $\mu = 15$: $P(X \leq 12 = .26761$

7.118 $P(X = 0$ with $\mu = 80/200) = \dfrac{e^{-\mu}\mu^{x}}{x!} = \dfrac{e^{-.4}(.4)^{0}}{0!} = .6703$

7.120 a. Table 2 with $\mu = 1.5$: $P(X \geq 2) = 1 - P(X \leq 1) = 1 - .5578 = .4422$

b. Table 2 $\mu = 6$: $P(X < 4) = P(X \leq 3) = .1512$

7.122   a. $P(X = 0 \text{ with } \mu = 1.5) = \dfrac{e^{-\mu}\mu^x}{x!} = \dfrac{e^{-1.5}(1.5)^0}{0!} = .2231$

       b.   Table 2 with $\mu = 4.5$: $P(X \le 5) = .7029$

       c.   Table 2 with $\mu = 3.0$: $P(X \ge 3) = 1 - P(X \le 2 = 1 - .4232 = .5768$

7.124   a. $E(X) = np = 40(.02) = .8$

       b. $P(X = 0) = \dfrac{40!}{0!(40-0)!}(.02)^0(1-.02)^{40-0} = .4457$

7.126   a. $P(X = 10 \text{ with } \mu = 8) = \dfrac{e^{-\mu}\mu^x}{x!} = \dfrac{e^{-8}(8)^{10}}{10!} = .0993$

       b.   Table 2 with $\mu = 8$: $P(X > 5) = P(X \ge 6) = 1 - P(X \le 5) = 1 - .1912 = .8088$

       c.   Table 2 with $\mu = 8$: $P(X < 12) = P(X \le 11) = .8881$

7.128   Table 1 with $n = 10$ and $p = .3$: $P(X > 5) = P(X \ge 6) = 1 - P(X \le 5) = 1 - .9527 = .0473$

7.130   Table 1 with $n = 10$ and $p = .20$: $P(X \ge 6) = 1 - P(X \le 5) = 1 - .9936 = .0064$

7.132   a.   Excel with $n = 80$ and $p = .70$: $P(X > 65) = P(X \ge 66) = 1 - P(X \le 65) = 1 - .99207 = .00793$

       b. $E(X) = np = 80(.70) = 56$

       c. $\sigma = \sqrt{np(1-p)} = \sqrt{80(.70)(1-.70)} = 4.10$

7.134   Table 1 with $n = 25$ and $p = .40$:

       a. $P(X = 10) = P(X \le 10) - P(X \le 9) = .5858 - .4246 = .1612$

       b. $P(X < 5) = P(X \le 4) = .0095$

       c. $P(X > 15) = P(X \ge 16) = 1 - P(X \le 15) = 1 - .9868 = .0132$

7.136 a. $\mu = E(X) = \sum xP(x) = 0(.36) + 1(.22) + 2(.20) + 3(.09) + 4(.08) + 5(.05) = 1.46$

$\sigma^2 = V(X) = \sum (x - \mu)^2 P(x) = (0-1.46)^2 (.36) + (1-1.46)^2 (.22) + (2-1.46)^2 (.20)$

$+ (3-1.46)^2 (.09) + (4-1.46)^2 (.08) + (5-1.46)^2 (.05) = 2.23$

$\sigma = \sqrt{\sigma^2} = \sqrt{2.23} = 1.49$

b. $\mu = E(X) = \sum xP(x) = 0(.15) + 1(.18) + 2(.23) + 3(.26) + 4(.10) + 5(.08) = 2.22$

$\sigma^2 = V(X) = \sum (x - \mu)^2 P(x) = (0-2.22)^2 (.15) + (1-2.22)^2 (.18) + (2-2.22)^2 (.23)$

$+ (3-2.22)^2 (.26) + (4-2.22)^2 (.10) + (5-2.22)^2 (.08) = 2.11$

$\sigma = \sqrt{\sigma^2} = \sqrt{2.11} = 1.45$

7.138 $p = .08755$ because $P(X \geq 1) = 1 - P(X = 0$ with $n = 10$ and $p = .08755) = 1 - .40 = .60$

7.140   Binomial with $n = 5$ and $p = .01$. (using Excel)

x	p(x)
0	.95099
1	.04803
2	.00097
3	.00001
4	0
5	0

Chapter 8

8.2   a. $P(X > 45) \approx \dfrac{(60-45) \times 3}{50 \times 15} + \dfrac{(75-60) \times 3}{50 \times 15} = .1200$

        b. $P(10 < X < 40) \approx \dfrac{(15-10) \times 17}{50 \times 15} + \dfrac{(30-15) \times 7}{50 \times 15} + \dfrac{(40-30) \times 6}{50 \times 15} = .3333$

        c. $P(X < 25) \approx \dfrac{(-30-[-45]) \times 5}{50 \times 15} + \dfrac{(-15-[-30]) \times 5}{50 \times 15} + \dfrac{(0-[-15]) \times 2}{50 \times 15} + \dfrac{(15-0) \times 16}{50 \times 15} + \dfrac{(25-15) \times 8}{50 \times 15} = .6667$

        d. $P(35 < X < 65) \approx \dfrac{(45-35) \times 8}{50 \times 15} + \dfrac{(60-45) \times 3}{50 \times 15} + \dfrac{(65-60) \times 3}{50 \times 15} = .1867$

8.4   a.

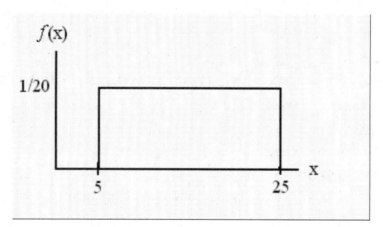

        b. $P(X > 25) = 0$

        c. $P(10 < X < 15) = (15-10)\dfrac{1}{20} = .25$

        d. $P(5.0 < X < 5.1) = (5.1-5)\dfrac{1}{20} = .005$

8.6 $f(x) = \dfrac{1}{(60-30)} = \dfrac{1}{30} \qquad 30 < x < 60$

        a. $P(X > 55) = (60-55)\dfrac{1}{30} = .1667$

        b. $P(30 < X < 40) = (40-30)\dfrac{1}{30} = .3333$

        c. $P(X = 37.23) = 0$

8.8 $.10 \times (60-30) = 3$; The top decile = 60–3 = 57 minutes

8.10   .20(175–110) = 13. Bottom 20% lie below (110 + 13) = 123

For Exercises 8.12 and 8.14 we calculate probabilities by determining the area in a triangle. That is,
 Area in a triangle = (.5)(height)(base)

8.12   a.

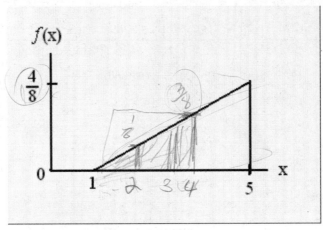

b.   P(2 < X < 4) = P(X < 4) – P(X < 2) = (.5)(3/8)(4–1) – (.5)(1/8)(2–1) = .5625 – .0625 = .5

c.   P(X < 3) = (.5)(2/8)(3–1) = .25

8.14   a.   f(x) = .10 – .005x   0 ≤ x ≤ 20

b.   P(X > 10) = (.5)(.05)(20–10) = .25

c.   P(6 < X < 12) = P(X > 6) – PX > 12) = (.5)(.07)(20–6) – (.5)(.04)(20–12) = .49 – .16 = .33

8.16   P(Z < 1.51) = .9345

8.18   P(Z < –1.59) = .0559

8.20   P(Z < – 2.30) = .0107

8.22   P(Z > –1.44) = 1 – P(Z < –1.44) = 1 – .0749 = .9251

8.24   P(Z > 1.67) = 1 – P(Z < 1.67) = 1 – .9525 = .0475

8.26   P(1.14 < Z < 2.43) = P(Z < 2.43) – P(Z < 1.14) = .9925 – .8729 = .1196

8.28   P(Z > 3.09) = .5 – P(0 < Z < 3.09) = .5 – .4990 = .0010

8.30   P(Z > 4.0) = 0

8.32   P(Z < $z_{.045}$) = 1 – .045 = .9550; $z_{.045}$ = 1.70

8.34 $P(X > 145) = P\left(\dfrac{X-\mu}{\sigma} > \dfrac{145-100}{20}\right) = P(Z > 2.25) = 1 - P(Z < 2.25) = 1 - .9878 = .0122$

8.36 $P(800 < X < 1100) = P\left(\dfrac{800-1,000}{250} < \dfrac{X-\mu}{\sigma} < \dfrac{1,100-1,000}{250}\right) = P(-.8 < Z < .4)$

       $= P(Z < .4) - P(Z < -.8) = .6554 - .2119 = .4435$

8.38   a. $P(5 < X < 10) = P\left(\dfrac{5-6.3}{2.2} < \dfrac{X-\mu}{\sigma} < \dfrac{10-6.3}{2.2}\right) = P(-.59 < Z > 1.68)$

         $= P(Z < 1.68) - P(Z < -.59) = .9535 - .2776 = .6759$

   b. $P(X > 7) = P\left(\dfrac{X-\mu}{\sigma} > \dfrac{7-6.3}{2.2}\right) = P(Z > .32) = 1 - P(Z < .32) = 1 - .6255 = .3745$

   c. $P(X < 4) = P\left(\dfrac{X-\mu}{\sigma} < \dfrac{4-6.3}{2.2}\right) = P(Z < -1.05) = .1469$

8.40 $P(X > 5,000) = P\left(\dfrac{X-\mu}{\sigma} > \dfrac{5,000-5,100}{200}\right) = P(Z > -.5) = 1 - P(Z < -.5) = 1 - .3085 = .6915$

8.42   a. $P(X > 12,000) = P\left(\dfrac{X-\mu}{\sigma} > \dfrac{12,000-10,000}{2,400}\right) = P(Z > .83) = 1 - P(Z < .83) = 1 - .7967 = .2033$

   b. $P(X < 9,000) = P\left(\dfrac{X-\mu}{\sigma} < \dfrac{9,000-10,000}{2,400}\right) = P(Z < -.42) = .3372$

8.44   a. $P(X > 70) = P\left(\dfrac{X-\mu}{\sigma} > \dfrac{70-65}{4}\right) = P(Z > 1.25) = 1 - P(Z < 1.25) = 1 - .8944 = .1056$

   b. $P(X < 60) = P\left(\dfrac{X-\mu}{\sigma} < \dfrac{60-65}{4}\right) = P(Z < -1.25) = .1056$

   c. $P(55 < X < 70) = P\left(\dfrac{55-65}{4} < \dfrac{X-\mu}{\sigma} < \dfrac{70-65}{4}\right) = P(-2.50 < Z < 1.25)$

         $= P(Z < 1.25) - P(Z < -2.50) = .8944 - .0062 = .8882$

8.46   Top 5%: $P(Z < z_{.05}) = 1 - .05 = .9500$; $z_{.05} = 1.645$; $z_{.05} = \dfrac{x-\mu}{\sigma}$; $1.645 = \dfrac{x-32}{1.5}$; $x = 34.4675$

       Bottom 5%: $P(Z < -z_{.05}) = .0500$; $-z_{.05} = -1.645$; $-z_{.05} = \dfrac{x-\mu}{\sigma}$; $-1.645 = \dfrac{x-32}{1.5}$;

       $x = 29.5325$

8.48 $P(X > 8) = P\left(\dfrac{X-\mu}{\sigma} > \dfrac{8-7.2}{.667}\right) = P\,(Z > 1.20) = 1 - P(Z < 1.20) = 1 - .8849 = .1151$

8.50   a. $P(X > 10) = P\left(\dfrac{X-\mu}{\sigma} > \dfrac{10-7.5}{2.1}\right) = P\,Z > 1.19) = 1 - P(Z < 1.19) = 1 - .8830 = .1170$

       b. $P(7 < X < 9) = P\left(\dfrac{7-7.5}{2.1} < \dfrac{X-\mu}{\sigma} < \dfrac{9-7.5}{2.1}\right) = P(-.24 < Z < .71)$

            $= P(Z < .71) - P(0 < Z < -.24) = .7611 - .4052 = .3559$

       c. $P(X < 3) = P\left(\dfrac{X-\mu}{\sigma} < \dfrac{3-7.5}{2.1}\right) = P\,Z < -2.14) = .0162$

       d. $P(Z < -z_{.05}) = .0500; \quad -z_{.05} = -1.645; \quad -z_{.05} = \dfrac{x-\mu}{\sigma}; \quad -1.645 = \dfrac{x-7.5}{2.1}; x = 4.05$ hours

8.52 $P(Z < -z_{.01}) = .0100; \quad -z_{.05} = -2.33; -z_{.01} = \dfrac{x-\mu}{\sigma}; \quad -2.33 = \dfrac{x-11,500}{800}; x = 9,636$

8.54   a. $P(X > 30) = P\left(\dfrac{X-\mu}{\sigma} > \dfrac{30-27}{7}\right) = P(Z > .43) = 1 - P(Z < .43) = 1 - .6664 = .3336$

       b. $P(X > 40) = P\left(\dfrac{X-\mu}{\sigma} > \dfrac{40-27}{7}\right) = P(Z > 1.86) = 1 - P(Z < 1.86) = 1 - .9686 = .0314$

       c. $P(X < 15) = P\left(\dfrac{X-\mu}{\sigma} < \dfrac{15-27}{7}\right) = P(Z < -1.71) = .0436$

       d. $P(Z < z_{.20}) = 1 - .20 = .8000; \quad z_{.20} = .84; \; z_{.20} = \dfrac{x-\mu}{\sigma}; \; .84 = \dfrac{x-27}{7}; x = 32.88$

8.56   a. $P(X < 10) = P\left(\dfrac{X-\mu}{\sigma} < \dfrac{10-16.40}{2.75}\right) = P(Z < -2.33) = .0099$

       b. $P(Z < -z_{.10}) = .1000; \quad -z_{.10} = -1.28; \; -z_{.10} = \dfrac{x-\mu}{\sigma}; \; -1.28 = \dfrac{x-16.40}{2.75}; x = 12.88$

8.58 $P(Z < z_{.02}) = 1 - .02 = .9800; \quad z_{.02} = 2.05; \; z_{.02} = \dfrac{x-\mu}{\sigma}; \; 2.05 = \dfrac{x-100}{16}; x = 132.80$ (rounded to 133)

8.60 $P(X < 45,000) = P\left(\dfrac{X-\mu}{\sigma} < \dfrac{45,000-41,825}{13,444}\right) = P(Z < .24) = .5948$

8.62 $P(x > 150,000) = P\left(\dfrac{X-\mu}{\sigma} < \dfrac{150,000-99,700}{30,000}\right) = P(Z > 1.68) = 1 - P(Z < 1.68) = 1 - .9535 = .0465$

8.64 $P(Z < z_{.20}) = 1 - .20 = .8000;\ z_{.20} = .84;\ z_{.20} = \dfrac{x - \mu}{\sigma};\ .84 = \dfrac{x - 150}{25};\ x = 171$

8.66 $P(Z < z_{.40}) = 1 - .40 = .6000;\ z_{.40} = .25;\ z_{.40} = \dfrac{x - \mu}{\sigma};\ .25 = \dfrac{x - 850}{90};\ .x = 872.5$ (rounded to 873)

8.68 $P(X < 150) = P\left(\dfrac{X - \mu}{\sigma} < \dfrac{150 - 145}{5.57}\right) = P(Z < .90) = .8159$

8.70 a. $P(X < 0) = P\left(\dfrac{X - \mu}{\sigma} < \dfrac{0 - 10.60}{14.56}\right) = P(Z < -.73) = .2327$

b. $P(X > 20) = P\left(\dfrac{X - \mu}{\sigma} > \dfrac{20 - 10.60}{14.56}\right) = P(Z > .65) = 1 - P(Z < .65) = 1 - .7422 = .2578$

8.72

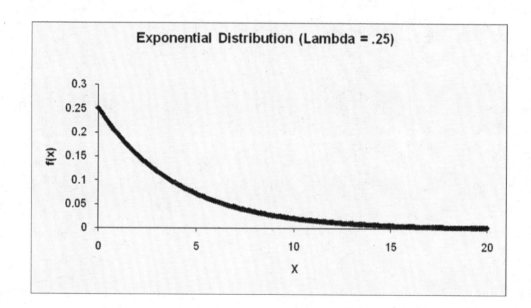

8.74 a. $P(X > 2) = e^{-.3(2)} = e^{-.6} = .5488$

b. $P(X < 4) = 1 - e^{-.3(4)} = 1 - e^{-1.2} = 1 - .3012 = .6988$

c. $P(1 < X < 2) = e^{-.3(1)} - e^{-.3(2)} = e^{-.3} - e^{-.6} = .7408 - .5488 = .1920$

d. $P(X = 3) = 0$

8.76 $\mu = 1/\lambda = 25\ \text{hours};\ \lambda = .04$ breakdowns/hour
$P(X > 50) = e^{-.04(50)} = e^{-2} = .1353$

8.78 $\mu = 1/\lambda = 5$ minutes; $\lambda = .2$ customer/minute
       $P(X < 10) = 1 - e^{-.2(10)} = 1 - e^{-2} = 1 - .1353 = .8647$

8.80 $\mu = 1/\lambda = 7.5$ minutes; $\lambda = .133$ service/minute
       $P(X < 5) = 1 - e^{-.133(5)} = 1 - e^{-.665} = 1 - .5143 = .4857$

8.82 $\mu = 1/\lambda = 6$ minutes; $\lambda = .167$ customers/minute
       $P(X > 10) = e^{-.167(10)} = e^{-1.67} = .1889$

	a.		b.		c.		d.	
8.84	a.	2.724	b.	1.282	c.	2.132	d.	2.528
8.86	a.	1.6556	b.	2.6810	c.	1.9600	d.	1.6602
8.88	a.	.1744	b.	.0231	c.	.0251	d.	.0267
8.90	a.	17.3	b.	50.9	c.	2.71	d.	53.5
8.92	a.	33.5705	b.	866.911	c.	24.3976	d.	261.058
8.94	a.	.4881	b.	.9158	c.	.9988	d.	.9077
8.96	a.	2.84	b.	1.93	c.	3.60	d.	3.37
8.98	a.	1.5204	b.	1.5943	c.	2.8397	d.	1.1670
8.100	a.	.1050	b.	.1576	c.	.0001	d.	.0044

Chapter 9

9.2   a. $P(\overline{X}=1)=P(1,1)=1/36$

        b. $P(\overline{X}=6)=P(6,6)=1/36$

9.4   The variance of $\overline{X}$ is smaller than the variance of X.

9.6   No, because the sample mean is approximately normally distributed.

9.8   a. $P(\overline{X}>1050)=P\left(\dfrac{\overline{X}-\mu}{\sigma/\sqrt{n}}>\dfrac{1050-1000}{200/\sqrt{25}}\right)=P(Z>1.25)=1-P(Z<1.25)=1-.8944=.1056$

        b. $P(\overline{X}<960)=P\left(\dfrac{\overline{X}-\mu}{\sigma/\sqrt{n}}<\dfrac{960-1000}{200/\sqrt{25}}\right)=P(Z<-1.00)=.1587$

        c. $P(\overline{X}>1100)=P\left(\dfrac{\overline{X}-\mu}{\sigma/\sqrt{n}}>\dfrac{1100-1000}{200/\sqrt{25}}\right)=P(Z>2.50)=1-P(Z<2.50)=1-.9938=.0062$

9.10   a. $P(49<\overline{X}<52)=P\left(\dfrac{49-50}{5/\sqrt{4}}<\dfrac{\overline{X}-\mu}{\sigma/\sqrt{n}}<\dfrac{52-50}{5/\sqrt{4}}\right)=P(-.40<Z<.80)$

                $=P(Z<.80)-P(Z<-.40)=.7881-.3446=.4435$

        b. $P(49<\overline{X}<52)=P\left(\dfrac{49-50}{5/\sqrt{16}}<\dfrac{\overline{X}-\mu}{\sigma/\sqrt{n}}<\dfrac{52-50}{5/\sqrt{16}}\right)=P(-.80<Z<1.60)$

                $=P(Z<1.60)-P(Z<-.80)=.9452-.2119=.7333$

        c. $P(49<\overline{X}<52)=P\left(\dfrac{49-50}{5/\sqrt{25}}<\dfrac{\overline{X}-\mu}{\sigma/\sqrt{n}}<\dfrac{52-50}{5/\sqrt{25}}\right)=P(-1.00<Z<2.00)$

                $=P(Z<2.00)-P(Z<-1.00)=.9772-.1587=.8185$

9.12   a. $P(49<\overline{X}<52)=P\left(\dfrac{49-50}{20/\sqrt{4}}<\dfrac{\overline{X}-\mu}{\sigma/\sqrt{n}}<\dfrac{52-50}{20/\sqrt{4}}\right)=P(-.10<Z<.20)$

                $=P(Z<.20)-P(Z<-.10)=.5793-.4602=.1191$

        b. $P(49<\overline{X}<52)=P\left(\dfrac{49-50}{20/\sqrt{16}}<\dfrac{\overline{X}-\mu}{\sigma/\sqrt{n}}<\dfrac{52-50}{20/\sqrt{16}}\right)=P(-.20<Z<.40)$

                $=P(Z<.40)-P(Z<-.20)=.6554-.4207=.2347$

        c. $P(49<\overline{X}<52)=P\left(\dfrac{49-50}{20/\sqrt{25}}<\dfrac{\overline{X}-\mu}{\sigma/\sqrt{n}}<\dfrac{52-50}{20/\sqrt{25}}\right)=P(-.25<Z<.50)$

                $=P(Z<.50)-P(Z<-.25)=.6915-.4013=.2902$

9.14   a. $\sigma_{\bar{x}} = \dfrac{\sigma}{\sqrt{n}}\sqrt{\dfrac{N-n}{N-1}} = \dfrac{500}{\sqrt{1,000}}\sqrt{\dfrac{10,000-1,000}{10,000-1}} = 15.00$

       b. $\sigma_{\bar{x}} = \dfrac{\sigma}{\sqrt{n}}\sqrt{\dfrac{N-n}{N-1}} = \dfrac{500}{\sqrt{500}}\sqrt{\dfrac{10,000-500}{10,000-1}} = 21.80$

       c. $\sigma_{\bar{x}} = \dfrac{\sigma}{\sqrt{n}}\sqrt{\dfrac{N-n}{N-1}} = \dfrac{500}{\sqrt{100}}\sqrt{\dfrac{10,000-100}{10,000-1}} = 49.75$

9.16   We can answer part (c) and possibly part (b) depending on how nonnormal the population is.

9.18   a. $P(X > 60) = P\left(\dfrac{X-\mu}{\sigma} > \dfrac{60-52}{6}\right) = P(Z > 1.33) = 1 - P(Z < 1.33) = 1 - .9082 = .0918$

       b. $P(\bar{X} > 60) = P\left(\dfrac{\bar{X}-\mu}{\sigma/\sqrt{n}} > \dfrac{60-52}{6/\sqrt{3}}\right) = P(Z > 2.31) = 1 - P(Z < 2.31) = 1 - .9896 = .0104$

       c. $[P(X > 60)]^3 = [.0918]^3 = .00077$

9.20   a. $P(X < 75) = P\left(\dfrac{X-\mu}{\sigma} < \dfrac{75-78}{6}\right) = P(Z < -.50) = .3085$

       b. $P(\bar{X} < 75) = P\left(\dfrac{\bar{X}-\mu}{\sigma/\sqrt{n}} < \dfrac{75-78}{6/\sqrt{50}}\right) = P(Z < -3.54) = 1 - P(Z < 3.54) = 1 - 1 = 0$

9.22   a. $P(\bar{X} < 5.97) = P\left(\dfrac{\bar{X}-\mu}{\sigma/\sqrt{n}} < \dfrac{5.97-6.05}{.18/\sqrt{36}}\right) = P(Z < -2.67) = .0038$

       b.   It appears to be false.

9.24   The professor needs to know the mean and standard deviation of the population of the weights of elevator users and that the distribution is not extremely nonnormal.

9.26 $P(\text{Total time} > 300) = P(\bar{X} > 300/60) = P(\bar{X} > 5) = P\left(\dfrac{\bar{X}-\mu}{\sigma/\sqrt{n}} > \dfrac{5-4.8}{1.3/\sqrt{60}}\right) = P(Z > 1.19)$

       $= 1 - P(Z < 1.19) = 1 - .8830 = .1170$

9.28 $P(\text{Total number of cups} > 240) = P(\bar{X} > 240/125) = P(\bar{X} > 1.92) = P\left(\dfrac{\bar{X}-\mu}{\sigma/\sqrt{n}} > \dfrac{1.92-2.0}{.6/\sqrt{125}}\right)$

       $= P(Z > -1.49) = 1 - P(Z < -1.49) = 1 - .0681 = .9319$

9.30 a. $P(\hat{P} > .60) = P\left(\dfrac{\hat{P}-p}{\sqrt{p(1-p)/n}} > \dfrac{.60-.5}{\sqrt{(.5)(1-.5)/300}}\right) = P(Z > 3.46) = 0$

b. $P(\hat{P} > .60) = P\left(\dfrac{\hat{P}-p}{\sqrt{p(1-p)/n}} > \dfrac{.60-.55}{\sqrt{(.55)(1-.55)/300}}\right) = P(Z > 1.74) = 1 - P(Z < 1.74)$

$= 1 - .9591 = .0409$

c. $P(\hat{P} > .60) = P\left(\dfrac{\hat{P}-p}{\sqrt{p(1-p)/n}} > \dfrac{.60-.6}{\sqrt{(.6)(1-.6)/300}}\right) = P(Z > 0) = 1 - P(Z < 0) = 1 - .5 = .5$

9.32 $P(\hat{P} < .75) = P\left(\dfrac{\hat{P}-p}{\sqrt{p(1-p)/n}} > \dfrac{.75-.80}{\sqrt{(.80)(1-.80)/100}}\right) = P(Z < -1.25) = .1056$

9.34 $P(\hat{P} < .49) = P\left(\dfrac{\hat{P}-p}{\sqrt{p(1-p)/n}} < \dfrac{.49-.55}{\sqrt{(.55)(1-.55)/500}}\right) = P(Z < -2.70) = .0035$

9.36 a. $P(\hat{P} < .50) = P\left(\dfrac{\hat{P}-p}{\sqrt{p(1-p)/n}} < \dfrac{.50-.53}{\sqrt{(.53)(1-.53)/400}}\right) = P(Z < -1.20) = .1151$; the claim may be true

b. $P(\hat{P} < .50) = P\left(\dfrac{\hat{P}-p}{\sqrt{p(1-p)/n}} < \dfrac{.50-.53}{\sqrt{(.53)(1-.53)/1,000}}\right) = P(Z < -1.90) = .0287$; the claim appears to be

false

9.38 $P(\hat{P} > .05) = P\left(\dfrac{\hat{P}-p}{\sqrt{p(1-p)/n}} > \dfrac{.05-.03}{\sqrt{(.03)(1-.03)/400}}\right) = P(Z > 2.34) = 1 - P(Z < 2.34) = 1 - .9904$

$= .0096$; the commercial appears to be dishonest

9.40 a. $P(\hat{P} < .45) = P\left(\dfrac{\hat{P}-p}{\sqrt{p(1-p)/n}} < \dfrac{.45-.50}{\sqrt{(.50)(1-.50)/600}}\right) = P(Z < -2.45) = .0071$

b. The claim appears to be false.

9.42 $P(\hat{P} < .70) = P\left(\dfrac{\hat{P}-p}{\sqrt{p(1-p)/n}} < \dfrac{.70-.75}{\sqrt{(.75)(1-.75)/460}}\right) = P(Z < -2.48) = .0066$

9.44 The claim appears to be false.

9.46 $P(\overline{X}_1 - \overline{X}_2 > 25) = P\left(\dfrac{(\overline{X}_1 - \overline{X}_2) - (\mu_1 - \mu_2)}{\sqrt{\dfrac{\sigma_1^2}{n_1} + \dfrac{\sigma_2^2}{n_2}}} > \dfrac{25 - (280 - 270)}{\sqrt{\dfrac{25^2}{50} + \dfrac{30^2}{50}}} \right) = P(Z > 2.72) = 1 - P(Z < 2.72)$

$= 1 - .9967 = .0033$

9.48 $P(\overline{X}_1 - \overline{X}_2 > 0) = P\left(\dfrac{(\overline{X}_1 - \overline{X}_2) - (\mu_1 - \mu_2)}{\sqrt{\dfrac{\sigma_1^2}{n_1} + \dfrac{\sigma_2^2}{n_2}}} > \dfrac{0 - (40 - 38)}{\sqrt{\dfrac{6^2}{25} + \dfrac{8^2}{25}}} \right) = P(Z > -1.00) = 1 - P(Z < -1.00)$

$1 - .1587 = .8413$

9.50 $P(\overline{X}_1 - \overline{X}_2 > 0) = P\left(\dfrac{(\overline{X}_1 - \overline{X}_2) - (\mu_1 - \mu_2)}{\sqrt{\dfrac{\sigma_1^2}{n_1} + \dfrac{\sigma_2^2}{n_2}}} > \dfrac{0 - (140 - 138)}{\sqrt{\dfrac{6^2}{25} + \dfrac{8^2}{25}}} \right) = P(Z > -1.00) = 1 - P(Z < -1.00)$

$= 1 - .1587 = .8413$

9.52 $P(\overline{X}_1 - \overline{X}_2 > 0) = P\left(\dfrac{(\overline{X}_1 - \overline{X}_2) - (\mu_1 - \mu_2)}{\sqrt{\dfrac{\sigma_1^2}{n_1} + \dfrac{\sigma_2^2}{n_2}}} > \dfrac{0 - (73 - 77)}{\sqrt{\dfrac{12^2}{4} + \dfrac{10^2}{4}}} \right) = P(Z > .51) = 1 - P(Z < .51)$

$= 1 - .6950 = .3050$

9.54 $P(\overline{X}_1 - \overline{X}_2 < 0) = P\left(\dfrac{(\overline{X}_1 - \overline{X}_2) - (\mu_1 - \mu_2)}{\sqrt{\dfrac{\sigma_1^2}{n_1} + \dfrac{\sigma_2^2}{n_2}}} < \dfrac{0 - (10 - 15)}{\sqrt{\dfrac{3^2}{25} + \dfrac{3^2}{25}}} \right) = P(Z < 5.89) = 1$

Chapter 10

10.2   An unbiased estimator of a parameter is an estimator whose expected value equals the parameter.

10.4

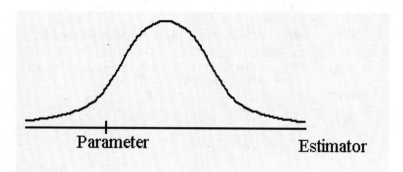

10.6

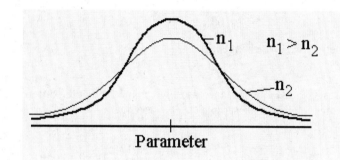

10.8

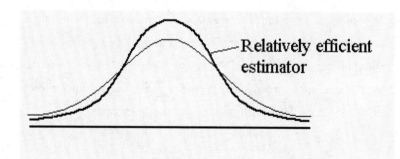

10.10   a. $\bar{x} \pm z_{\alpha/2}\sigma/\sqrt{n} = 200 \pm 1.96(50/\sqrt{25}) = 200 \pm 19.60$; LCL = 180.40, UCL = 219.60

        b. $\bar{x} \pm z_{\alpha/2}\sigma/\sqrt{n} = 200 \pm 1.96(25/\sqrt{25}) = 200 \pm 9.80$; LCL = 190.20, UCL = 209.80

        c. $\bar{x} \pm z_{\alpha/2}\sigma/\sqrt{n} = 200 \pm 1.96(10/\sqrt{25}) = 200 \pm 3.92$; LCL = 196.08, UCL = 203.92

        d.   The interval narrows.

10.12   a. $\bar{x} \pm z_{\alpha/2}\sigma/\sqrt{n} = 500 \pm 2.33(12/\sqrt{50}) = 500 \pm 3.95$; LCL = 496.05, UCL = 503.95

        b. $\bar{x} \pm z_{\alpha/2}\sigma/\sqrt{n} = 500 \pm 1.96(12/\sqrt{50}) = 500 \pm 3.33$; LCL = 496.67, UCL = 503.33

c. $\bar{x} \pm z_{\alpha/2} \sigma / \sqrt{n} = 500 \pm 1.645(12/\sqrt{50}) = 500 \pm 2.79$; LCL = 497.21, UCL = 502.79

d.   The interval narrows.

10.14   a. $\bar{x} \pm z_{\alpha/2} \sigma / \sqrt{n} = 10 \pm 1.645(5/\sqrt{100}) = 10 \pm .82$; LCL = 9.18, UCL = 10.82

       b. $\bar{x} \pm z_{\alpha/2} \sigma / \sqrt{n} = 10 \pm 1.645(5/\sqrt{25}) = 10 \pm 1.64$; LCL = 8.36, UCL = 11.64

       c. $\bar{x} \pm z_{\alpha/2} \sigma / \sqrt{n} = 10 \pm 1.645(5/\sqrt{10}) = 10 \pm 2.60$; LCL = 7.40, UCL = 12.60

       d.   The interval widens.

10.16   a. $\bar{x} \pm z_{\alpha/2} \sigma / \sqrt{n} = 400 \pm 2.575(5/\sqrt{100}) = 400 \pm 1.29$; LCL = 398.71, UCL = 401.29

       b. $\bar{x} \pm z_{\alpha/2} \sigma / \sqrt{n} = 200 \pm 2.575(5/\sqrt{100}) = 200 \pm 1.29$; LCL = 198.71, UCL = 201.29

       c. $\bar{x} \pm z_{\alpha/2} \sigma / \sqrt{n} = 100 \pm 2.575(5/\sqrt{100}) = 100 \pm 1.29$; LCL = 98.71, UCL = 101.29

       d.   The width of the interval is unchanged.

10.18   The variance decreases as the sample size increases, which means that the difference between the estimator and the parameter grows smaller as the sample size grows larger.

10.20   a.   sample median $\pm z_{\alpha/2} \dfrac{1.2533\,\sigma}{\sqrt{n}} = 500 \pm 1.645 \dfrac{1.2533(12)}{\sqrt{50}} = 500 \pm 3.50$

       b.   The 90% confidence interval estimate of the population mean using the sample mean is 500 ± 2.79. The 90% confidence interval of the population mean using the sample median is wider than that using the sample mean because the variance of the sample median is larger. The median is calculated by placing all the observations in order. Thus, the median loses the potential information contained in the actual values in the sample. This results in a wider interval estimate.

10.22 $\bar{x} \pm z_{\alpha/2} \sigma / \sqrt{n} = 43.75 \pm 1.96(10/\sqrt{8}) = 43.75 \pm 6.93$; LCL = 36.82, UCL = 50.68
We estimate that the mean age of men who frequent bars lies between 36.82 and 50.68. This type of estimate is correct 95% of the time.

10.24 $\bar{x} \pm z_{\alpha/2} \sigma / \sqrt{n} = 9.85 \pm 1.645(8/\sqrt{20}) = 9.85 \pm 2.94$; LCL = 6.91, UCL = 12.79

10.26 $\bar{x} \pm z_{\alpha/2} \sigma / \sqrt{n} = 16.9 \pm 2.575(5/\sqrt{10}) = 16.9 \pm 4.07$; LCL = 12.83, UCL = 20.97
10.28 $\bar{x} \pm z_{\alpha/2} \sigma / \sqrt{n} = 13.15 \pm 1.645(6/\sqrt{13}) = 13.15 \pm 2.74$; LCL = 10.41, UCL = 15.89

10.30 $\bar{x} \pm z_{\alpha/2} \sigma / \sqrt{n} = 252.38 \pm 1.96(30/\sqrt{400}) = 252.38 \pm 2.94$; LCL = 249.44, UCL = 255.32

10.32 $\bar{x} \pm z_{\alpha/2}\sigma/\sqrt{n} = 12.10 \pm 1.645(2.1/\sqrt{200}) = 12.10 \pm .24$; LCL = 11.86, UCL = 12.34. We estimate that the mean rate of return on all real estate investments lies between 11.86% and 12.34%. This type of estimate is correct 90% of the time.

10.34 $\bar{x} \pm z_{\alpha/2}\sigma/\sqrt{n} = .510 \pm 2.575(.1/\sqrt{250}) = .510 \pm .016$; LCL = .494, UCL = .526. We estimate that the mean growth rate of this type of grass lies between .494 and .526 inch. This type of estimate is correct 99% of the time.

10.36 $\bar{x} \pm z_{\alpha/2}\sigma/\sqrt{n} = 19.28 \pm 1.645(6/\sqrt{250}) = 19.28 \pm .62$; LCL = 18.66, UCL = 19.90. We estimate that the mean leisure time per week of Japanese middle managers lies between 18.66 and 19.90 hours. This type of estimate is correct 90% of the time.

10.38 $\bar{x} \pm z_{\alpha/2}\sigma/\sqrt{n} = 585,063 \pm 1.645(30,000/\sqrt{80}) = 585,063 \pm 5,518$; LCL = 579,545, UCL = 590,581. We estimate that the mean annual income of all company presidents lies between \$579,545 and \$590,581. This type of estimate is correct 90% of the time.

10.40 $\bar{x} \pm z_{\alpha/2}\sigma/\sqrt{n} = 27.19 \pm 1.96(8/\sqrt{100}) = 27.19 \pm 1.57$; LCL = 25.62, UCL = 28.76

10.42 a. The sample size increases.

      b. The sample size increases.

      c. The sample size decreases.

10.44 a. The sample size decreases.

      b. the sample size decreases.

      c. The sample size increases.

10.46 a. $\bar{x} \pm z_{\alpha/2}\dfrac{\sigma}{\sqrt{n}} = 150 \pm 1.645\dfrac{5}{\sqrt{271}} = 150 \pm .5$

      b. $\bar{x} \pm z_{\alpha/2}\dfrac{\sigma}{\sqrt{n}} = 150 \pm 1.645\dfrac{20}{\sqrt{271}} = 150 \pm 2$

10.48 a. $n = \left(\dfrac{z_{\alpha/2}\sigma}{W}\right)^2 = \left(\dfrac{1.96 \times 200}{10}\right)^2 = 1,537$

      b. 500 ± 10

10.50 a. The width of the confidence interval estimate is equal to what was specified.

      b. The width of the confidence interval estimate is smaller than what was specified.

      c. The width of the confidence interval estimate is larger than what was specified.

10.52 $\quad n = \left(\dfrac{z_{\alpha/2}\sigma}{B}\right)^2 = \left(\dfrac{2.575 \times 360}{20}\right)^2 = 2{,}149$

10.54 $\quad n = \left(\dfrac{z_{\alpha/2}\sigma}{B}\right)^2 = \left(\dfrac{1.645 \times 20}{1}\right)^2 = 1{,}083$

10.56 $\quad n = \left(\dfrac{z_{\alpha/2}\sigma}{B}\right)^2 = \left(\dfrac{1.96 \times 15}{2}\right)^2 = 217$

Chapter 11

11.2 H_0 : I will complete the Ph.D.

       H_1 : I will not be able to complete the Ph.D.

11.4 H_0 : Risky investment is more successful

       H_1 : Risky investment is not more successful

11.6   The defendant in both cases was O. J. Simpson. The verdicts were logical because in the criminal trial the amount of evidence to convict is greater than the amount of evidence required in a civil trial. The two juries concluded that there was enough (preponderance of) evidence in the civil trial, but not enough evidence (beyond a reasonable doubt) in the criminal trial.

All p-values and probabilities of Type II errors were calculated manually using Table 3 in Appendix B.

11.8   Rejection region: $z > z_{.03} = 1.88$

$$z = \frac{\bar{x} - \mu}{\sigma / \sqrt{n}} = \frac{51 - 50}{5 / \sqrt{9}} = .60$$

p-value = $P(Z > .60) = 1 - .7257 = .2743$

There is not enough evidence to infer that $\mu > 50$.

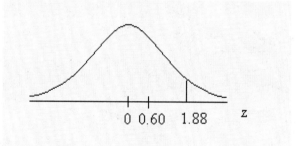

11.10   Rejection region: $z < -z_{.025} = -1.96$ or $z > z_{.025} = 1.96$

$$z = \frac{\bar{x} - \mu}{\sigma / \sqrt{n}} = \frac{100 - 100}{10 / \sqrt{100}} = 0$$

p-value = $2P(Z > 0) = 2(.5) = 1.00$

There is not enough evidence to infer that $\mu \neq 100$.

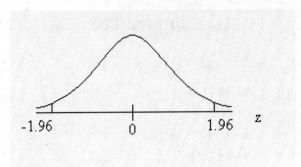

11.12 Rejection region: $z < -z_{.05} = -1.645$

$$z = \frac{\bar{x} - \mu}{\sigma / \sqrt{n}} = \frac{48 - 50}{15 / \sqrt{100}} = -1.33$$

p-value = $P(Z < -1.33) = .0918$

There is not enough evidence to infer that $\mu < 50$.

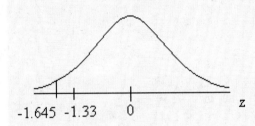

11.14 a. $z = \dfrac{\bar{x} - \mu}{\sigma / \sqrt{n}} = \dfrac{190 - 200}{50 / \sqrt{9}} = -.60$

p-value = $P(Z < -.60) = .5 - .2257 = .2743$

b. $z = \dfrac{\bar{x} - \mu}{\sigma / \sqrt{n}} = \dfrac{190 - 200}{30 / \sqrt{9}} = -1.00$

p-value = $P(Z < -1.00) = .1587$

c. $z = \dfrac{\bar{x} - \mu}{\sigma / \sqrt{n}} = \dfrac{190 - 200}{10 / \sqrt{9}} = -3.00$

p-value = $P(Z < -3.00) = .0013$

d.   The value of the test statistic decreases and the p-value decreases.

11.16 a. $z = \dfrac{\bar{x} - \mu}{\sigma / \sqrt{n}} = \dfrac{99 - 100}{8 / \sqrt{100}} = -1.25$

p-value = $2P(Z < -1.25) = 2(.1056) = .2112$

112

b. $z = \dfrac{\overline{x} - \mu}{\sigma / \sqrt{n}} = \dfrac{99 - 100}{8 / \sqrt{50}} = -.88$

p-value $= 2P(Z < -.88) = 2(.1894) = .3788$

c. $z = \dfrac{\overline{x} - \mu}{\sigma / \sqrt{n}} = \dfrac{99 - 100}{8 / \sqrt{20}} = -.56$

p-value $= 2P(Z < -.56) = 2(.2877) = .5754$

d. The value of the test statistic increases and the p-value increases.

11.18 a. $z = \dfrac{\overline{x} - \mu}{\sigma / \sqrt{n}} = \dfrac{72 - 60}{20 / \sqrt{25}} = 3.00$

p-value $= P(Z > 3.00) = 1 - .9987 = .0013$

b. $z = \dfrac{\overline{x} - \mu}{\sigma / \sqrt{n}} = \dfrac{68 - 60}{20 / \sqrt{25}} = 2.00$

p-value $= P(Z > 2.00) = 1 - .9772 = .0228$

c. $z = \dfrac{\overline{x} - \mu}{\sigma / \sqrt{n}} = \dfrac{64 - 60}{20 / \sqrt{25}} = 1.00$

p-value $= P(Z > 1.00) = 1 - .8413 = .1587$

d. The value of the test statistic decreases and the p-value increases.

11.20 a. $z = \dfrac{\overline{x} - \mu}{\sigma / \sqrt{n}} = \dfrac{178 - 170}{35 / \sqrt{400}} = 4.57$

p-value $= P(Z > 4.57) = 0.$

b. $z = \dfrac{\overline{x} - \mu}{\sigma / \sqrt{n}} = \dfrac{178 - 170}{100 / \sqrt{400}} = 1.60$

p-value $= P(Z > 1.60) = 1 - .9452 = .0548$

The value of the test statistic decreases and the p-value increases.

11.22 a. $z = \dfrac{\overline{x} - \mu}{\sigma / \sqrt{n}} = \dfrac{21.63 - 22}{6 / \sqrt{100}} = -.62$

p-value $= P(Z < -.62) = .2676$

b. $z = \dfrac{\overline{x} - \mu}{\sigma / \sqrt{n}} = \dfrac{21.63 - 22}{6 / \sqrt{500}} = -1.38$

p-value $= P(Z < -1.38) = .0838$

The value of the test statistic decreases and the p-value decreases.

11.24 $\bar{x}$ $z = \dfrac{\bar{x} - 22}{6 / \sqrt{220}}$ p-value

$\bar{x}$	z	p-value
22.0	0	.5
21.8	−.49	.3121
21.6	−.99	.1611
21.4	−1.48	.0694
21.2	−1.98	.0239
21.0	−2.47	.0068
20.8	−2.97	.0015
20.6	−3.46	0
20.4	−3.96	0

11.26   a. $z = \dfrac{\bar{x} - \mu}{\sigma / \sqrt{n}} = \dfrac{17.55 - 17.09}{2 / \sqrt{100}} = 2.30$

p-value $= 2P(Z > 2.30) = 2(1 - .9893) = 2(.0107) = .0214$

     b. $z = \dfrac{\bar{x} - \mu}{\sigma / \sqrt{n}} = \dfrac{17.55 - 17.09}{10 / \sqrt{100}} = .46$

p-value $= 2P(Z > .46) = 2(1 - .6772) = 2(.3228) = .6456$

The value of the test statistic decreases and the p-value increases.

11.28 $H_0 : \mu = 5$

     $H_1 : \mu > 5$

     $z = \dfrac{\bar{x} - \mu}{\sigma / \sqrt{n}} = \dfrac{6 - 5}{1.5 / \sqrt{10}} = 2.11$

p-value $= P(Z > 2.11) = 1 - .9826 = .0174$

There is enough evidence to infer that the mean is greater than 5 cases.

11.30 $H_0 : \mu = 12$

     $H_1 : \mu < 12$

     $z = \dfrac{\bar{x} - \mu}{\sigma / \sqrt{n}} = \dfrac{11.00 - 12}{3 / \sqrt{15}} = -1.29$

p-value $= P(Z < -1.29) = .0985$

There is enough evidence to infer that the average number of golf balls lost is less than 12.

11.32 $H_0 : \mu = 6$

     $H_1 : \mu > 6$

     $z = \dfrac{\bar{x} - \mu}{\sigma / \sqrt{n}} = \dfrac{6.60 - 6}{2 / \sqrt{10}} = .95$

p-value $= P(Z > .95) = 1 - .8289 = .1711$

There is not enough evidence to infer that the mean time spent putting on the 18th green is greater than 6 minutes.

11.34 $H_0 : \mu = 25$

$H_1 : \mu > 25$

$z = \dfrac{\bar{x} - \mu}{\sigma / \sqrt{n}} = \dfrac{30.22 - 25}{12 / \sqrt{18}} = 1.85$

p-value = $P(Z > 1.85) = 1 - .9678 = .0322$

There is not enough evidence to conclude that the manager is correct.

11.36 $H_0 : \mu = 30,000$

$H_1 : \mu < 30,000$

$z = \dfrac{\bar{x} - \mu}{\sigma / \sqrt{n}} = \dfrac{29,120 - 30,000}{8,000 / \sqrt{350}} = -2.06$

p-value = $(P(Z < -2.06) = .0197$

There is enough evidence to infer that the president is correct

11.38   a. $H_0 : \mu = 17.85$

$H_1 : \mu \qquad > 17.85$

$z = \dfrac{\bar{x} - \mu}{\sigma / \sqrt{n}} = \dfrac{19.13 - 17.85}{3.87 / \sqrt{25}} = 1.65$

p-value = $P(Z > 1.65) = 1 - .9505 = .0495$

There is enough evidence to infer that the campaign was successful.

b.   We must assume that the population standard deviation is unchanged.

11.40 $H_0 : \mu = 55$

$H_1 : \mu > 55$

$z = \dfrac{\bar{x} - \mu}{\sigma / \sqrt{n}} = \dfrac{55.80 - 55}{5 / \sqrt{200}} = 2.26$

p-value = $P(Z > 2.26) = 1 - .9881 = .0119$

There is not enough evidence to support the officer's belief.

11.42 $H_0 : \mu = 20$

$H_1 : \mu < 20$

$z = \dfrac{\bar{x} - \mu}{\sigma / \sqrt{n}} = \dfrac{19.39 - 20}{3 / \sqrt{36}} = -1.22$

p-value = $P(Z < -1.22) = .1112$

There is not enough evidence to infer that the manager is correct.

11.44 $H_0 : \mu = 4$

$H_1 : \mu \neq 4$

$z = \dfrac{\bar{x} - \mu}{\sigma / \sqrt{n}} = \dfrac{4.84 - 4}{2 / \sqrt{63}} = 3.33$

p-value = 2P(Z > 3.33) = 0

There is enough evidence to infer that the average Alpine skier does not ski 4 times per year.

11.46 $H_0 : \mu = 32$

$H_1 : \mu < 32$

$z = \dfrac{\bar{x} - \mu}{\sigma / \sqrt{n}} = \dfrac{29.92 - 32}{8 / \sqrt{110}} = -2.73$

p-value = P(Z < –2.73) = 1– .9968 = .0032

There is enough evidence to infer that there has been a decrease in the mean time away from desks. A type I error occurs when we conclude that the plan decreases the mean time away from desks when it actually does not. This error is quite expensive. Consequently we demand a low p-value. The p-value is small enough to infer that there has been a decrease.

11.48   Rejection region: $\dfrac{\bar{x} - \mu}{\sigma / \sqrt{n}} > z_{\alpha/2}$ or $\dfrac{\bar{x} - \mu}{\sigma / \sqrt{n}} < -z_{\alpha/2}$

$\dfrac{\bar{x} - 200}{10 / \sqrt{100}} > z_{.025} = 1.96$ or $\dfrac{\bar{x} - 200}{10 / \sqrt{100}} < -1.96$

$\bar{x} > 201.96$ or $\bar{x} < 198.04$

β = P(198.04 < $\bar{x}$ < 201.96 given μ = 203)

$= P\left(\dfrac{198.04 - 203}{10 / \sqrt{100}} < \dfrac{\bar{x} - \mu}{\sigma / \sqrt{n}} < \dfrac{201.96 - 203}{10 / \sqrt{100}} \right) = P(-4.96 < z < -1.04) = .1492 - 0 = .1492$

11.50   Rejection region: $\dfrac{\bar{x} - \mu}{\sigma / \sqrt{n}} < -z_{\alpha}$

$\dfrac{\bar{x} - 50}{10 / \sqrt{40}} < -z_{.05} = -1.645$

$\bar{x} < 47.40$

β = P($\bar{x}$ > 47.40 given μ = 48) = $P\left(\dfrac{\bar{x} - \mu}{\sigma / \sqrt{n}} > \dfrac{47.40 - 48}{10 / \sqrt{40}} \right)$ = P(z > –.38) = 1 – .3520 = .6480

11.52   a.   Rejection region: $\dfrac{\overline{x}-\mu}{\sigma/\sqrt{n}} > z_\alpha$

$\dfrac{\overline{x}-100}{20/\sqrt{100}} > z_{.10} = 1.28$

$\overline{x} > 102.56$

$\beta = P(\overline{x} < 102.56 \text{ given } \mu = 102) = P\left(\dfrac{\overline{x}-\mu}{\sigma/\sqrt{n}} < \dfrac{102.56-102}{20/\sqrt{100}}\right) = P(z < .28) = .6103$

   b.   Rejection region: $\dfrac{\overline{x}-\mu}{\sigma/\sqrt{n}} > z_\alpha$

$\dfrac{\overline{x}-100}{20/\sqrt{100}} > z_{.02} = 2.55$

$\overline{x} > 104.11$

$\beta = P(\overline{x} < 104.11 \text{ given } \mu = 102) = P\left(\dfrac{\overline{x}-\mu}{\sigma/\sqrt{n}} < \dfrac{104.11-102}{20/\sqrt{100}}\right) = P(z < 1.06) = .8554$

   c. β increases.

11.54
Exercise 11.52 a

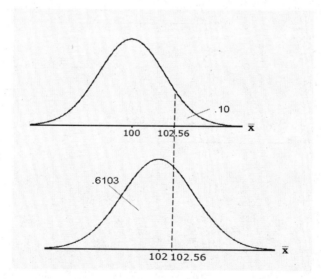

Exercise 11.52 b

117

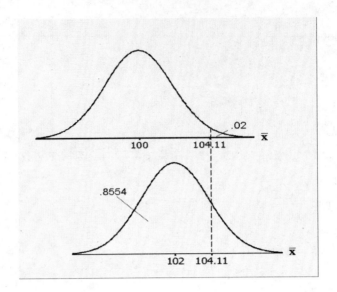

Exercise 11.53 a

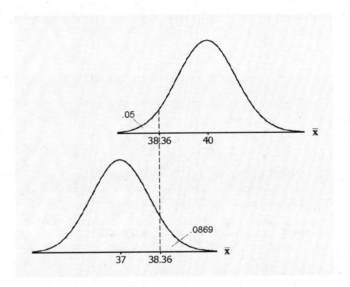

Exercise 11.53 b

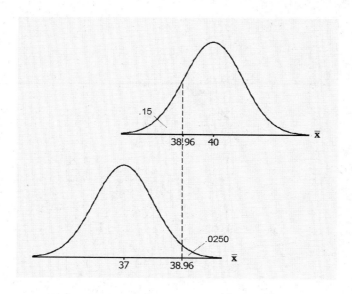

11.56   a.   Rejection region: $\dfrac{\bar{x} - \mu}{\sigma / \sqrt{n}} > z_\alpha$

$$\dfrac{\bar{x} - 300}{50 / \sqrt{81}} > z_{.05} = 1.645$$

$\bar{x} > 309.14$

$$\beta = P(\bar{x} < 309.14 \text{ given } \mu = 310) = P\left(\dfrac{\bar{x} - \mu}{\sigma / \sqrt{n}} < \dfrac{309.14 - 310}{50 / \sqrt{81}} \right) = P(z < -.15) = .4404$$

   b.   Rejection region: $\dfrac{\bar{x} - \mu}{\sigma / \sqrt{n}} > z_\alpha$

$$\dfrac{\bar{x} - 300}{50 / \sqrt{36}} > z_{.05} = 1.645$$

$\bar{x} > 313.71$

$$\beta = P(\bar{x} < 313.71 \text{ given } \mu = 310) = P\left(\dfrac{\bar{x} - \mu}{\sigma / \sqrt{n}} < \dfrac{313.71 - 310}{50 / \sqrt{36}} \right) = P(z < .45) = .6736$$

   c. β increases.

11.58

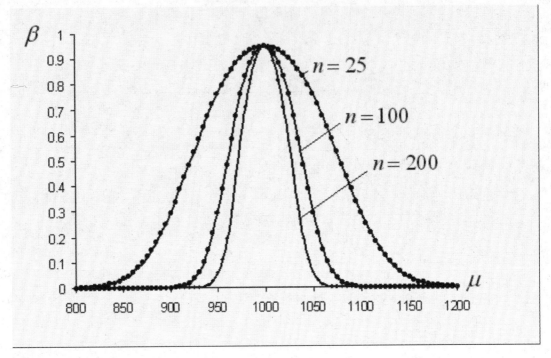

11.60 $H_0 : \mu = 170$

$H_1 : \mu < 170$

A Type I error occurs when we conclude that the new system is not cost effective when it actually is. A Type II error occurs when we conclude that the new system is cost effective when it actually is not.

The test statistic is the same. However, the p-value equals 1 minus the p-value calculated Example 11.1. That is,

 p-value $= 1 - .0069 = .9931$

We conclude that there is no evidence to infer that the mean is less than 170. That is, there is no evidence to infer that the new system will not be cost effective.

11.62   Rejection region: $\dfrac{\overline{x} - \mu}{\sigma / \sqrt{n}} < -z_\alpha$

$\dfrac{\overline{x} - 22}{6 / \sqrt{220}} < -z_{.10} = -1.28$

$\overline{x} < 21.48$

$\beta = P(\overline{x} > 21.48 \text{ given } \mu = 21) = P\left(\dfrac{\overline{x} - \mu}{\sigma / \sqrt{n}} > \dfrac{21.48 - 21}{6 / \sqrt{220}} \right) = P(z > 1.19) = 1 - .8830 = .1170$

The company can decide whether the sample size and significance level are appropriate.

11.64   Rejection region: $\dfrac{\overline{x}-\mu}{\sigma/\sqrt{n}} < -z_\alpha$

$\dfrac{\overline{x}-32}{8/\sqrt{110}} < -z_{.05} = -1.645$

$\overline{x} < 30.75$

$\beta = P(\overline{x} > 30.75 \ \text{given} \ \mu = 30) = P\left(\dfrac{\overline{x}-\mu}{\sigma/\sqrt{n}} > \dfrac{30.75-30)}{8/\sqrt{110}}\right) = P(z > .98) = 1 - .8365 = .1635$

β can be decreased by increasing α and/or increasing the sample size.

11.66   A Type I error occurs when we conclude that the site is feasible when it is not. The consequence of this decision is to conduct further testing. A Type II error occurs when we do not conclude that a site is feasible when it actually is. We will do no further testing on this site, and as a result we will not build on a good site. If there are few other sits, this could be an expensive mistake.

Chapter 12

12.2   a. $\bar{x} \pm t_{\alpha/2}s/\sqrt{n} = 1{,}500 \pm 1.984(300/\sqrt{100}) = 1{,}500 \pm 59.52$; LCL = 1,440.48, UCL = 1,559.52

    b. $\bar{x} \pm t_{\alpha/2}s/\sqrt{n} = 1{,}500 \pm 1.984(200/\sqrt{100}) = 1{,}500 \pm 39.68$; LCL = 1,460.32, UCL = 1,539.68

    c. $\bar{x} \pm t_{\alpha/2}s/\sqrt{n} = 1{,}500 \pm 1.984(100/\sqrt{100}) = 1{,}500 \pm 19.84$; LCL = 1,480.16, UCL = 1,519.84

    d.   The interval narrows.

12.4   a. $\bar{x} \pm t_{\alpha/2}s/\sqrt{n} = 10 \pm 1.984(1/\sqrt{100}) = 10 \pm .20$; LCL = 9.80, UCL = 10.20

    b. $\bar{x} \pm t_{\alpha/2}s/\sqrt{n} = 10 \pm 1.984(4/\sqrt{100}) = 10 \pm .79$; LCL = 9.21, UCL = 10.79

    c. $\bar{x} \pm t_{\alpha/2}s/\sqrt{n} = 10 \pm 1.984(10/\sqrt{100}) = 10 \pm 1.98$; LCL = 8.02, UCL = 11.98

    d.   The interval widens.

12.6   a. $\bar{x} \pm t_{\alpha/2}s/\sqrt{n} = 63 \pm 1.990(8/\sqrt{81}) = 63 \pm 1.77$; LCL = 61.23, UCL = 64.77

    b. $\bar{x} \pm t_{\alpha/2}s/\sqrt{n} = 63 \pm 2.000(8/\sqrt{64}) = 63 \pm 2.00$; LCL = 61.00, UCL = 65.00

    c. $\bar{x} \pm t_{\alpha/2}s/\sqrt{n} = 63 \pm 2.030(8/\sqrt{36}) = 63 \pm 2.71$; LCL = 60.29, UCL = 65.71

    d.   The interval widens.

12.8 $H_0 : \mu = 180$

    $H_1 : \mu \neq 180$

    Rejection region: $t < -t_{\alpha/2,n-1} = -t_{.025,199} \approx -1.972$ or $t > t_{\alpha/2,n-1} = t_{.025,199} = 1.972$

    a. $t = \dfrac{\bar{x}-\mu}{s/\sqrt{n}} = \dfrac{175-180}{22/\sqrt{200}} = -3.21$, p-value = .0015. There is enough evidence to infer that the population

       mean is not equal to 180.

    b. $t = \dfrac{\bar{x}-\mu}{s/\sqrt{n}} = \dfrac{175-180}{45/\sqrt{200}} = -1.57$, p-value = .1177. There is not enough evidence to infer that the

       population mean is not equal to 180.

    c. $t = \dfrac{\bar{x}-\mu}{s/\sqrt{n}} = \dfrac{175-180}{60/\sqrt{200}} = -1.18$, p-value = .2400. There is not enough evidence to infer that the

       population mean is not equal to 180.

    d.   As the s increases, the test statistic increases and the p-value increases.

12.10 $H_0 : \mu = 50$

$H_0 : \mu \neq 50$

a. Rejection region: $t < -t_{\alpha/2,n-1} = -t_{.05,24} = -1.711$ or $t > t_{\alpha/2,n-1} = t_{.05,24} = 1.711$

$t = \dfrac{\bar{x} - \mu}{s/\sqrt{n}} = \dfrac{52 - 50}{15/\sqrt{25}} = .67$, p-value = .5113. There is not enough evidence to infer that the population

mean is not equal to 50.

b. Rejection region: $t < -t_{\alpha/2,n-1} = -t_{.05,14} = -1.761$ or $t > t_{\alpha/2,n-1} = t_{.05,14} = 1.761$

$t = \dfrac{\bar{x} - \mu}{s/\sqrt{n}} = \dfrac{52 - 50}{15/\sqrt{15}} = .52$, p-value = .6136. There is not enough evidence to infer that the population

mean is not equal to 50.

c. Rejection region: $t < -t_{\alpha/2,n-1} = -t_{.05,4} = -2.132$ or $t > t_{\alpha/2,n-1} = t_{.05,4} = -2.132$

$t = \dfrac{\bar{x} - \mu}{s/\sqrt{n}} = \dfrac{52 - 50}{15/\sqrt{5}} = .30$, p-value = .7804. There is not enough evidence to infer that the population

mean is not equal to 50.

d. The test statistic decreases and the p-value increases.

12.12 Rejection region: $t > t_{\alpha,n-1} = t_{.01,99} \approx 2.364$

a. $t = \dfrac{\bar{x} - \mu}{s/\sqrt{n}} = \dfrac{106 - 100}{35/\sqrt{100}} = 1.71$, p-value = .0448. There is not enough evidence to infer that the

population mean is greater than 100.

b. $t = \dfrac{\bar{x} - \mu}{s/\sqrt{n}} = \dfrac{106 - 100}{25/\sqrt{100}} = 2.40$, p-value = .0091. There is enough evidence to infer that the population

mean is greater than 100.

c. $t = \dfrac{\bar{x} - \mu}{s/\sqrt{n}} = \dfrac{106 - 100}{15/\sqrt{100}} = 4.00$, p-value = .0001. There is enough evidence to infer that the population

mean is greater than 100

d. The test statistic increases and the p-value decreases.

12.14 a. $\bar{x} \pm t_{\alpha/2} s/\sqrt{n} = 175 \pm 2.132(30/\sqrt{5}) = 175 \pm 28.60$; LCL = 146.40, UCL = 203.60

b. $\bar{x} \pm z_{\alpha/2} \sigma/\sqrt{n} = 175 \pm 1.645(30/\sqrt{5}) = 175 \pm 22.07$; LCL = 152.93, UCL = 197.07

c. The student t distribution is more widely dispersed than the standard normal; thus, $z_{\alpha/2}$ is smaller than

$t_{\alpha/2}$.

12.16   a. $\bar{x} \pm t_{\alpha/2} s/\sqrt{n} = 350 \pm 2.576(100/\sqrt{500}) = 350 \pm 11.52$; LCL = 338.48, UCL = 361.52

        b. $\bar{x} \pm z_{\alpha/2} \sigma/\sqrt{n} = 350 \pm 2.575(100/\sqrt{500}) = 350 \pm 11.52$; LCL = 338.48, UCL = 361.52

        c.   With n = 500 the student t distribution with 999 degrees of freedom is almost identical to the standard normal distribution.

12.18 $H_0 : \mu = 110$

            $H_0 : \mu < 110$

        a.   Rejection region: $t < -t_{\alpha,n-1} = -t_{.10,9} = -1.383$

$$t = \frac{\bar{x} - \mu}{s/\sqrt{n}} = \frac{103 - 110}{17/\sqrt{10}} = -1.30,$$ p-value = .1126. There is not enough evidence to infer that the population mean is less than 110.

        b.   Rejection region: $z < -z_{\alpha} = z_{.10} = -1.28$

$$z = \frac{\bar{x} - \mu}{\sigma/\sqrt{n}} = \frac{103 - 110}{17/\sqrt{10}} = -1.30,$$ p-value = P(Z < −1.30) = .0968. There is enough evidence to infer that the population mean is less than 110.

        c.   The Student t distribution is more dispersed than the standard normal.

12.20   a.   Rejection region: $t > t_{\alpha,n-1} = t_{.05,999} = 1.645$

$$t = \frac{\bar{x} - \mu}{s/\sqrt{n}} = \frac{405 - 400}{100/\sqrt{1,000}} = 1.58,$$ p-value = .0569. There is not enough evidence to infer that the population mean is less than 15.

        b.   Rejection region: $z > z_{\alpha} = z_{.05} = 1.645$

$$t = \frac{\bar{x} - \mu}{s/\sqrt{n}} = \frac{405 - 400}{100/\sqrt{1,000}} = 1.58,$$ p-value = P(Z > 1.58) = 1 − .9429 = .0571. There is not enough evidence to infer that the population mean is less than 15.

        c.   With n = 1,000 the student t distribution with 999 degrees of freedom is almost identical to the standard normal distribution.

12.22 $\bar{x} \pm t_{\alpha/2} s/\sqrt{n} = 24{,}051 \pm 2.145(17{,}386/\sqrt{15}) = 24{,}051 \pm 9{,}628$; LCL = 14,422, UCL = 33,680

12.24 $H_0 : \mu = 8$

$H_0 : \mu < 8$

Rejection region: $t < -t_{\alpha,n-1} = -t_{.01,17} = -2.567$

$t = \dfrac{\bar{x} - \mu}{s / \sqrt{n}} = \dfrac{7.91 - 8}{.085 / \sqrt{18}} = -4.49$, p-value = .0002. There is enough evidence to conclude that the average container is mislabeled.

12.26 $\bar{x} \pm t_{\alpha/2} s / \sqrt{n} = 26.67 \pm 1.796(16.52 / \sqrt{12}) = 26.67 \pm 8.56$; LCL = 18.11, UCL = 35.23

12.28 $H_0 : \mu = 10$

$H_0 : \mu < 10$

Rejection region: $t < -t_{\alpha,n-1} = -t_{.10,9} = -1.383$

$t = \dfrac{\bar{x} - \mu}{s / \sqrt{n}} = \dfrac{7.10 - 10}{3.75 / \sqrt{10}} = -2.45$, p-value = .0185. There is enough evidence to infer that the mean proportion of returns is less than 10%.

12.30 $\bar{x} \pm t_{\alpha/2} s / \sqrt{n} = 4.66 \pm 2.576(2.37 / \sqrt{240}) = 4.66 \pm .39$; LCL = 4.27, UCL = 5.05

Total number: LCL = 100 million (4.27) = 427 million, UCL = 100 million (5.05) = 505 million

12.32 $\bar{x} \pm t_{\alpha/2} s / \sqrt{n} = 15,137 \pm 1.96(5,263 / \sqrt{306} = 15,137 \pm 590$; LCL = 14,547, UCL = 15,727

Total credit card debt: LCL = 50 million (14,547) = \$727,350 million, UCL = 50 million (15,727) = \$786,350 million

12.34 $\bar{x} \pm t_{\alpha/2} s / \sqrt{n} = 2.67 \pm 1.973(2.50 / \sqrt{188}) = 2.67 \pm .36$; LCL = 2.31, UCL = 3.03

12.36 $\bar{x} \pm t_{\alpha/2} s / \sqrt{n} = 422.36 \pm 1.973(122.77 / \sqrt{176}) = 422.36 \pm 18.26$; LCL = 404.10, UCL = 440.62

Total cost of congestion: LCL = 128 million (404.10) = \$51,725 million, UCL = 128 million (440.62) = \$56,399 million

12.38 $H_0 : \mu = 15$

$H_0 : \mu > 15$

Rejection region: $t > t_{\alpha,n-1} = t_{.05,115} \approx 1.658$

$t = \dfrac{\bar{x} - \mu}{s / \sqrt{n}} = \dfrac{15.27 - 15}{5.72 / \sqrt{116}} = .51$, p-value = .3061. There is not enough evidence to infer that the mean number of commercials is greater than 15.

12.40 $H_0 : \mu = 85$

$H_0 : \mu > 85$

Rejection region: $t > t_{\alpha, n-1} = t_{.05,84} \approx 1.663$

$t = \dfrac{\bar{x} - \mu}{s / \sqrt{n}} = \dfrac{89.27 - 85}{17.30 / \sqrt{85}} = 2.28$, p-value = .0127. There is enough evidence to infer that an e-grocery will be successful.

12.42 $H_0 : \mu = 450$

$H_0 : \mu > 450$

Rejection region: $t > t_{\alpha, n-1} = t_{.05,49} \approx 1.676$

$t = \dfrac{\bar{x} - \mu}{s / \sqrt{n}} = \dfrac{460.38 - 450}{38.83\sqrt{50}} = 1.89$, p-value = .0323. There is enough evidence to infer that the belief is correct

12.44 $H_0 : \sigma^2 = 100$

$H_1 : \sigma^2 < 100$

a. Rejection region: $\chi^2 < \chi^2_{1-\alpha, n-1} = \chi^2_{.99,49} \approx 29.7$

$\chi^2 = \dfrac{(n-1)s^2}{\sigma^2} = \dfrac{(50-1)(80)}{100} = 39.20$, p-value = .1596. There is not enough evidence to infer that the

population variance is less than 100.

b. Rejection region: $\chi^2 < \chi^2_{1-\alpha, n-1} = \chi^2_{.99,99} \approx 70.1$

$\chi^2 = \dfrac{(n-1)s^2}{\sigma^2} = \dfrac{(100-1)(80)}{100} = 79.20$, p-value = .0714. There is not enough evidence to infer that the

population variance is less than 100.

c. Increasing the sample size increases the test statistic and decreases the p-value.

12.46 $\text{LCL} = \dfrac{(n-1)s^2}{\chi^2_{\alpha/2, n-1}} = \dfrac{(n-1)s^2}{\chi^2_{.05,7}} = \dfrac{(8-1)(.00093)}{14.1} = .00046$,

$\text{UCL} = \dfrac{(n-1)s^2}{\chi^2_{1-\alpha/2, n-1}} = \dfrac{(n-1)s^2}{\chi^2_{.95,7}} = \dfrac{(8-1)(.00093)}{2.17} = .00300$

12.48 $H_0 : \sigma^2 = 23$

$H_1 : \sigma^2 \neq 23$

Rejection region: $\chi^2 < \chi^2_{1-\alpha/2, n-1} = \chi^2_{.95,7} = 2.17$ or $\chi^2 > \chi^2_{\alpha/2, n-1} = \chi^2_{.05,7} = 14.1$

$\chi^2 = \dfrac{(n-1)s^2}{\sigma^2} = \dfrac{(8-1)(16.50)}{23} = 5.02$, p-value = .6854. There is not enough evidence to infer that the population variance has changed.

12.50 a. $H_0 : \sigma^2 = 250$

$H_1 : \sigma^2 \neq 250$

Rejection region: $\chi^2 < \chi^2_{1-\alpha/2, n-1} = \chi^2_{.975,24} = 12.4$ or $\chi^2 > \chi^2_{\alpha/2, n-1} = \chi^2_{.025,24} = 39.4$

$\chi^2 = \dfrac{(n-1)s^2}{\sigma^2} = \dfrac{(25-1)(270.58)}{250} = 25.98$, p-value = .7088. There is not enough evidence to infer that

the population variance is not equal to 250.

b.   Demand is required to be normally distributed.

c.   The histogram is approximately bell shaped.

12.52 $LCL = \dfrac{(n-1)s^2}{\chi^2_{\alpha/2, n-1}} = \dfrac{(n-1)s^2}{\chi^2_{.05,89}} = \dfrac{(90-1)(4.72)}{113} = 3.72$

$UCL = \dfrac{(n-1)s^2}{\chi^2_{1-\alpha/2, n-1}} = \dfrac{(n-1)s^2}{\chi^2_{.95,89}} = \dfrac{(90-1)(4.72)}{69.1} = 6.08$

12.54 $LCL = \dfrac{(n-1)s^2}{\chi^2_{\alpha/2, n-1}} = \dfrac{(n-1)s^2}{\chi^2_{.025,24}} = \dfrac{(25-1)(19.68)}{39.4} = 11.99$

$UCL = \dfrac{(n-1)s^2}{\chi^2_{1-\alpha/2, n-1}} = \dfrac{(n-1)s^2}{\chi^2_{.975,24}} = \dfrac{(25-1)(19.68)}{12.4} = 38.09$

12.56 a. $\hat{p} \pm z_{\alpha/2}\sqrt{\hat{p}(1-\hat{p})/n} = .50 \pm 1.96\sqrt{.50(1-.50)/400} = .50 \pm .0490$

b. $\hat{p} \pm z_{\alpha/2}\sqrt{\hat{p}(1-\hat{p})/n} = .33 \pm 1.96\sqrt{.33(1-.33)/400} = .33 \pm .0461$

c. $\hat{p} \pm z_{\alpha/2}\sqrt{\hat{p}(1-\hat{p})/n} = .10 \pm 1.96\sqrt{.10(1-.10)/400} = .10 \pm .0294$

d.   The interval narrows.

12.58 a. $z = \dfrac{\hat{p}-p}{\sqrt{p(1-p)/n}} = \dfrac{.73-.70}{\sqrt{.70(1-.70)/100}} = .65$, p-value = $P(Z > .65) = 1 - .7422 = .2578$

b. $z = \dfrac{\hat{p}-p}{\sqrt{p(1-p)/n}} = \dfrac{.72-.70}{\sqrt{.70(1-.70)/100}} = .44$, p-value = $P(Z > .44) = 1 - .6700 = .3300$

c. $z = \dfrac{\hat{p}-p}{\sqrt{p(1-p)/n}} = \dfrac{.71-.70}{\sqrt{.70(1-.70)/100}} = .22$, p-value = $P(Z > .22) = 1 - .5871 = .4129$

d.   The z statistic decreases and the p-value increases.

12.60 a. $.5 \pm .03$

   b. Yes, because the sample size was chosen to produce this interval.

12.62 $n = \left(\dfrac{z_{\alpha/2}\sqrt{\hat{p}(1-\hat{p})}}{B}\right)^2 = \left(\dfrac{1.645\sqrt{.75(1-.75)}}{.03}\right)^2 = 564$

12.64 a. $\hat{p} \pm z_{\alpha/2}\sqrt{\hat{p}(1-\hat{p})/n} = .92 \pm 1.645\sqrt{.92(1-.92)/564} = .92 \pm .0188$

   b. The interval is narrower.

   c. Yes, because the interval estimate is better than specified.

12.66 $\hat{p} = 259/373 = .69$

   $\hat{p} \pm z_{\alpha/2}\sqrt{\hat{p}(1-\hat{p})/n} = .69 \pm 1.96\sqrt{.69(1-.69)/373} = .69 \pm .0469;$ LCL = .6431, UCL = .7369

12.68 $\hat{p} = 204/314 = .65$

   $\hat{p} \pm z_{\alpha/2}\sqrt{\hat{p}(1-\hat{p})/n} = .65 \pm 1.645\sqrt{.65(1-.65)/314} = .65 \pm .0443;$ LCL = .6057, UCL = .6943

12.70 $\hat{p} = 97/344 = .28$

   $\hat{p} \pm z_{\alpha/2}\sqrt{\hat{p}(1-\hat{p})/n} = .28 \pm 1.96\sqrt{.28(1-.28)/344} = .28 \pm .0474;$ LCL = .2326, UCL = .3274

12.72 LCL = .1332(1,000,000)(3.00) = \$399,600, UCL = .2068(1,000,000)(3.00) = \$620,400

12.74 $\tilde{p} = \dfrac{x+2}{n+4} = \dfrac{3+2}{374+4} = .0132$

   $\tilde{p} \pm z_{\alpha/2}\sqrt{\dfrac{\tilde{p}(1-\tilde{p})}{n+4}} = .0132 \pm 1.645\sqrt{\dfrac{.0132(1-.0132)}{374+4}} = .0132 \pm .0097;$ LCL = .0035, UCL = .0229

12.76 a. $\hat{p} \pm z_{\alpha/2}\sqrt{\hat{p}(1-\hat{p})/n} = .1056 \pm 1.96\sqrt{.1056(1-.1056)/521} = .1056 \pm .0264;$ LCL = .0792, UCL
      = .1320

12.78 $\hat{p} \pm z_{\alpha/2}\sqrt{\hat{p}(1-\hat{p})/n} = .7584 \pm 1.96\sqrt{.7584(1-.7584)/567} = .7584 \pm .0352;$ LCL = .7232,
      UCL = .7936

12.80 $\hat{p} \pm z_{\alpha/2} \sqrt{\hat{p}(1-\hat{p})/n} = .2333 \pm 1.96\sqrt{.2333(1-.2333)/120} = .2333 \pm .0757;$ LCL = .1576,

UCL = .3090

12.82 a. $\hat{p} \pm z_{\alpha/2} \sqrt{\hat{p}(1-\hat{p})/n} = .7840 \pm 1.96\sqrt{.7840(1-.7840)/426} = .7840 \pm .0391;$ LCL = .7449,

UCL = .8231

12.84 Codes 1, 2, and 3 have been recoded to 5.

$H_0 : p = .90$

$H_1 : p > .90$

$z = \dfrac{\hat{p}-p}{\sqrt{p(1-p)/n}} = \dfrac{.96-.90}{\sqrt{.90(1-.90)/100}} = 2.00,$ p-value = $P(Z > 2.00) = 1 - .9772 = .0228.$ There is enough

evidence to conclude that more than 90% of all business students would rate the book as at least adequate.

12.86 $H_0 : p = .12$

$H_1 : p > .12$

$z = \dfrac{\hat{p}-p}{\sqrt{p(1-p)/n}} = \dfrac{.1625-.12}{\sqrt{.12(1-.12)/400}} = 2.62,$ p-value = $P(Z > 2.62) = 1 - .9956 = .0044.$ There is enough

evidence to infer that the proposed newspaper will be financially viable.

12.88 a. $\hat{p} \pm z_{\alpha/2} \sqrt{\hat{p}(1-\hat{p})/n} = .2031 \pm 1.96\sqrt{.2031(1-.2031)/650} = .2031 \pm .0309;$ LCL = .1722,

UCL = .2340

Number: LCL = 5 million (.1722) = .861 million, UCL = 5 million (.2340) = 1.17 million

12.90 Codes 3 and 4 were changed to 5

$\hat{p} \pm z_{\alpha/2} \sqrt{\hat{p}(1-\hat{p})/n} = .7305 \pm 1.96\sqrt{.7305(1-.7305)/475} = .7305 \pm .0399;$ LCL = .6906,
UCL = .7704; Market segment size: LCL = 19,108,000 (.6906) = 13,195,985,
UCL = 19,108,000 (.7704) = 14,720,803

12.92 a. $\hat{p} \pm z_{\alpha/2} \sqrt{\hat{p}(1-\hat{p})/n} = .2919 \pm 1.96\sqrt{.2919(1-.2919)/1836} = .2919 \pm .0208;$ LCL = .2711,

UCL = .3127

b. LCL = 107,194,000 (.2711) = 29,060,293, UCL = 107,194,000 (.3127) = 33,519,564

12.94 $\hat{p} \pm z_{\alpha/2} \sqrt{\hat{p}(1-\hat{p})/n} = .1748 \pm 1.645\sqrt{.1748(1-.1748)/412} = .1748 \pm .0308;$ LCL = .1440,
UCL = .2056; Number: LCL = 187 million(.1440) = 26.928 million, UCL = 187 million(.2056) = 38.447
million

12.96 $\hat{p} = 4/80 = .05$; $\hat{p} \pm z_{\alpha/2}\sqrt{\hat{p}(1-\hat{p})/n} = .05 \pm 1.96\sqrt{.05(1-.05)/80} = .05 \pm .0478$; LCL = .0022, UCL = .0978; Number: LCL = 2,453(.0022) = 5.4 (rounded to 5), UCL = 2,453(.0978) = 239.9 (rounded to 240)

12.98 $\bar{x} \pm t_{\alpha/2}s/\sqrt{n} = 229.18 \pm 1.96(67.36/\sqrt{500}) = 229.18 \pm 5.92$; LCL = 223.26, UCL = 235.10
Total value: LCL = 73,544(223.26) = \$16,419,433, UCL = 73,544(235.10) = \$17,290,194

12.100 a. $\hat{p} = 5/85 = .0588$; $\hat{p} \pm z_{\alpha/2}\sqrt{\dfrac{\hat{p}(1-\hat{p})}{n}}\sqrt{\dfrac{N-n}{N-1}} = .0588 \pm 1.645\sqrt{\dfrac{.0588(1-.0588)}{85}}\sqrt{\dfrac{1,864-85}{1,864-1}}$

    $= .0588 \pm .0410$;

    LCL = .0178, UCL = .0998; Number: LCL = 1,864(.0178) = 33, UCL = 1,864(.0998) = 186

12.102 $\hat{p} = 18/200 = .09$; $\hat{p} \pm z_{\alpha/2}\sqrt{\dfrac{\hat{p}(1-\hat{p})}{n}}\sqrt{\dfrac{N-n}{N-1}} = .09 \pm 1.96\sqrt{\dfrac{.09(1-.09)}{200}}\sqrt{\dfrac{3,745-200}{3,745-1}} = .09 \pm .0386$; LCL = .0514, UCL = .1286; Number: LCL = 3,745(.0514) = 192, UCL = 3,745(.1286) = 482

12.104 $\hat{p} = 38/317 = .1199$; $\hat{p} \pm z_{\alpha/2}\sqrt{\hat{p}(1-\hat{p})/n} = .1199 \pm 1.96\sqrt{.1199(1-.1199)/317} = .1199 \pm .0358$; LCL = .0841, UCL = .1557; Number: LCL = 102,412(.0841) = 8,613, UCL = 102,412(.1557) = 15,946

12.106 $H_0 : \mu = 60$
      $H_1 : \mu < 60$

	A	B	C	D
1	t-Test: Mean			
2				
3				*Times*
4	Mean			57.79
5	Standard Deviation			6.58
6	Hypothesized Mean			60
7	df			23
8	t Stat			-1.64
9	P(T<=t) one-tail			0.0569
10	t Critical one-tail			1.7139
11	P(T<=t) two-tail			0.1138
12	t Critical two-tail			2.0687

    $t = -1.64$, p-value = .0569. There is not enough evidence to conclude that the supplier's assertion is correct.

12.108

	A	B
1	**z-Estimate: Proportion**	
2		*Resolution*
3	Sample Proportion	0.358
4	Observations	215
5	LCL	0.304
6	UCL	0.412

LCL = .304, UCL = .412

12.110

	A	B	C	D
1	**t-Estimate: Mean**			
2				
3				*Points*
4	Mean			117.54
5	Standard Deviation			50.24
6	LCL			108.19
7	UCL			126.89

LCL = 108.19, UCL = 126.89

12.112 a.

	A	B	C	D
1	**t-Estimate: Mean**			
2				
3				*Times*
4	Mean			6.91
5	Standard Deviation			0.23
6	LCL			6.84
7	UCL			6.98

LCL = 6.84, UCL = 6.98

b.　The histogram is bell shaped.

c. $H_0 : \mu = 7$

$H_1 : \mu < 7$

	A	B	C	D
1	**t-Test: Mean**			
2				
3				*Times*
4	Mean			6.91
5	Standard Deviation			0.23
6	Hypothesized Mean			7
7	df			74
8	t Stat			-3.48
9	P(T<=t) one-tail			0.0004
10	t Critical one-tail			1.2931
11	P(T<=t) two-tail			0.0008
12	t Critical two-tail			1.6657

$t = -3.48$, p-value = .0004; there is enough evidence to infer that postal workers are spending less than seven hours doing their jobs.

12.114

	A	B	C	D
1	**t-Estimate: Mean**			
2				
3				*Times*
4	Mean			5.79
5	Standard Deviation			2.86
6	LCL			5.11
7	UCL			6.47

LCL = 5.11, UCL = 6.47

12.116 $H_0 : \sigma^2 = 4$

$H_1 : \sigma^2 > 4$

	A	B	C	D
1	**Chi Squared Test: Variance**			
2				
3				*Lengths*
4	Sample Variance			6.52
5	Hypothesized Variance			4
6	df			99
7	chi-squared Stat			161.25
8	P (CHI<=chi) one-tail			0.0001
9	chi-squared Critical one tail	Left-tail		77.0463
10		Right-tail		123.2252
11	P (CHI<=chi) two-tail			0.0002
12	chi-squared Critical two tail	Left-tail		73.3611
13		Right-tail		128.4220

$\chi^2 = 161.25$, p-value = .0001; there is enough evidence to conclude that the number of springs requiring reworking is unacceptably large.

12.118

	A	B	C	D
1	**t-Estimate: Mean**			
2				
3				*Service*
4	Mean			1.10
5	Standard Deviation			0.98
6	LCL			0.94
7	UCL			1.26

LCL = .94, UCL = 1.26

12.120 $n = \left(\dfrac{z_{\alpha/2} \sqrt{\hat{p}(1-\hat{p})}}{B} \right)^2 = \left(\dfrac{2.575\sqrt{.5(1-.5)}}{.02} \right)^2 = 4144$

12.122 Number of cars:

$H_0 : \mu = 125$

$H_1 : \mu > 125$

	A	B	C	D
1	t-Test: Mean			
2				
3				Cars
4	Mean			125.80
5	Standard Deviation			3.90
6	Hypothesized Mean			125
7	df			4
8	t Stat			0.46
9	P(T<=t) one-tail			0.3351
10	t Critical one-tail			3.7469
11	P(T<=t) two-tail			0.6702
12	t Critical two-tail			4.6041

t = .46, p-value = .3351; there is not enough evidence to infer that the employee is stealing by lying about the number of cars.

Amount of time

$H_0 : \mu = 3.5$

$H_1 : \mu > 3.5$

	A	B	C	D
1	t-Test: Mean			
2				
3				Time
4	Mean			3.61
5	Standard Deviation			0.40
6	Hypothesized Mean			3.5
7	df			628
8	t Stat			7.00
9	P(T<=t) one-tail			0
10	t Critical one-tail			2.3323
11	P(T<=t) two-tail			0
12	t Critical two-tail			2.5837

t = 7.00, p-value = 0; there is enough evidence to infer that the employee is stealing by lying about the amount of time.

Chapter 13

13.2 $H_0 : (\mu_1 - \mu_2) = 0$

$H_1 : (\mu_1 - \mu_2) \neq 0$

a. Equal-variances test statistic

Rejection region: $t < -t_{\alpha/2,v} = -t_{.025,22} = -2.074$ or $t > t_{\alpha/2,v} = t_{.025,22} = 2.074$

$$t = \frac{(\bar{x}_1 - \bar{x}_2) - (\mu_1 - \mu_2)}{\sqrt{s_p^2 \left(\frac{1}{n_1} + \frac{1}{n_2}\right)}} = \frac{(74-71)-0}{\sqrt{\left(\frac{(12-1)18^2 + (12-1)16^2}{12+12-2}\right)\left(\frac{1}{12} + \frac{1}{12}\right)}} = .43, \text{ p-value} = .6703. \text{ There is not}$$

enough evidence to infer that the population means differ.

b. Equal-variances test statistic

Rejection region: $t < -t_{\alpha/2,v} = -t_{.025,22} = -2.074$ or $t > t_{\alpha/2,v} = t_{.025,22} = 2.074$

$$t = \frac{(\bar{x}_1 - \bar{x}_2) - (\mu_1 - \mu_2)}{\sqrt{s_p^2 \left(\frac{1}{n_1} + \frac{1}{n_2}\right)}} = \frac{(74-71)-0}{\sqrt{\left(\frac{(12-1)210^2 + (12-1)198^2}{12+12-2}\right)\left(\frac{1}{12} + \frac{1}{12}\right)}} = .04, \text{ p-value} = .9716. \text{ There is}$$

not enough evidence to infer that the population means differ.

c. The value of the test statistic decreases and the p-value increases.

d. Equal-variances test statistic

Rejection region: $t < -t_{\alpha/2,v} = -t_{.025,298} = -1.960$ or $t > t_{\alpha/2,v} = t_{.025,298} = 1.960$

$$t = \frac{(\bar{x}_1 - \bar{x}_2) - (\mu_1 - \mu_2)}{\sqrt{s_p^2 \left(\frac{1}{n_1} + \frac{1}{n_2}\right)}} = \frac{(74-71)-0}{\sqrt{\left(\frac{(150-1)18^2 + (150-1)16^2}{150+150-2}\right)\left(\frac{1}{150} + \frac{1}{150}\right)}} = 1.53, \text{ p-value} = .1282.$$

There is not enough evidence to infer that the population means differ.

e. The value of the test statistic increases and the p-value decreases.

f. Rejection region: $t < -t_{\alpha/2,v} = -t_{.025,22} = -2.074$ or $t > t_{\alpha/2,v} = t_{.025,22} = 2.074$

$$t = \frac{(\bar{x}_1 - \bar{x}_2) - (\mu_1 - \mu_2)}{\sqrt{s_p^2 \left(\frac{1}{n_1} + \frac{1}{n_2}\right)}} = \frac{(76-71)-0}{\sqrt{\left(\frac{(12-1)18^2 + (12-1)16^2}{12+12-2}\right)\left(\frac{1}{12} + \frac{1}{12}\right)}} = .72, \text{ p-value} = .4796. \text{ There is}$$

not enough evidence to infer that the population means differ.

g. The value of the test statistic increases and the p-value decreases.

13.4 $H_0 : (\mu_1 - \mu_2) = 0$

$H_1 : (\mu_1 - \mu_2) > 0$

a. Unequal-variances test statistic

$$\nu = \frac{(s_1^2 / n_1 + s_2^2 / n_2)^2}{\dfrac{(s_1^2 / n_1)^2}{n_1 - 1} + \dfrac{(s_2^2 / n_2)^2}{n_2 - 1}} = 200.4 \text{ (rounded to 200)}$$

Rejection region: $t > t_{\alpha,\nu} = t_{.05,200} = 1.653$

$$t = \frac{(\bar{x}_1 - \bar{x}_2) - (\mu_1 - \mu_2)}{\sqrt{\left(\dfrac{s_1^2}{n_1} + \dfrac{s_2^2}{n_2}\right)}} = \frac{(412 - 405) - 0}{\sqrt{\left(\dfrac{128^2}{150} + \dfrac{54^2}{150}\right)}} = .62, \text{ p-value} = .2689. \text{ There is not enough evidence to}$$

infer that μ_1 is greater than μ_2.

b. Unequal-variances test statistic

$$\nu = \frac{(s_1^2 / n_1 + s_2^2 / n_2)^2}{\dfrac{(s_1^2 / n_1)^2}{n_1 - 1} + \dfrac{(s_2^2 / n_2)^2}{n_2 - 1}} = 223.1 \text{ (rounded to 223)}$$

Rejection region: $t > t_{\alpha,\nu} = t_{.05,223} \approx 1.645$

$$t = \frac{(\bar{x}_1 - \bar{x}_2) - (\mu_1 - \mu_2)}{\sqrt{\left(\dfrac{s_1^2}{n_1} + \dfrac{s_2^2}{n_2}\right)}} = \frac{(412 - 405) - 0}{\sqrt{\left(\dfrac{31^2}{150} + \dfrac{16^2}{150}\right)}} = 2.46, \text{ p-value} = .0074. \text{ There is enough evidence to infer}$$

that μ_1 is greater than μ_2.

c. The value of the test statistic increases and the p-value decreases.

d. Unequal-variances test statistic

$$\nu = \frac{(s_1^2 / n_1 + s_2^2 / n_2)^2}{\dfrac{(s_1^2 / n_1)^2}{n_1 - 1} + \dfrac{(s_2^2 / n_2)^2}{n_2 - 1}} = 25.6 \text{ (rounded to 26)}$$

Rejection region: $t > t_{\alpha,\nu} = t_{.05,26} = 1.706$

$$t = \frac{(\bar{x}_1 - \bar{x}_2) - (\mu_1 - \mu_2)}{\sqrt{\left(\dfrac{s_1^2}{n_1} + \dfrac{s_2^2}{n_2}\right)}} = \frac{(412 - 405) - 0}{\sqrt{\left(\dfrac{128^2}{20} + \dfrac{54^2}{20}\right)}} = .23, \text{ p-value} = .4118. \text{ There is not enough evidence to}$$

infer that μ_1 is greater than μ_2.

e. The value of the test statistic decreases and the p-value increases.

f. Unequal-variances test statistic

Rejection region: $t > t_{\alpha,v} = t_{.05,200} = 1.653$

$$t = \frac{(\bar{x}_1 - \bar{x}_2) - (\mu_1 - \mu_2)}{\sqrt{\left(\dfrac{s_1^2}{n_1} + \dfrac{s_2^2}{n_2}\right)}} = \frac{(409 - 405) - 0}{\sqrt{\left(\dfrac{128^2}{150} + \dfrac{54^2}{150}\right)}} = .35,$$ p-value = .3624. There is not enough evidence to

infer that μ_1 is greater than μ_2.

g. The value of the test statistic decreases and the p-value increases.

13.6 a. In all cases the equal-variances t-test degrees of freedom is greater than the unequal-variances t-test degrees of freedom.

13.8 $H_0 : (\mu_1 - \mu_2) = 0$
$H_1 : (\mu_1 - \mu_2) < 0$
Two-tail F test: F = 1.02, p-value = .9823; use equal-variances test statistic
Rejection region: $t < -t_{\alpha,v} = -t_{.10,18} = -1.330$

$$t = \frac{(\bar{x}_1 - \bar{x}_2) - (\mu_1 - \mu_2)}{\sqrt{s_p^2\left(\dfrac{1}{n_1} + \dfrac{1}{n_2}\right)}} = \frac{(5.10 - 7.30) - 0}{\sqrt{\left(\dfrac{(10-1)5.88 + (10-1)5.79}{10+10-2}\right)\left(\dfrac{1}{10} + \dfrac{1}{10}\right)}} = -2.04,$$ p-value = .0283. There is

enough evidence to infer that there are fewer errors when the yellow ball is used.

13.10 $H_0 : (\mu_1 - \mu_2) = 0$
$H_1 : (\mu_1 - \mu_2) \neq 0$
Two-tail F test: F = 1.04, p-value = .9873; use equal-variances test statistic
Rejection region: $t < -t_{\alpha/2,v} = -t_{.05,13} = -1.771$ or $t > t_{\alpha/2,v} = t_{.05,13} = 1.771$

$$t = \frac{(\bar{x}_1 - \bar{x}_2) - (\mu_1 - \mu_2)}{\sqrt{s_p^2\left(\dfrac{1}{n_1} + \dfrac{1}{n_2}\right)}} = \frac{(3{,}372 - 4{,}093) - 0}{\sqrt{\left(\dfrac{(9-1)755{,}196 + (6-1)725{,}778}{9+6-2}\right)\left(\dfrac{1}{9} + \dfrac{1}{6}\right)}} = -1.59,$$ p-value = .1368. There is

not enough evidence to infer a difference between the two types of vacation expenses.

13.12 $H_0 : (\mu_1 - \mu_2) = 0$
$H_1 : (\mu_1 - \mu_2) \neq 0$
Two-tail F test: F = .99, p-value = .9571; use equal-variances test statistic
Rejection region: $t < -t_{\alpha/2,v} = -t_{.025,238} = -1.960$ or $t > t_{\alpha/2,v} = t_{.025,238} = 1.960$

$$t = \frac{(\bar{x}_1 - \bar{x}_2) - (\mu_1 - \mu_2)}{\sqrt{s_p^2\left(\dfrac{1}{n_1} + \dfrac{1}{n_2}\right)}} = \frac{(10.01 - 9.12) - 0}{\sqrt{\left(\dfrac{(120-1)4.43^2 + (120-1)4.45^2}{120+120-2}\right)\left(\dfrac{1}{120} + \dfrac{1}{120}\right)}} = 1.55,$$ p-value = .1204. There

is not enough evidence to infer that oat bran is different from other cereals in terms of cholesterol reduction?

13.14 a. $H_0 : (\mu_1 - \mu_2) = 0$

$H_1 : (\mu_1 - \mu_2) > 0$

Two-tail F test: F = 1.01, p-value = .9619; use equal-variances test statistic

Rejection region: $t > t_{\alpha,\nu} = t_{.05,282} \approx 1.645$

$$t = \frac{(\bar{x}_1 - \bar{x}_2) - (\mu_1 - \mu_2)}{\sqrt{s_p^2\left(\dfrac{1}{n_1} + \dfrac{1}{n_2}\right)}} = \frac{(59.81 - 57.40) - 0}{\sqrt{\left(\dfrac{(125-1)7.02^2 + (159-1)6.99^2}{125 + 159 - 2}\right)\left(\dfrac{1}{125} + \dfrac{1}{159}\right)}} = 2.88, \text{ p-value} = .0021.$$

There is enough evidence to infer that the cruise ships are attracting younger customers.

b. $(\bar{x}_1 - \bar{x}_2) \pm t_{\alpha/2}\sqrt{s_p^2\left(\dfrac{1}{n_1} + \dfrac{1}{n_2}\right)} = (59.81 - 57.40)$

$$\pm 2.576\sqrt{\left(\frac{(125-1)7.02^2 + (159-1)6.99^2}{125 + 159 - 2}\right)\left(\frac{1}{125} + \frac{1}{159}\right)}$$

$= 2.41 \pm 2.16;$

LCL = .25, UCL = 4.57

13.16 $H_0 : (\mu_1 - \mu_2) = 0$
$H_1 : (\mu_1 - \mu_2) > 0$
Two-tail F test: F = .98, p-value = .9520; use equal-variances test statistic
Rejection region: $t > t_{\alpha,\nu} = t_{.05,58} \approx 1.671$

$$t = \frac{(\bar{x}_1 - \bar{x}_2) - (\mu_1 - \mu_2)}{\sqrt{s_p^2\left(\dfrac{1}{n_1} + \dfrac{1}{n_2}\right)}} = \frac{(115.50 - 110.20) - 0}{\sqrt{\left(\dfrac{(30-1)21.69^2 + (30-1)21.93^2}{30 + 30 - 2}\right)\left(\dfrac{1}{30} + \dfrac{1}{30}\right)}} = .94, \text{ p-value} = .1753. \text{ There is}$$

not enough evidence to retain supplier A - switch to supplier B.

13.18 a. $H_0 : (\mu_1 - \mu_2) = 0$

$H_1 : (\mu_1 - \mu_2) \neq 0$

Two-tail F test: F = 5.18, p-value = .0019; use unequal-variances test statistic

$$\nu = \frac{(s_1^2 / n_1 + s_2^2 / n_2)^2}{\dfrac{(s_1^2 / n_1)^2}{n_1 - 1} + \dfrac{(s_2^2 / n_2)^2}{n_2 - 1}} = 33.9 \text{ (rounded to 34)}$$

Rejection region: $t < -t_{\alpha/2,\nu} = -t_{.005,34} \approx -2.724$ or $t > t_{\alpha/2,\nu} = t_{.005,34} \approx 2.724$

$$t = \frac{(\bar{x}_1 - \bar{x}_2) - (\mu_1 - \mu_2)}{\sqrt{\dfrac{s_1^2}{n_1} + \dfrac{s_2^2}{n_2}}} = \frac{(70.42 - 56.44) - 0}{\sqrt{\dfrac{20.54^2}{24} + \dfrac{9.03^2}{16}}} = 2.94, \text{ p-value} = .0060. \text{ There is enough evidence to}$$

conclude that the two packages differ in the amount of time needed to learn how to use them.

b. $(\overline{x}_1 - \overline{x}_2) \pm t_{\alpha/2}\sqrt{\left(\dfrac{s_1^2}{n_1} + \dfrac{s_2^2}{n_2}\right)} = (70.42 - 56.44) \pm 2.030\sqrt{\left(\dfrac{20.54^2}{24} + \dfrac{9.03^2}{16}\right)} = 13.98 \pm 9.67;$

LCL = 4.31, UCL = 23.65

c. The amount of time is required to be normally distributed.

d. The histograms are somewhat bell shaped.

13.20 $H_0 : (\mu_1 - \mu_2) = 0$

$H_1 : (\mu_1 - \mu_2) > 0$

Two-tail F test: F = .73, p-value = .0699; use equal-variances test statistic

Rejection region: $t > t_{\alpha,v} = t_{.05,268} \approx 1.645$

$t = \dfrac{(\overline{x}_1 - \overline{x}_2) - (\mu_1 - \mu_2)}{\sqrt{s_p^2\left(\dfrac{1}{n_1} + \dfrac{1}{n_2}\right)}} = \dfrac{(.646 - .601) - 0}{\sqrt{\left(\dfrac{(125-1).045^2 + (145-1).053^2}{125 + 145 - 2}\right)\left(\dfrac{1}{125} + \dfrac{1}{145}\right)}} = 7.54$, p-value = 0. There is

enough evidence to conclude that the reaction time of drivers using cell phones is slower that for non-cell phone users.

13.22 $H_0 : (\mu_1 - \mu_2) = 0$

$H_1 : (\mu_1 - \mu_2) > 0$

Two-tail F test: F = .97, p-value = .9054; use equal-variances test statistic

Rejection region: $t > t_{\alpha,v} = t_{.05,143} \approx 1.656$

$t = \dfrac{(\overline{x}_1 - \overline{x}_2) - (\mu_1 - \mu_2)}{\sqrt{s_p^2\left(\dfrac{1}{n_1} + \dfrac{1}{n_2}\right)}} = \dfrac{(6.18 - 5.94) - 0}{\sqrt{\left(\dfrac{(64-1)1.59^2 + (81-1)1.61^2}{64 + 81 - 2}\right)\left(\dfrac{1}{64} + \dfrac{1}{81}\right)}} = .90$, p-value = .1858. There is not

enough evidence to infer that people spend more time researching for a financial planner than they do for a stock broker.

13.24 $H_0 : (\mu_1 - \mu_2) = 0$

$H_1 : (\mu_1 - \mu_2) \neq 0$

Two-tail F test: F = .85, p-value = .2494; use equal-variances test statistic

Rejection region: $t < -t_{\alpha/2,v} = -t_{.025,413} \approx -1.960$ or $t > t_{\alpha/2,v} = t_{.025,413} \approx 1.960$

$t = \dfrac{(\overline{x}_1 - \overline{x}_2) - (\mu_1 - \mu_2)}{\sqrt{s_p^2\left(\dfrac{1}{n_1} + \dfrac{1}{n_2}\right)}} = \dfrac{(149.85 - 154.43) - 0}{\sqrt{\left(\dfrac{(213-1)21.82^2 + (202-1)23.64^2}{213 + 202 - 2}\right)\left(\dfrac{1}{213} + \dfrac{1}{202}\right)}} = -2.05$, p-value = .0412.

There is enough evidence to conclude that there are differences in service times between the two chains.

13.26   a. $H_0 : (\mu_1 - \mu_2) = 0$

$H_1 : (\mu_1 - \mu_2) \neq 0$

Two-tail F test: F = 1.51, p-value = .0402; use unequal-variances test statistic

$$\nu = \frac{(s_1^2 / n_1 + s_2^2 / n_2)^2}{\dfrac{(s_1^2 / n_1)^2}{n_1 - 1} + \dfrac{(s_2^2 / n_2)^2}{n_2 - 1}} = 190$$

Rejection region: $t < -t_{\alpha/2, \nu} = -t_{.025, 190} \approx -1.973$ or $t > t_{\alpha/2, \nu} = t_{.025, 190} \approx 1.973$

$$t = \frac{(\overline{x}_1 - \overline{x}_2) - (\mu_1 - \mu_2)}{\sqrt{\left(\dfrac{s_1^2}{n_1} + \dfrac{s_2^2}{n_2}\right)}} = \frac{(130.93 - 126.14) - 0}{\sqrt{\left(\dfrac{31.99^2}{100} + \dfrac{26.00^2}{100}\right)}} = 1.16,$$ p-value = .2467. There is not enough

evidence to infer that differences exist between the two types of customers.

13.28 $H_0 : (\mu_1 - \mu_2) = 0$

$H_1 : (\mu_1 - \mu_2) < 0$

Two-tail F test: F = .95, p-value = .8252; use equal-variances test statistic

Rejection region: $t > t_{\alpha, \nu} = t_{.05, 178} \approx 1.653$

$$t = \frac{(\overline{x}_1 - \overline{x}_2) - (\mu_1 - \mu_2)}{\sqrt{s_p^2 \left(\dfrac{1}{n_1} + \dfrac{1}{n_2}\right)}} = \frac{60,245 - 63,563) - 0}{\sqrt{\left(\dfrac{(90-1)10,506^2 + (90-1)10,755^2}{20 + 20 - 2}\right)\left(\dfrac{1}{90} + \dfrac{1}{90}\right)}} = -2.09$$

$t = -2.09$, p-value = .0189. There is enough evidence to conclude that commission salespeople outperform fixed-salary salespersons

13.30 $H_0 : (\mu_1 - \mu_2) = 0$

$H_1 : (\mu_1 - \mu_2) > 0$

Two-tail F test: F = .41, p-value = 0; use unequal-variances test statistic

$$\nu = \frac{(s_1^2 / n_1 + s_2^2 / n_2)^2}{\dfrac{(s_1^2 / n_1)^2}{n_1 - 1} + \dfrac{(s_2^2 / n_2)^2}{n_2 - 1}} = 222$$

Rejection region: $t > t_{\alpha, \nu} = -t_{.05, 222} \approx -1.645$

$$t = \frac{(\overline{x}_1 - \overline{x}_2) - (\mu_1 - \mu_2)}{\sqrt{\left(\dfrac{s_1^2}{n_1} + \dfrac{s_2^2}{n_2}\right)}} = \frac{(14.20 - 11.27) - 0}{\sqrt{\left(\dfrac{2.84^2}{130} + \dfrac{4.42^2}{130}\right)}} = 6.28,$$ p-value = 0. There is enough evidence to conclude

that bottles of wine with metal caps are perceived to be cheaper.

13.32   Assuming that the volunteers were randomly assigned to eat either oat bran or another grain cereal the data are experimental.

13.34   a.   The data are observational because the students decided themselves which package each would use.

b.   The professor can randomly assign one of the two packages to each student.

c.   Better students tend to choose Program B and better students learn how to use computer software more quickly.

13.36   a.   Let students select the section they wish to attend and compare test results.

b.   Randomly assign students to either section and compare test results.

13.38   a.   Randomly select finance and marketing MBA graduates and determine their starting salaries.

b.   Randomly assign some MBA students to major in finance and others to major in marketing. Compare starting salaries after they graduate.

c.   Better students may be attracted to finance and better students draw higher starting salaries.

13.40 $H_0 : \mu_D = 0$

$H_1 : \mu_D < 0$

Rejection region: $t < -t_{\alpha,v} = -t_{.05,7} = -1.895$

$t = \dfrac{\overline{x}_D - \mu_D}{s_D / \sqrt{n_D}} = \dfrac{-4.75 - 0}{4.17 / \sqrt{8}} = -3.22$, p-value = .0073. There is enough evidence to infer that the Brand A is better than Brand B.

13.42 $H_0 : \mu_D = 0$

$H_1 : \mu_D > 0$

Rejection region: $t > t_{\alpha,v} = t_{.05,6} = 1.943$

$t = \dfrac{\overline{x}_D - \mu_D}{s_D / \sqrt{n_D}} = \dfrac{1.86 - 0}{2.48 / \sqrt{7}} = 1.98$, p-value = .0473. There is enough evidence to infer that the camera reduces the number of red-light runners.

13.44   a. $H_0 : \mu_D = 0$

$H_1 : \mu_D > 0$

Rejection region: $t > t_{\alpha,v} = t_{.05,11} = 1.796$

$t = \dfrac{\overline{x}_D - \mu_D}{s_D / \sqrt{n_D}} = \dfrac{3.08 - 0}{5.88 / \sqrt{12}} = 1.82$, p-value = .0484. There is enough evidence to infer that companies with exercise programs have lower medical expenses.

b. $\overline{x}_D \pm t_{\alpha/2} \dfrac{s_D}{\sqrt{n_D}} = 3.08 \pm 2.201 \dfrac{5.88}{\sqrt{12}} = 3.08 \pm 3.74$; LCL = −.66, UCL = 6.82

c.   Yes because medical expenses will vary by the month of the year.

13.46 $H_0 : \mu_D = 0$

       $H_1 : \mu_D \neq 0$

       Rejection region: $t < -t_{\alpha/2,\nu} = -t_{.025,49} \approx -2.009$ or $t > t_{\alpha/2,\nu} = t_{.025,49} \approx 2.009$

       $t = \dfrac{\overline{x}_D - \mu_D}{s_D / \sqrt{n_D}} = \dfrac{-1.16 - 0}{2.22 / \sqrt{50}} = -3.70$, p-value = .0006. There is enough evidence to infer that waiters and

       waitresses earn different amounts in tips.

13.48   a. $H_0 : \mu_D = 0$

            $H_1 : \mu_D > 0$

            Rejection region: $t > t_{\alpha,\nu} = t_{.10,14} = 1.345$

            $t = \dfrac{\overline{x}_D - \mu_D}{s_D / \sqrt{n_D}} = \dfrac{57.40 - 0}{13.14 / \sqrt{15}} = 16.92$, p-value = 0. There is enough evidence to conclude that heating

            costs for insulated homes is less than that for uninsulated homes.

      b. $\overline{x}_D \pm t_{\alpha/2} \dfrac{s_D}{\sqrt{n_D}} = 57.40 \pm 2.145 \dfrac{13.14}{\sqrt{15}} = 57.40 \pm 7.28$; LCL = 50.12, UCL = 64.68

      c.   Differences are required to be normally distributed.

13.50 $H_0 : \mu_D = 0$

       $H_1 : \mu_D < 0$

       Rejection region: $t < -t_{\alpha,\nu} = -t_{.05,169} \approx -1.654$

       $t = \dfrac{\overline{x}_D - \mu_D}{s_D / \sqrt{n_D}} = \dfrac{-183.35 - 0}{1568.94 / \sqrt{170}} = -1.52$, p-value = .0647. There is not enough to infer stock holdings have

       decreased.

13.52 $H_0 : \mu_D = 0$

       $H_1 : \mu_D > 0$

       Rejection region: $t > t_{\alpha,\nu} = t_{.05,54} \approx 1.676$

       $t = \dfrac{\overline{x}_D - \mu_D}{s_D / \sqrt{n_D}} = \dfrac{520.85 - 0}{1854.92 / \sqrt{55}} = 2.08$, p-value = .0210. There is enough evidence to infer that company 1's

       calculated tax payable is higher than company 2's.

13.54   The matched pairs experiment reduced the variation caused by different drivers.

13.56   Salary offers and undergraduate GPA are not as strongly linked as are salary offers and MBA GPA.

13.58   a. $H_0 : \sigma_1^2 / \sigma_2^2 = 1$

$H_1 : \sigma_1^2 / \sigma_2^2 \neq 1$

Rejection region: $F > F_{\alpha/2, v_1, v_2} = F_{.05,29,29} \approx 1.88$ or

$F < F_{1-\alpha/2, v_1, v_2} = 1/F_{\alpha/2, v_2, v_1} = 1/F_{.05,29,29} \approx 1/1.88 = .53$

$F = s_1^2 / s_2^2 = 350/700 = .50$, p-value = .0669. There is enough evidence to conclude that the population variances differ.

   b.   Rejection region: $F > F_{\alpha/2, v_1, v_2} = F_{.025,14,14} = 2.98$ or

$F < F_{1-\alpha/2, v_1, v_2} = 1/F_{\alpha/2, v_2, v_1} = 1/F_{.025,14,14} = 1/2.98 = .34$

$F = s_1^2 / s_2^2 = 350/700 = .50$, p-value = .2071. There is not enough evidence to conclude that the population variances differ.

   c.   The value of the test statistic is unchanged and in this exercise the conclusion changed as well..

13.60 $H_0 : \sigma_1^2 / \sigma_2^2 = 1$
$H_1 : \sigma_1^2 / \sigma_2^2 \neq 1$
Rejection region: $F > F_{\alpha/2, v_1, v_2} = F_{.025,9,10} = 3.78$ or
$F < F_{1-\alpha/2, v_1, v_2} = 1/F_{\alpha/2, v_2, v_1} = 1/F_{.025,10,9} = 1/3.96 = .25$
$F = s_1^2 / s_2^2 = .0000057/.0000114 = .50$, p-value = .3179. There is not enough evidence to conclude that the two machines differ in their consistency of fills.

13.62 $H_0 : \sigma_1^2 / \sigma_2^2 = 1$
$H_1 : \sigma_1^2 / \sigma_2^2 \neq 1$
Rejection region: $F > F_{\alpha/2, v_1, v_2} = F_{.025,10,10} = 3.72$ or
$F < F_{1-\alpha/2, v_1, v_2} = 1/F_{\alpha/2, v_2, v_1} = 1/F_{.025,10,10} = 1/3.72 = .269$
$F = s_1^2 / s_2^2 = 193.67/60.00 = 3.23$, p-value = .0784. There is not enough evidence to infer that the variances of the marks differ between the two sections.

13.64 $H_0 : \sigma_1^2 / \sigma_2^2 = 1$
$H_1 : \sigma_1^2 / \sigma_2^2 \neq 1$
Rejection region: $F > F_{\alpha/2, v_1, v_2} = F_{.025,99,99} \approx 1.48$ or
$F < F_{1-\alpha/2, v_1, v_2} = 1/F_{\alpha/2, v_2, v_1} = 1/F_{.025,99,99} \approx 1/1.48 = .68$
$F = s_1^2 / s_2^2 = 41,309/19,850 = 2.08$, p-value = .0003. There is enough evidence to conclude that the variances differ.

13.66 $H_0 : \sigma_1^2 / \sigma_2^2 = 1$

        $H_1 : \sigma_1^2 / \sigma_2^2 \neq 1$

        Rejection region: $F > F_{\alpha/2, \nu_1, \nu_2} = F_{.05,99,99} \approx 1.39$ or $F < F_{1-\alpha, \nu_1, \nu_2} = 1/F_{\alpha, \nu_2, \nu_1} = 1/F_{.05,99,99} \approx 1/1.39 = .72$

        $F = s_1^2 / s_2^2 = 3.35/10.95 = .31$, p-value = 0. There is enough evidence to conclude that the variance in service times differ.

13.68 $H_0 : (p_1 - p_2) = 0$

        $H_1 : (p_1 - p_2) \neq 0$

   a. $z = \dfrac{(\hat{p}_1 - \hat{p}_2)}{\sqrt{\hat{p}(1-\hat{p})\left(\dfrac{1}{n_1} + \dfrac{1}{n_2}\right)}} = \dfrac{(.60 - .55)}{\sqrt{.575(1-.575)\left(\dfrac{1}{225} + \dfrac{1}{225}\right)}} = 1.07$, p-value $= 2P(Z > 1.07) = 2(1 - .8577)$

       $= .2846$

   b. $z = \dfrac{(\hat{p}_1 - \hat{p}_2)}{\sqrt{\hat{p}(1-\hat{p})\left(\dfrac{1}{n_1} + \dfrac{1}{n_2}\right)}} = \dfrac{(.95 - .90)}{\sqrt{.925(1-.925)\left(\dfrac{1}{225} + \dfrac{1}{225}\right)}} = 2.01$, p-value $= 2P(Z > 2.01) = 2(1 - .9778)$

       $= .0444$.

   c.   The p-value decreases.

   d. $z = \dfrac{(\hat{p}_1 - \hat{p}_2)}{\sqrt{\hat{p}(1-\hat{p})\left(\dfrac{1}{n_1} + \dfrac{1}{n_2}\right)}} = \dfrac{(.10 - .05)}{\sqrt{.075(1-.075)\left(\dfrac{1}{225} + \dfrac{1}{225}\right)}} = 2.01$,   p-value $= 2P(Z > 2.01)$

       $= 2(1 - .94778)$

       $= .0444$.

   e.   The p-value decreases.

13.70 $H_0 : (p_1 - p_2) = 0$

        $H_1 : (p_1 - p_2) > 0$

        $z = \dfrac{(\hat{p}_1 - \hat{p}_2)}{\sqrt{\hat{p}(1-\hat{p})\left(\dfrac{1}{n_1} + \dfrac{1}{n_2}\right)}} = \dfrac{(.205 - .140)}{\sqrt{.177(1-.177)\left(\dfrac{1}{229} + \dfrac{1}{178}\right)}} = 1.70$, p-value $= P(Z > 1.70) = 1 - .9554 = .0446$.

        There is enough evidence to conclude that those who paid the regular price are more likely to buy an extended warranty.

13.72 $H_0 : (p_1 - p_2) = 0$

$H_1 : (p_1 - p_2) > 0$

$$z = \frac{(\hat{p}_1 - \hat{p}_2)}{\sqrt{\hat{p}(1-\hat{p})\left(\dfrac{1}{n_1} + \dfrac{1}{n_2}\right)}} = \frac{(.0196 - .0087)}{\sqrt{.0132(1-.0132)\left(\dfrac{1}{562} + \dfrac{1}{804}\right)}} = 1.74,\ \text{p-value} = P(Z > 1.74) = 1 - .9591$$

$= .0409.$

There is enough evidence to conclude that those who score under 600 are more likely to default than those who score 60 or more.

13.74 $H_0 : (p_1 - p_2) = -.08$

$H_1 : (p_1 - p_2) < -.08$

Rejection region: $z < -z_\alpha = -z_{.01} = -2.33$

$$z = \frac{(\hat{p}_1 - \hat{p}_2) - (p_1 - p_2)}{\sqrt{\dfrac{\hat{p}_1(1-\hat{p}_1)}{n_1} + \dfrac{\hat{p}_2(1-\hat{p}_2)}{n_2}}} = \frac{(.11 - .28) - (-.08)}{\sqrt{\dfrac{.11(1-.11)}{300} + \dfrac{.28(1-.28)}{300}}} = -2.85,\ \text{p-value} = P(Z < -2.85) = 1 - .9978$$

$= .0022.$

There is enough evidence to conclude that management should adopt process 1.

13.76 a. $H_0 : (p_1 - p_2) = 0$

$H_1 : (p_1 - p_2) < 0$

Rejection region: $z < -z_\alpha = -z_{.05} = -1.645$

$$z = \frac{(\hat{p}_1 - \hat{p}_2)}{\sqrt{\hat{p}(1-\hat{p})\left(\dfrac{1}{n_1} + \dfrac{1}{n_2}\right)}} = \frac{(.093 - .115)}{\sqrt{.104(1-.104)\left(\dfrac{1}{6281} + \dfrac{1}{6281}\right)}} = -4.04,\ \text{p-value} = 0.\ \text{There is enough}$$

evidence to infer that Plavix is effective.

13.78 $H_0 : (p_1 - p_2) = 0$

$H_1 : (p_1 - p_2) > 0$

Rejection region: $z > z_\alpha = z_{.05} = 1.645$

$\hat{p}_1 = \dfrac{1,084}{11,000} = .0985$ $\hat{p}_2 = \dfrac{997}{11,000} = .0906$ $\hat{p} = \dfrac{1,084 + 997}{22,000} = .0946$

$$z = \frac{(\hat{p}_1 - \hat{p}_2)}{\sqrt{\hat{p}(1-\hat{p})\left(\dfrac{1}{n_1} + \dfrac{1}{n_2}\right)}} = \frac{(.0985 - .0906)}{\sqrt{.0946(1-.0946)\left(\dfrac{1}{11,000} + \dfrac{1}{11,000}\right)}} = 2.00,\ \text{p-value} = P(Z > 2.00) = 1 - .9772$$

$= .0228.$

There is enough evidence to infer that aspirin leads to more cataracts.

13.80 $H_0 : (p_1 - p_2) = 0$

$H_1 : (p_1 - p_2) < 0$

Rejection region: $z < -z_\alpha = -z_{.05} = -1.645$

$$\hat{p}_1 = \frac{88}{395} = .2228 \quad \hat{p}_2 = \frac{105}{406} = .2586 \quad \hat{p} = \frac{88+105}{395+406} = .2409$$

$$z = \frac{(\hat{p}_1 - \hat{p}_2)}{\sqrt{\hat{p}(1-\hat{p})\left(\frac{1}{n_1} + \frac{1}{n_2}\right)}} = \frac{(.2228 - .2586)}{\sqrt{.2409(1-.2409)\left(\frac{1}{395} + \frac{1}{406}\right)}} = -1.19, \text{ p-value} = P(Z < -1.19) = .1170. \text{ There}$$

is not enough evidence to infer that exercise training reduces mortality.

13.82 $H_0 : (p_1 - p_2) = 0$

$H_1 : (p_1 - p_2) > 0$

Rejection region: $z > z_\alpha = z_{.10} = 1.28$

$$z = \frac{(\hat{p}_1 - \hat{p}_2)}{\sqrt{\hat{p}(1-\hat{p})\left(\frac{1}{n_1} + \frac{1}{n_2}\right)}} = \frac{(.2632 - .0741)}{\sqrt{.11(1-.11)\left(\frac{1}{38} + \frac{1}{162}\right)}} = 3.35, \text{ p-value} = 0. \text{ There is enough evidence to}$$

conclude that smokers have a higher incidence of heart diseases than nonsmokers.

b. $(\hat{p}_1 - \hat{p}_2) \pm z_{\alpha/2} \sqrt{\dfrac{\hat{p}_1(1-\hat{p}_1)}{n_1} + \dfrac{\hat{p}_2(1-\hat{p}_2)}{n_2}}$

$$= (.2632 - 0741) \pm 1.645 \sqrt{\frac{.2632(1-.2632)}{38} + \frac{.0741(1-.0741)}{162}} = .1891 \pm .1223; \text{ LCL} = .0668, \text{ UCL} = .3114$$

13.84 $H_0 : (p_1 - p_2) = 0$

$H_1 : (p_1 - p_2) > 0$

Rejection region: $z > z_\alpha = z_{.05} = 1.645$

$$z = \frac{(\hat{p}_1 - \hat{p}_2)}{\sqrt{\hat{p}(1-\hat{p})\left(\frac{1}{n_1} + \frac{1}{n_2}\right)}} = \frac{(.3585 - .3420)}{\sqrt{.3504(1-.3504)\left(\frac{1}{477} + \frac{1}{462}\right)}} = .53, \text{ p-value} = P(Z > .53) = 1 - .7019$$

$= .2981.$

There is not enough evidence to infer that the use of illicit drugs in the United States has increased in the past decade.

13.86 $H_0 : (p_1 - p_2) = 0$

$H_1 : (p_1 - p_2) > 0$

Rejection region: $z > z_\alpha = z_{.05} = 1.645$

$$z = \frac{(\hat{p}_1 - \hat{p}_2)}{\sqrt{\hat{p}(1-\hat{p})\left(\frac{1}{n_1} + \frac{1}{n_2}\right)}} = \frac{(.1385 - .0905)}{\sqrt{.1035(1-.1035)\left(\frac{1}{231} + \frac{1}{619}\right)}} \quad z = 2.04, \text{ p-value} = P(Z > 2.04) = 1 - .9793$$

$= .0207.$

There is enough evidence to conclude that health conscious adults are more likely to buy Special X.

13.88 $H_0 : (p_1 - p_2) = 0$

$H_1 : (p_1 - p_2) \neq 0$

Rejection region: $z < -z_{\alpha/2} = -z_{.025} = -1.96$ or $z > z_{\alpha/2} = z_{.025} = 1.96$

$$z = \frac{(\hat{p}_1 - \hat{p}_2)}{\sqrt{\hat{p}(1-\hat{p})\left(\dfrac{1}{n_1} + \dfrac{1}{n_2}\right)}} = \frac{(.0995 - .1297)}{\sqrt{.1132(1-.1132)\left(\dfrac{1}{382} + \dfrac{1}{316}\right)}} = -1.25, \text{ p-value} = 2P(Z < -1.25) = 2(.1056) =$$

.2112.

There is not enough evidence to infer differences between the two sources.

13.90   Gross sales must increase by 50/.20 = \$250 to pay for ads.

$H_0 : (\mu_1 - \mu_2) = 250$

$H_1 : (\mu_1 - \mu_2) > 250$

	A	B	C
1	t-Test: Two-Sample Assuming Equal Variances		
2			
3		*During*	*Before*
4	Mean	5746.07	5372.13
5	Variance	167289	194772
6	Observations	15	24
7	Pooled Variance	184373	
8	Hypothesized Mean Difference	250	
9	df	37	
10	t Stat	0.88	
11	P(T<=t) one-tail	0.1931	
12	t Critical one-tail	1.6871	
13	P(T<=t) two-tail	0.3862	
14	t Critical two-tail	2.0262	

t = .88, p-value = .1931. There is not enough evidence to conclude that the ads are profitable.

13.92 $H_0: \mu_D = 0$

   $H_1: \mu_D < 0$

	A	B	C
1	t-Test: Paired Two Sample for Means		
2			
3		Drug	Placebo
4	Mean	18.43	22.03
5	Variance	30.39	66.37
6	Observations	100	100
7	Pearson Correlation	0.69	
8	Hypothesized Mean Difference	0	
9	df	99	
10	t Stat	-6.09	
11	P(T<=t) one-tail	0.0000	
12	t Critical one-tail	1.6604	
13	P(T<=t) two-tail	0.0000	
14	t Critical two-tail	1.9842	

t = –6.09, p-value = 0. There is enough evidence to infer that the new drug is effective.

13.94 $H_0: (p_1 - p_2) = 0$

   $H_1: (p_1 - p_2) < 0$

	A	B	C	D
1	z-Test: Two Proportions			
2				
3			Last Year	This Year
4	Sample Proportions		0.6758	0.7539
5	Observations		327	382
6	Hypothesized Difference		0	
7	z Stat		-2.30	
8	P(Z<=z) one tail		0.0106	
9	z Critical one-tail		1.6449	
10	P(Z<=z) two-tail		0.0212	
11	z Critical two-tail		1.96	

z = –2.30, p-value = .0106. There is enough evidence to infer an increase in seatbelt use.

13.96　a.　$H_0 : (\mu_1 - \mu_2) = 0$

$H_1 : (\mu_1 - \mu_2) \neq 0$

	A	B	C
1	t-Test: Two-Sample Assuming Equal Variances		
2			
3		*Male*	*Female*
4	Mean	39.75	49.00
5	Variance	803.88	733.16
6	Observations	20	20
7	Pooled Variance	768.52	
8	Hypothesized Mean Difference	0	
9	df	38	
10	t Stat	-1.06	
11	P(T<=t) one-tail	0.1490	
12	t Critical one-tail	1.3042	
13	P(T<=t) two-tail	0.2980	
14	t Critical two-tail	1.6860	

$t = -1.06$, p-value = .2980. There is not enough evidence to conclude that men and women differ in the amount of time spent reading magazines.

b.　$H_0 : (\mu_1 - \mu_2) = 0$

$H_1 : (\mu_1 - \mu_2) < 0$

	A	B	C
1	t-Test: Two-Sample Assuming Unequal Variances		
2			
3		*Low*	*High*
4	Mean	33.10	56.84
5	Variance	278.69	1047.81
6	Observations	21.00	19
7	Hypothesized Mean Difference	0.00	
8	df	26.00	
9	t Stat	-2.87	
10	P(T<=t) one-tail	0.0040	
11	t Critical one-tail	1.3150	
12	P(T<=t) two-tail	0.0080	
13	t Critical two-tail	1.7056	

$t = -2.87$, p-value = .0040. There is enough evidence to conclude that high-income individuals devote more time to reading magazines than do low-income individuals.

13.98 $H_0 : (p_1 - p_2) = 0$

       $H_1 : (p_1 - p_2) > 0$

	A	B	C	D
1	**z-Test: Two Proportions**			
2				
3			*This Year*	*3 Years Ago*
4	Sample Proportions		0.4351	0.3558
5	Observations		393	385
6	Hypothesized Difference		0	
7	z Stat		2.26	
8	P(Z<=z) one tail		0.0119	
9	z Critical one-tail		1.2816	
10	P(Z<=z) two-tail		0.0238	
11	z Critical two-tail		1.6449	

z = 2.26, p-value = .0119. There is enough evidence to infer that Americans have become more distrustful of television and newspaper reporting this year than they were three years ago.

13.100 $H_0 : (p_1 - p_2) = 0$

       $H_1 : (p_1 - p_2) \neq 0$

The totals in columns A through D are 5788, 265, 5154, and 332, respectively.

	A	B	C	D	E
1	**z-Test of the Difference Between Two Proportions (Case 1)**				
2					
3		**Sample 1**	**Sample 2**	**z Stat**	**-4.28**
4	**Sample proportion**	0.045800	0.064400	**P(Z<=z) one-tail**	**0.0000**
5	**Sample size**	5788	5154	**z Critical one-tail**	**1.6449**
6	**Alpha**	0.05		**P(Z<=z) two-tail**	**0.0000**
7				**z Critical two-tail**	**1.9600**

z = –4.28, p-value = 0. There is enough evidence to infer that the defective rate differs between the two machines.

13.102 a.　　$H_0 : (\mu_1 - \mu_2) = 0$

　　　　　$H_1 : (\mu_1 - \mu_2) < 0$

	A	B	C
1	t-Test: Two-Sample Assuming Equal Variances		
2			
3		20-year-old	40-year-old
4	Mean	125.74	129.93
5	Variance	31.90	31.95
6	Observations	26	24
7	Pooled Variance	31.92	
8	Hypothesized Mean Difference	0	
9	df	48	
10	t Stat	-2.62	
11	P(T<=t) one-tail	0.0059	
12	t Critical one-tail	1.2994	
13	P(T<=t) two-tail	0.0119	
14	t Critical two-tail	1.6772	

$t = -2.62$, p-value = .0059. There is enough evidence to infer that 40-year-old men have more iron in their bodies than do 20-year-old men.

b.　　$H_0 : (\mu_1 - \mu_2) = 0$

　　　$H_1 : (\mu_1 - \mu_2) < 0$

	A	B	C
1	t-Test: Two-Sample Assuming Equal Variances		
2			
3		20-year-old	40-year-old
4	Mean	134.02	141.11
5	Variance	36.15	39.47
6	Observations	26	24
7	Pooled Variance	37.74	
8	Hypothesized Mean Difference	0	
9	df	48	
10	t Stat	-4.08	
11	P(T<=t) one-tail	0.0001	
12	t Critical one-tail	1.2994	
13	P(T<=t) two-tail	0.0002	
14	t Critical two-tail	1.6772	

$t = -4.08$, p-value = .0001. There is enough evidence to infer that 40-year-old women have more iron in their bodies than do 20-year-old women.

13.104 a. $H_0 : (\mu_1 - \mu_2) = 0$

   $H_1 : (\mu_1 - \mu_2) > 0$

	A	B	C
1	t-Test: Two-Sample Assuming Unequal Variances		
2			
3		*Exercise*	*Drug*
4	Mean	13.52	9.92
5	Variance	5.76	13.16
6	Observations	25	25
7	Hypothesized Mean Difference	0	
8	df	42	
9	t Stat	4.14	
10	P(T<=t) one-tail	0.0001	
11	t Critical one-tail	2.4185	
12	P(T<=t) two-tail	0.0002	
13	t Critical two-tail	2.6981	

$t = 4.14$, p-value $= .0001$. There is enough evidence that exercise is more effective than medication in reducing hypertension.

b.

	A	B	C	D	E	F
1	t-Estimate of the Difference Between Two Means (Unequal-Variances)					
2						
3		Sample 1	Sample 2	Confidence Interval Estimate		
4	Mean	13.52	9.92	3.60	±	1.76
5	Variance	5.76	13.16	Lower confidence limit		1.84
6	Sample size	25	25	Upper confidence limit		5.36
7	Degrees of freedom	41.63				
8	Confidence level	0.95				

LCL = 1.84, UCL = 5.36

c.   The histograms are bell shaped.

13.106 $H_0 : \mu_D = 0$

$H_1 : \mu_D < 0$

	A	B	C
1	t-Test: Paired Two Sample for Means		
2			
3		Group 1	Group 2
4	Mean	7.53	8.57
5	Variance	29.77	43.37
6	Observations	50	50
7	Pearson Correlation	0.89	
8	Hypothesized Mean Difference	0	
9	df	49	
10	t Stat	-2.40	
11	P(T<=t) one-tail	0.0100	
12	t Critical one-tail	1.6766	
13	P(T<=t) two-tail	0.0201	
14	t Critical two-tail	2.0096	

$t = -2.40$, p-value $= .0100$. There is enough evidence to conclude that people who exercise moderately more frequently lose weight faster

13.108 $H_0 : (p_1 - p_2) = 0$

$H_1 : (p_1 - p_2) > 0$

	A	B	C	D
1	z-Test: Two Proportions			
2				
3			Special K	Other
4	Sample Proportions		0.575	0.515
5	Observations		200	200
6	Hypothesized Difference		0	
7	z Stat		1.20	
8	P(Z<=z) one tail		0.1141	
9	z Critical one-tail		1.6449	
10	P(Z<=z) two-tail		0.2282	
11	z Critical two-tail		1.9600	

$z = 1.20$, p-value $= .1141$. There is not enough evidence to conclude that Special K buyers are more likely to think the ad is effective.

13.110 $H_0 : (\mu_1 - \mu_2) = 0$

$H_1 : (\mu_1 - \mu_2) > 0$

	A	B	C
1	t-Test: Two-Sample Assuming Unequal Variances		
2			
3		Computer	No Computer
4	Mean	69,933	48,246
5	Variance	63,359,040	101,588,525
6	Observations	89	61
7	Hypothesized Mean Difference	0	
8	df	109	
9	t Stat	14.07	
10	P(T<=t) one-tail	0.0000	
11	t Critical one-tail	1.2894	
12	P(T<=t) two-tail	0.0000	
13	t Critical two-tail	1.6590	

t = 14.07, p-value = 0. There is enough evidence to conclude that single-person businesses that use a PC earn more.

13.112 $H_0 : (\mu_1 - \mu_2) = 0$

$H_1 : (\mu_1 - \mu_2) < 0$

	A	B	C
1	t-Test: Two-Sample Assuming Equal Variances		
2			
3		Supplement	Placebo
4	Mean	19.02	21.85
5	Variance	41.34	25.49
6	Observations	48	48
7	Pooled Variance	33.41	
8	Hypothesized Mean Difference	0	
9	df	94	
10	t Stat	-2.40	
11	P(T<=t) one-tail	0.0092	
12	t Critical one-tail	1.6612	
13	P(T<=t) two-tail	0.0183	
14	t Critical two-tail	1.9855	

t = –2.40, p-value = .0092. There is enough evidence to infer that taking vitamin and mineral supplements daily increases the body's immune system?

13.114 $H_0 : (\mu_1 - \mu_2) = 0$
$H_1 : (\mu_1 - \mu_2) \neq 0$

	A	B	C
1	t-Test: Two-Sample Assuming Equal Variances		
2			
3		*Female*	*Male*
4	Mean	7.27	7.02
5	Variance	2.57	2.85
6	Observations	103	97
7	Pooled Variance	2.71	
8	Hypothesized Mean Difference	0	
9	df	198	
10	t Stat	1.08	
11	P(T<=t) one-tail	0.1410	
12	t Critical one-tail	1.6526	
13	P(T<=t) two-tail	0.2820	
14	t Critical two-tail	1.9720	

t = 1.08, p-value = .2820. There is not enough evidence to conclude that female and male high school students differ in the amount of time spent at part-time jobs.

13.116 $H_0 : (\mu_1 - \mu_2) = 0$
$H_1 : (\mu_1 - \mu_2) > 0$

	A	B	C
1	t-Test: Two-Sample Assuming Unequal Variances		
2			
3		*Teenagers*	*20-to-30*
4	Mean	18.18	14.30
5	Variance	357.32	130.79
6	Observations	176	154
7	Hypothesized Mean Difference	0	
8	df	293	
9	t Stat	2.28	
10	P(T<=t) one-tail	0.0115	
11	t Critical one-tail	1.6501	
12	P(T<=t) two-tail	0.0230	
13	t Critical two-tail	1.9681	

t = 2.28, p-value = .0115. There is enough evidence to infer that teenagers see more movies than do twenty to thirty year olds.

13.118 $H_0 : (\mu_1 - \mu_2) = 0$

$H_1 : (\mu_1 - \mu_2) > 0$

	A	B	C
1	t-Test: Two-Sample Assuming Unequal Variances		
2			
3		Group 1	Groups 2-4
4	Mean	11.58	10.60
5	Variance	9.28	21.41
6	Observations	269	981
7	Hypothesized Mean Difference	0	
8	df	644	
9	t Stat	4.15	
10	P(T<=t) one-tail	0.0000	
11	t Critical one-tail	1.6472	
12	P(T<=t) two-tail	0.0000	
13	t Critical two-tail	1.9637	

$t = 4.15$, p-value = 0. There is enough evidence to conclude that on average the market segment concerned about eating healthy food (group 1) outspends the other market segments.

13.120 $H_0 : (\mu_1 - \mu_2) = 0$

$H_1 : (\mu_1 - \mu_2) < 0$

	A	B	C
1	t-Test: Two-Sample Assuming Equal Variances		
2			
3		No	Yes
4	Mean	91,467	97,836
5	Variance	461,917,705	401,930,840
6	Observations	466	55
7	Pooled Variance	455,676,297	
8	Hypothesized Mean Difference	0	
9	df	519	
10	t Stat	-2.09	
11	P(T<=t) one-tail	0.0184	
12	t Critical one-tail	1.6478	
13	P(T<=t) two-tail	0.0369	
14	t Critical two-tail	1.9645	

$t = -2.09$, p-value = .0184. There is enough evidence to infer that professors aged 55 to 64 who plan to retire early have higher salaries than those who don't plan to retire early.

Appendix 13

A13.2 a.   z-test of $p_1 - p_2$ (case 1)

$$H_0 : (p_1 - p_2) = 0$$

$$H_1 : (p_1 - p_2) > 0$$

$$z = \frac{(\hat{p}_1 - \hat{p}_2)}{\sqrt{\hat{p}(1-\hat{p})\left(\dfrac{1}{n_1} + \dfrac{1}{n_2}\right)}}$$

	A	B	C	D	E
1	z-Test of the Difference Between Two Proportions (Case 1)				
2					
3		Sample 1	Sample 2	z Stat	2.83
4	Sample proportion	0.4336	0.2414	P(Z<=z) one-tail	0.0024
5	Sample size	113	87	z Critical one-tail	1.6449
6	Alpha	0.05		P(Z<=z) two-tail	0.0047
7				z Critical two-tail	1.9600

$z = 2.83$, p-value = .0024. There is enough evidence to infer that customers who see the ad are more likely to make a purchase than those who do not see the ad.

b.   Equal-variances t-test of $\mu_1 - \mu_2$

$$H_0 : (\mu_1 - \mu_2) = 0$$

$$H_1 : (\mu_1 - \mu_2) > 0$$

$$t = \frac{(\overline{x}_1 - \overline{x}_2) - (\mu_1 - \mu_2)}{\sqrt{s_p^2\left(\dfrac{1}{n_1} + \dfrac{1}{n_2}\right)}}$$

	A	B	C
1	t-Test: Two-Sample Assuming Equal Variances		
2			
3		Ad	No Ad
4	Mean	97.38	92.01
5	Variance	621.97	283.26
6	Observations	49	21
7	Pooled Variance	522.35	
8	Hypothesized Mean Difference	0	
9	df	68	
10	t Stat	0.90	
11	P(T<=t) one-tail	0.1853	
12	t Critical one-tail	1.6676	
13	P(T<=t) two-tail	0.3705	
14	t Critical two-tail	1.9955	

t = .90, p-value = .1853. There is not enough evidence to infer that customers who see the ad and make a purchase spend more than those who do not see the ad and make a purchase.

c.   z-estimator of p

$$\hat{p} \pm z_{\alpha/2} \sqrt{\frac{\hat{p}(1-\hat{p})}{n}}$$

	A	B	C	D	E
1	**z-Estimate of a Proportion**				
2					
3	**Sample proportion**	0.4336	**Confidence Interval Estimate**		
4	**Sample size**	113	0.4336	±	0.0914
5	**Confidence level**	0.95	**Lower confidence limit**		0.3423
6			**Upper confidence limit**		0.5250

We estimate that between 34.23% and 52.50% of all customers who see the ad will make a purchase.

d.   t-estimator of μ

$$\bar{x} \pm t_{\alpha/2} \frac{s}{\sqrt{n}}$$

	A	B	C	D
1	**t-Estimate: Mean**			
2				
3				*Ad*
4	Mean			97.38
5	Standard Deviation			24.94
6	LCL			90.22
7	UCL			104.55

We estimate that the mean amount spent by customers who see the ad and make a purchase lies between $90.22 and $104.55.

A13.4   Frequency of accidents: z -test of $p_1 - p_2$ (case 1)

$H_0 : (p_1 - p_2) = 0$

$H_1 : (p_1 - p_2) > 0$

$$z = \frac{(\hat{p}_1 - \hat{p}_2)}{\sqrt{\hat{p}(1-\hat{p})\left(\frac{1}{n_1} + \frac{1}{n_2}\right)}}$$

	A	B	C	D	E
1	z-Test of the Difference Between Two Proportions (Case 1)				
2					
3		Sample 1	Sample 2	z Stat	0.47
4	Sample proportion	0.0840	0.0760	P(Z<=z) one-tail	0.3205
5	Sample size	500	500	z Critical one-tail	1.6449
6	Alpha	0.05		P(Z<=z) two-tail	0.6410
7				z Critical two-tail	1.9600

z = .47, p-value = .32053. There is not enough evidence to infer that ABS-equipped cars have fewer accidents than cars without ABS.

Severity of accidents Equal-variances t-test of $\mu_1 - \mu_2$

$H_0 : (\mu_1 - \mu_2) = 0$

$H_1 : (\mu_1 - \mu_2) > 0$

$$t = \frac{(\bar{x}_1 - \bar{x}_2) - (\mu_1 - \mu_2)}{\sqrt{s_p^2\left(\frac{1}{n_1} + \frac{1}{n_2}\right)}}$$

	A	B	C
1	t-Test: Two-Sample Assuming Equal Variances		
2			
3		No ABS	ABS
4	Mean	2075	1714
5	Variance	450,343	390,409
6	Observations	42	38
7	Pooled Variance	421,913	
8	Hypothesized Mean Difference	0	
9	df	78	
10	t Stat	2	
11	P(T<=t) one-tail	0.0077	
12	t Critical one-tail	1.6646	
13	P(T<=t) two-tail	0.0153	
14	t Critical two-tail	1.9908	

Estimate of the difference between two means (equal-variances)

	A	B	C	D	E	F
1	t-Estimate of the Difference Between Two Means (Equal-Variances)					
2						
3		Sample 1	Sample 2	Confidence Interval Estimate		
4	Mean	2075	1714	360.48	±	290
5	Variance	450,343	390,409	Lower confidence limit		71
6	Sample size	42	38	Upper confidence limit		650
7	Pooled Variance	421,913				
8	Confidence level	0.95				

We estimate that the mean repair cost for non-ABS-equipped cars will be between $71 and $650 more than the mean repair cost for ABS-equipped cars.

A13.6 Speeds: Equal-variances t-test of $\mu_1 - \mu_2$

$H_0 : (\mu_1 - \mu_2) = 0$

$H_1 : (\mu_1 - \mu_2) > 0$

$$t = \frac{(\bar{x}_1 - \bar{x}_2) - (\mu_1 - \mu_2)}{\sqrt{s_p^2 \left(\dfrac{1}{n_1} + \dfrac{1}{n_2} \right)}}$$

	A	B	C
1	t-Test: Two-Sample Assuming Equal Variances		
2			
3		*Speeds Before*	*Speeds After*
4	Mean	31.74	31.42
5	Variance	4.50	4.41
6	Observations	100	100
7	Pooled Variance	4.45	
8	Hypothesized Mean Difference	0	
9	df	198	
10	t Stat	1.07	
11	P(T<=t) one-tail	0.1424	
12	t Critical one-tail	1.6526	
13	P(T<=t) two-tail	0.2849	
14	t Critical two-tail	1.9720	

t = 1.07, p-value = .1424. There is not enough evidence to infer that speed bumps reduce speeds.

Proper stops: Equal-variances t-test of $\mu_1 - \mu_2$

$H_0 : (\mu_1 - \mu_2) = 0$

$H_1 : (\mu_1 - \mu_2) < 0$

$$t = \frac{(\bar{x}_1 - \bar{x}_2) - (\mu_1 - \mu_2)}{\sqrt{s_p^2 \left(\dfrac{1}{n_1} + \dfrac{1}{n_2} \right)}}$$

	A	B	C
1	t-Test: Two-Sample Assuming Equal Variances		
2			
3		*Stops Before*	*Stops After*
4	Mean	7.82	7.98
5	Variance	1.83	1.84
6	Observations	100	100
7	Pooled Variance	1.83	
8	Hypothesized Mean Difference	0	
9	df	198	
10	t Stat	-0.84	
11	P(T<=t) one-tail	0.2021	
12	t Critical one-tail	1.6526	
13	P(T<=t) two-tail	0.4042	
14	t Critical two-tail	1.9720	

t = −.84, p-value = .2021. There is not enough evidence to infer that speed bumps increase the number of proper stops.

A13.8   t-test of μ_D

$H_0 : \mu_D = 0$

$H_1 : \mu_D > 0$

$$t = \frac{\bar{x}_D - \mu_D}{s_D / \sqrt{n_D}}$$

	A	B	C
1	t-Test: Paired Two Sample for Means		
2			
3		*Before*	*After*
4	Mean	28.94	26.22
5	Variance	61.45	104.30
6	Observations	50	50
7	Pearson Correlation	0.87	
8	Hypothesized Mean Difference	0	
9	df	49	
10	t Stat	3.73	
11	P(T<=t) one-tail	0.000	
12	t Critical one-tail	1.677	
13	P(T<=t) two-tail	0.000	
14	t Critical two-tail	2.010	

t = 3.73, p-value = .0002. There is enough evidence to infer that the law discourages bicycle use.

A13.10 t-test of μ

$H_0 : \mu = 200$

$H_1 : \mu > 200$

$$t = \frac{\bar{x} - \mu}{s / \sqrt{n}}$$

	A	B	C	D
1	**t-Test: Mean**			
2				
3				*Pedestrians*
4	Mean			209.13
5	Standard Deviation			60.01
6	Hypothesized Mean			200
7	df			39
8	t Stat			0.96
9	P(T<=t) one-tail			0.1711
10	t Critical one-tail			1.6849
11	P(T<=t) two-tail			0.3422
12	t Critical two-tail			2.0227

t = .96, p-value = .1711. There is not enough evidence to infer that the franchiser should build on this site.

A13.2 F-test of σ_1^2 / σ_2^2

$H_0 : \sigma_1^2 / \sigma_2^2 = 1$

$H_1 : \sigma_1^2 / \sigma_2^2 > 1$

$F = \dfrac{s_1^2}{s_2^2}$

	A	B	C
1	F-Test Two-Sample for Variances		
2			
3		Brand A	Brand B
4	Mean	145.95	144.78
5	Variance	16.45	4.25
6	Observations	100	100
7	df	99	99
8	F	3.87	
9	P(F<=f) one-tail	0.0000	
10	F Critical one-tail	1.3941	

F = 3.87, p-value = 0. There is overwhelming evidence to infer that Brand B is superior to Brand A.

A13.14 z-test of $p_1 - p_2$ (case 1)

$H_0 : p_1 - p_2 = 0$

$H_1 : p_1 - p_2 > 0$

$z = \dfrac{(\hat{p}_1 - \hat{p}_2)}{\sqrt{\hat{p}(1-\hat{p})\left(\dfrac{1}{n_1} + \dfrac{1}{n_2}\right)}}$

	A	B	C	D
1	**z-Test: Two Proportions**			
2				
3			Exercisers	Watchers
4	Sample Proportions		0.4250	0.3675
5	Observations		400	400
6	Hypothesized Difference		0	
7	z Stat		1.66	
8	P(Z<=z) one tail		0.0482	
9	z Critical one-tail		1.6449	
10	P(Z<=z) two-tail		0.0964	
11	z Critical two-tail		1.9600	

z = 1.66, p-value = .0482. There is evidence to infer that exercisers are more likely to remember the sponsor's brand name than those who only watch.

A13.16 t-tests of μ_D

    a. $H_0 : \mu_D = 40$

           $H_1 : \mu_D > 40$

$$t = \frac{\bar{x}_D - \mu_D}{s_D / \sqrt{n_D}}$$

	A	B	C
1	t-Test: Paired Two Sample for Means		
2			
3		SAT after	SAT before
4	Mean	1235	1162
5	Variance	37970	28844
6	Observations	40	40
7	Pearson Correlation	0.94	
8	Hypothesized Mean Difference	40	
9	df	39	
10	t Stat	2.98	
11	P(T<=t) one-tail	0.0024	
12	t Critical one-tail	1.6849	
13	P(T<=t) two-tail	0.0049	
14	t Critical two-tail	2.0227	

t = 2.98, p-value = .0024. There is enough evidence to conclude that the ETS claim is false.

    b. $H_0 : \mu_D = 110$

           $H_1 : \mu_D < 110$

$$t = \frac{\bar{x}_D - \mu_D}{s_D / \sqrt{n_D}}$$

	A	B	C
1	t-Test: Paired Two Sample for Means		
2			
3		SAT after	SAT before
4	Mean	1235	1162
5	Variance	37970	28844
6	Observations	40	40
7	Pearson Correlation	0.94	
8	Hypothesized Mean Difference	110	
9	df	39	
10	t Stat	-3.39	
11	P(T<=t) one-tail	0.0008	
12	t Critical one-tail	1.6849	
13	P(T<=t) two-tail	0.0016	
14	t Critical two-tail	2.0227	

t = –3.39, p-value = .0008. There is enough evidence to conclude that the Kaplan claim is also false.

Chapter 14

14.2   a. $\bar{\bar{x}} = \dfrac{4(20) + 4(22) + 4(25)}{4 + 4 + 4} = 22.33$

$SST = \sum n_j(\bar{x}_j - \bar{\bar{x}})^2 = 4(20 - 22.33)^2 + 4(22 - 22.33)^2 + 4(25 - 22.33)^2 = 50.67$

$SSE = \sum (n_j - 1)s_j^2 = (4-1)(10) + (4-1)(10) + (4-1)(10) = 90$

ANOVA Table

Source	Degrees of Freedom	Sum of Squares	Mean Squares	F
Treatments	$k - 1 = 2$	$SST = 50.67$	$\dfrac{SST}{k-1} = \dfrac{50.67}{2} = 25.33$	$\dfrac{MST}{MSE} = \dfrac{25.33}{10} = 2.53$
Error	$n - k = 9$	$SSE = 90$	$\dfrac{SSE}{n - k1} = \dfrac{90}{9} = 10$	

b. $SSE = \sum (n_j - 1)s_j^2 = (4-1)(25) + (4-1)(25) + (4-1)(25) = 225$

ANOVA Table

Source	Degrees of Freedom	Sum of Squares	Mean Squares	F
Treatments	$k - 1 = 2$	$SST = 50.67$	$\dfrac{SST}{k-1} = \dfrac{50.67}{2} = 25.33$	$\dfrac{MST}{MSE} = \dfrac{25.33}{25.0} = 1.01$
Error	$n - k = 9$	$SSE = 225$	$\dfrac{SSE}{n - k} = \dfrac{225}{9} = 25.0$	

c.   The F statistic decreases.

14.4 $H_0 : \mu_1 = \mu_2 = \mu_3$

$H_1 :$ At least two means differ.

Rejection region: $F > F_{\alpha, k-1, n-k} = F_{.05, 2, 9} = 4.26$

	Finance	Marketing	Management
Mean	2.25	3.25	5.75
Variance	2.25	2.92	2.92

Grand mean = 3.75

$SST = \sum n_j(\bar{x}_j - \bar{\bar{x}})^2 = 4(2.25 - 3.75)^2 + 4(3.25 - 3.75)^2 + 4(5.75 - 3.75)^2 = 26.00$

$SSE = \sum (n_j - 1)s_j^2 = (4-1)(2.25) + (4-1)(2.92) + (4-1)(2.92) = 24.25$

ANOVA table

Source	Degrees of Freedom	Sum of Squares	Mean Squares	F
Treatments	$k-1=2$	$SST = 26.00$	$\dfrac{SST}{k-1} = \dfrac{26.00}{2} = 13.00$	$\dfrac{MST}{MSE} = \dfrac{13.00}{2.69} = 4.82$
Error	$n-k=9$	$SSE = 24.25$	$\dfrac{SSE}{n-k} = \dfrac{24.25}{9} = 2.69$	

$F = 4.82$, p-value $= .0377$. There is enough evidence to conclude that there are differences in the number of job offers between the three MBA majors.

14.6 $H_0 : \mu_1 = \mu_2 = \mu_3$

H_1 : At least two means differ.

Rejection region: $F > F_{\alpha,k-1,n-k} = F_{.05,2,12} = 3.89$

	BA	BSc	BBA
Mean	3.94	4.78	5.76
Variance	1.26	.92	1.00

Grand mean $= 4.83$

$SST = \sum n_j(\overline{x}_j - \overline{\overline{x}})^2 = 5(3.94 - 4.83)^2 + 5(4.78 - 4.83)^2 + 5(5.76 - 4.83)^2 = 8.30$

$SSE = \sum (n_j - 1)s_j^2 = (5-1)(1.26) + (5-1)(.92) + (5-1)(1.00) = 12.73$

ANOVA table

Source	Degrees of Freedom	Sum of Squares	Mean Squares	F
Treatments	$k-1=2$	$SST = 8.30$	$\dfrac{SST}{k-1} = \dfrac{8.30}{2} = 4.15$	$\dfrac{MST}{MSE} = \dfrac{4.15}{1.06} = 3.91$
Error	$n-k=12$	$SSE = 12.73$	$\dfrac{SSE}{n-k} = \dfrac{12.73}{12} = 1.06$	

$F = 3.91$, p-value $= .0493$. There is enough evidence to conclude that students in different degree program differ in their summer earnings.

14.8 $H_0 : \mu_1 = \mu_2 = \mu_3$

H_1 : At least two means differ.

Rejection region: $F > F_{\alpha,k-1,n-k} = F_{.05,3,8} = 4.07$

	IBM	Dell	HP	Other
Mean	13.33	11.00	9.67	17.00
Variance	12.33	79.00	22.33	39.00

Grand mean $= 12.75$

$SST = \sum n_j(\overline{x}_j - \overline{\overline{x}})^2 = 3(13.33 - 12.75)^2 + 3(11.00 - 12.75)^2 + 3(9.67 - 12.75)^2 + 3(17.00 - 12.75)^2 = 92.92$

$SSE = \sum (n_j - 1)s_j^2 = (3-1)(12.33) + (3-1)(79.00) + (3-1)(22.33) + (3-1)(39.00) = 305.33$

ANOVA table

Source	Degrees of Freedom	Sum of Squares	Mean Squares	F
Treatments	$k-1=3$	SST = 92.92	$\dfrac{SST}{k-1}=\dfrac{92.92}{3}=30.97$	$\dfrac{MST}{MSE}=\dfrac{30.97}{38.17}=.81$
Error	$n-k=8$	SSE = 305.33	$\dfrac{SSE}{n-k}=\dfrac{305.33}{8}=38.17$	

F = .81, p-value = .5224. There is not enough evidence to conclude that there are differences in age between the computer brands.

14.10   a. $H_0 : \mu_1 = \mu_2 = \mu_3 = \mu_4$

H_1 : At least two means differ.

Rejection region: $F > F_{\alpha,k-1,n-k} = F_{.05,3,116} \approx 2.68$

Grand mean = 101.0

$SST = \sum n_j(\bar{x}_j - \bar{\bar{x}})^2$

$= 30(90.17 - 101.0)^2 + 30(95.77 - 101.0)^2 + 30(106.8 - 101.0)^2 + 30(111.17 - 101.0)^2 = 8,464$

$SSE = \sum (n_j - 1)s_j^2$

$= (30-1)(991.52) + (30-1)(900.87) + (30-1)(928.70) + (30-1)(1,023.04) = 111,480$

ANOVA table

Source	Degrees of Freedom	Sum of Squares	Mean Squares	F
Treatments	$k-1=3$	SST = 8,464	$\dfrac{SST}{k-1}=\dfrac{8,464}{3}=2,821$	$\dfrac{MST}{MSE}=\dfrac{2,821}{961.0}=2.94$
Error	$n-k=116$	SSE = 111,480	$\dfrac{SSE}{n-k}=\dfrac{111,480}{116}=961.0$	

F = 2.94, p-value = .0363. There is enough evidence to infer that there are differences between the completion times of the four income tax forms.

b.   The times for each form must be normally distributed with the same variance.

c.   The histograms are approximately bell-shaped and the sample variances are similar.

14.12 $H_0 : \mu_1 = \mu_2 = \mu_3 = \mu_4 = \mu_5$
H_1 : At least two means differ.
Rejection region: $F > F_{\alpha,k-1,n-k} = F_{.01,4,120} = 3.48$
Grand mean = 173.3
$SST = \sum n_j(\bar{x}_j - \bar{\bar{x}})^2 = 25(164.6 - 173.3)^2 + 25(185.6 - 173.3)^2 + 25(154.8 - 173.3)^2$
$+ 25(182.6 - 173.3)^2 + 25(178.9 - 173.3)^2 = 17,251$
$SSE = \sum (n_j - 1)s_j^2 = (25-1)(1,164) + (25-1)(1,720) + (25-1)(1,114) + (25-1)(1,658)$
$+ (25-1)(841.8) = 155,941$

ANOVA table

Source	Degrees of Freedom	Sum of Squares	Mean Squares	F
Treatments	$k-1=4$	$SST = 17{,}251$	$\dfrac{SST}{k-1} = \dfrac{17{,}251}{4} = 4{,}312.6$	$\dfrac{MST}{MSE} = \dfrac{4{,}312.6}{1{,}299.5} = 3.32$
Error	$n-k=120$	$SSE = 155{,}941$	$\dfrac{SSE}{n-k} = \dfrac{155{,}941}{120} = 1{,}299.5$	

$F = 3.32$, p-value = .0129. There is not enough evidence to allow the manufacturer to conclude that differences exist between the five lacquers.

b. The times until first sign of corrosion for each lacquer must be normally distributed with a common variance.

c. The histograms are approximately bell-shaped with similar sample variances.

14.14 $H_0 : \mu_1 = \mu_2 = \mu_3$

H_1 : At least two means differ.

Rejection region: $F > F_{\alpha,k-1,n-k} = F_{.05,2,57} \approx 3.15$

Grand mean = 562.6

$SST = \sum n_j (\overline{x}_j - \overline{\overline{x}})^2 = 20(551.50 - 562.6)^2 + 20(576.75 - 562.6)^2 + 20(559.45 - 562.6)^2 = 6{,}667$

$SSE = \sum (n_j - 1)s_j^2 = (20-1)(2{,}741.95) + (20-1)(2{,}641.14) + (20-1)(3{,}129.31) = 161{,}736$

ANOVA table

Source	Degrees of Freedom	Sum of Squares	Mean Squares	F
Treatments	$k-1=2$	$SST = 6{,}667$	$\dfrac{SST}{k-1} = \dfrac{6{,}667}{2} = 3{,}334$	$\dfrac{MST}{MSE} = \dfrac{3{,}334}{2{,}837} = 1.17$
Error	$n-k=57$	$SSE = 161{,}736$	$\dfrac{SSE}{n-k} = \dfrac{161{,}736}{57} = 2{,}837$	

$F = 1.17$, p-value = .3162. There is not enough evidence of a difference between fertilizers in terms of crop yields.

14.16 $H_0 : \mu_1 = \mu_2 = \mu_3 = \mu_4$

H_1 : At least two means differ.

Rejection region: $F > F_{\alpha,k-1,n-k} = F_{.05,3,116} \approx 2.68$

Grand mean = 77.39

$SST = \sum n_j (\overline{x}_j - \overline{\overline{x}})^2 = 30(74.10 - 77.39)^2 + 30(75.67 - 77.39)^2 + 30(78.50 - 77.39)^2$
$+ 30(81.30 - 77.39)^2 = 909.42$

$SSE = \sum (n_j - 1)s_j^2 = (30-1)(249.96) + (30-1)(184.23) + (30-1)(233.36) + (30-1)(242.91) = 26{,}403$

ANOVA table

Source	Degrees of Freedom	Sum of Squares	Mean Squares	F
Treatments	$k-1=3$	SST = 909.4	$\dfrac{SST}{k-1}=\dfrac{909.4}{3}=303.1$	$\dfrac{MST}{MSE}=\dfrac{303.1}{227.6}=1.33$
Error	$n-k=116$	SSE = 26,403	$\dfrac{SSE}{n-k}=\dfrac{26,403}{116}=227.6$	

$F = 1.33$, p-value = .2675. There is not enough evidence of a difference between the four groups of companies.

14.18 $H_0 : \mu_1 = \mu_2 = \mu_3 = \mu_4$

      H_1 : At least two means differ.

a.   Ages: Rejection region: $F > F_{\alpha,k-1,n-k} = F_{.05,3,291} \approx 2.61$

     Grand mean = 36.23

$$SST = \sum n_j(\overline{x}_j - \overline{\overline{x}})^2 = 63(31.30 - 36.23)^2 + 81(34.42 - 36.23)^2 + 40(37.38 - 36.23)^2$$

$$+ 111(39.93 - 36.23)^2 = 3,366$$

$$SSE = \sum (n_j - 1)s_j^2 = (63-1)(28.34) + (81-1)(23.20) + (40-1)(31.16) + (111-1)(72.03) = 12,752$$

ANOVA table

Source	Degrees of Freedom	Sum of Squares	Mean Squares	F
Treatments	$k-1=3$	SST =3,366	$\dfrac{SST}{k-1}=\dfrac{3,366}{3}=1,122$	$\dfrac{MST}{MSE}=\dfrac{1,122}{43.82}=25.60$
Error	$n-k=291$	SSE = 12,752	$\dfrac{SSE}{n-k}=\dfrac{12,752}{291}=43.82$	

$F = 25.60$, p-value = 0. There is sufficient evidence to infer that the ages of the four groups of cereal buyers differ.

b.   Incomes: Rejection region: $F > F_{\alpha,k-1,n-k} = F_{.05,3,291} \approx 2.61$

     Grand mean = 39.97

$$SST = \sum n_j(\overline{x}_j - \overline{\overline{x}})^2 = 63(37.22 - 39.97)^2 + 81(38.91 - 39.97)^2 + 40(41.48 - 39.97)^2$$

$$+ 111(41.75 - 39.97)^2 = 1,008$$

$$SSE = \sum (n_j - 1)s_j^2 = (63-1)(39.82) + (81-1)(40.85) + (40-1)(61.38) + (111-1)(46.59) = 13,256$$

ANOVA table

Source	Degrees of Freedom	Sum of Squares	Mean Squares	F
Treatments	$k-1=3$	SST =1,008	$\dfrac{SST}{k-1}=\dfrac{1,008}{3}=336.0$	$\dfrac{MST}{MSE}=\dfrac{336.0}{45.55}=7.37$
Error	$n-k=291$	SSE = 13,256	$\dfrac{SSE}{n-k}=\dfrac{13,256}{291}=45.55$	

F = 7.37, p-value = .0001. There is sufficient evidence to conclude that incomes differ between the four groups of cereal buyers.

c.   Education: Rejection region: $F > F_{\alpha,k-1,n-k} = F_{.05,3,291} \approx 2.61$

Grand mean = 11.98

$$SST = \sum n_j(\overline{x}_j - \overline{\overline{x}})^2 = 63(11.75 - 11.98)^2 + 81(12.41 - 11.98)^2 + 40(11.73 - 11.98)^2$$

$$+ 111(11.89 - 11.98)^2 = 21.71$$

$$SSE = \sum (n_j - 1)s_j^2 = (63 - 1)(3.93) + (81 - 1)(3.39) + (40 - 1)(4.26) + (111 - 1)(4.30) = 1,154$$

ANOVA table

Source	Degrees of Freedom	Sum of Squares	Mean Squares	F
Treatments	$k-1 = 3$	SST = 21.71	$\dfrac{SST}{k-1} = \dfrac{21.71}{3} = 7.24$	$\dfrac{MST}{MSE} = \dfrac{7.24}{3.97} = 1.82$
Error	$n-k = 291$	SSE = 1,154	$\dfrac{SSE}{n-k} = \dfrac{1,154}{291} = 3.97$	

F = 1.82, p-value = .1428. There is not enough evidence to infer that education differs between the four groups of cereal buyers.

d.   Using the F-tests and the descriptive statistics we see that the mean ages and mean household incomes are in ascending order. For example, Sugar Smacks buyers are younger and earn less than the buyers of the other three cereals. Cheerio purchasers are older and earn the most.

14.20 $H_0 : \mu_1 = \mu_2 = \mu_3$

H_1 : At least two means differ.

Rejection region: $F > F_{\alpha,k-1,n-k} = F_{.05,2,232} \approx 3.07$

Grand mean = 19.50

$$SST = \sum n_j(\overline{x}_j - \overline{\overline{x}})^2 = 61(18.54 - 19.50)^2 + 83(19.34 - 19.50)^2 + 91(20.29 - 19.50)^2 = 114.5$$

$$SSE = \sum (n_j - 1)s_j^2 = (61 - 1)(177.95) + (83 - 1)(171.42) + (91 - 1)(297.50) = 51,508$$

ANOVA table

Source	Degrees of Freedom	Sum of Squares	Mean Squares	F
Treatments	$k-1 = 2$	SST = 114.5	$\dfrac{SST}{k-1} = \dfrac{114.5}{2} = 57.3$	$\dfrac{MST}{MSE} = \dfrac{57.3}{222.0} = .26$
Error	$n-k = 232$	SSE = 51,508	$\dfrac{SSE}{n-k} = \dfrac{51,508}{232} = 222.0$	

F = .26, p-value = .7730. There is not enough evidence of a difference between the three segments.

14.22   a. $\alpha = .05$: $t_{\alpha/2, n-k} = t_{.025, 20} = 2.086$

$$LSD = t_{\alpha/2, n-k} \sqrt{MSE\left(\frac{1}{n_i} + \frac{1}{n_j}\right)} = 2.086 \sqrt{125\left(\frac{1}{5} + \frac{1}{5}\right)} = 14.75$$

Treatment		Means	Difference
$i = 1, j = 2$	227	205	22
$i = 1, j = 3$	227	219	8
$i = 1, j = 4$	227	248	−21
$i = 1, j = 5$	227	202	25
$i = 2, j = 3$	205	219	−14
$i = 2, j = 4$	205	248	−43
$i = 2, j = 5$	205	202	3
$i = 3, j = 4$	219	248	−29
$i = 3, j = 5$	219	202	17
$i = 4, j = 5$	248	202	46

Conclusion: The following pairs of means differ. μ_1 and μ_2, μ_1 and μ_4, μ_1 and μ_5, μ_2 and μ_4, μ_3 and μ_4, μ_3 and μ_5, and μ_4 and μ_5.

b. $C = 5(4)/2 = 10$, $\alpha_E = .05$, $\alpha = \alpha_E / C = .005$ $t_{\alpha/2, n-k} = t_{.0025, 20} = 3.153$ (from Excel)

$$LSD = t_{\alpha/2, n-k} \sqrt{MSE\left(\frac{1}{n_i} + \frac{1}{n_j}\right)} = 3.153 \sqrt{125\left(\frac{1}{5} + \frac{1}{5}\right)} = 22.30$$

Treatment		Means	Difference
$i = 1, j = 2$	227	205	22
$i = 1, j = 3$	227	219	8
$i = 1, j = 4$	227	248	−21
$i = 1, j = 5$	227	202	25
$i = 2, j = 3$	205	219	−14
$i = 2, j = 4$	205	248	−43
$i = 2, j = 5$	205	202	3
$i = 3, j = 4$	219	248	−29
$i = 3, j = 5$	219	202	17
$i = 4, j = 5$	248	202	46

Conclusion: The following pairs of means differ. μ_1 and μ_5, μ_2 and μ_4, μ_3 and μ_4, and μ_4 and μ_5.

c. $q_{\alpha}(k, \nu) = q_{.05}(5, 20) = 4.23 \;\varpi = q_{\alpha}(k, \nu)\sqrt{\dfrac{MSE}{n_g}} = 4.23\sqrt{\dfrac{125}{5}} = 21.15$

Treatment	Means		Difference
$i = 1, j = 2$	227	205	22
$i = 1, j = 3$	227	219	8
$i = 1, j = 4$	227	248	−21
$i = 1, j = 5$	227	202	25
$i = 2, j = 3$	205	219	−14
$i = 2, j = 4$	205	248	−43
$i = 2, j = 5$	205	202	3
$i = 3, j = 4$	219	248	−2
$i = 3, j = 5$	219	202	17
$i = 4, j = 5$	248	202	46

Conclusion: The following pairs of means differ. μ_1 and μ_2, μ_1 and μ_5, μ_2 and μ_4, μ_3 and μ_4, and μ_4 and μ_5.

14.24 a. $LSD = t_{\alpha/2, n-k}\sqrt{MSE\left(\dfrac{1}{n_i} + \dfrac{1}{n_j}\right)} = 1.782\sqrt{1.06\left(\dfrac{1}{5} + \dfrac{1}{5}\right)} = 1.16$

Treatment	Means		Difference
$i = 1, j = 2$	3.94	4.78	−.84
$i = 1, j = 3$	3.94	5.76	−1.82
$i = 2, j = 3$	4.78	5.76	−1.02

Means of BAs and BBAs differ.

b. $C = 3(2)/2 = 3,\; \alpha_E = .10,\; \alpha = \alpha_E / C = .0333$: $t_{\alpha/2, n-k} = t_{.0167, 12} = 2.404$ (from Excel)

$LSD = t_{\alpha/2, n-k}\sqrt{MSE\left(\dfrac{1}{n_i} + \dfrac{1}{n_j}\right)} = 2.404\sqrt{1.06\left(\dfrac{1}{5} + \dfrac{1}{5}\right)} = 1.57$

Treatment	Means		Difference
$i = 1, j = 2$	3.94	4.78	−.84
$i = 1, j = 3$	3.94	5.76	−1.82
$i = 2, j = 3$	4.78	5.76	−1.02

Means of BAs and BBAs differ.

14.26 Tukey's method: $q_\alpha(k, \nu) = q_{.05}(4, 116) \approx 3.68$ $\varpi = 3.68\sqrt{\dfrac{961.0}{30}} = 20.83$

LSD method with the Bonferroni adjustment: $C = 4(3)/2 = 6, \alpha_E = .05, \alpha = \alpha_E / C = .0083$

$$LSD = t_{\alpha/2, n-k}\sqrt{MSE\left(\dfrac{1}{n_i} + \dfrac{1}{n_j}\right)} = 2.64\sqrt{961.0\left(\dfrac{1}{30} + \dfrac{1}{30}\right)} = 21.13$$

Treatment		Means	Difference	Tukey	LSD
$i = 1, j = 2$	90.17	95.77	−5.60	20.83	21.13
$i = 1, j = 3$	90.17	106.8	−16.67	20.83	21.13
$i = 1, j = 4$	90.17	111.17	−21.00	20.83	21.13
$i = 2, j = 3$	95.77	106.8	−11.07	20.83	21.13
$i = 2, j = 4$	95.77	111.17	−15.40	20.83	21.13
$i = 3, j = 4$	106.8	111.17	−4.33	20.83	21.13

a. The means for Forms 1 and 4 differ.

b. No means differ.

14.28 a. LSD method: $C = 5(4)/2 = 10, \alpha_E = .05, \alpha = \alpha_E / C = .005$ $t_{\alpha/2, n-k} = t_{.0025, 120} = 2.860$ (from Excel)

$$LSD = t_{\alpha/2, n-k}\sqrt{MSE\left(\dfrac{1}{n_i} + \dfrac{1}{n_j}\right)} = 2.860\sqrt{1300\left(\dfrac{1}{25} + \dfrac{1}{25}\right)} = 29.17$$

b. Tukey's method: $q_\alpha(k, \nu) = q_{.05}(5, 120) = 3.92$ $\varpi = 3.92\sqrt{\dfrac{1300}{25}} = 28.27$

Treatment		Means	Difference
$i = 1, j = 2$	164.6	185.6	−21.0
$i = 1, j = 3$	164.6	154.8	9.8
$i = 1, j = 4$	164.6	182.6	−18.0
$i = 1, j = 5$	164.6	178.9	−14.3
$i = 2, j = 3$	185.6	154.8	30.8
$i = 2, j = 4$	185.6	182.6	3.0
$i = 2, j = 5$	185.6	178.9	6.7
$i = 3, j = 4$	154.8	182.6	−27.8
$i = 3, j = 5$	154.8	178.9	−24.1
$i = 4, j = 5$	182.6	178.9	3.7

a. The means of lacquers 2 and 3 differ

b. The means of lacquers 2 and 3 differ.

14.30 Tukey's method: $q_\alpha(k,v) = q_{.05}(3,57) \approx 3.40$ $\varpi = 3.40\sqrt{\dfrac{2{,}838}{20}} = 40.50$

LSD method: $C = 3(2)/2 = 3, \alpha_E = .05, \alpha = \alpha_E/C = .0167$ $t_{\alpha/2,n-k} = t_{.0083,57} = 2.466$ (from Excel)

$$LSD = t_{\alpha/2,n-k}\sqrt{MSE\left(\dfrac{1}{n_i} + \dfrac{1}{n_j}\right)} = 2.466\sqrt{2{,}838\left(\dfrac{1}{20} + \dfrac{1}{20}\right)} = 41.54$$

Treatment		Means		Difference
I = 1, j = 2	551.5		576.8	−25.3
I = 1, j = 3	551.5		559.5	−8.0
i = 2, j = 3	576.8		559.5	17.3

a. There are no differences.

b. There are no differences.

14.32

ANOVA Table

Source	Degrees of Freedom	Sum of Squares	Mean Squares	F
Treatments	4	1,500	375.0	16.50
Blocks	11	1,000	90.91	4.00
Error	44	1,000	22.73	
Total	59	3,500		

a. Rejection region: $F > F_{\alpha,k-1,n-k-b+1} = F_{.01,4,44} \approx 3.83$

$F = 16.50$, p-value = 0. There is enough evidence to conclude that the treatment means differ.

b. Rejection region: $F > F_{\alpha,b-1,n-k-b+1} = F_{.01,11,44} \approx 2.80$

Conclusion: $F = 4.00$, p-value = .0005. There is enough evidence to conclude that the block means differ.

14.34 Rejection region: $F > F_{\alpha,k-1,n-k-b+1} = F_{.05,2,14} = 3.74$

a.

ANOVA Table

Source	Degrees of Freedom	Sum of Squares	Mean Squares	F
Treatments	2	1,500	750.0	7.00
Blocks	7	500	71.43	.67
Error	14	1,500	107.1	
Total	23	3,500		

Conclusion: F = 7.00, p-value = .0078. There is enough evidence to conclude that the treatment means differ.

b.

ANOVA Table

Source	Degrees of Freedom	Sum of Squares	Mean Squares	F
Treatments	2	1,500	750.0	10.50
Blocks	7	1000	142.86	2.00
Error	14	1,000	71.43	
Total	23	3,500		

Conclusion: F = 10.50, .0016. There is enough evidence to conclude that the treatment means differ

c.

ANOVA Table

Source	Degrees of Freedom	Sum of Squares	Mean Squares	F
Treatments	2	1,500	750.0	21.00
Blocks	7	1,500	214.3	6.00
Error	14	500	35.71	
Total	23	3,500		

Conclusion: F = 21.00, p-value = .0001. There is enough evidence to conclude that the treatment means differ

d. The test statistic increases.

14.36 a. $k = 4$, $b = 3$, Grand mean = 5.6

$$SS(Total) = \sum_{j=1}^{k} \sum_{i=1}^{b} (x_{ij} - \bar{\bar{x}})^2 = (6-5.6)^2 + (8-5.6)^2 + (7-5.6)^2 + (5-5.6)^2 + (5-5.6)^2 + (6-5.6)^2$$

$$+ (4-5.6)^2 + (5-5.6)^2 + (5-5.6)^2 + (4-5.6)^2 + (6-5.6)^2 + (6-5.6)^2 = 14.9$$

$$SST = \sum_{j=1}^{k} b(\bar{x}[T]_j - \bar{\bar{x}})^2 = 3[(7-5.6)^2 + (5.3-5.6)^2 + (4.7-5.6)^2 + (5.3-5.6)^2] = 8.9$$

$$SSB = \sum_{i=1}^{b} k(\bar{x}[B]_i - \bar{\bar{x}})^2 = 4[(4.8-5.6)^2 + (6-5.6)^2 + (6-5.6)^2 = 4.2$$

$$SSE = SS(Total) - SST - SSB = 14.9 - 8.9 - 4.2 = 1.8$$

b. $SS(Total) = \sum_{j=1}^{k} \sum_{i=1}^{b} (x_{ij} - \overline{\overline{x}})^2 = (6-5.6)^2 + (8-5.6)^2 + (7-5.6)^2 + (5-5.6)^2 + (5-5.6)^2 + (6-5.6)^2$

$+ (4-5.6)^2 + (5-5.6)^2 + (5-5.6)^2 + (4-5.6)^2 + (6-5.6)^2 + (6-5.6)^2 = 14.9$

$SST = \sum_{j=1}^{k} b(\overline{x}[T]_j - \overline{\overline{x}})^2 = 3[(7-5.6)^2 + (5.3-5.6)^2 + (4.7-5.6)^2 + (5.3-5.6)^2] = 8.9$

$SSE = SS(Total) - SST = 14.9 - 8.9 = 6.0$

c.   The variation between all the data is the same for both designs.

d.   The variation between treatments is the same for both designs.

e.   Because the randomized block design divides the sum of squares for error in the one-way analysis of variance into two parts.

14.38 $H_0 : \mu_1 = \mu_2 = \mu_3 = \mu_4$

H_1 : At least two means differ.

Rejection region: $F > F_{\alpha, k-1, n-k-b+1} = F_{.01,3,12} = 5.95$

$k = 4, b = 5$, Grand mean $= 8.3$

$SS(Total) = \sum_{j=1}^{k} \sum_{i=1}^{b} (x_{ij} - \overline{\overline{x}})^2$

$= (5-8.3)^2 + (4-8.3)^2 + (6-8.3)^2 + (7-8.3)^2 + (9-8.3)^2$

$+ (2-8.3)^2 + (7-8.3)^2 + (12-8.3)^2 + (11-8.3)^2 + (8-8.3)^2$

$+ (6-8.3)^2 + (8-8.3)^2 + (9-8.3)^2 + (16-8.3)^2 + (15-8.3)^2$

$+ (8-8.3)^2 + (10-8.3)^2 + (2-8.3)^2 + (7-8.3)^2 + (14-8.3)^2 = 286.2$

$SST = \sum_{j=1}^{k} b(\overline{x}[T]_j - \overline{\overline{x}})^2 = 5[(6.2-8.3)^2 + (8.0-8.3)^2 + (10.8-8.3)^2 + (8.2-8.3)^2] = 53.8$

$SSB = \sum_{i=1}^{b} k(\overline{x}[B]_i - \overline{\overline{x}})^2$

$= 4[(5.25-8.3)^2 + (7.25-8.3)^2 + (7.25-8.3)^2 + (10.25-8.3)^2 + (11.5-8.3)^2] = 102.2$

$SSE = SS(Total) - SST - SSB = 286.2 - 53.8 - 102.2 = 130.2$

ANOVA Table

Source	Degrees of Freedom	Sum of Squares	Mean Squares	F
Treatments	3	53.8	17.93	1.65
Blocks	4	102.2	25.55	2.35
Error	12	130.2	10.85	
Total	19	286.2		

F = 1.65, p-value = .2296. There is not enough evidence to conclude there are differences between the four diets.

14.40

ANOVA Table

Source	Degrees of Freedom	Sum of Squares	Mean Squares	F
Treatments	2	7,131	3,566	123.36
Blocks	19	177,465	9,340	323.16
Error	38	1,098	28.90	

a. $H_0 : \mu_1 = \mu_2 = \mu_3$

H_1 : At least two means differ.

Rejection region: $F > F_{\alpha, k-1, n-k-b+1} = F_{.05, 2, 38} \approx 3.23$

F = 123.36, p-value = 0. There is sufficient evidence to conclude that the three fertilizers differ with respect to crop yield.

b.   F = 323.16, p-value = 0. There is sufficient evidence to indicate that there are differences between the plots.

14.42

ANOVA Table

Source	Degrees of Freedom	Sum of Squares	Mean Squares	F
Treatments	3	4,206	1,402	21.16
Blocks	29	126,843	4,374	66.02
Error	87	5,764	66.25	

a. $H_0 : \mu_1 = \mu_2 = \mu_3 = \mu_4$

H_1 : At least two means differ.

Rejection region: $F > F_{\alpha, k-1, n-k-b+1} = F_{.01, 3, 87} \approx 4.01$

F = 21.16, p-value = 0. There is sufficient evidence to conclude that differences in completion times exist between the four forms.

b. $H_0 : \mu_1 = \mu_2 = \ldots = \mu_{30}$

H_1 : At least two means differ.

F = 66.02, p-value = 0. There is sufficient evidence to indicate that there are differences between the taxpayers, which tells us that this experimental design is recommended.

14.44

ANOVA Table

Source	Degrees of Freedom	Sum of Squares	Mean Squares	F
Treatments	4	1,406	351,6	10.72
Blocks	35	7,310	208.9	6.36
Error	140	4,594	32.81	

a. $H_0 : \mu_1 = \mu_2 = \mu_3 = \mu_4 = \mu_5$

   H_1 : At least two means differ.

$F = 10.72$, p-value = 0. There is enough evidence to infer differences between medical specialties.

b. $H_0 : \mu_1 = \mu_2 = \ldots = \mu_{36}$

   H_1 : At least two means differ.

$F = 6.36$, p-value = 0. There is sufficient evidence to indicate that there are differences between the physicians' ages, which tells us that this experimental design is recommended.

14.46

ANOVA Table

Source	Degrees of Freedom	Sum of Squares	Mean Squares	F
Factor A	2	1,560	780	5.86
Factor B	3	2,880	960	7.18
Interaction	6	7,605	1268	9.53
Error	228	30,405	133	
Total	239	42,450		

a.   Rejection region: $F > F_{\alpha,(a-1)(b-1),n-ab} = F_{.01,6,228} \approx 2.80$

$F = 9.53$. There is enough evidence to conclude that factors A and B interact. The F-tests in Parts b and c are irrelevant.

14.48

ANOVA Table

ANOVA Table

	A	B	C	D	E	F	G
23	ANOVA						
24	*Source of Variation*	*SS*	*df*	*MS*	*F*	*P-value*	*F crit*
25	Sample	5.33	1	5.33	1.23	0.2995	5.32
26	Columns	56.33	1	56.33	13.00	0.0069	5.32
27	Interaction	1.33	1	1.33	0.31	0.5943	5.32
28	Within	34.67	8	4.33			
29							
30	Total	97.67	11				

a. $F = .31$, p-value = .5943. There is not enough evidence to conclude that factors A and B interact.

b. $F = 1.23$, p-value = .2995. There is not enough evidence to conclude that differences exist between the levels of factor A.

c. $F = 13.00$, p-value = .0069. There is enough evidence to conclude that differences exist between the levels of factor B.

14.49

ANOVA Table

	A	B	C	D	E	F	G
35	ANOVA						
36	*Source of Variation*	*SS*	*df*	*MS*	*F*	*P-value*	*F crit*
37	Sample	135.85	3	45.28	4.49	0.0060	2.7318
38	Columns	151.25	1	151.25	15.00	0.0002	3.9739
39	Interaction	6.25	3	2.08	0.21	0.8915	2.7318
40	Within	726.20	72	10.09			
41							
42	Total	1019.55	79				

The test for interaction yields ($F = .21$, p-value = .8915) and the test for the differences between educational levels ($F = 4.49$, p-value = .0060) is the same as in Example 14.4. However, in this exercise there is evidence of a difference between men and women ($F = 15.00$, p-value = .0002).

14.52 a. There are 12 treatments.

b. There are two factors, tax form and income group.

c.   There are a = 4 forms and b = 3 income groups.

	A	B	C	D	E	F	G
28							
29	ANOVA						
30	*Source of Variation*	*SS*	*df*	*MS*	*F*	*P-value*	*F crit*
31	Sample	6719	2	3359.4	4.11	0.0190	3.08
32	Columns	6280	3	2093.3	2.56	0.0586	2.69
33	Interaction	5102	6	850.3	1.04	0.4030	2.18
34	Within	88217	108	816.8			
35							
36	Total	106317	119				

d. $F = 1.04$, p-value $= .4030$. There is not enough evidence to conclude that forms and income groups interact

e. $F = 2.56$, p-value $= .0586$. There is not enough evidence to conclude that differences exist between the forms.

f. $F = 4.11$, p-value $= .0190$. There is enough evidence to conclude that differences exist between the three income groups.

14.54 a.   Factor A is the drug mixture and factor B is the schedule.

b.   The response variable is the improvement index.

c.   There are a = 4 drug mixtures and b = 2 schedules.

	A	B	C	D	E	F	G
23	ANOVA						
24	*Source of Variation*	*SS*	*df*	*MS*	*F*	*P-value*	*F crit*
25	Sample	14.40	1	14.40	0.57	0.4548	4.15
26	Columns	581.80	3	193.93	7.71	0.0005	2.90
27	Interaction	548.60	3	182.87	7.27	0.0007	2.90
28	Within	804.80	32	25.15			
29							
30	Total	1949.60	39				

d.   Test for interaction: $F = 7.27$, p-value $= .0007$. There is sufficient evidence to conclude that the schedules and drug mixtures interact. There is sufficient evidence to conclude that detergents and temperatures interact. The F-tests in Parts e and f are irrelevant.

14.56

	A	B	C	D	E	F	G
23	ANOVA						
24	*Source of Variation*	*SS*	*df*	*MS*	*F*	*P-value*	*F crit*
25	Sample	16.04	1	16.04	14.74	0.0005	4.11
26	Columns	6.77	1	6.77	6.22	0.0173	4.11
27	Interaction	0.025	1	0.025	0.023	0.8814	4.11
28	Within	39.17	36	1.09			
29							
30	Total	62.00	39				

The p-values for interaction, machines, and alloys are .8814, .0173, .0005, and, respectively. Both machines and alloys are sources of variation.

14.58

	A	B	C	D	E	F	G
29	ANOVA						
30	*Source of Variation*	*SS*	*df*	*MS*	*F*	*P-value*	*F crit*
31	Sample	211.78	2	105.89	21.04	0.0000	3.22
32	Columns	0.59	1	0.59	0.12	0.7348	4.07
33	Interaction	0.13	2	0.0640	0.0127	0.9874	3.22
34	Within	211.42	42	5.03			
35							
36	Total	423.91	47				

The p-values for interaction, methods, and skills are .9874, .7348, 0, and. The only source of variation is skill level.

14.60   a. $H_0 : \mu_1 = \mu_2 = \mu_3 = \mu_4$

H_1 : At least two means differ.

	A	B	C	D	E	F	G
11	ANOVA						
12	*Source of Variation*	*SS*	*df*	*MS*	*F*	*P-value*	*F crit*
13	Between Groups	9.90	3	3.30	7.67	0.0001	2.70
14	Within Groups	41.33	96	0.43			
15							
16	Total	51.23	99				

F = 7.67, p-value = .0001. There is sufficient evidence to infer that differences in productivity exist between the four groups of companies.

b.

	A	B	C	D	E
1	**Multiple Comparisons**				
2					
3				LSD	Omega
4	Treatment	Treatment	Difference	Alpha = 0.0083	Alpha = 0.05
5	*Extensive*	*Some*	0.534	0.500	0.483
6		*Little*	0.722	0.500	0.483
7		*No*	0.811	0.500	0.483
8	*Some*	*Little*	0.188	0.500	0.483
9		*No*	0.277	0.500	0.483
10	*Little*	*No*	0.089	0.500	0.483

Using either the Bonferroni adjustment or Tukey's method we conclude that μ_1 differs from μ_2, μ_3 and μ_4. Companies that offered extensive training have productivity levels different from the other companies.

14.62 $H_0 : \mu_1 = \mu_2 = \mu_3 = \mu_4$

H_1 : At least two means differ.

	A	B	C	D	E	F	G
31	ANOVA						
32	*Source of Variation*	SS	df	MS	F	P-value	F crit
33	Rows	43980	19	2314.72	21.58	0.0000	1.77
34	Columns	4438	3	1479.21	13.79	0.0000	2.77
35	Error	6113	57	107.25			
36							
37	Total	54530	79				

F = 13.79, p-value = 0. There is sufficient evidence to conclude that the reading speeds differ between the four typefaces. The typeface that was read the fastest should be used.

14.64 $H_0 : \mu_1 = \mu_2 = \mu_3$

H_1 : At least two means differ

	A	B	C	D	E	F	G
17	ANOVA						
18	*Source of Variation*	SS	df	MS	F	P-value	F crit
19	Rows	195.33	6	32.56	11.55	0.0002	3.00
20	Columns	43.52	2	21.76	7.72	0.0070	3.89
21	Error	33.81	12	2.82			
22							
23	Total	272.67	20				

F = 7.72, p-value = .0070. There is enough evidence to infer that differences in attention span exist between the three products.

14.66 a. $H_0 : \mu_1 = \mu_2 = \mu_3$

H$_1$: At least two means differ.

	A	B	C	D	E	F	G
10	ANOVA						
11	*Source of Variation*	*SS*	*df*	*MS*	*F*	*P-value*	*F crit*
12	Between Groups	1769.5	2	884.74	136.58	0.0000	3.02
13	Within Groups	2409.8	372	6.48			
14							
15	Total	4179.3	374				

F = 136.58, p-value = 0. There is sufficient evidence to infer that differences exist between the effects of the three teaching approaches.

b.

	A	B	C	D	E
1	**Multiple Comparisons**				
2					
3				LSD	Omega
4	Treatment	Treatment	Difference	Alpha = 0.0167	Alpha = 0.05
5	*hole Langua*	*Embedded*	-0.856	0.774	0.754
6		*Pure*	-4.976	0.774	0.754
7	*Embedded*	*Pure*	-4.120	0.774	0.754

All three means differ from one another. From the sample means we may infer that the pure method is best, followed by embedded, and by whole-language.

14.68 $H_0 : \mu_1 = \mu_2 = \mu_3 = \mu_4$

H$_1$: At least two means differ.

	A	B	C	D	E	F	G
11	ANOVA						
12	*Source of Variation*	*SS*	*df*	*MS*	*F*	*P-value*	*F crit*
13	Between Groups	5990284	3	1996761	14.47	0.0000	2.64
14	Within Groups	40024172	290	138014			
15							
16	Total	46014456	293				

F = 14.47, p-value = 0. There is enough evidence to infer differences in debt levels between the four types of degrees.

14.70 $H_0 : \mu_1 = \mu_2 = \mu_3 = \mu_4$

H_1 : At least two means differ.

	A	B	C	D	E	F	G
11	ANOVA						
12	*Source of Variation*	*SS*	*df*	*MS*	*F*	*P-value*	*F crit*
13	Between Groups	3007	3	1002.3	13.84	0.0000	2.67
14	Within Groups	10576	146	72.4			
15							
16	Total	13583	149				

F = 13.84, p-value = 0. There is enough evidence to infer that the length of time depends on the size of the party

14.72 $H_0 : \mu_1 = \mu_2 = \mu_3$

H_1 : At least two means differ.

	A	B	C	D	E	F	G
10	ANOVA						
11	*Source of Variation*	*SS*	*df*	*MS*	*F*	*P-value*	*F crit*
12	Between Groups	1.57	2	0.787	1.62	0.202233	3.09
13	Within Groups	46.98	97	0.484			
14							
15	Total	48.55	99				

F = 1.62, p-value = .2022. There is no evidence to infer that at least one buy indicator is useful.

14.74 $H_0 : \mu_1 = \mu_2 = \mu_3$

H_1 : At least two means differ.

	A	B	C	D	E	F	G
1	ANOVA						
2	*Source of Variation*	*SS*	*df*	*MS*	*F*	*P-value*	*F crit*
3	Between Groups	52.82	2	26.41	3.24	0.0414	3.04
4	Within Groups	1607.82	197	8.16			
5							
6	Total	1660.6	199				

F = 3.24, p-value = .0414. There is enough evidence to infer that the distances driven differ between drivers who have had 0, 1, or 2 accidents.

een the three types of treatments.

Appendix 14

A14.2 t-test of μ_D

$H_0 : \mu_D = 0$

$H_1 : \mu_D < 0$

$$t = \frac{\overline{x}_D - \mu_D}{s_D / \sqrt{n_D}}$$

	A	B	C
1	t-Test: Paired Two Sample for Means		
2			
3		*Price shown*	*Price not shown*
4	Mean	56.15	60.31
5	Variance	243.68	467.71
6	Observations	100	100
7	Pearson Correlation	0.79	
8	Hypothesized Mean Difference	0	
9	df	99	
10	t Stat	-3.12	
11	P(T<=t) one-tail	0.0012	
12	t Critical one-tail	1.6604	
13	P(T<=t) two-tail	0.0024	
14	t Critical two-tail	1.9842	

$t = -3.12$, p-value = .0012. There is overwhelming evidence to conclude that ads with no price shown are more effective in generating interest than ads that show the price.

A14.4 a. z-test of $p_1 - p_2$ (case 1)

$H_0 : p_1 - p_2 = 0$

$H_1 : p_1 - p_2 > 0$

$$z = \frac{(\hat{p}_1 - \hat{p}_2)}{\sqrt{\hat{p}(1-\hat{p})\left(\frac{1}{n_1} + \frac{1}{n_2}\right)}}$$

	A	B	C	D
1	**z-Test: Two Proportions**			
2				
3			*Topiramate*	*Placebo*
4	Sample Proportions		0.2364	0.1042
5	Observations		55	48
6	Hypothesized Difference		0	
7	z Stat		1.76	
8	P(Z<=z) one tail		0.0390	
9	z Critical one-tail		1.6449	
10	P(Z<=z) two-tail		0.0780	
11	z Critical two-tail		1.96	

$z = 1.76$, p-value = .0390. There is enough evidence to conclude that topiramate is effective in causing abstinence for the first month.

b. z-test of $p_1 - p_2$ (case 1)

$H_0 : p_1 - p_2 = 0$

$H_1 : p_1 - p_2 > 0$

$$z = \frac{(\hat{p}_1 - \hat{p}_2)}{\sqrt{\hat{p}(1-\hat{p})\left(\dfrac{1}{n_1} + \dfrac{1}{n_2}\right)}}$$

	A	B	C	D
1	**z-Test: Two Proportions**			
2				
3			*Topiramate*	*Placebo*
4	Sample Proportions		0.5091	0.1667
5	Observations		55	48
6	Hypothesized Difference		0	
7	z Stat		3.64	
8	P(Z<=z) one tail		0.0001	
9	z Critical one-tail		1.6449	
10	P(Z<=z) two-tail		0.0002	
11	z Critical two-tail		1.96	

$z = 3.64$, p-value = .0001. There is enough evidence to conclude that topiramate is effective in causing alcoholics to refrain from binge drinking in the final month.

A14.6 a. One-way analysis of variance

	A	B	C	D	E	F	G
11	ANOVA						
12	*Source of Variation*	*SS*	*df*	*MS*	*F*	*P-value*	*F crit*
13	Between Groups	25113	3	8371.2	85.98	0.0000	2.63
14	Within Groups	30766	316	97.36			
15							
16	Total	55880	319				

$F = 85.98$, p-value = 0.

Two-factor analysis of variance

	A	B	C	D	E	F	G
23	ANOVA						
24	*Source of Variation*	*SS*	*df*	*MS*	*F*	*P-value*	*F crit*
25	Sample	17024	1	17024	174.85	0.0000	3.87
26	Columns	7411	1	7411	76.12	0.0000	3.87
27	Interaction	679	1	678.6	6.97	0.0087	3.87
28	Within	30766	316	97.36			
29							
30	Total	55880	319				

Interaction: F = 6.97; p-value = .0087. There is enough evidence to infer that differences are caused by interaction. There is no need to conduct the other two tests.

A14.8   Two-way analysis of variance

$H_0 : \mu_1 = \mu_2 = \mu_3$

$H_1 :$ At least two means differ.

	A	B	C	D	E	F	G
35	ANOVA						
36	*Source of Variation*	*SS*	*df*	*MS*	*F*	*P-value*	*F crit*
37	Rows	31,154,590	24	1,298,108	15.05	5.20E-15	1.75
38	Columns	913,217	2	456,608	5.29	0.0084	3.19
39	Error	4,141,276	48	86,277			
40							
41	Total	36,209,083	74				

F = 5.29; p-value = .0084. There is sufficient evidence to infer that differences exist between the estimated repair costs from different appraisers.

A14.10   z-test of $p_1 - p_2$ (case 2)

$H_0 : p_1 - p_2 = -.15$

$H_1 : p_1 - p_2 < -.15$

$$z = \frac{(\hat{p}_1 - \hat{p}_2) - (p_1 - p_2)}{\sqrt{\dfrac{\hat{p}_1(1 - \hat{p}_1)}{n_1} + \dfrac{\hat{p}_2(1 - \hat{p}_2)}{n_2}}}$$

	A	B	C
1	**z-Test: Two Proportions**		
2			
3		*Comm 1*	*Comm 2*
4	Sample Proportions	0.268	0.486
5	Observations	500	500
6	Hypothesized Difference	-0.15	
7	z Stat	-2.28	
8	P(Z<=z) one tail	0.0114	
9	z Critical one-tail	1.6449	
10	P(Z<=z) two-tail	0.0228	
11	z Critical two-tail	1.9600	

z = –2.28, p-value = .0114. There is evidence to indicate that the second commercial is viable.

A14.12 Two-factor analysis of variance

	A	B	C	D	E	F	G
29	ANOVA						
30	*Source of Variation*	SS	df	MS	F	P-value	F crit
31	Sample	427.61	2	213.81	39.97	0.0000	3.06
32	Columns	20.17	1	20.17	3.77	0.0541	3.91
33	Interaction	17.77	2	8.89	1.66	0.1935	3.06
34	Within	770.32	144	5.35			
35							
36	Total	1235.87	149				

Interaction: $F = 1.66$, p-value = .1935. There is no evidence of interaction.
Gender (Columns) : $F = 3.77$, p-value = .0541. There is not enough evidence of a difference between men and women.
Fitness (Sample): $F = 39.97$, p-value = 0. There is overwhelming evidence of differences among the three levels of fitness.

A14.14 One-way analysis of variance

	A	B	C	D	E	F	G
10	ANOVA						
11	*Source of Variation*	SS	df	MS	F	P-value	F crit
12	Between Groups	1813.7	2	906.87	6.46	0.0030	3.16
13	Within Groups	7998.0	57	140.32			
14							
15	Total	9811.7	59				

Multiple comparisons

	A	B	C	D	E
1	**Multiple Comparisons**				
2					
3				LSD	Omega
4	Treatment	Treatment	Difference	Alpha = 0.0167	Alpha = 0.05
5	*Price: $34*	*Price: $39*	-12.9	9.24	9.01
6		*Price: $44*	-3.1	9.24	9.01
7	*Price: $39*	*Price: $44*	9.8	9.24	9.01

Sales with $34 and $44 dollar prices do not differ. Sales with $39 differ from sales with $34 and $44 prices.

A14.16 Two-way analysis of variance

	A	B	C	D	E	F	G
24	ANOVA						
25	*Source of Variation*	*SS*	*df*	*MS*	*F*	*P-value*	*F crit*
26	Rows	335.17	13	25.78	16.86	0.0000	2.12
27	Columns	10.90	2	5.45	3.57	0.0428	3.37
28	Error	39.76	26	1.53			
29							
30	Total	385.83	41				

a. $H_0 : \mu_1 = \mu_2 = \mu_3$

H_1 : At least two means differ.

$F = 3.57$, p-value = .0428. There is enough evidence to conclude that there are differences in waiting times between the three resorts.

b. The waiting times are required to be normally distributed with the same variance at all three resorts.

c. Histograms are used to check the normality requirement.

A14.18 a   z-estimate of p

	A	B	C	D	E
1	**z-Estimate of a Proportion**				
2					
3	**Sample proportion**	0.3569	**Confidence Interval Estimate**		
4	**Sample size**	1328	**0.357**	±	**0.026**
5	**Confidence level**	0.95	**Lower confidence limit**		**0.331**
6			**Upper confidence limit**		**0.383**

Estimate of the number of households with at least one dog

LCL = 112 million × .331 = 37.072 million

UCL = 112 million × .383 = 42.896 million

b.

	A	B	C	D	E
1	**z-Estimate of a Proportion**				
2					
3	**Sample proportion**	0.316	**Confidence Interval Estimate**		
4	**Sample size**	1328	**0.316**	±	**0.025**
5	**Confidence level**	0.95	**Lower confidence limit**		**0.291**
6			**Upper confidence limit**		**0.341**

Number of households with at least one cat

LCL = 112 million × .291 = 32.592 million

UCL = 112 million × .341 = 38.192 million

c.   t-estimate of μ

$$\bar{x} \pm t_{\alpha/2}\frac{s}{\sqrt{n}}$$

	A	B	C	D
1	**t-Estimate: Mean**			
2				
3				*Dogs*
4	Mean			247.19
5	Standard Deviation			133.16
6	LCL			235.17
7	UCL			259.20

Estimate of the total amount spent on dogs

LCL = 40 million ×235.17 = \$9.407 billion

UCL = 40 million ×259.29 = \$10.368 billion,

d.   t-estimate of μ

$$\bar{x} \pm t_{\alpha/2}\frac{s}{\sqrt{n}}$$

	A	B	C	D
1	**t-Estimate: Mean**			
2				
3				*Cats*
4	Mean			158.07
5	Standard Deviation			88.94
6	LCL			149.53
7	UCL			166.61

Estimate of the total amount spent on cats

LCL = 35 million ×149.53 = \$5.234 billion

UCL = 35 million ×166.61 = \$5.831 billion

Chapter 15

15.2 $H_0 : p_1 = .1,\ p_2 = .2,\ p_3 = .3,\ p_4 = .2,\ p_5 = .2$

H_1 : At least one p_i is not equal to its specified value.

Cell i	f_i	e_i	$(f_i - e_i)$	$(f_i - e_i)^2 / e_i$
1	12	$150(.1) = 15$	-3	.60
2	32	$150(.2) = 30$	2	.13
3	42	$150(.3) = 45$	-3	.20
4	36	$150(.2) = 30$	6	1.20
5	28	$150(.2) = 30$	-2	.13
Total	150	150		$\chi^2 = 2.26$

Rejection region: $\chi^2 > \chi^2_{\alpha, k-1} = \chi^2_{.01,4} = 13.3$

$\chi^2 = 2.26$, p-value = .6868. There is not enough evidence to infer that at least one p_i is not equal to its specified value.

15.4 The χ^2 statistic decreases.

15.6 $H_0 : p_1 = .3,\ p_2 = .3,\ p_3 = .2,\ p_4 = .2$

H_1 : At least one p_i is not equal to its specified value.

Cell i	f_i	e_i	$(f_i - e_i)$	$(f_i - e_i)^2 / e_i$
1	76	$300(.3) = 90$	-14	2.18
2	100	$300(.3) = 90$	10	1.11
3	76	$300(.2) = 60$	16	4.27
4	48	$300(.2) = 60$	-12	2.40
Total	300	300		$\chi^2 = 9.96$

Rejection region: $\chi^2 > \chi^2_{\alpha, k-1} = \chi^2_{.05,3} = 7.81$

$\chi^2 = 9.96$, p-value = .0189. There is enough evidence to infer that at least one p_i is not equal to its specified value.

15.8 $H_0 : p_1 = .15, \; p_2 = .40, \; p_3 = .35, \; p_4 = .10$

H_1 : At least one p_i is not equal to its specified value.

Cell i	f_i	e_i	$(f_i - e_i)$	$(f_i - e_i)^2 / e_i$
1	41	$233(.15) = 34.95$	6.05	1.05
2	107	$233(.40) = 93.20$	13.80	2.04
3	66	$233(.35) = 81.55$	-15.55	2.97
4	19	$233(.10) = 23.30$	-4.30	0.79
Total	233	233		$\chi^2 = 6.85$

Rejection region: $\chi^2 > \chi^2_{\alpha,k-1} = \chi^2_{.05,3} = 7.81$

$\chi^2 = 6.85$, p-value = .0769. There is not enough evidence to infer that at least one p_i is not equal to its specified value.

15.10 $H_0 : p_1 = .05, \; p_2 = .25 \; p_3 = .40, \; p_4 = .25 \; p_5 = .05$

H_1 : At least one p_i is not equal to its specified value.

Cell i	f_i	e_i	$(f_i - e_i)$	$(f_i - e_i)^2 / e_i$
1	11	$150(.05) = 7.5$	3.5	1.63
2	32	$150(.25) = 37.5$	-5.5	0.81
3	62	$150(.40) = 60.0$	2.0	0.07
4	29	$150(.25) = 37.5$	-8.5	1.93
5	16	$150(.05) = 7.5$	8.5	9.63
Total	150	150		$\chi^2 = 14.07$

Rejection region: $\chi^2 > \chi^2_{\alpha,k-1} = \chi^2_{.10,4} = 7.78$

$\chi^2 = 14.07$, p-value = .0071. There is enough evidence to infer that grades are distributed differently from grades in the past.

15.12 $H_0 : p_1 = .72, \; p_2 = .15, \; p_3 = .10, \; p_4 = .03$

H_1 : At least one p_i is not equal to its specified value.

Cell i	f_i	e_i	$(f_i - e_i)$	$(f_i - e_i)^2 / e_i$
1	159	$250(.72) = 180.0$	-21.0	2.45
2	28	$250(.15) = 37.5$	-9.5	2.41
3	47	$250(.10) = 25.0$	22.0	19.36
4	16	$250(.03) = 7.5$	8.5	9.63
Total	250	250		$\chi^2 = 33.85$

Rejection region: $\chi^2 > \chi^2_{\alpha, k-1} = \chi^2_{.05,3} = 7.81$

$\chi^2 = 33.85$, p-value = 0. There is enough evidence to infer that the aging schedule has changed.

15.14 $H_0 : p_1 = .31, \ p_2 = .51, \ p_3 = .18$
H_1 : At least one p_i is not equal to its specified value.

Cell i	f_i	e_i	$(f_i - e_i)$	$(f_i - e_i)^2 / e_i$
1	408	$1200(.31) = 372$	36	3.48
2	571	$1200(.51) = 612$	-41	2.75
3	221	$1200(.18) = 216$	5	0.12
Total	1200	1200		$\chi^2 = 6.35$

Rejection region: $\chi^2 > \chi^2_{\alpha, k-1} = \chi^2_{.10,2} = 4.61$

$\chi^2 = 6.35$, p-value = .0419. There is enough evidence to infer that voter support has changed since the election.

15.16 $H_0 : p_1 = .23, \ p_2 = .40, \ p_3 = .15, \ p_4 = .22$
H_1 : At least one p_i is not equal to its specified value.

Cell i	f_i	e_i	$(f_i - e_i)$	$(f_i - e_i)^2 / e_i$
1	63	$320(.23) = 73.6$	-10.6	1.53
2	125	$320(.40) = 128.0$	-3.0	0.07
3	45	$320(.15) = 48.0$	-3.0	0.19
4	87	$320(.22) = 70.4$	16.6	3.91
Total	320	320		$\chi^2 = 5.70$

Rejection region: $\chi^2 > \chi^2_{\alpha, k-1} = \chi^2_{.05,3} = 7.81$

$\chi^2 = 5.70$, p-value = .1272. There is not enough evidence to infer that there has been a change in proportions.

15.18 H_0 : The two variables are independent
H_1 : The two variables are dependent

Cell i	f_i	e_i	$(f_i - e_i)$	$(f_i - e_i)^2 / e_i$
1	14	$48(42)/188 = 21.45$	-7.45	2.59
2	34	$48(52)/188 = 26.55$	7.45	2.09
3	28	$46(42)/188 = 20.55$	7.45	2.70
4	18	$46(52)/188 = 25.45$	-7.45	2.18
Total	94	94		$\chi^2 = 9.56$

Rejection region: $\chi^2 > \chi^2_{\alpha,(r-1)(c-1)} = \chi^2_{.05,1} = 3.84$

$\chi^2 = 9.56$, p-value $= .0020$. There is enough evidence to infer that the two classifications L and M are dependent.

15.20 The χ^2 statistic decreases.

15.22 H_0 : The two variables (responses and employee group) are independent

H_1 : The two variables are dependent

Cell i	f_i	e_i	$(f_i - e_i)$	$(f_i - e_i)^2 / e_i$
1	67	$110(130)/200 = 71.50$	-4.50	0.28
2	32	$110(50)/200 = 27.50$	4.50	0.74
3	11	$110(20)/200 = 11.00$	0	0.00
4	63	$90(130)/200 = 58.50$	4.50	0.35
5	18	$90(50)/200 = 22.50$	-4.50	0.90
6	9	$90(20)/200 = 9.00$	0	0.00
Total	200	200		$\chi^2 = 2.27$

Rejection region: $\chi^2 > \chi^2_{\alpha,(r-1)(c-1)} = \chi^2_{.05,2} = 5.99$

$\chi^2 = 2.27$, p-value $= .3221$. There is not enough evidence to infer that responses differ among the three groups of employees.

15.24 H_0 : The two variables economic option and political affiliation) are independent

H_1 : The two variables are dependent

Cell i	f_i	e_i	$(f_i - e_i)$	$(f_i - e_i)^2 / e_i$
1	101	$444(331)/1000 = 146.96$	-45.96	14.376
2	282	$444(557)/1000 = 233.99$	48.01	9.852
3	61	$444(142)/1000 = 63.05$	-2.05	0.067
4	38	$130(331)/1000 = 43.03$	-5.03	0.588
5	67	$130(557)/1000 = 68.51$	-1.51	0.033
6	25	$130(142)/1000 = 18.46$	6.54	2.317
7	131	$250(331)/1000 = 82.75$	48.25	28.134
8	88	$250(557)/1000 = 131.75$	-43.75	14.528
9	31	$250(142)/1000 = 35.50$	-4.50	0.570
10	61	$176(331)/1000 = 58.26$	2.74	0.129
11	90	$176(557)/1000 = 92.75$	-2.75	0.082
12	25	$176(142)/1000 = 24.99$	0.01	0.000
Total	1000	1000		$\chi^2 = 70.675$

Rejection region: $\chi^2 > \chi^2_{\alpha,(r-1)(c-1)} = \chi^2_{.01,6} = 16.8$

$\chi^2 = 70.675$, p-value = 0. There is sufficient evidence to infer that political affiliation affects support for economic options.

15.26 H_0 : The two variables (newspaper and occupation) are independent

H_1 : The two variables are dependent

Cell i	f_i	e_i	$(f_i - e_i)$	$(f_i - e_i)^2 / e_i$
1	27	120(89)/354=30.2	-3.2	.33
2	18	120(112)/354=38.0	-20.0	10.50
3	38	120(81)/354=27.5	10.5	4.05
4	37	120(72)/354=24.4	12.6	6.50
5	29	108(89)/354=27.2	1.8	.13
6	43	108(112)/354=34.2	8.8	2.28
7	21	108(81)/354=24.7	-3.7	.56
8	15	108(72)/354=22.0	-7.0	2.21
9	33	126(89)/354=31.7	1.3	.06
10	51	126(112)/354=39.9	11.1	3.11
11	22	126(81)/354=28.8	-6.8	1.62
12	20	126(72)/354=25.6	-5.6	1.24
Total	354	354		$\chi^2 = 32.57$

Rejection region: $\chi^2 > \chi^2_{\alpha,(r-1)(c-1)} = \chi^2_{.05,6} = 12.6$

$\chi^2 = 32.57$, p-value = 0. There is sufficient evidence to infer that occupation and newspaper are related.

15.28 H_0 : The two variables (last purchase and second-last purchase) are independent

H_1 : The two variables are dependent

Cell i	f_i	e_i	$(f_i - e_i)$	$(f_i - e_i)^2/e_i$
1	39	$149(153)/559 = 40.78$	-1.78	.08
2	36	$149(134)/559 = 35.72$	.28	0
3	51	$149(190)/559 = 50.64$	.36	0
4	23	$149(82)/559 = 21.86$	1.14	.06
5	36	$134(153)/559 = 36.68$	$-.68$	.01
6	32	$134(134)/559 = 32.12$	$-.12$	0
7	46	$134(190)/559 = 45.55$	.45	0
8	20	$134(82)/559 = 19.66$	.34	.01
9	54	$194(153)/559 = 53.10$	.90	.02
10	46	$194(134)/559 = 46.50$	$-.50$	.01
11	65	$194(190)/559 = 65.94$	$-.94$	.01
12	29	$194(82)/559 = 28.46$	.54	.01
13	24	$82(153)/559 = 22.44$	1.56	.11
14	20	$82(134)/559 = 19.66$	.34	.01
15	28	$82(190)/559 = 27.87$	.13	0
16	10	$82(82)/558 = 12.03$	-2.03	.34
Total	559	559		$\chi^2 = .67$

Rejection region: $\chi^2 > \chi^2_{\alpha,(r-1)(c-1)} = \chi^2_{.05,9} = 16.9$

$\chi^2 = .67$, p-value = .9999. There is no evidence of a relationship.

15.30 H_0 : The two variables (education and smoker) are independent

        H_1 : The two variables are dependent

Cell i	f_i	e_i	$(f_i - e_i)$	$(f_i - e_i)^2 / e_i$
1	60	121(369)/658 =67.9	-7.9	.91
2	23	121(116)/658=21.3	1.7	.13
3	13	121(65)/658=12.0	1.0	.09
4	25	121(108)/658=19.9	5.1	1.33
5	65	126(369)/658=70.7	-5.7	.45
6	19	126(116)/658=22.2	-3.2	.46
7	14	126(65)/658=12.4	1.6	.19
8	28	126(108)/658=20.7	7.3	2.59
9	73	132(369)/658=74.0	-1.0	.01
10	26	132(116)/658=23.3	2.7	.32
11	9	132(65)/658=13.0	-4.0	1.25
12	24	132(108)/658=21.7	2.3	.25
13	67	95(369)/658=53.3	13.7	3.54
14	11	95(116)/658=16.7	-5.7	1.97
15	10	95(65)/658=9.4	0.6	.04
16	7	95(108)/658=15.6	-8.6	4.74
17	57	96(369)/658=53.8	3.2	.19
18	16	96(116)/658=16.9	-.9	.05
19	9	96(65)/658=9.5	-.5	.02
20	14	96(108)/658=15.8	-1.8	.20
21	47	88(369)/658=49.3	-2.3	.11
22	21	88(116)/658=15.5	5.5	1.94
23	10	88(65)/658=8.7	1.3	.20
24	10	88(108)/658=14.4	-4.4	1.37
Total	658	658		$\chi^2 = 22.36$

Rejection region: $\chi^2 > \chi^2_{\alpha,(r-1)(c-1)} = \chi^2_{.05,15} = 25.0$

$\chi^2 = 22.36$, p-value = .0988. There is not enough evidence to infer that there is a relationship between an adult's source of news and his or her heartburn condition.

15.32 H_0 : The two variables (results and financial ties) are independent

H_1 : The two variables are dependent

Cell i	f_i	e_i	$(f_i - e_i)$	$(f_i - e_i)^2 / e_i$
1	29	30(48)/70 = 20.57	8.43	3.45
2	1	30(22)/70 = 9.43	-8.43	7.54
3	10	17(48)/70 = 11.66	-1.66	.24
4	7	17(22)/70 = 5.34	1.66	.52
5	9	23(48)/70 = 15.77	-6.77	2.91
6	14	23(22)/70 = 7.23	6.77	6.34
Total	70	70		$\chi^2 = 21.00$

Rejection region: $\chi^2 > \chi^2_{\alpha,(r-1)(c-1)} = \chi^2_{.05,2} = 5.99$

$\chi^2 = 21.00$, p-value = 0. There is sufficient evidence to infer that the research findings are related to whether drug companies fund the research.

15.34 H_0 : The data are normally distributed

H_1 : The data are not normally distributed

Interval	Probability	Expected Value e_i	Observed Value f_i	$f_i - e_i$	$(f_i - e_i)^2 / e_i$
$Z \le -1.5$	.0668	6.68	10	3.32	1.65
$-1.5 < Z \le -0.5$	.2417	24.17	18	-6.17	1.58
$-0.5 < Z \le 0.5$	.3829	38.29	48	9.71	2.46
$0.5 < Z \le 1.5$	.2417	24.17	16	8.17	2.76
$Z > 1.5$	.0668	6.68	8	1.32	0.26
Total	1	100	100		$\chi^2 = 8.71$

Rejection region: $\chi^2 > \chi^2_{\alpha,k-3} = \chi^2_{.05,2} = 5.99$

$\chi^2 = 8.71$, p-value = .0128. There is enough evidence to infer that the data are not normally distributed.

15.36 H_0 : Times are normally distributed

H_1 : Times are not normally distributed.

	A	B	C	D
1	**Chi-Squared Test of Normality**			
2				
3		*Hours*		
4	Mean	7.15		
5	Standard deviation	1.65		
6	Observations	200		
7				
8	Intervals	Probability	Expected	Observed
9	(z <= -1.5)	0.0668	13.36	11
10	(-1.5 < z <= -0.5)	0.2417	48.35	55
11	(-0.5 < z <= 0.5)	0.3829	76.59	52
12	(0.5 < z <= 1.5)	0.2417	48.35	67
13	(z > 1.5)	0.0668	13.36	15
14				
15				
16	chi-squared Stat	16.62		
17	df	2		
18	p-value	0.0002		
19	chi-squared Critical	5.9915		

χ^2 = 16.62, p-value = .0002. There is sufficient evidence to infer that the amount of time at part-time jobs is not normally distributed.

15.38   Successful firms:

H_0 : Productivity in successful firms is normally distributed

H_1 : Productivity in successful firms is not normally distributed

	A	B	C	D
1	**Chi-Squared Test of Normality**			
2				
3		*Successful*		
4	Mean	5.02		
5	Standard deviation	1.39		
6	Observations	200		
7				
8	Intervals	Probability	Expected	Observed
9	(z <= -1.5)	0.0668	13.36	12
10	(-1.5 < z <= -0.5)	0.2417	48.35	52
11	(-0.5 < z <= 0.5)	0.3829	76.59	72
12	(0.5 < z <= 1.5)	0.2417	48.35	55
13	(z > 1.5)	0.0668	13.36	9
14				
15				
16	chi-squared Stat	3.0288		
17	df	2		
18	p-value	0.2199		
19	chi-squared Critical	5.9915		

$\chi^2 = 3.03$, p-value = .2199. There is not enough evidence to infer that productivity in successful firms is not normally distributed.

Unsuccessful firms:

H_0 : Productivity in unsuccessful firms is normally distributed

H_1 : Productivity in unsuccessful firms is not normally distributed

	A	B	C	D
1	**Chi-Squared Test of Normality**			
2				
3		*Unsuccessful*		
4	Mean	7.80		
5	Standard deviation	3.09		
6	Observations	200		
7				
8	Intervals	Probability	Expected	Observed
9	(z <= -1.5)	0.0668	13.36	12
10	(-1.5 < z <= -0.5)	0.2417	48.35	47
11	(-0.5 < z <= 0.5)	0.3829	76.59	83
12	(0.5 < z <= 1.5)	0.2417	48.35	44
13	(z > 1.5)	0.0668	13.36	14
14				
15				
16	chi-squared Stat	1.1347		
17	df	2		
18	p-value	0.567		
19	chi-squared Critical	5.9915		

$\chi^2 = 1.13$, p-value = .5670. There is not enough evidence to infer that productivity in unsuccessful firms is not normally distributed.

15.40 H_0 : Matched pairs differences of sales are normally distributed

   H_1 : Matched pairs differences of sales are not normally distributed

	A	B	C	D
1	**Chi-Squared Test of Normality**			
2				
3		*Difference*		
4	Mean	19.75		
5	Standard deviation	30.63		
6	Observations	40		
7				
8	Intervals	Probability	Expected	Observed
9	$(z \le -1)$	0.1587	6.35	6
10	$(-1 < z \le 0)$	0.3413	13.65	14
11	$(0 < z \le 1)$	0.3413	13.65	14
12	$(z > 1)$	0.1587	6.35	6
13				
14				
15				
16	chi-squared Stat	0.0553		
17	df	1		
18	p-value	0.8140		
19	chi-squared Critical	2.7055		

$\chi^2 = .055$, p-value $= .8140$. There is not enough evidence to infer that matched pairs difference of sales is not normally distributed.

15.42 $H_0 : p_1 = .2, \ p_2 = .2, \ p_3 = .2, \ p_4 = .2, \ p_5 = .2$

$H_1 :$ At least one p_i is not equal to its specified value.

Cell i	f_i	e_i	$(f_i - e_i)$	$(f_i - e_i)^2 / e_i$
1	87	$362(.2) = 72.4$	14.6	2.94
2	62	$362(.2) = 72.4$	-10.4	1.49
3	71	$362(.2) = 72.4$	-1.4	0.03
4	68	$362(.2) = 72.4$	-4.4	0.27
5	74	$362(.2) = 72.4$	1.6	0.04
Total	362	362		$\chi^2 = 4.77$

Rejection region: $\chi^2 > \chi^2_{\alpha, k-1} = \chi^2_{.05,4} = 9.49$

$\chi^2 = 4.77$, p-value $= .3119$. There is not enough evidence to infer that absenteeism is higher on some days of the week.

15.44　H_0 : The two variables (satisfaction and relationship) are independent

H_1 : The two variables are dependent

Cell i	f_i	e_i	$(f_i - e_i)$	$(f_i - e_i)^2 / e_i$
1	21	171(91)/447 = 34.81	-13.81	5.48
2	25	171(122)/447 = 46.67	-21.67	10.06
3	54	171(114)/447 = 43.61	10.39	2.48
4	71	171(120)/447 = 45.91	25.09	13.72
5	39	176(91)/447 = 35.83	3.17	0.28
6	49	176(122)/447 = 48.04	0.96	0.02
7	50	176(114)/447 = 44.89	5.11	0.58
8	38	176(120)/447 = 47.25	-9.25	1.81
9	31	100(91)/447 = 20.36	10.64	5 56
10	48	100(122)/447 = 27.29	20.71	15.71
11	10	100(114)/447 = 25.50	-15.50	9.42
12	11	100(120)/447 = 26.85	-15.85	9.35
Total	447	447		$\chi^2 = 74.47$

Rejection region: $\chi^2 > \chi^2_{\alpha,(r-1)(c-1)} = \chi^2_{.05,6} = 12.6$

$\chi^2 = 74.47$, p-value = 0. There is sufficient evidence to infer that the level of job satisfaction depends on boss/employee gender relationship.

15.46　H_0 : The two variables (method and quit) are independent

H_1 : The two variables are dependent

	A	B	C	D	E	F	G
1	**Contingency Table**						
2							
3		*Quit*					
4	*Method*		1	2	3	4	TOTAL
5		1	104	125	32	49	310
6		2	14	17	5	9	45
7		TOTAL	118	142	37	58	355
8							
9							
10		chi-squared Stat			0.5803		
11		df			3		
12		p-value			0.9009		
13		chi-squared Critical			7.8147		

$\chi^2 = .5803$, p-value = .9009. There is not enough evidence to infer that the four methods differ in their success rates.

15.48 a   The expected frequency is 1/49.

    b $H_0 : p_1 = 1/49, \ p_2 = 1/49, \ldots, \ p_{49} = 1/49$

    H_1 : At least one p_i is not equal to its specified value.

Number i	f_i	e_i	$(f_i - e_i)$	$(f_i - e_i)^2 / e_i$
1	5	312(1/49) = 6.37	-1.38	0.29
2	6	312(1/49) = 6.37	-0.38	0.02
3	7	312(1/49) = 6.37	0.63	0.06
.		.		
.		.		
.		.		
47	6	312(1/49) = 6.37	-0.37	0.02
48	10	312(1/49) = 6.37	3.63	2.07
49	6	312(1/49) = 6.37	-0.37	0.02
Total	312	312		$\chi^2 = 38.22$

$\chi^2 = 38.22$, p-value = .8427. There is not enough evidence to infer that the numbers were not generated randomly.

15.50   Binomial probabilities with n = 5 and p = .5: P(X = 0) = .0313, P(X = 1) = .1563, P(X = 2) = .3125, P(X = 3) = .3125, P(X = 4) = .1563, P(X = 5) = .0313

    $H_0 : p_0 = .0313, p_1 = .1563, \ p_2 = .3125, \ p_3 = .3125, \ p_4 = .1563, \ p_5 = .0313$
    H_1 : At least one p_i is not equal to its specified value.

Cell i	f_i	e_i	$(f_i - e_i)$	$(f_i - e_i)^2 / e_i$
0	8	200(.0313) = 6.26	1.74	0.48
1	35	200(.1563) = 31.26	3.74	0.45
2	57	200(.3125) = 62.50	-5.50	0.48
3	69	200(.3125) = 62.50	6.50	0.68
4	28	200(.1563) = 31.26	-3.26	0.34
5	3	200(.0313) = 6.26	-3.26	1.70
Total	200	200		$\chi^2 = 4.13$

Rejection region: $\chi^2 > \chi^2_{\alpha,6-1} = \chi^2_{.05,5} = 11.1$

$\chi^2 = 4.13$, p-value = .5310. There is not enough evidence to infer that at the number of boys in families with 5 children is not a binomial random variable with p =.5.

15.52 H_0 : The two variables (faculty and retire) are independent

H_1 : The two variables are dependent

	A	B	C	D	E	F	G	H
1	**Contingency Table**							
2								
3		*Retire*						
4	*Faculty*		1	2	3	4	5	TOTAL
5		1	174	51	113	42	86	466
6		2	13	7	22	7	6	55
7		TOTAL	187	58	135	49	92	521
8								
9								
10		chi-squared Stat			9.732			
11		df			4			
12		p-value			0.0452			
13		chi-squared Critical			9.4877			

$\chi^2 = 9.732$, p-value = .0452. There is enough evidence to infer that whether a professor wishes to retire is related to the faculty.

15.54 H_0 : The two variables (network and ask) are independent

H_1 : The two variables are dependent

	A	B	C	D	E	F
1	**Contingency Table**					
2						
3		*Ask*				
4	*Network*		1	2	3	TOTAL
5		1	19	30	43	92
6		2	104	107	123	334
7		TOTAL	123	137	166	426
8						
9						
10		chi-squared Stat			4.573	
11		df			2	
12		p-value			0.1016	
13		chi-squared Critical			5.9915	

$\chi^2 = 4.573$, p-value = .1016. There is not enough evidence to conclude that there are differences in responses between the three network news shows.

15.56 a H_0 : The two variables (education and group) are independent

H_1 : The two variables are dependent

	A	B	C	D	E	F	G
1	**Contingency Table**						
2							
3		*Group*					
4	*Education*		1	2	3	4	TOTAL
5		1	5	113	73	40	231
6		2	70	305	189	55	619
7		TOTAL	75	418	262	95	850
8							
9							
10		chi-squared Stat			26.7059		
11		df			3		
12		p-value			0		
13		chi-squared Critical			7.8147		

$\chi^2 = 26.7059$, p-value = 0. There is enough evidence to infer that there are differences in educational attainment between those who belong and those who do not belong to the health conscious group.

b. H_0 : The two variables (education and buy Special X) are independent

H_1 : The two variables are dependent

	A	B	C	D	E	F	G
1	**Contingency Table**						
2							
3		*Buy Sp X*					
4	*Education*		1	2	3	4	TOTAL
5		1	70	376	229	87	762
6		2	5	42	33	8	88
7		TOTAL	75	418	262	95	850
8							
9							
10		chi-squared Stat			2.9416		
11		df			3		
12		p-value			0.4007		
13		chi-squared Critical			7.8147		

$\chi^2 = 2.9416$, p-value = .4007. There is not enough evidence to infer that there is a relationship between the four education groups and whether a person buys Special X.

15.58   a H_0 : The two variables (gender and vote) are independent

        H_1 : The two variables are dependent

	A	B	C	D	E
1	**Contingency Table**				
2					
3		*Votes*			
4	*Gender*		1	2	TOTAL
5		1	189	169	358
6		2	203	204	407
7		TOTAL	392	373	765
8					
9					
10		chi-squared Stat			0.6483
11		df			1
12		p-value			0.4207
13		chi-squared Critical			3.8415

χ^2 = .6483, p-value = .4207. There is not enough evidence to infer that voting and gender are

related.

   b H_0 : The two variables (education and vote) are independent

        H_1 : The two variables are dependent

	A	B	C	D	E	F	G
1	**Contingency Table**						
2							
3		*Votes*					
4	*Educ*		1	2	3	4	TOTAL
5		1	48	164	107	39	358
6		2	34	178	134	61	407
7		TOTAL	82	342	241	100	765
8							
9							
10		chi-squared Stat			7.7214		
11		df			3		
12		p-value			0.0521		
13		chi-squared Critical			7.8147		

χ^2 = 7.7214, p-value = .0521. There is not enough evidence to infer that voting and educational
level are related.

c H_0 : The two variables (income category and vote) are independent

        H_1 : The two variables are dependent

	A	B	C	D	E	F	G
1	**Contingency Table**						
2							
3		*Votes*					
4	*Income*		1	2	3	4	TOTAL
5		1	38	186	105	29	358
6		2	21	185	128	73	407
7		TOTAL	59	371	233	102	765
8							
9							
10		chi-squared Stat			23.108		
11		df			3		
12		p-value			0		
13		chi-squared Critical			7.8147		

$\chi^2 = 23.108$, p-value = 0. There is enough evidence to infer that voting and income are related.

15.60 H_0 : The two variables (value and segment) are independent

        H_1 : The two variables are dependent

	A	B	C	D	E	F
1	**Contingency Table**					
2						
3		*Segment*				
4	*Value*		1	2	3	TOTAL
5		1	147	135	136	418
6		2	221	155	160	536
7		3	339	254	289	882
8		TOTAL	707	544	585	1836
9						
10						
11		chi-squared Stat			4.5122	
12		df			4	
13		p-value			0.3411	
14		chi-squared Critical			9.4877	

$\chi^2 = 4.5122$, p-value = .3411. There is not enough evidence to infer that there are differences in the definition of value between the three market segments.

Appendix 15

A15.2 t-test of μ_D

$H_0 : \mu_D = 0$

$H_1 : \mu_D < 0$

$$t = \frac{\bar{x}_D - \mu_D}{s_D / \sqrt{n_D}}$$

	A	B	C
1	t-Test: Paired Two Sample for Means		
2			
3		*First Sat*	*Second SAT*
4	Mean	1175	1190
5	Variance	28422	35392
6	Observations	40	40
7	Pearson Correlation	0.91	
8	Hypothesized Mean Difference	0	
9	df	39	
10	t Stat	-1.20	
11	P(T<=t) one-tail	0.1182	
12	t Critical one-tail	1.6849	
13	P(T<=t) two-tail	0.2365	
14	t Critical two-tail	2.0227	

$t = -1.20$, p-value = .1182. There is not enough evidence to indicate that repeating the SAT produces higher exam scores.

A15.4 a.   t-estimator of μ

$$\bar{x} \pm t_{\alpha/2} \frac{s}{\sqrt{n}}$$

	A	B	C	D
1	t-Estimate: Mean			
2				
3				*Overdue*
4	Mean			7.09
5	Standard Deviation			6.97
6	LCL			6.40
7	UCL			7.77

LCL = 6.40, UCL = 7.77

b.   LCL = 50,000($.25)(6.40) = $80,000

UCL = 50,000($.25)(7.77) = $97,125

It does appear that not all fines are collected

A15.6 Chi-squared test of a contingency table

H_0 : The two variables (income category and mutual fund ownership) are independent

H_1 : The two variables are dependent

$$\chi^2 = \sum \frac{(f_i - e_i)^2}{e_i}$$

	A	B	C	D	E
1	**Contingency Table**				
2					
3		Income category			
4	Mutual fund		1	2	TOTAL
5		1	71	13	84
6		2	59	28	87
7		3	86	55	141
8		4	87	157	244
9		5	32	145	177
10		6	58	205	263
11		TOTAL	393	603	996
12					
13					
14		chi-squared Stat			196.77
15		df			5
16		p-value			0
17		chi-squared Critical			11.0705

$\chi^2 = 196.77$; p-value = 0. There is overwhelming evidence to infer that household income and ownership of mutual funds are related

A15.8 z-test of $p_1 - p_2$ (case 1) Code 3 results were omitted.

$H_0 : (p_1 - p_2) = 0$

$H_1 : (p_1 - p_2) < 0$

$$z = \frac{(\hat{p}_1 - \hat{p}_2)}{\sqrt{\hat{p}(1-\hat{p})\left(\frac{1}{n_1} + \frac{1}{n_2}\right)}}$$

	A	B	C	D
1	**z-Test: Two Proportions**			
2				
3			Folic acid	Placebo
4	Sample Proportions		0.0101	0.0343
5	Observations		597	612
6	Hypothesized Difference		0	
7	z Stat		-2.85	
8	P(Z<=z) one tail		0.0022	
9	z Critical one-tail		1.6449	
10	P(Z<=z) two-tail		0.0044	
11	z Critical two-tail		1.9600	

z = −2.85, p-value = .0022. There is overwhelming evidence to conclude that folic acid reduces the incidence of spina bifida.

A15.10 one-way analysis of variance

$H_0 : \mu_1 = \mu_2 = \mu_3$

$H_1 :$ At least two means differ

	A	B	C	D	E	F	G
10	ANOVA						
11	*Source of Variation*	*SS*	*df*	*MS*	*F*	*P-value*	*F crit*
12	Between Groups	626046	2	313023	58.37	0.0000	3.03
13	Within Groups	1523047	284	5363			
14							
15	Total	2149093	286				

F = 58.37, p-value = 0. There is enough evidence to conclude that there are differences between the three groups.

Multiple Comparisons

	A	B	C	D	E
1	**Multiple Comparisons**				
2					
3				LSD	Omega
4	Treatment	Treatment	Difference	Alpha = 0.0167	Alpha = 0.05
5	*Before 1976*	*After 1986*	122.62	28.03	25.46
6		*Canadian*	78.04	24.67	25.46
7	*After 1986*	*Canadian*	-44.58	25.75	25.46

All three groups differ from each other.

A15.12 t-estimator of μ

$$\bar{x} \pm t_{\alpha/2} \frac{s}{\sqrt{n}}$$

	A	B	C	D
1	**t-Estimate: Mean**			
2				
3				*Cars*
4	Mean			165.79
5	Standard Deviation			51.59
6	LCL			157.17
7	UCL			174.41

Five minute interval: LCL = 157.17, UCL = 174.41

Twenty-four hour day (12 5-minute intervals, 24 hours per day):

LCL = $12 \times 24 \times 157.17$ = 45,265

UCL = $12 \times 24 \times 174.41$ = 50,230

A15.14 Equal-variances t-test of $\mu_1 - \mu_2$

$H_0 : (\mu_1 - \mu_2) = 0$

$H_1 : (\mu_1 - \mu_2) < 0$

$$t = \frac{(\overline{x}_1 - \overline{x}_2) - (\mu_1 - \mu_2)}{\sqrt{s_p^2 \left(\dfrac{1}{n_1} + \dfrac{1}{n_2} \right)}}$$

	A	B	C
1	t-Test: Two-Sample Assuming Equal Variances		
2			
3		*Activity*	*Usual*
4	Mean	57.06	87.28
5	Variance	296.18	215.42
6	Observations	67	67
7	Pooled Variance	255.80	
8	Hypothesized Mean Difference	0.00	
9	df	132	
10	t Stat	-10.94	
11	P(T<=t) one-tail	0.0000	
12	t Critical one-tail	1.6565	
13	P(T<=t) two-tail	0.0000	
14	t Critical two-tail	1.9781	

$t = -10.94$, p-value = 0. There is enough evidence to indicate to infer that graded activity is effective.

A15.16 z-estimator of p

$$\hat{p} \pm z_{\alpha/2} \sqrt{\hat{p}(1-\hat{p})/n}$$

	A	B	C	D	E
1	z-Estimate of a Proportion				
2					
3	Sample proportion	0.774	Confidence Interval Estimate		
4	Sample size	780	0.774	±	0.0294
5	Confidence level	0.95	Lower confidence limit		0.7446
6			Upper confidence limit		0.8034

Total number of on-time departures:
LCL = 7,140,596(.7446) = 5,316,888
UCL = 7,140,596(.8034) = 5,736,755

Chapter 16

16.2   a.

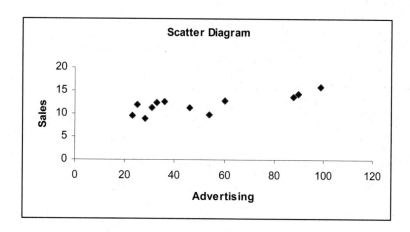

b.

x_i	y_i	x_i^2	y_i^2	$x_i y_i$
23	9.6	529	92.16	220.8
46	11.3	2,116	127.69	519.8
60	12.8	3,600	163.84	768.0
54	9.8	2,916	96.04	529.2
28	8.9	784	79.21	249.2
33	12.5	1,089	156.25	412.5
25	12.0	625	144.00	300.0
31	11.4	961	129.96	353.4
36	12.6	1,296	158.76	453.6
88	13.7	7,744	187.69	1205.6
90	14.4	8,100	207.36	1296.0
99	15.9	9,801	252.81	1,574.1
Total 613	144.9	39,561	1,795.77	7,882.2

$$\sum_{i=1}^{n} x_i = 613 \quad \sum_{i=1}^{n} y_i = 144.9 \quad \sum_{i=1}^{n} x_i^2 = 39,561 \quad \sum_{i=1}^{n} x_i y_i = 7,882.2$$

$$s_{xy} = \frac{1}{n-1}\left[\sum_{i=1}^{n} x_i y_i - \frac{\sum_{i=1}^{n} x_i \sum_{i=1}^{n} y_i}{n}\right] = \frac{1}{12-1}\left[7,882.2 - \frac{(613)(144.9)}{12}\right] = 43.66$$

$$s_x^2 = \frac{1}{n-1}\left[\sum_{i=1}^{n} x_i^2 - \frac{\left(\sum_{i=1}^{n} x_i\right)^2}{n}\right] = \frac{1}{12-1}\left[39,561 - \frac{(613)^2}{12}\right] = 749.7$$

$$b_1 = \frac{s_{xy}}{s_x^2} = \frac{43.66}{749.7} = .0582$$

$$\bar{x} = \frac{\sum x_i}{n} = \frac{613}{12} = 51.08$$

$$\bar{y} = \frac{\sum y_i}{n} = \frac{144.9}{12} = 12.08$$

$$b_0 = \bar{y} - b_1\bar{x} = 12.08 - (.0582)(51.08) = 9.107$$

The sample regression line is

$$\hat{y} = 9.107 + .0582x$$

The slope tells us that for each additional thousand dollars of advertising sales increase on average by .0582 million. The y-intercept has no practical meaning.

16.4   a.

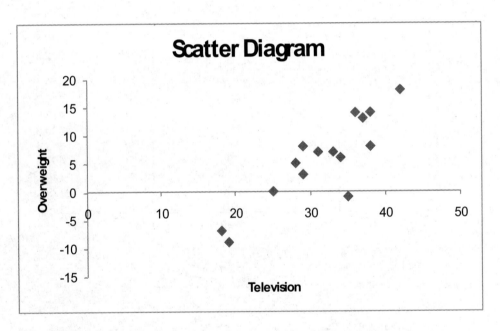

b.

x_i	y_i	x_i^2	y_i^2	$x_i y_i$
42	18	1,764	324	756
34	6	1,156	36	204
25	0	625	0	0
35	−1	1,225	1	−35
37	13	1,369	169	481
38	14	1,444	196	532
31	7	961	49	217
33	7	1,089	49	231
19	−9	361	81	−171
29	8	841	64	232
38	8	1,444	64	304
28	5	784	25	140
29	3	841	9	87
36	14	1,296	196	504
18	−7	324	49	−126
Total 472	86	15,524	1,312	3,356

$$\sum_{i=1}^{n} x_i = 472 \quad \sum_{i=1}^{n} y_i = 86 \quad \sum_{i=1}^{n} x_i^2 = 15,524 \quad \sum_{i=1}^{n} x_i y_i = 3,356$$

$$s_{xy} = \frac{1}{n-1}\left[\sum_{i=1}^{n} x_i y_i - \frac{\sum_{i=1}^{n} x_i \sum_{i=1}^{n} y_i}{n}\right] = \frac{1}{15-1}\left[3,356 - \frac{(472)(86)}{15}\right] = 46.42$$

$$s_x^2 = \frac{1}{n-1}\left[\sum_{i=1}^{n} x_i^2 - \frac{\left(\sum_{i=1}^{n} x_i\right)^2}{n}\right] = \frac{1}{15-1}\left[15,524 - \frac{(472)^2}{15}\right] = 47.98$$

$$b_1 = \frac{s_{xy}}{s_x^2} = \frac{46.42}{47.98} = .9675$$

$$\bar{x} = \frac{\sum x_i}{n} = \frac{472}{15} = 31.47$$

$$\bar{y} = \frac{\sum y_i}{n} = \frac{86}{15} = 5.73$$

$$b_0 = \bar{y} - b_1 \bar{x} = 5.73 - (.9675)(31.47) = -24.72$$

The sample regression line is

$$\hat{y} = -24.72 + .9675x$$

The slope coefficient indicates that for each additional hour of television weight increases on average by .9675 pounds. The y-intercept is the point at which the regression line hits the y–axis; it has no practical meaning.

16.6 a.

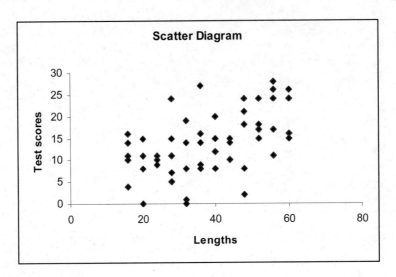

b. $b_1 = \dfrac{s_{xy}}{s_x^2} = \dfrac{51.86}{193.9} = .2675$, $b_0 = \overline{y} - b_1\overline{x} = 13.80 - .2675(38.00) = 3.635$

Regression line: $\hat{y} = 3.635 + .2675x$ (Excel: $\hat{y} = 3.636 + .2675x$)

c. $b_1 = .2675$; for each additional second of commercial, the memory test score increases on average by .2675. $b_0 = 3.64$ is the y-intercept.

16.8 a.

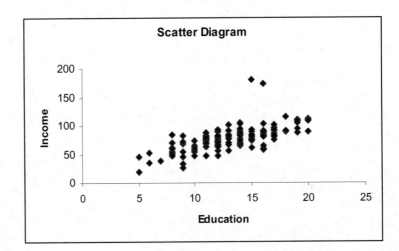

b. $b_1 = \dfrac{s_{xy}}{s_x^2} = \dfrac{46.02}{11.12} = 4.138$, $b_0 = \overline{y} - b_1\overline{x} = 78.13 - 4.138(13.17) = 23.63$.

Regression line: $\hat{y} = 23.63 + 4.138x$ (Excel: $\hat{y} = 23.63 + 4.137x$)

c. The slope coefficient tells us that for each additional year of education income increases on average by \$4.138 thousand (\$4,138). The y-intercept has no meaning.

16.10 a. $b_1 = \dfrac{s_{xy}}{s_x^2} = \dfrac{20.55}{108.3} = .1898$, $b_0 = \bar{y} - b_1\bar{x} = 14.43 - .1898(37.64) = 7.286$.

Regression line: $\hat{y} = 7.286 + .1898x$ (Excel: $\hat{y} = 7.287 + .1897x$)

b. For each additional cigarette the number of days absent from work increases on average by .1898. The y-intercept has no meaning.

16.12 a. $b_1 = \dfrac{s_{xy}}{s_x^2} = \dfrac{30{,}945}{688.2} = 44.97$, $b_0 = \bar{y} - b_1\bar{x} = 6{,}465 - 44.97(53.93) = 4040$.

Regression line: $\hat{y} = 4040 + 44.97x$ (Excel: $\hat{y} = 4040 + 44.97x$)

b. For each additional thousand square feet the price increases on average by \$44.97 thousand.

16.14 $b_1 = \dfrac{s_{xy}}{s_x^2} = \dfrac{310.0}{4.84} = 64.05$, $b_0 = \bar{y} - b_1\bar{x} = 762.6 - 64.05(4.75) = 458.4$.

Regression line: $\hat{y} = 458.4 + 64.05x$ (Excel: : $\hat{y} = 458.9 + 64.00x$)
For each additional occupant the electrical use increases on average by 64.05.

16.16 a. $b_1 = \dfrac{s_{xy}}{s_x^2} = \dfrac{-10.78}{35.47} = -.3039$, $b_0 = \bar{y} - b_1\bar{x} = 17.20 - (-.3039)(11.33) = 20.64$.

Regression line: $\hat{y} = 20.64 - .3039x$ (Excel: $\hat{y} = 20.64 - .3038x$)

b. The slope indicates that for each additional one percentage point increase in the vacancy rate rents on average decrease by \$.3039.

16.18 $b_1 = \dfrac{s_{xy}}{s_x^2} = \dfrac{.8258}{16.07} = .0514$, $b_0 = \bar{y} - b_1\bar{x} = 93.89 - .0514(79.47) = 89.81$.

Regression line: $\hat{y} = 89.81 + .0514x$ (Excel: $\hat{y} = 89.81 + .0514x$)
For each additional mark on the test the number of non-defective products increases on average by .0514.

16.20 For each number of years of education incomes are normally distributed with constant variance and a mean that is a linear function of the number of years of education.

16.22 b

x_i	y_i	x_i^2	y_i^2	$x_i y_i$
1	1	1	1	1
3	8	9	64	24
4	15	16	225	60
6	33	36	1089	198
9	75	81	5625	675
8	70	64	4900	560
10	95	100	9025	950
Total 41	297	307	20,929	2,468

$$\sum_{i=1}^{n} x_i = 41 \qquad \sum_{i=1}^{n} y_i = 297 \qquad \sum_{i=1}^{n} x_i^2 = 307 \qquad \sum_{i=1}^{n} y_i^2 = 20{,}929 \qquad \sum_{i=1}^{n} x_i y_i = 2{,}468$$

$$s_{xy} = \frac{1}{n-1}\left[\sum_{i=1}^{n} x_i y_i - \frac{\sum_{i=1}^{n} x_i \sum_{i=1}^{n} y_i}{n}\right] = \frac{1}{7-1}\left[2{,}468 - \frac{(41)(297)}{7}\right] = 121.4$$

$$s_x^2 = \frac{1}{n-1}\left[\sum_{i=1}^{n} x_i^2 - \frac{\left(\sum_{i=1}^{n} x_i\right)^2}{n}\right] = \frac{1}{7-1}\left[307 - \frac{(41)^2}{7}\right] = 11.14$$

$$s_y^2 = \frac{1}{n-1}\left[\sum_{i=1}^{n} y_i^2 - \frac{\left(\sum_{i=1}^{n} y_i\right)^2}{n}\right] = \frac{1}{7-1}\left[20{,}929 - \frac{(297)^2}{7}\right] = 1{,}388.0$$

$$b_1 = \frac{s_{xy}}{s_x^2} = \frac{121.4}{11.14} = 10.90$$

$$SSE = (n-1)\left(s_y^2 - \frac{s_{xy}^2}{s_x^2}\right) = (7-1)\left(1{,}388.0 - \frac{(121.4)^2}{11.14}\right) = 390.1$$

$$s_\varepsilon = \sqrt{\frac{SSE}{n-2}} = \sqrt{\frac{390.1}{7-2}} = 8.83 \text{ (Excel: } s_\varepsilon = 8.85)$$

$$H_0 : \beta_1 = 0$$

$$H_1 : \beta_1 \neq 0$$

Rejection region: $t > t_{\alpha/2, n-2} = t_{.025,5} = 2.571$ or $t < -t_{\alpha/2, n-2} = -t_{.025,5} = -2.571$

$$s_{b_1} = \frac{s_\varepsilon}{\sqrt{(n-1)s_x^2}} = \frac{8.83}{\sqrt{(7-1)(11.14)}} = 1.08$$

$$t = \frac{b_1 - \beta_1}{s_{b_1}} = \frac{10.90 - 0}{.1.08} = 10.09 \text{ (Excel: } t = 10.90, \text{ p–value} = .0002. \text{ There is enough evidence}$$

to infer a linear relationship.

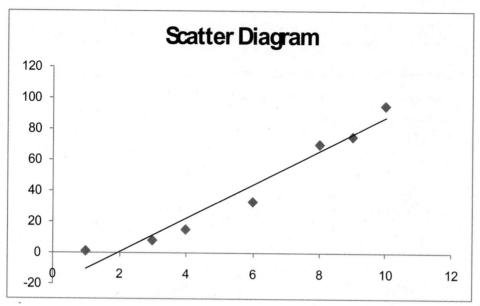

There does appear to be a linear relationship.

16.24 a. $$s_y^2 = \frac{1}{n-1}\left[\sum_{i=1}^{n} y_i^2 - \frac{\left(\sum_{i=1}^{n} y_i\right)^2}{n}\right] = \frac{1}{12-1}\left[1{,}795.77 - \frac{(144.9)^2}{12}\right] = 4.191$$

$$SSE = (n-1)\left(s_y^2 - \frac{s_{xy}^2}{s_x^2}\right) = (12-1)\left(4.191 - \frac{(43.66)^2}{749.7}\right) = 18.13$$

$$s_\varepsilon = \sqrt{\frac{SSE}{n-2}} = \sqrt{\frac{18.13}{12-2}} = 1.347 \;(\text{Excel: } s_\varepsilon = 1.347)$$

b. $H_0 : \beta_1 = 0$

$H_1 : \beta_1 \neq 0$

Rejection region: $t > t_{\alpha/2,n-2} = t_{.025,10} = 2.228$ or $t < -t_{\alpha/2,n-2} = -t_{.025,10} = -2.228$

$$s_{b_1} = \frac{s_\varepsilon}{\sqrt{(n-1)s_x^2}} = \frac{1.347}{\sqrt{(12-1)(749.7)}} = .0148$$

$$t = \frac{b_1 - \beta_1}{s_{b_1}} = \frac{.0582 - 0}{.0148} = 3.93 \;(\text{Excel: } t = 3.93, \; p\text{–value} = .0028. \text{ There is enough evidence to}$$

infer a linear relationship between advertising and sales.

c. $b_1 \pm t_{\alpha/2,n-2} s_{b_1} = .0582 \pm 2.228(.0148) = .0582 \pm .0330$ LCL = .0252, UCL = .0912

d. $R^2 = \dfrac{s_{xy}^2}{s_x^2 s_y^2} = \dfrac{(43.66)^2}{(749.7)(4.191)} = .6067$ (Excel: $R^2 = .6066$). 60.67% of the variation in sales is

explained by the variation in advertising.

e. There is evidence of a linear relationship. For each additional dollar of advertising sales increase, on average by .0582.

16.26 $s_y^2 = \dfrac{1}{n-1}\left[\displaystyle\sum_{i=1}^{n} y_i^2 - \dfrac{\left(\displaystyle\sum_{i=1}^{n} y_i\right)^2}{n}\right] = \dfrac{1}{15-1}\left[1{,}312 - \dfrac{(86)^2}{15}\right] = 58.50$

$SSE = (n-1)\left(s_y^2 - \dfrac{s_{xy}^2}{s_x^2}\right) = (15-1)\left(58.50 - \dfrac{(46.42)^2}{47.98}\right) = 190.2$

$s_\varepsilon = \sqrt{\dfrac{SSE}{n-2}} = \sqrt{\dfrac{190.2}{15-2}} = 3.825$

$H_0 : \beta_1 = 0$

$H_1 : \beta_1 \neq 0$

Rejection region: $t > t_{\alpha/2, n-2} = t_{.025,13} = 2.160$ or $t < -t_{\alpha/2, n-2} = -t_{.025,13} = -2.160$

$s_{b_1} = \dfrac{s_\varepsilon}{\sqrt{(n-1)s_x^2}} = \dfrac{3.825}{\sqrt{(15-1)(47.98)}} = .1476$

$t = \dfrac{b_1 - \beta_1}{s_{b_1}} = \dfrac{.9675 - 0}{.1476} = 6.55$ (Excel: t = 6.55, p–value = 0.) There is enough evidence to conclude

that there is a linear relationship between hours of television viewing and how overweight the child is.

16.28 a. $SSE = (n-1)\left(s_y^2 - \dfrac{s_{xy}^2}{s_x^2}\right) = (60-1)\left(47.96 - \dfrac{(51.86)^2}{193.9}\right) = 2{,}011$

$s_\varepsilon = \sqrt{\dfrac{SSE}{n-2}} = \sqrt{\dfrac{2{,}011}{60-2}} = 5.888$ (Excel: $s_\varepsilon = 5.888$). Relative to the values of the dependent

variable the standard error of estimate appears to be large indicating a weak linear relationship.

b. $R^2 = \dfrac{s_{xy}^2}{s_x^2 s_y^2} = \dfrac{(51.86)^2}{(193.9)(47.96)} = .2892$ (Excel: $R^2 = .2893$).

c. $H_0 : \beta_1 = 0$

$H_1 : \beta_1 \neq 0$

Rejection region: $t > t_{\alpha/2, n-2} = t_{.025,58} \approx 2.000$ or $t < -t_{\alpha/2, n-2} = -t_{.025,58} = -2.000$

$s_{b_1} = \dfrac{s_\varepsilon}{\sqrt{(n-1)s_x^2}} = \dfrac{5.888}{\sqrt{(60-1)(193.9)}} = .0550$

$t = \dfrac{b_1 - \beta_1}{s_{b_1}} = \dfrac{.2675 - 0}{.0550} = 4.86$ (Excel: t = 4.86, p–value = 0). There is enough evidence to infer a

linear relationship between memory test scores and length of commercial.

d.　$b_1 \pm t_{\alpha/2, n-2} s_{b_1} = .2675 \pm 1.671(.0550) = .2675 \pm .0919$ LCL = .1756, UCL = .3594

16.30　$SSE = (n-1)\left(s_y^2 - \dfrac{s_{xy}^2}{s_x^2}\right) = (150-1)\left(437.9 - \dfrac{(46.02)^2}{11.12}\right) = 36,870$

$s_\varepsilon = \sqrt{\dfrac{SSE}{n-2}} = \sqrt{\dfrac{36,870}{150-2}} = 15.78$

$H_0 : \beta_1 = 0$

$H_1 : \beta_1 \neq 0$

Rejection region: $t > t_{\alpha/2, n-2} = t_{.025,148} \approx 1.977$ or $t < -t_{\alpha/2, n-2} = -t_{.025,148} = -1.977$

$s_{b_1} = \dfrac{s_\varepsilon}{\sqrt{(n-1)s_x^2}} = \dfrac{15.78}{\sqrt{(150-1)(11.12)}} = .3877$

$t = \dfrac{b_1 - \beta_1}{s_{b_1}} = \dfrac{4.138 - 0}{.3877} = 10.67$ (Excel: t = 10.67, p–value = 0.) There is evidence of a linear

relationship between education and income.

16.32　$SSE = (n-1)\left(s_y^2 - \dfrac{s_{xy}^2}{s_x^2}\right) = (231-1)\left(19.80 - \dfrac{(20.55)^2}{108.3}\right) = 3657$

$s_\varepsilon = \sqrt{\dfrac{SSE}{n-2}} = \sqrt{\dfrac{3657}{231-2}} = 3.996$

$H_0 : \beta_1 = 0$

$H_1 : \beta_1 > 0$

Rejection region: $t > t_{\alpha/2, n-2} = t_{.025,229} \approx 1.960$ or $t < -t_{\alpha/2, n-2} = -t_{.025,229} \approx -1.960$

$s_{b_1} = \dfrac{s_\varepsilon}{\sqrt{(n-1)s_x^2}} = \dfrac{3.996}{\sqrt{(231-1)(108.3)}} = .02532$

$t = \dfrac{b_1 - \beta_1}{s_{b_1}} = \dfrac{.1898 - 0}{.02532} = 7.50$ (Excel: t =7.49, p–value = 0.) There is evidence of a positive linear

relationship between cigarettes smoked and the number of sick days.

16.34　$SSE = (n-1)\left(s_y^2 - \dfrac{s_{xy}^2}{s_x^2}\right) = (40-1)\left(11,918,489 - \dfrac{(30,945)^2}{688.2}\right) = 410,554,683$

a.　$s_\varepsilon = \sqrt{\dfrac{SSE}{n-2}} = \sqrt{\dfrac{410,554,683}{40-2}} = 3,287$ (Excel: $s_\varepsilon = 3,287$). There is a weak linear

relationship.

b. $H_0 : \beta_1 = 0$

        $H_1 : \beta_1 \neq 0$

Rejection region: $t > t_{\alpha/2, n-2} = t_{.025,38} \approx 2.021$ or $t < -t_{\alpha/2, n-2} = -t_{.025,38} \approx -2.021$

$$s_{b_1} = \frac{s_\varepsilon}{\sqrt{(n-1)s_x^2}} = \frac{3,287}{\sqrt{(40-1)(688.2)}} = 20.06$$

$$t = \frac{b_1 - \beta_1}{s_{b_1}} = \frac{44.97 - 0}{20.06} = 2.24 \text{ (Excel: } t = 2.24, \text{ p–value} = .0309.) \text{ There is enough evidence of a}$$

linear relationship.

c. $R^2 = \frac{s_{xy}^2}{s_x^2 s_y^2} = \frac{(30,945)^2}{(688.2)(11,918,489)} = .1167 \text{ (Excel: } R^2 = .1168) \text{ } 11.67\% \text{ of the variation in}$

percent damage is explained by the variation in distance to the fire station.

16.36 $\text{SSE} = (n-1)\left(s_y^2 - \frac{s_{xy}^2}{s_x^2}\right) = (200-1)\left(56,725 - \frac{(310.0)^2}{4.84}\right) = 7,337,056$

$$s_\varepsilon = \sqrt{\frac{\text{SSE}}{n-2}} = \sqrt{\frac{7,337,056}{200-2}} = 191.1 \text{ (Excel: } s_\varepsilon = 192.5).$$

$$R^2 = \frac{s_{xy}^2}{s_x^2 s_y^2} = \frac{(310.0)^2}{(4.84)(56,725)} = .3500 \text{ (Excel: } R^2 = .3496) \text{ } 35.00\% \text{ of the variation in the electricity}$$

use is explained by the variation in the number of occupants.

$H_0 : \beta_1 = 0$

$H_1 : \beta_1 \neq 0$

Rejection region: $t > t_{\alpha/2, n-2} = t_{.025,198} \approx 1.972$ or $t < -t_{\alpha/2, n-2} = -t_{.025,198} \approx -1.972$

$$s_{b_1} = \frac{s_\varepsilon}{\sqrt{(n-1)s_x^2}} = \frac{191.1}{\sqrt{(200-1)(4.84)}} = 6.16$$

$$t = \frac{b_1 - \beta_1}{s_{b_1}} = \frac{64.05 - 0}{6.16} = 10.39 \text{ (Excel: } t = 10.32, \text{ p–value} = 0.) \text{ There is enough evidence of a}$$

linear relationship.

16.38 $\text{SSE} = (n-1)\left(s_y^2 - \frac{s_{xy}^2}{s_x^2}\right) = (30-1)\left(11.24 - \frac{(-10.78)^2}{35.47}\right) = 230.9$

$$s_\varepsilon = \sqrt{\frac{\text{SSE}}{n-2}} = \sqrt{\frac{230.9}{30-2}} = 2.872 \text{ (Excel: } s_\varepsilon = 2.873).$$

$H_0 : \beta_1 = 0$

$H_1 : \beta_1 \neq 0$

Rejection region: $t > t_{\alpha/2, n-2} = t_{.025,28} = 2.048$ or $t < -t_{\alpha/2, n-2} = -t_{.025,28} = -2.048$

$$s_{b_1} = \frac{s_\varepsilon}{\sqrt{(n-1)s_x^2}} = \frac{2.872}{\sqrt{(30-1)(35.47)}} = .08955$$

$$t = \frac{b_1 - \beta_1}{s_{b_1}} = \frac{-.3039 - 0}{.08955} = -3.39 \text{ (Excel: } t = -3.39, \text{ p–value} = .0021.) \text{ There is sufficient evidence}$$

to conclude that office rents and vacancy rates are linearly related.

16.40   a. $R^2 = \dfrac{s_{xy}^2}{s_x^2 s_y^2} = \dfrac{(.8258)^2}{(16.07)(1.283)} = .0331$ (Excel: $R^2 = .0331$) 3.31% of the variation in

percentage of defectives is explained by the variation in aptitude test scores.

b. $SSE = (n-1)\left(s_y^2 - \dfrac{s_{xy}^2}{s_x^2} \right) = (45-1)\left(1.283 - \dfrac{(.8258)^2}{16.07} \right) = 54.58$

$$s_\varepsilon = \sqrt{\frac{SSE}{n-2}} = \sqrt{\frac{54.58}{45-2}} = 1.127 \text{ (Excel: } s_\varepsilon = 1.127).$$

$H_0 : \beta_1 = 0$

$H_1 : \beta_1 \neq 0$

Rejection region: $t > t_{\alpha/2,n-2} = t_{.025,43} \approx 2.014$ or $t < -t_{\alpha/2,n-2} = -t_{.025,43} \approx -2.014$

$$s_{b_1} = \frac{s_\varepsilon}{\sqrt{(n-1)s_x^2}} = \frac{1.127}{\sqrt{(45-1)(16.07)}} = .04238$$

$$t = \frac{b_1 - \beta_1}{s_{b_1}} = \frac{.0516 - 0}{.04238} = 1.22 \text{ (Excel: } t = 1.21, \text{ p–value} = .2319) \text{ There is not enough evidence to}$$

conclude that aptitude test scores and percentage of defectives are linearly related.

16.42 $H_0 : \rho = 0$

$H_1 : \rho \neq 0$

Rejection region: $t > t_{\alpha/2,n-2} = t_{.025,58} \approx 2.000$ or $t < -t_{\alpha/2,n-2} = -t_{.025,58} = -2.000$

$$r = \frac{s_{xy}}{s_x s_y} = \frac{51.86}{\sqrt{(193.9)(47.96)}} = .5378$$

$$t = r\sqrt{\frac{n-2}{1-r^2}} = (.5378)\sqrt{\frac{60-2}{1-(.5378)^2}} = 4.86 \text{ (Excel: } t = 4.86, \text{ p–value} = 0) \text{ This result is identical to}$$

the one produced in Exercise 16.6.

16.44 $H_0 : \rho = 0$

$H_1 : \rho > 0$

Rejection region: $t > t_{\alpha,n-2} = t_{.05,229} \approx 1.645$

$$r = \frac{s_{xy}}{s_x s_y} = \frac{20.55}{\sqrt{(108.3)(19.80)}} = .4438$$

$$t = r\sqrt{\frac{n-2}{1-r^2}} = (.4438)\sqrt{\frac{231-2}{1-(.4438)^2}} = 7.49 \text{ (Excel: } t = 7.49, \text{ p–value} = 0.) \text{ There is evidence of a}$$

positive linear relationship between cigarettes smoked and the number of sick days.

16.46 $\hat{y} = b_0 + b_1 x_g = 91.07 + .0582(90) = 14.35$

Prediction interval: $\hat{y} \pm t_{\alpha/2, n-2} s_\varepsilon \sqrt{1 + \dfrac{1}{n} + \dfrac{(x_g - \bar{x})^2}{(n-1)s_x^2}}$ (where $t_{\alpha/2, n-2} = t_{.05,10} = 1.812$)

$$= 14.35 \pm 1.812(1.347)\sqrt{1 + \frac{1}{12} + \frac{(90-51.08)^2}{(12-1)(749.7)}} = 14.35 \pm 2.747$$

Lower prediction limit = 11.60, Upper prediction limit = 17.10 (Excel: 11.59, 17.09)

16.48 $\hat{y} = b_0 + b_1 x_g = -24.72 + .9675(30) = 4.305$

a. Prediction interval: $\hat{y} \pm t_{\alpha/2, n-2} s_\varepsilon \sqrt{1 + \dfrac{1}{n} + \dfrac{(x_g - \bar{x})^2}{(n-1)s_x^2}}$ (where $t_{\alpha/2, n-2} = t_{.05,13} = 1.771$)

$$= 4.305 \pm 1.771(3.825)\sqrt{1 + \frac{1}{15} + \frac{(30-31.47)^2}{(15-1)(47.98)}} = 4.305 \pm 7.007$$

Lower prediction limit = –2.702, Upper prediction limit = 11.31 (Excel: –2.692, 11.32)

b. Confidence interval estimate: $\hat{y} \pm t_{\alpha/2, n-2} s_\varepsilon \sqrt{\dfrac{1}{n} + \dfrac{(x_g - \bar{x})^2}{(n-1)s_x^2}}$

$$= 4.305 \pm 1.771(3.825)\sqrt{\frac{1}{15} + \frac{(30-31.47)^2}{(15-1)(47.98)}} = 4.305 \pm 1.791$$

LCL = 2.514, UCL = 6.096 (Excel: 2.524, 6.105)

16.50 $\hat{y} = b_0 + b_1 x_g = 3.636 + .2675(36) = 13.27$

a. Prediction interval: $\hat{y} \pm t_{\alpha/2, n-2} s_\varepsilon \sqrt{1 + \dfrac{1}{n} + \dfrac{(x_g - \bar{x})^2}{(n-1)s_x^2}}$ (where $t_{\alpha/2, n-2} = t_{.025,58} \approx 2.000$)

$$= 13.27 \pm 2.000(5.888)\sqrt{1 + \frac{1}{60} + \frac{(36-38)^2}{(60-1)(193.9)}} = 13.27 \pm 11.88$$

Lower prediction limit =1.39, Upper prediction limit = 25.15 (Excel: 1.378, 25.15)

b. Confidence interval estimate: $\hat{y} \pm t_{\alpha/2, n-2} s_\varepsilon \sqrt{\dfrac{1}{n} + \dfrac{(x_g - \bar{x})^2}{(n-1)s_x^2}}$

$$= 13.27 \pm 2.000(5.888)\sqrt{\frac{1}{60} + \frac{(36-38)^2}{(60-1)(193.9)}} = 13.27 \pm 1.536$$

LCL = 11.73, UCL = 14.81 (Excel: 11.73, 14.80)

16.52 $\hat{y} = b_0 + b_1 x_g = 23.63 + 4.138(15) = 85.70$

Confidence interval estimate: $\hat{y} \pm t_{\alpha/2,n-2} s_\varepsilon \sqrt{\dfrac{1}{n} + \dfrac{(x_g - \bar{x})^2}{(n-1)s_x^2}}$ (where $t_{\alpha/2,n-2} = t_{.05,148} \approx 1.656$)

$= 85.70 \pm 1.656(15.78)\sqrt{\dfrac{1}{150} + \dfrac{(15-13.17)^2}{(150-1)(11.12)}} = 85.70 \pm 2.436$

LCL = 83.26, UCL = 88.14 (Excel:83.25, 88.18)

16.54 $\hat{y} = b_0 + b_1 x_g = 7.286 + .1898(30) = 12.98$

Prediction interval: $\hat{y} \pm t_{\alpha/2,n-2} s_\varepsilon \sqrt{1 + \dfrac{1}{n} + \dfrac{(x_g - \bar{x})^2}{(n-1)s_x^2}}$ (where $t_{\alpha/2,n-2} = t_{.025,229} \approx 1.960$)

$= 12.98 \pm 1.960(3.996)\sqrt{1 + \dfrac{1}{231} + \dfrac{(30-37.64)^2}{(231-1)(108.3)}} = 12.98 \pm 7.858$

Lower prediction limit = 5.12, Upper prediction limit = 20.84 (Excel: 5.078, 20.88)

16.56 $\hat{y} = b_0 + b_1 x_g = 4,040 + 44.97(50) = 6,289$

Confidence interval estimate: $\hat{y} \pm t_{\alpha/2,n-2} s_\varepsilon \sqrt{\dfrac{1}{n} + \dfrac{(x_g - \bar{x})^2}{(n-1)s_x^2}}$ (where $t_{\alpha/2,n-2} = t_{.025,38} \approx 2.021$)

$= 6,289 \pm 2.021(3,287)\sqrt{\dfrac{1}{40} + \dfrac{(50-53.93)^2}{(40-1)(688.2)}} = 6,289 \pm 1,062$

LCL = 5,227, UCL = 7,351 (Excel: LCL = 5,224, UCL = 7,352)

16.58 $\hat{y} = b_0 + b_1 x_g = 458.4 + 64.05(5) = 778.65$

Confidence interval estimate: $\hat{y} \pm t_{\alpha/2,n-2} s_\varepsilon \sqrt{\dfrac{1}{n} + \dfrac{(x_g - \bar{x})^2}{(n-1)s_x^2}}$ (where $t_{\alpha/2,n-2} = t_{.05,198} \approx 1.653$)

$= 778.65 \pm 1.653(191.1)\sqrt{\dfrac{1}{200} + \dfrac{(5-4.75)^2}{(200-1)(4.84)}} = 778.65 \pm 22.48$

LCL = 756.17, UCL = 801.13 (Excel: 756.27,801.57)

16.60 $\hat{y} = b_0 + b_1 x_g = 20.64 - .3039(10) = 17.60$

Prediction interval: $\hat{y} \pm t_{\alpha/2,n-2} s_\varepsilon \sqrt{1 + \dfrac{1}{n} + \dfrac{(x_g - \bar{x})^2}{(n-1)s_x^2}}$ (where $t_{\alpha/2,n-2} = t_{.025,28} = 2.048$)

$= 17.60 \pm 2.048(2.872)\sqrt{1 + \dfrac{1}{30} + \dfrac{(10-11.33)^2}{(30-1)(35.47)}} = 17.60 \pm 5.984$

Lower prediction limit = 11.62 , Upper prediction limit = 23.58 (Excel: 11.61, 23.59)

16.62　$\hat{y} = b_0 + b_1 x_g = 89.81 + .0514(75) = 93.64$

Confidence interval estimate: $\hat{y} \pm t_{\alpha/2,n-2} s_\varepsilon \sqrt{\dfrac{1}{n} + \dfrac{(x_g - \overline{x})^2}{(n-1)s_x^2}}$ where $t_{\alpha/2,n-2} = t_{.025,43} \approx 2.014)$

$= 93.64 \pm 2.014(1.127)\sqrt{\dfrac{1}{45} + \dfrac{(75 - 79.47)^2}{(45-1)(16.07)}} = 93.64 \pm .510$

LCL = 93.13, UCL = 94.15　(Excel: 93.15, 94.17)

16.64

x_i	y_i	$\hat{y}_i = 9.107 - .0582x$	$e_i = y_i - \hat{y}_i$
23	9.6	10.45	−.85
46	11.3	11.78	−.48
60	12.8	12.60	.20
54	9.8	12.25	−2.45
28	8.9	10.74	−1.84
33	12.5	11.03	1.47
25	12.0	10.56	1.44
31	11.4	10.91	.49
36	12.6	11.20	1.40
88	13.7	14.23	−.53
90	14.4	14.35	.06
99	15.9	14.87	1.03

16.66 a & b

x_i	y_i	$\hat{y} = -24.72 + .9675x$	$e_i = y_i - \hat{y}_i$
42	18	15.92	2.09
34	6	8.18	−2.18
25	0	−.53	.53
35	−1	9.14	−10.14
37	13	11.08	1.92
38	14	12.05	1.96
31	7	5.27	1.73
33	7	7.21	−.21
19	−9	−6.34	−2.66
29	8	3.34	4.66
38	8	12.05	−4.05
28	5	2.37	2.63
29	3	3.34	−.34
36	14	10.11	3.89
18	−7	−7.31	.31

c.

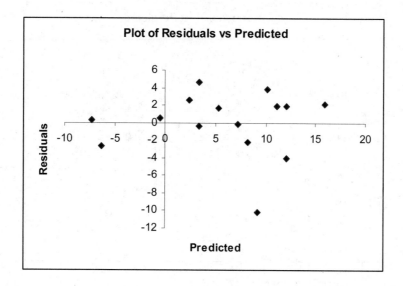

The histograms drawn below are of the standardized residuals, which make it easier to see whether the shape is extremely nonnormal. It also makes it easier to identify outliers. The shape of the resulting histogram is identical to the histogram of the residuals using the equivalent class limits.

16.68   b & c

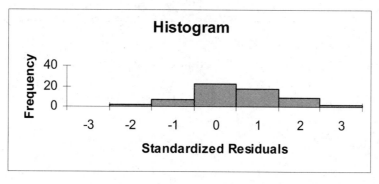

Because the histogram is approximately bell shaped the errors appear to be normally distributed. There are two residuals whose absolute value exceeds 2.0.

d.

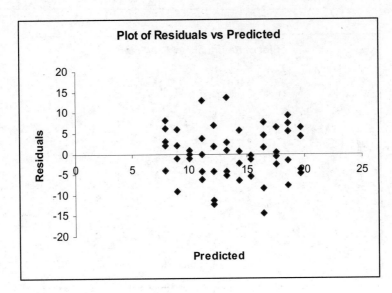

Plot of Residuals vs Predicted

There is no indication of heteroscedasticity.

16.70

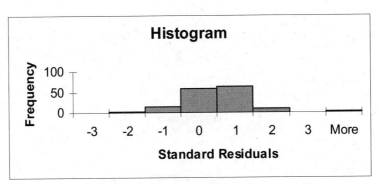

Histogram

The normality requirement appears to be satisfied. There are two outliers.

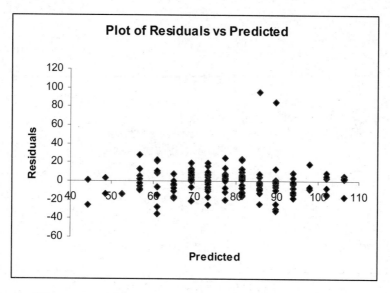

The variance of the error variable appears to be constant. The two outliers are clearly seen.

16.72

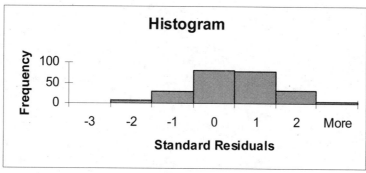

The error variable appears to be normally distributed.

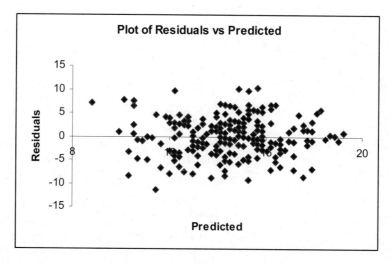

The variance of the error variable is constant.

16.74

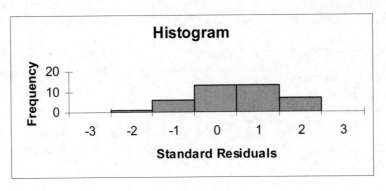

The error variable appears to be normally distributed.

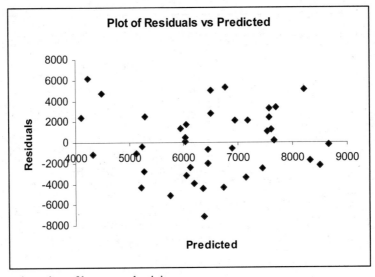

There is no clear sign of heteroscedasticity.

16.76

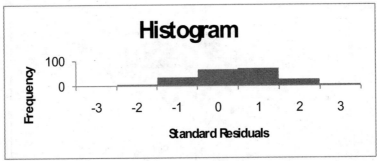

The error variable appears to be normal.

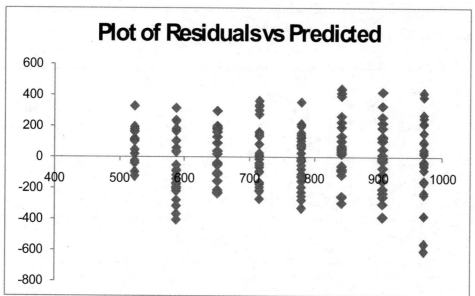

Plot of Residuals vs Predicted

The variance of the error variable is constant.

16.78

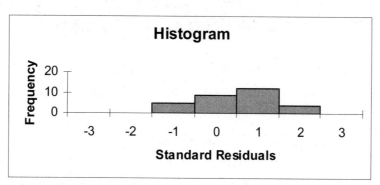

Histogram

The error variable appears to be normal.

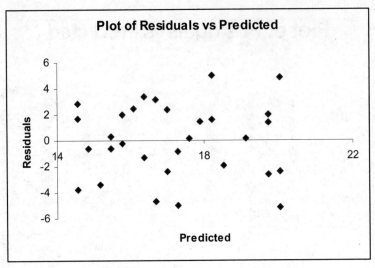

The variance of the error variable is constant.

16.80

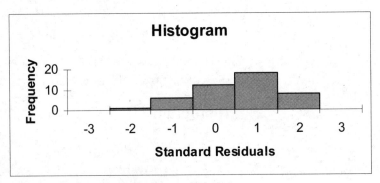

The error variable appears to be normal.

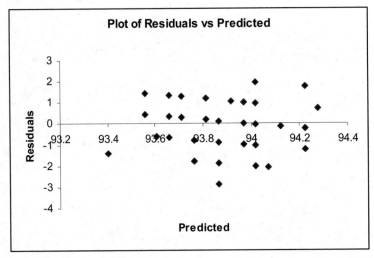

The variance of the error variable is constant.

234

16.82   a. $b_1 = \dfrac{s_{xy}}{s_x^2} = \dfrac{936.82}{378.77} = 2.47$ $b_0 = \bar{y} - b_1\bar{x} = 395.21 - 2.47(113.35) = 115.24.$

Regression line: $\hat{y} = 115.24 + 2.47x$ (Excel: $\hat{y} = 114.85 + 2.47x$)

   b. $b_1 = 2.47$; for each additional month of age, repair costs increase on average by \$2.47.

$b_0 = 114.85$ is the y-intercept.

   c. $R^2 = \dfrac{s_{xy}^2}{s_x^2 s_y^2} = \dfrac{(936.82)^2}{(378.77)(4,094.79)} = .5659$ (Excel: $R^2 = .5659$) 56.59% of the variation in

repair costs s explained by the variation in ages.

   d. $SSE = (n-1)\left(s_y^2 - \dfrac{s_{xy}^2}{s_x^2}\right) = (20-1)\left(4,094.79 - \dfrac{(936.82)^2}{378.77}\right) = 33,777$

$s_\varepsilon = \sqrt{\dfrac{SSE}{n-2}} = \sqrt{\dfrac{33,777}{20-2}} = 43.32$ (Excel: $s_\varepsilon = 43.32$).

$H_0 : \beta_1 = 0$

$H_1 : \beta_1 \neq 0$

Rejection region: $t > t_{\alpha/2,n-2} = t_{.025,18} = 2.101$ or $t < -t_{\alpha/2,n-2} = -t_{.025,18} = -2.101$

$s_{b_1} = \dfrac{s_\varepsilon}{\sqrt{(n-1)s_x^2}} = \dfrac{43.32}{\sqrt{(20-1)(378.77)}} = .511$

$t = \dfrac{b_1 - \beta_1}{s_{b_1}} = \dfrac{2.47 - 0}{.511} = 4.84$ (Excel: $t = 4.84$, p–value = .0001. There is enough evidence to

infer that repair costs and age are linearly related.

   e. $\hat{y} = b_0 + b_1 x_g = 115.24 + 2.47(120) = 411.64$

Prediction interval: $\hat{y} \pm t_{\alpha/2,n-2} s_\varepsilon \sqrt{1 + \dfrac{1}{n} + \dfrac{(x_g - \bar{x})^2}{(n-1)s_x^2}}$ (where $t_{\alpha/2,n-2} = t_{.025,18} = 2.101$)

$= 411.64 \pm 2.101(43.32)\sqrt{1 + \dfrac{1}{20} + \dfrac{(120 - 113.35)^2}{(20-1)(378.77)}} = 411.64 \pm 93.54$

Lower prediction limit = 318.1, upper prediction limit = 505.2 (Excel: 318.1, 505.2)

16.84   a. $H_0 : \rho = 0$

$H_1 : \rho \neq 0$

	A	B
1	**Correlation**	
2		
3	*Tar and Nicotine*	
4	Pearson Coefficient of Correlation	0.9766
5	t Stat	21.78
6	df	23
7	P(T<=t) one tail	0
8	t Critical one tail	1.7139
9	P(T<=t) two tail	0
10	t Critical two tail	2.0687

r = .9766, t = 21.78, p–value = 0. There is sufficient evidence to infer that levels of tar and nicotine are linearly related.

b. $H_0 : \rho = 0$

$H_1 : \rho \neq 0$

	A	B
1	**Correlation**	
2		
3	*Nicotine and CO*	
4	Pearson Coefficient of Correlation	0.9259
5	t Stat	11.76
6	df	23
7	P(T<=t) one tail	0
8	t Critical one tail	1.7139
9	P(T<=t) two tail	0
10	t Critical two tail	2.0687

r = .9259, t = 11.76, p–value = 0. There is sufficient evidence to infer that levels of nicotine and carbon monoxide are linearly related.

16.86 $H_0 : \rho = 0$

$H_1 : \rho \neq 0$

Rejection region: $t > t_{\alpha/2, n-2} = t_{.025, 48} \approx 2.009$ or $t < -t_{\alpha/2, n-2} = -t_{.025, 48} = -2.009$

$$r = \frac{s_{xy}}{s_x s_y} = \frac{13.08}{\sqrt{(90.97)(11.84)}} = .3985 \, (\text{Excel: } .3984)$$

$$t = r\sqrt{\frac{n-2}{1-r^2}} = (.3985)\sqrt{\frac{50-2}{1-(.3985)^2}} = 3.01 \, (\text{Excel: } t = 3.01, \text{ p–value} = .0042).$$ There is enough evidence of a linear relationship. The theory appears to be valid.

16.88 $H_0 : \rho = 0$
         $H_1 : \rho > 0$

	A	B	C	D
1	**Correlation**			
2				
3	*Time and Sales*			
4	Pearson Coefficient of Correlation			0.2791
5	t Stat			1.67
6	df			33
7	P(T<=t) one tail			0.0522
8	t Critical one tail			1.6924
9	P(T<=t) two tail			0.1044
10	t Critical two tail			2.0345

t = 1.67, p-value = .0522. There is not enough evidence to infer that when the times between movies increase so do sales.

16.90 $H_0 : \rho = 0$
         $H_1 : \rho \neq 0$

	A	B
1	**Correlation**	
2		
3	*Times and Amount*	
4	Pearson Coefficient of Correlation	0.7976
5	t Stat	29.51
6	df	498
7	P(T<=t) one tail	0
8	t Critical one tail	1.6479
9	P(T<=t) two tail	0
10	t Critical two tail	1.9647

t = 29.51, p–value = 0. There is overwhelming evidence of a linear relationship between listening times and amounts spent on music.

Appendix 16

A16.2 Two-way analysis of variance

$H_0 : \mu_1 = \mu_2 = \mu_3 = \mu_4$

H_1 : At least two means differ

	A	B	C	D	E	F	G
40	ANOVA						
41	*Source of Variation*	*SS*	*df*	*MS*	*F*	*P-value*	*F crit*
42	Rows	3708.8	28	132.46	8.63	6.52E-15	1.61
43	Columns	997.0	3	332.33	21.64	1.77E-10	2.71
44	Error	1289.8	84	15.35			
45							
46	Total	5995.5	115				

F = 21.64; p-value = 0. There is enough evidence to conclude that there are differences in the decrease in test scores between the four types of breakfast meals.

A16.4 t-test of ρ or t-test of β_1

$H_0 : \rho = 0$

$H_1 : \rho > 0$

$$t = r\sqrt{\frac{n-2}{1-r^2}}$$

	A	B	C	D
1	**Correlation**			
2				
3	*Age and Duration*			
4	Pearson Coefficient of Correlation			0.558
5	t Stat			7.90
6	df			138
7	P(T<=t) one tail			0
8	t Critical one tail			1.6560
9	P(T<=t) two tail			0
10	t Critical two tail			1.9773

t = 7.90; p-value = 0. There is overwhelming evidence to infer that the older the patient the longer it takes for the symptoms to disappear?

A16.6   Question 1: Equal-variances t-test of $\mu_1 - \mu_2$

$$H_0 : (\mu_1 - \mu_2) = 0$$

$$H_1 : (\mu_1 - \mu_2) < 0$$

$$t = \frac{(\bar{x}_1 - \bar{x}_2) - (\mu_1 - \mu_2)}{\sqrt{s_p^2 \left(\dfrac{1}{n_1} + \dfrac{1}{n_2} \right)}}$$

	A	B	C
1	t-Test: Two-Sample Assuming Equal Variances		
2			
3		US Days	Canada Days
4	Mean	26.98	29.44
5	Variance	55.90	56.82
6	Observations	300	300
7	Pooled Variance	56.36	
8	Hypothesized Mean Difference	0	
9	df	598	
10	t Stat	-4.00	
11	P(T<=t) one-tail	0.0000	
12	t Critical one-tail	1.6474	
13	P(T<=t) two-tail	0.0001	
14	t Critical two-tail	1.9639	

t = –4.00, p-value = 0. There is enough evidence to indicate that recovery is faster in the United States.

Question 2: z-tests of $p_1 - p_2$ (case 1)

$$H_0 : (p_1 - p_2) = 0$$

$$H_1 : (p_1 - p_2) < 0$$

$$z = \frac{(\hat{p}_1 - \hat{p}_2)}{\sqrt{\hat{p}(1 - \hat{p}) \left(\dfrac{1}{n_1} + \dfrac{1}{n_2} \right)}}$$

	A	B	C	D
1	z-Test: Two Proportions			
2				
3			U.S.	Canada
4	Sample Proportions		0.6267	0.6867
5	Observations		300	300
6	Hypothesized Difference		0	
7	z Stat		-1.55	
8	P(Z<=z) one tail		0.0609	
9	z Critical one-tail		1.6449	
10	P(Z<=z) two-tail		0.1218	
11	z Critical two-tail		1.9600	

z = –1.55, p-value = .0609. There is not enough evidence to infer that recovery is faster in the United States.

6 months after heart attack:

	A	B	C	D
1	**z-Test: Two Proportions**			
2				
3			*U.S.*	*Canada*
4	Sample Proportions		0.1867	0.1733
5	Observations		300	300
6	Hypothesized Difference		0	
7	z Stat		0.43	
8	P(Z<=z) one tail		0.3354	
9	z Critical one-tail		1.6449	
10	P(Z<=z) two-tail		0.6708	
11	z Critical two-tail		1.9600	

z = .43, p-value = 1 - .3354 = .6646. There is no evidence to infer that recovery is faster in the United States.

12 months after heart attack

	A	B	C	D
1	**z-Test: Two Proportions**			
2				
3			*U.S.*	*Canada*
4	Sample Proportions		0.1167	0.1100
5	Observations		300	300
6	Hypothesized Difference		0	
7	z Stat		0.26	
8	P(Z<=z) one tail		0.3984	
9	z Critical one-tail		1.6449	
10	P(Z<=z) two-tail		0.7968	
11	z Critical two-tail		1.9600	

z = .26, p-value = 1 − .3984 = .6016. There is no evidence to infer that recovery is faster in the United States.

A16.8   t-test of μ_D

$H_0 : \mu_D = 0$

$H_1 : \mu_D < 0$

$$t = \frac{\bar{x}_D - \mu_D}{s_D / \sqrt{n_D}}$$

	A	B	C
1	t-Test: Paired Two Sample for Means		
2			
3		No-Slide	Slide
4	Mean	3.73	3.78
5	Variance	0.0653	0.0727
6	Observations	25	25
7	Pearson Correlation	0.96	
8	Hypothesized Mean Difference	0	
9	df	24	
10	t Stat	-3.04	
11	P(T<=t) one-tail	0.0028	
12	t Critical one-tail	1.7109	
13	P(T<=t) two-tail	0.0057	
14	t Critical two-tail	2.0639	

t = –3.04, p-value = .0028. There is overwhelming evidence to indicate that sliding is slower.

A16.10 Simple linear regression with cholesterol reduction (Before – After) as the dependent variable

a. t-test of $\beta 1$ or test of ρ

$H_0 : \beta_1 = 0$

$H_1 : \beta_1 \neq 0$

We used the t-test of $\beta 1$ because parts (b) and (c) use the regression equation to predict and estimate.

	A	B	C	D	E	F
1	SUMMARY OUTPUT					
2						
3	Regression Statistics					
4	Multiple R	0.7138				
5	R Square	0.5095				
6	Adjusted R Square	0.4993				
7	Standard Error	10.53				
8	Observations	50				
9						
10	ANOVA					
11		df	SS	MS	F	Significance F
12	Regression	1	5528	5528.5	49.87	5.92E-09
13	Residual	48	5322	110.9		
14	Total	49	10850			
15						
16		Coefficients	Standard Error	t Stat	P-value	
17	Intercept	2.05	3.94	0.52	0.6051	
18	Exercise	0.0909	0.0129	7.06	5.92E-09	

t = 7.06; p-value = 0. There is overwhelming evidence to infer that exercise and cholesterol reduction are related.

b.   Prediction interval

$$\hat{y} \pm t_{\alpha/2,n-2} s_{\varepsilon} \sqrt{1 + \frac{1}{n} + \frac{(x_g - \overline{x})^2}{(n-1)s_x^2}}$$

	A	B	C
1	**Prediction Interval**		
2			
3			Reduction
4			
5	Predicted value		11.14
6			
7	Prediction Interval		
8	Lower limit		-10.76
9	Upper limit		33.05
10			
11	Interval Estimate of Expected Valu		
12	Lower limit		5.54
13	Upper limit		16.75

The cholesterol reduction is predicted to fall between −10.76 and 33.05.

c.   Confidence interval estimator of the expected value of y

$$\hat{y} \pm t_{\alpha/2,n-2} s_{\varepsilon} \sqrt{\frac{1}{n} + \frac{(x_g - \overline{x})^2}{(n-1)s_x^2}}$$

	A	B	C
1	**Prediction Interval**		
2			
3			Reduction
4			
5	Predicted value		12.96
6			
7	Prediction Interval		
8	Lower limit		-8.83
9	Upper limit		34.76
10			
11	Interval Estimate of Expected Valu		
12	Lower limit		7.79
13	Upper limit		18.14

We estimate that the mean reduction in cholesterol lies between 7.79 and 18.14.

A16.12 a. One-way analysis of variance

$H_0 : \mu_1 = \mu_2 = \mu_3$

H_1 : At least two means differ

	A	B	C	D	E	F	G
10	ANOVA						
11	*Source of Variation*	*SS*	*df*	*MS*	*F*	*P-value*	*F crit*
12	Between Groups	1.65	2	0.823	0.1332	0.8753	3.0259
13	Within Groups	1847.2	299	6.18			
14							
15	Total	1848.9	301				

F = .1332; p-value = .8753. There is no evidence to infer that there are differences between the three groups of patients.

b. One-way analysis of variance

$H_0 : \mu_1 = \mu_2 = \mu_3$

H_1 : At least two means differ

	A	B	C	D	E	F	G
10	ANOVA						
11	*Source of Variation*	*SS*	*df*	*MS*	*F*	*P-value*	*F crit*
12	Between Groups	247.0	2	123.48	15.81	2.96E-07	3.03
13	Within Groups	2334.6	299	7.81			
14							
15	Total	2581.6	301				

F = 15.81; p-value = 0. There is overwhelming evidence to conclude that there are differences between the three groups of patients.

Multiple comparisons

	A	B	C	D	E
1	**Multiple Comparisons**				
2					
3				LSD	Omega
4	Treatment	Treatment	Difference	Alpha = 0.0167	Alpha = 0.05
5	*Group 1 After*	*Group 2 After*	0.099	0.949	0.922
6		*Group 3 After*	-1.867	0.942	0.922
7	*Group 2 After*	*Group 3 After*	-1.965	0.954	0.922

Group 3 differs from both group 1 and group 2. Groups 1 and 2 do not differ.

c. The test assures researchers that the three groups of patients were very similar prior to treatments.

A16.14 a. Chi-squared test of a contingency table

H_0 : The two variables (year and party) are independent

H_1 : The two variables are dependent

$$\chi^2 = \sum_{i=1}^{8} \frac{(f_i - e_i)^2}{e_i}$$

	A	B	C	D	E	F
1	**Contingency Table**					
2						
3		*1990*	*1996*	*2000*	*2004*	TOTAL
4	*Democrats*	154	161	159	152	626
5	*Republican*	99	100	97	87	383
6	*Other*	22	42	56	60	180
7	TOTAL	275	303	312	299	1189
8						
9	chi-squared Stat			19.27		
10	df			6		
11	p-value			0.0037		
12	chi-squared Critical			12.5916		

$\chi^2 = 19.27$; p-value = .0037. There is overwhelming evidence to infer that party affiliation in Broward County changed over the four years.

b. Chi-squared test of a contingency table

H_0 : The two variables (year and party) are independent

H_1 : The two variables are dependent

$$\chi^2 = \sum_{i=1}^{8} \frac{(f_i - e_i)^2}{e_i}$$

	A	B	C	D	E	F
1	**Contingency Table**					
2						
3		*1990*	*1996*	*2000*	*2004*	TOTAL
4	*Democrats*	173	157	136	146	612
5	*Republican*	117	128	117	122	484
6	*Other*	25	43	56	63	187
7	TOTAL	315	328	309	331	1283
8						
9	chi-squared Stat			22.65		
10	df			6		
11	p-value			0.0009		
12	chi-squared Critical			12.5916		

$\chi^2 = 22.65$; p-value = .0009. There is overwhelming evidence to infer that party affiliation in Miami-Dade changed over the four years.

c. Chi-squared test of a contingency table

H_0 : The two variables (County and party in 2004) are independent

H_1 : The two variables are dependent

$$\chi^2 = \sum_{i=1}^{6} \frac{(f_i - e_i)^2}{e_i}$$

	A	B	C	D
1	**Contingency Table**			
2				
3		*Broward*	*Miami-Dade*	TOTAL
4	*Democrats*	152	146	298
5	*Republicans*	87	122	209
6	*Other*	60	63	123
7	TOTAL	299	331	630
8				
9	chi-squared Stat			4.44
10	df			2
11	p-value			0.1085
12	chi-squared Critical			5.9915

$\chi^2 = 4.44$; p-value = 1095. There is not enough evidence to infer that party affiliation differ between Broward County and Miami-Dade County.

A16.16 t-estimator of μ

$$\bar{x} \pm t_{\alpha/2} \frac{s}{\sqrt{n}}$$

	A	B	C	D
1	**t-Estimate: Mean**			
2				
3				*Commute*
4	Mean			24.54
5	Standard Deviation			11.63
6	LCL			23.64
7	UCL			25.45

Total time spent commuting by all workers:
LCL = 129,142,000 (23.64) = 3,052,916,880 minutes
UCL = 129,142,000 (25.45) = 3,286,663,900 minutes

Chapter 17

17.2

	A	B	C	D	E	F
1	SUMMARY OUTPUT					
2						
3	*Regression Statistics*					
4	Multiple R	0.8734				
5	R Square	0.7629				
6	Adjusted R Square	0.7453				
7	Standard Error	3.75				
8	Observations	30				
9						
10	ANOVA					
11		*df*	*SS*	*MS*	*F*	*Significance F*
12	Regression	2	1223.2	611.59	43.43	0.0000
13	Residual	27	380.2	14.08		
14	Total	29	1603.4			
15						
16		*Coefficients*	*Standard Error*	*t Stat*	*P-value*	
17	Intercept	13.01	3.53	3.69	0.0010	
18	Assignment	0.194	0.200	0.97	0.3417	
19	Midterm	1.11	0.122	9.12	0.0000	

a. $\hat{y} = 13.01 + .194x_1 + 1.11x_2$

b. The standard error of estimate is $s_\varepsilon = 3.75$. It is an estimate of the standard deviation of the error variable.

c. The coefficient of determination is $R^2 = .7629$; 76.29% of the variation in final exam marks is explained by the model.

d. $H_0 : \beta_1 = \beta_2 = 0$

H_1 : At least one β_i is not equal to zero

F = 43.43, p-value = 0. There is enough evidence to conclude that the model is valid.

e. $b_1 = .194$; for each addition mark on assignments the final exam mark on average increases by .194 provided that the other variable remains constant.

$b_2 = 1.112$; for each addition midterm mark the final exam mark on average increases by 1.112 provided that the other variable remains constant.

f. $H_0 : \beta_1 = 0$

$H_1 : \beta_1 \neq 0$

t = .97, p-value = .3417. There is not enough evidence to infer that assignment marks and final exam marks are linearly related.

g $H_0 : \beta_2 = 0$

$H_1 : \beta_2 \neq 0$

$t = 9.12$, p-value = 0. There is sufficient evidence to infer that midterm marks and final exam marks are linearly related.

H.

	A	B	C	D
1	**Prediction Interval**			
2				
3			Final	
4				
5	Predicted value		31	
6				
7	Prediction Interval			
8	Lower limit		23	
9	Upper limit		39	
10				
11	Interval Estimate of Expected Value			
12	Lower limit		29	
13	Upper limit		33	

Pat's final exam mark is predicted to lie between 23 and 39

Pat's predicted final grade: LCL = 12 + 14 + 23 = 49, UCL = 12 + 14 + 39 = 65

17.4   a.

	A	B	C	D	E	F
1	SUMMARY OUTPUT					
2						
3	*Regression Statistics*					
4	Multiple R	0.5926				
5	R Square	0.3511				
6	Adjusted R Square	0.3352				
7	Standard Error	6.99				
8	Observations	126				
9						
10	ANOVA					
11		*df*	*SS*	*MS*	*F*	*Significance F*
12	Regression	3	3228	1075.87	22.01	0.0000
13	Residual	122	5965	48.89		
14	Total	125	9192			
15						
16		*Coefficients*	*Standard Error*	*t Stat*	*P-value*	
17	Intercept	-1.97	9.55	-0.21	0.8369	
18	Minor HR	0.666	0.087	7.64	0.0000	
19	Age	0.136	0.524	0.26	0.7961	
20	Years Pro	1.18	0.671	1.75	0.0819	

b $b_1 = .666$; for each additional minor league home run the number of major league home runs increases on average by .666 provided that the other variables remain constant.

$b_2 = .136$; for each additional year of age the number of major league home runs increases on average by .14 provided that the other variables remain constant.

$b_3 = 1.18$; for each additional year as a professional the number of major league home runs increases on average by 1.18 provided that the other variables remain constant.

c. $s_\varepsilon = 6.99$ and $R^2 = .3511$; the model's fit is not very good.

d. $H_0 : \beta_1 = \beta_2 = \beta_3 = 0$

H_1 : At least one β_i is not equal to zero

$F = 22.01$, p-value = 0. There is enough evidence to conclude that the model is valid.

e. $H_0 : \beta_i = 0$

$H_1 : \beta_i \neq 0$

Minor league home runs: $t = 7.64$, p-value = 0

Age: $t = .26$, p-value = .7961

Years professional: $t = 1.75$, p-value = .0819

At the 5% significance level only the number of minor league home runs is linearly related to the number of major league home runs.

f.

	A	B	C	D
1	**Prediction Interval**			
2				
3			Major HR	
4				
5	Predicted value		24.31	
6				
7	Prediction Interval			
8	Lower limit		9.86	
9	Upper limit		38.76	
10				
11	Interval Estimate of Expected Value			
12	Lower limit		20.16	
13	Upper limit		28.45	

We predict that the player will hit between 9.86 (rounded to 10) and 38.76 (rounded to 39) home runs.

g.

	A	B	C	D
1	**Prediction Interval**			
2				
3			Major HR	
4				
5	Predicted value		19.56	
6				
7	Prediction Interval			
8	Lower limit		4.88	
9	Upper limit		34.25	
10				
11	Interval Estimate of Expected Value			
12	Lower limit		14.66	
13	Upper limit		24.47	

It is estimated that the average player will hit between 14.66 and 24.47 home runs.

17.6

	A	B	C	D	E	F
1	SUMMARY OUTPUT					
2						
3	*Regression Statistics*					
4	Multiple R	0.5369				
5	R Square	0.2882				
6	Adjusted R Square	0.2660				
7	Standard Error	2.0302				
8	Observations	100				
9						
10	ANOVA					
11		*df*	*SS*	*MS*	*F*	*Significance F*
12	Regression	3	160.23	53.41	12.96	0.0000
13	Residual	96	395.70	4.12		
14	Total	99	555.93			
15						
16		*Coefficients*	*Standard Error*	*t Stat*	*P-value*	
17	Intercept	0.721	1.87	0.39	0.7006	
18	HS GPA	0.611	0.101	6.06	0.0000	
19	SAT	0.00135	0.00144	0.94	0.3485	
20	Activities	0.0462	0.0641	0.72	0.4720	

b . The coefficient of determination is $R^2 = .2882$; 28.82% of the variation in university GPAs is explained by the model.

c . $H_0 : \beta_1 = \beta_2 = \beta_3 = 0$

H_1 : At least one β_i is not equal to zero

F = 12.96, p-value = 0. There is enough evidence to conclude that the model is valid.

d. $H_0 : \beta_i = 0$

$H_1 : \beta_i \neq 0$

High school GPA: t = 6.06,, p-value = 0

SAT: t = .94, p-value = .3485

Activities: t = .72, p-value = .4720

At the 5% significance level only the high school GPA is linearly related to the university GPA

e.

	A	B	C	D
1	**Prediction Interval**			
2				
3			Univ GPA	
4				
5	Predicted value		8.55	
6				
7	Prediction Interval			
8	Lower limit		4.45	
9	Upper limit		12.65	
10				
11	Interval Estimate of Expected Value			
12	Lower limit		7.79	
13	Upper limit		9.31	

We predict that the student's GPA will fall between 4.45 and 12.00 (12 is the maximum).

f.

	A	B	C	D
1	**Prediction Interval**			
2				
3			Univ GPA	
4				
5	Predicted value		7.56	
6				
7	Prediction Interval			
8	Lower limit		4.12	
9	Upper limit		10.99	
10				
11	Interval Estimate of Expected Value			
12	Lower limit		6.90	
13	Upper limit		8.22	

The mean GPA is estimated to lie between 6.90 and 8.22.

17.8   a.

	A	B	C	D	E	F
1	SUMMARY OUTPUT					
2						
3	*Regression Statistics*					
4	Multiple R	0.4125				
5	R Square	0.1702				
6	Adjusted R Square	0.1645				
7	Standard Error	3.67				
8	Observations	440				
9						
10	ANOVA					
11		*df*	*SS*	*MS*	*F*	*Significance F*
12	Regression	3	1205.93	401.98	29.80	1.52E-17
13	Residual	436	5880.39	13.49		
14	Total	439	7086.32			
15						
16		*Coefficients*	*Standard Error*	*t Stat*	*P-value*	
17	Intercept	7.19	1.09	6.59	1.30E-10	
18	HSize	0.0019	0.0006	3.21	0.0014	
19	Children	1.10	0.14	7.84	3.58E-14	
20	Adults	1.04	0.23	4.48	9.58E-06	

b. $H_0 : \beta_1 = \beta_2 = \beta_3 = 0$

H_1 : At least one β_i is not equal to zero

F = 29.80, p-value = 0. There is enough evidence to conclude that the model is valid.

c. b_1 = .0019; for each additional square foot the amount of garbage increases on average by .0019 pounds holding the other variables constant.

b_2 = 1.10; for each additional child in the home the amount of garbage increases on average by 1.10 holding the other variables constant.

b_3 = 1.04; for each additional adult at home during the day the amount of garbage increases on average by 1.04 holding the other variables constant.

d. $H_0 : \beta_i = 0$

$H_1 : \beta_i \neq 0$

House size : t = 3.21, p-value = .0014

Number of children: t = 7.84 p-value = 0

Number of adults at home: t = 4.48, p-value = 0

All three independent variable are linearly related to the amount of garbage.

17.10 a.

	A	B	C	D	E	F
1	SUMMARY OUTPUT					
2						
3	*Regression Statistics*					
4	Multiple R	0.8608				
5	R Square	0.7411				
6	Adjusted R Square	0.7301				
7	Standard Error	2.66				
8	Observations	100				
9						
10	ANOVA					
11		*df*	*SS*	*MS*	*F*	*Significance F*
12	Regression	4	1930	482.38	67.97	0.0000
13	Residual	95	674	7.10		
14	Total	99	2604			
15						
16		*Coefficients*	*Standard Error*	*t Stat*	*P-value*	
17	Intercept	3.24	5.42	0.60	0.5512	
18	Mother	0.451	0.0545	8.27	0.0000	
19	Father	0.411	0.0498	8.26	0.0000	
20	Gmothers	0.0166	0.0661	0.25	0.8028	
21	Gfathers	0.0869	0.0657	1.32	0.1890	

b. $H_0 : \beta_1 = \beta_2 = \beta_3 = 0$

H_1 : At least one β_i is not equal to zero

$F = 67.97$, p-value = 0. There is enough evidence to conclude that the model is valid.

c. $b_1 = .451$; for each one year increase in the mother's age the customer's age increases on average by .451 provided the other variables are constant (which may not be possible because of the multicollinearity).

$b_2 = .411$; for each one year increase in the father's age the customer's age increases on average by .411 provided the other variables are constant.

$b_3 = .0166$; for each one year increase in the grandmothers' mean age the customer's age increases on average by .0166 provided the other variables are constant.

$b_4 = .0869$; for each one year increase in the grandfathers' mean age the customer's age increases on average by .0869 provided the other variables are constant.

$H_0 : \beta_i = 0$

$H_1 : \beta_i \neq 0$

Mothers: $t = 8.27$, p-value = 0

Fathers: $t = 8.26$, p-value = 0

Grandmothers: $t = .25$, p-value .8028

Grandfathers: t = 1.32, p-value = .1890

The ages of mothers and fathers are linearly related to the ages of their children. The other two variables are not.

d.

	A	B	C	D
1	**Prediction Interval**			
2				
3			Longvity	
4				
5	Predicted value		71.43	
6				
7	Prediction Interval			
8	Lower limit		65.54	
9	Upper limit		77.31	
10				
11	Interval Estimate of Expected Value			
12	Lower limit		68.85	
13	Upper limit		74.00	

The man is predicted to live to an age between 65.54 and 77.31

e.

	A	B	C	D
1	**Prediction Interval**			
2				
3			Longvity	
4				
5	Predicted value		71.71	
6				
7	Prediction Interval			
8	Lower limit		65.65	
9	Upper limit		77.77	
10				
11	Interval Estimate of Expected Value			
12	Lower limit		68.75	
13	Upper limit		74.66	

The mean longevity is estimated to fall between 68.75 and 74.66.

17.12

	A	B	C	D	E	F
1	SUMMARY OUTPUT					
2						
3	*Regression Statistics*					
4	Multiple R	0.8984				
5	R Square	0.8072				
6	Adjusted R Square	0.7990				
7	Standard Error	7.07				
8	Observations	50				
9						
10	ANOVA					
11		*df*	*SS*	*MS*	*F*	*Significance F*
12	Regression	2	9,832	4,916	98.37	0.0000
13	Residual	47	2,349	49.97		
14	Total	49	12,181			
15						
16		*Coefficients*	*Standard Error*	*t Stat*	*P-value*	
17	Intercept	-28.43	6.89	-4.13	0.0001	
18	Boxes	0.604	0.0557	10.85	0.0000	
19	Weight	0.374	0.0847	4.42	0.0001	

a. $\hat{y} = -28.43 + .604x_1 + .374x_2$

b. $s_\varepsilon = 7.07$ and $R^2 = .8072$; the model fits well.

c. $b_1 = .604$; for each one additional box, the amount of time to unload increases on average by .604 minutes provided the weight is constant.

$b_2 = .374$; for each additional hundred pounds the amount of time to unload increases on average by 374 minutes provided the number of boxes is constant.

$H_0 : \beta_i = 0$

$H_1 : \beta_i \neq 0$

Boxes: t = 10.85, p-value = 0

Weight: t = 4.42, p-value = .0001

Both variables are linearly related to time to unload.

d & e

	A	B	C	D
1	**Prediction Interval**			
2				
3			Time	
4				
5	Predicted value		50.70	
6				
7	Prediction Interval			
8	Lower limit		35.16	
9	Upper limit		66.24	
10				
11	Interval Estimate of Expected Value			
12	Lower limit		44.43	
13	Upper limit		56.96	

d.   It is predicted that the truck will be unloaded in a time between 35.16 and 66.24 minutes.

e.   The mean time to unload the trucks is estimated to lie between 44.43 and 56.96 minutes.

17.14   a.

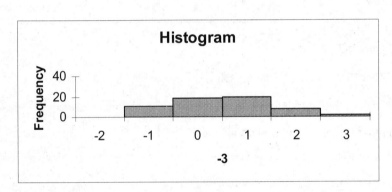

The normality requirement is satisfied.

b.

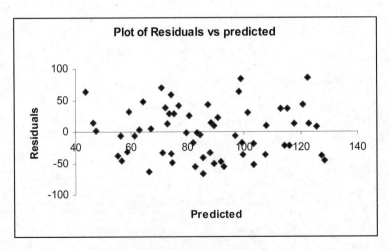

The variance of the error variable appears to be constant.

17.16   b.

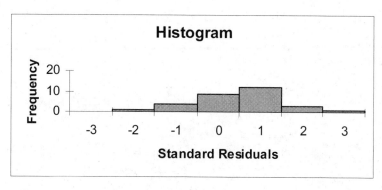

The normality requirement has not been violated.

c

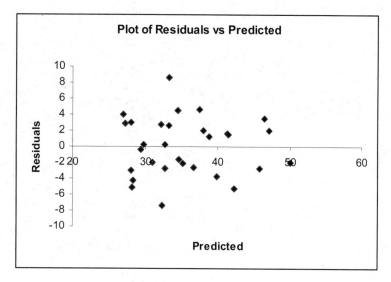

The variance of the error variable appears to be constant.

d.

	A	B	C
1		*Assignment*	*Midterm*
2	Assignment	1	
3	Midterm	0.1037	1

The lack of multicollinearity means that the t–tests were valid.

17.18   a.

	A	B	C	D
1		*Minor HR*	*Age*	*Years Pro*
2	Minor HR	1		
3	Age	0.0354	1	
4	Years Pro	-0.0392	0.7355	1

Age and years as a professional are highly correlated. The correlations of the other combinations are small.

b.   The t–tests may not be valid.

17.20

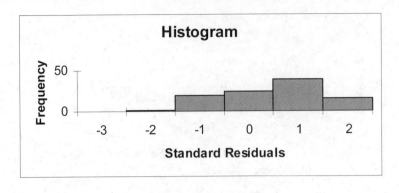

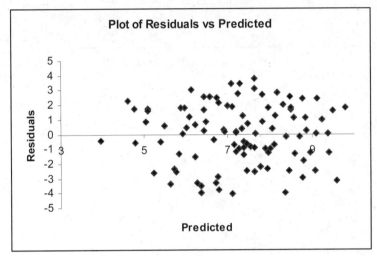

The error variable is approximately normally distributed and the variance is constant.

17.22

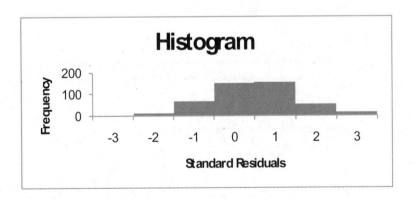

The error appears to be normally distributed.

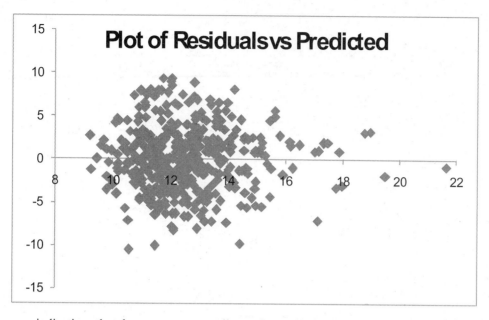

There are indications that the error grows smaller as the predicted value increases. However, overall the requirement of constant variance may be valid.

17.24   a.

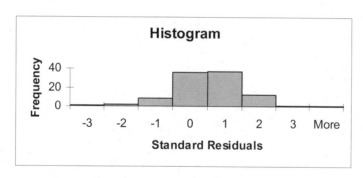

The normality requirement is satisfied.

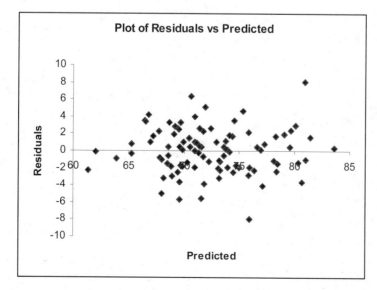

The variance of the error variable is constant.

c.

	A	B	C	D	E
1		*Mother*	*Father*	*Gmothers*	*Gfathers*
2	Mother	1			
3	Father	0.2766	1		
4	Gmothers	0.4343	0.2409	1	
5	Gfathers	0.3910	0.3752	-0.0077	1

The correlations are large enough to cause problems with the t–tests.

17.26

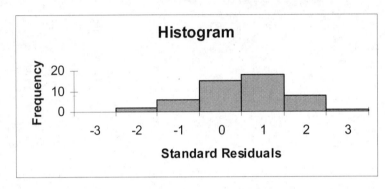

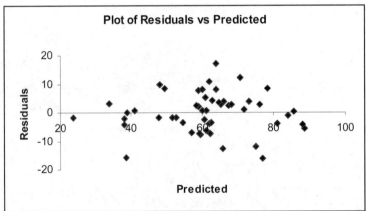

c.   The error variable appears to be normally distributed. The variance of the errors appears to be constant.

17.28

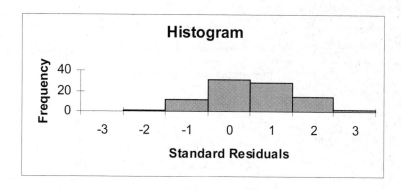

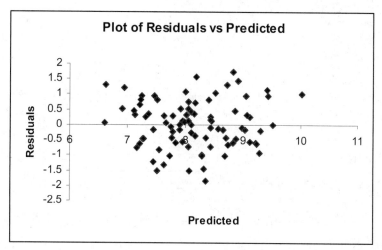

The requirements are satisfied.

17.30 $d_L = 1.16$, $d_U = 1.59$, $4 - d_U = 2.41$, $4 - d_L = 2.84$. There is evidence of negative first–order autocorrelation.

17.32 $d_L = 1.46$, $d_U = 1.63$. There is evidence of positive first–order autocorrelation.

17.34 $4 - d_U = 4 - 1.73 = 2.27$, $4 - d_L = 4 - 1.19 = 2.81$. There is no evidence of negative first–order autocorrelation.

17.36 a.   The regression equation is $\hat{y} = 2260 + .423x$

b.

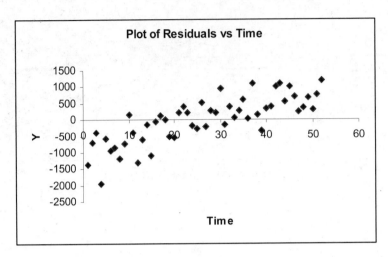

There appears to be a strong autocorrelation.

c.

	A	B	C
1	**Durbin-Watson Statistic**		
2			
3	d = 0.7859		

$d_L \approx 1.50$, $d_U \approx 1.59$, $4 - d_U \approx 2.41$, $4 - d_L \approx \approx 2.50$. There is evidence of first–order autocorrelation.

d.   The model is $y = \beta_0 + \beta_1 x + \beta_2 t + \varepsilon$

The regression equation is $\hat{y} = 446.2 + 1.10x + 38.92t$

e.

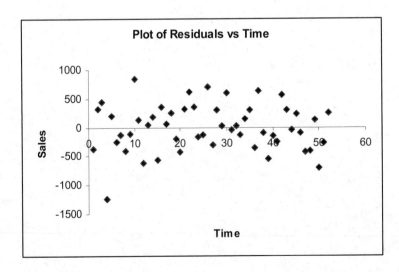

	A	B	C
1	**Durbin-Watson Statistic**		
2			
3	d = 2.2631		

There is no evidence of autocorrelation.

First model: $s_\varepsilon = 709.7$ and $R^2 = .0146$. Second model: $s_\varepsilon = 413.7$ and $R^2 = .6718$.
The second model fits better.

17.38

	A	B	C
1	**Durbin-Watson Statistic**		
2			
3	d = 2.2003		

$d = 2.2003$; $d_L = 1.30$, $d_U = 1.46$, $4 - d_U = 2.70$, $4 - d_L = 2.54$. There is no evidence of first–order

autocorrelation.

17.40 a.

	A	B	C	D	E	F
1	SUMMARY OUTPUT					
2						
3	*Regression Statistics*					
4	Multiple R	0.6894				
5	R Square	0.4752				
6	Adjusted R Square	0.4363				
7	Standard Error	63.08				
8	Observations	30				
9						
10	ANOVA					
11		*df*	*SS*	*MS*	*F*	*Significance F*
12	Regression	2	97283	48641	12.23	0.0002
13	Residual	27	107428	3979		
14	Total	29	204711			
15						
16		*Coefficients*	*Standard Error*	*t Stat*	*P-value*	
17	Intercept	164.01	35.9	4.57	9.60E-05	
18	Fetilizer	0.140	0.081	1.72	0.0974	
19	Water	0.0313	0.0067	4.64	8.08E-05	

For each additional unit of fertilizer crop yield increases on average by .140 (holding the amount of water
constant).

For each additional unit of water crop yield increases on average by .0313 (holding the fertilizer constant).

b. $H_0 : \beta_1 = 0$

$H_1 : \beta_1 \neq 0$

t = 1.72, p-value = .0974. There is not enough evidence to conclude that there is a linear relationship between crop yield and amount of fertilizer.

c. $H_0 : \beta_2 = 0$

       $H_1 : \beta_2 \neq 0$

t = 4.64, p-value = .0001. There is enough evidence to conclude that there is a linear relationship between crop yield and amount of water.

d. $s_\varepsilon = 63.08$ and $R^2 = .4752$; the model fits moderately well.

e.

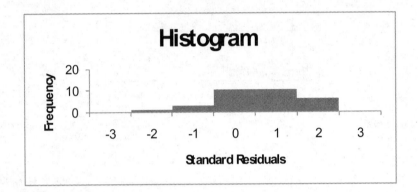

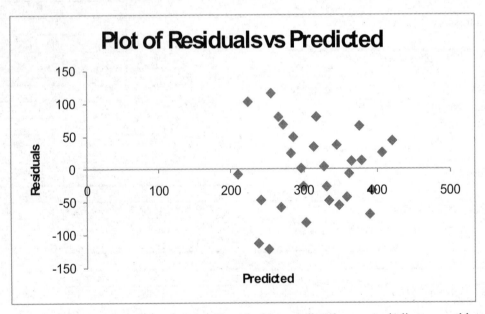

The errors appear to be normal, but the plot of residuals vs predicted aeems to indicate a problem.

f.

	A	B
1	**Prediction Interval**	
2		
3		Yield
4		
5	Predicted value	209.3
6		
7	Prediction Interval	
8	Lower limit	69.2
9	Upper limit	349.3
10		
11	Interval Estimate of Expected Value	
12	Lower limit	155.7
13	Upper limit	262.8
14		

We predict that the crop yield will fall between 69.2 and 349.3.

17.42 a.

	A	B	C	D	E	F
1	SUMMARY OUTPUT					
2						
3	*Regression Statistics*					
4	Multiple R	0.7825				
5	R Square	0.6123				
6	Adjusted R Square	0.5835				
7	Standard Error	2.16				
8	Observations	30				
9						
10	ANOVA					
11		*df*	*SS*	*MS*	*F*	*Significance F*
12	Regression	2	199.65	99.82	21.32	0.0000
13	Residual	27	126.44	4.68		
14	Total	29	326.09			
15						
16		*Coefficients*	*Standard Error*	*t Stat*	*P-value*	
17	Intercept	29.60	2.08	14.22	0.0000	
18	Vacancy	-0.309	0.067	-4.58	0.0001	
19	Unemployment	-1.11	0.24	-4.73	0.0001	

b. $R^2 = .6123$; 61.23 % of the variation in rents is explained by the independent variables.

c. $H_0 : \beta_1 = \beta_2 = 0$

H_1 : At least one β_i is not equal to zero

F = 21.32, p-value = 0. There is enough evidence to conclude that the model is valid.

d. $H_0 : \beta_i = 0$

$H_1 : \beta_i \neq 0$

Vacancy rate: $t = -4.58$, p-value = .0001

Unemployment rate: $t = -4.73$, p-value = .0001

Both vacancy and unemployment rates are linearly related to rents.

e.

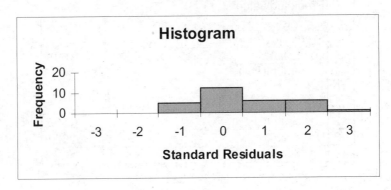

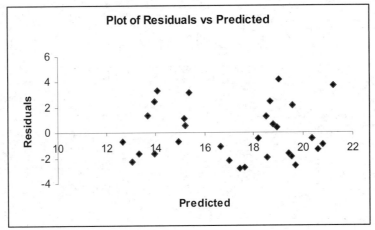

The error is approximately normally distributed with a constant variance.

f.

	A	B	C
1	**Durbin-Watson Statistic**		
2			
3	d = 2.0687		

$d_L = 1.28$, $d_U = 1.57$, $4 - d_U = 2.72$, $4 - d_L = 2.43$. There is no evidence of first–order autocorrelation.

g.

	A	B	C	D
1	**Prediction Interval**			
2				
3			Rent	
4				
5	Predicted value		18.72	
6				
7	Prediction Interval			
8	Lower limit		14.18	
9	Upper limit		23.27	
10				
11	Interval Estimate of Expected Value			
12	Lower limit		17.76	
13	Upper limit		19.68	

The city's office rent is predicted to lie between $14.18 and $23.27.

Appendix 17

A17.2 t-test of μ_D

H_0: $\mu_D = 0$

H_1: $\mu_D > 0$

$$t = \frac{\bar{x}_D - \mu_D}{s_D / \sqrt{n_D}}$$

	A	B	C
1	t-Test: Paired Two Sample for Means		
2			
3		*Eye-level*	*Lower shelf*
4	Mean	302.4	290.8
5	Variance	2482.2	6262.7
6	Observations	40	40
7	Pearson Correlation	0.7334	
8	Hypothesized Mean Difference	0	
9	df	39	
10	t Stat	1.35	
11	P(T<=t) one-tail	0.0922	
12	t Critical one-tail	1.6849	
13	P(T<=t) two-tail	0.1845	
14	t Critical two-tail	2.0227	

t = 1.35; p-value = .0922. There is not enough evidence to conclude that placement of the product at eye level significantly increases sales?

A17.4 Chi-squared test of a contingency table

H_0 : The two variables are independent

H_1 : The two variables are dependent

$$\chi^2 = \sum_{i=1}^{6} \frac{(f_i - e_i)^2}{e_i}$$

	A	B	C	D	E
1	**Contingency Table**				
2					
3		*Group*			
4	*Choice*		1	2	TOTAL
5		1	7	19	26
6		2	8	17	25
7		3	11	14	25
8		TOTAL	26	50	76
9					
10					
11		chi-squared Stat			1.73
12		df			2
13		p-value			0.4206
14		chi-squared Critical			5.9915

$\chi^2 = 1.73$, p-value = .4206. There is not enough evidence to infer that there is a relationship between choices students make and their level of intoxication.

A17.6   z-estimator of p

$$\hat{p} \pm z_{\alpha/2}\sqrt{\hat{p}(1-\hat{p})/n}$$

	A	B
1	**z-Estimate: Proportion**	
2		*Photography*
3	Sample Proportion	0.124
4	Observations	283
5	LCL	0.085
6	UCL	0.162

Confidence interval estimate of the total number of American adults who participate in photography
LCL = 205.8 million (.085) = 17.493 million
UCL = 205.8 million (.162) = 33.396 million

A17.8   Ch-squared test of a contingency table

H_0 : The two variables are independent

H_1 : The two variables are dependent

$$\chi^2 = \sum_{i=1}^{12} \frac{(f_i - e_i)^2}{e_i}$$

	A	B	C	D	E
1	**Contingency Table**				
2					
3		*Age category*			
4	*Mutual fund*		1	2	TOTAL
5		1	19	6	25
6		2	75	57	132
7		3	92	123	215
8		4	89	109	198
9		5	63	77	140
10		6	73	43	116
11		TOTAL	411	415	826
12					
13					
14		chi-squared Stat			24.84
15		df			5
16		p-value			0.0001
17		chi-squared Critical			11.0705

$\chi^2 = 24.84$; p-value = .0001. There is enough evidence to infer that the age of the head of the household is related to whether he or she owns mutual funds.

A17.10 Chi-squared test of a contingency table

H_0 : The two variables are independent

H_1 : The two variables are dependent

$$\chi^2 = \sum_{i=1}^{8} \frac{(f_i - e_i)^2}{e_i}$$

	A	B	C	D	E
1	**Contingency Table**				
2					
3		Weight category			
4	Hip/Knee		1	2	TOTAL
5		1	9	6	15
6		2	113	60	173
7		3	184	166	350
8		4	165	272	437
9		TOTAL	471	504	975
10					
11					
12		chi-squared Stat			42.89
13		df			3
14		p-value			0
15		chi-squared Critical			7.8147

$\chi^2 = 42.89$; p-value = 0. There is enough evidence to conclude that weight and the joint needing replacement are related.

A17.12

	A	B	C	D	E	F
1	SUMMARY OUTPUT					
2						
3	Regression Statistics					
4	Multiple R	0.8415				
5	R Square	0.7081				
6	Adjusted R Square	0.7021				
7	Standard Error	213.7				
8	Observations	100				
9						
10	ANOVA					
11		df	SS	MS	F	Significance F
12	Regression	2	10,744,454	5,372,227	117.6	0.0000
13	Residual	97	4,429,664	45,667		
14	Total	99	15,174,118			
15						
16		Coefficients	Standard Error	t Stat	P-value	
17	Intercept	576.8	514.0	1.12	0.2646	
18	Space	90.61	6.48	13.99	0.0000	
19	Water	9.66	2.41	4.00	0.0001	

a. The regression equation is $\hat{y} = 576.8 + 90.61x_1 + 9.66x_2$

b. The coefficient of determination is $R^2 = .7081$; 70.81% of the variation in electricity consumption is explained by the model. The model fits reasonably well.

c. $H_0 : \beta_1 = \beta_2 = 0$

H_1 : At least one β_i is not equal to zero

$F = 117.6$, p-value = 0. There is enough evidence to conclude that the model is valid.

d. & e.

	A	B	C	D
1	**Prediction Interval**			
2				
3			Consumption	
4				
5	Predicted value		8175	
6				
7	Prediction Interval			
8	Lower limit		7748	
9	Upper limit		8601	
10				
11	Interval Estimate of Expected Value			
12	Lower limit		8127	
13	Upper limit		8222	

e. We predict that the house will consume between 7748 and 8601 units of electricity.

f. We estimate that the average house will consume between 8127 and 8222 units of electricity.

A17.14 Multiple regression, test of coefficients

$$t = \frac{b_i - \beta_i}{s_{b_i}}$$

The ordinary multiple regression model fit quite well. The coefficient of determination is .7042 and the p-value of the F-test is 0. However, no independent variable is linearly related to salary. This is a clear sign of multicollinearity. Stepwise regression was used with the outcome shown below.

The only independent variables that are linearly related to salary are assists in 1992-93 and goals in 1992-93. It appears that players' salaries are most strongly related to the number of goals and the number of assists in the previous season.

	M	N	O	P	Q	R	S
1	**Results of stepwise regression**						
2							
3	**Step 1 - Entering variable: Ast92_93**						
4							
5	Summary measures						
6		Multiple R	0.7725				
7		R-Square	0.5967				
8		Adj R-Square	0.5883				
9		StErr of Est	380046.1250				
10							
11	ANOVA Table						
12		Source	df	SS	MS	F	p-value
13		Explained	1	10258242603399.2000	10258242603399.2000	71.0232	0.0000
14		Unexplained	48	6932882522112.0000	144435052544.0000		
15							
16	Regression coefficients						
17			Coefficient	Std Err	t-value	p-value	
18		Constant	38325.8711	82112.9297	0.4667	0.6428	
19		Ast92_93	25746.7754	3055.0806	8.4275	0.0000	
20							
21	**Step 2 - Entering variable: Goal92_93**						
22							
23	Summary measures			Change	% Change		
24		Multiple R	0.8086	0.0361	%4.7		
25		R-Square	0.6538	0.0571	%9.6		
26		Adj R-Square	0.6390	0.0507	%8.6		
27		StErr of Est	355859.9375	-24186.1875	-%6.4		
28							
29	ANOVA Table						
30		Source	df	SS	MS	F	p-value
31		Explained	2	11239219530119.2000	5619609765059.6100	44.3760	0.0000
32		Unexplained	47	5951905595392.0000	126636289263.6600		
33							
34	Regression coefficients						
35			Coefficient	Std Err	t-value	p-value	
36		Constant	65924.4297	77524.0313	0.8504	0.3994	
37		Ast92_93	14124.2783	5061.7593	2.7904	0.0076	
38		Goal92_93	18523.1426	6655.2490	2.7832	0.0077	

A17.16 t-estimator of μ

$$\bar{x} \pm t_{\alpha/2} \frac{s}{\sqrt{n}}$$

	A	B	C	D
1	**t-Estimate: Mean**			
2				
3				*Acres*
4	Mean			676.1
5	Standard Deviation			140.5
6	LCL			664.1
7	UCL			688.2

Estimate of total farmland:
LCL = 229,373(664.1) = 152,326,609 acres
UCL = 229,373(688.2) = 157,854,499 acres

Chapter 18

18.2   a.

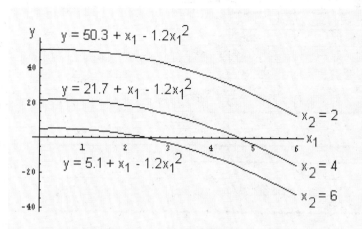

    b.

18.4   a.   First–order model: a Demand $= \beta_0 + \beta_1 \text{Price} + \varepsilon$

        Second–order model: a Demand $= \beta_0 + \beta_1 \text{Price} + \beta_2 \text{Price}^2 + \varepsilon$

        First–order model:

	A	B	C	D	E	F
1	SUMMARY OUTPUT					
2						
3	*Regression Statistics*					
4	Multiple R	0.9249				
5	R Square	0.8553				
6	Adjusted R Square	0.8473				
7	Standard Error	13.29				
8	Observations	20				
9						
10	ANOVA					
11		*df*	*SS*	*MS*	*F*	*Significance F*
12	Regression	1	18,798	18,798	106.44	0.0000
13	Residual	18	3,179	176.6		
14	Total	19	21,977			
15						
16		*Coefficients*	*Standard Error*	*t Stat*	*P-value*	
17	Intercept	453.6	15.18	29.87	0.0000	
18	Price	-68.91	6.68	-10.32	0.0000	

Second–order model:

	A	B	C	D	E	F
1	SUMMARY OUTPUT					
2						
3	*Regression Statistics*					
4	Multiple R	0.9862				
5	R Square	0.9726				
6	Adjusted R Square	0.9693				
7	Standard Error	5.96				
8	Observations	20				
9						
10	ANOVA					
11		*df*	*SS*	*MS*	*F*	*Significance F*
12	Regression	2	21,374	10,687	301.15	0.0000
13	Residual	17	603	35.49		
14	Total	19	21,977			
15						
16		*Coefficients*	*Standard Error*	*t Stat*	*P-value*	
17	Intercept	766.9	37.40	20.50	0.0000	
18	Price	-359.1	34.19	-10.50	0.0000	
19	Price-sq	64.55	7.58	8.52	0.0000	

c. The second order model fits better because its standard error of estimate is 5.96, whereas that of the first–order models is 13.29

d. $\hat{y} = 766.9 - 359.1(2.95) + 64.55(2.95)^2 = 269.3$

18.6　a.　MBA GPA $= \beta_0 + \beta_1 \text{UnderGPA} + \beta_2 \text{GMAT} + \beta_3 \text{Work} + \beta_4 \text{UnderGPA} \times \text{GMAT} + \varepsilon$

b.

	A	B	C	D	E	F
1	SUMMARY OUTPUT					
2						
3	*Regression Statistics*					
4	Multiple R	0.6836				
5	R Square	0.4674				
6	Adjusted R Square	0.4420				
7	Standard Error	0.790				
8	Observations	89				
9						
10	ANOVA					
11		*df*	*SS*	*MS*	*F*	*Significance F*
12	Regression	4	45.97	11.49	18.43	0.0000
13	Residual	84	52.40	0.62		
14	Total	88	98.37			
15						
16		*Coefficients*	*Standard Error*	*t Stat*	*P-value*	
17	Intercept	-11.11	14.97	-0.74	0.4601	
18	UnderGPA	1.19	1.46	0.82	0.4159	
19	GMAT	0.0311	0.0255	1.22	0.2265	
20	Work	0.0956	0.0312	3.06	0.0030	
21	UGPA-GMAT	-0.0019	0.0025	-0.78	0.4392	

$F = 18.43$, p-value $= 0$; $s_\varepsilon = .790$ and $R^2 = .4674$. The model is valid, but the fit is relatively poor.

c.　MBA example $s_\varepsilon = .788$ and $R^2 = .4635$. There is little difference between the fits of the two models.

18.8　a.

	A	B	C	D	E	F
1	SUMMARY OUTPUT					
2						
3	*Regression Statistics*					
4	Multiple R	0.9255				
5	R Square	0.8566				
6	Adjusted R Square	0.8362				
7	Standard Error	5.20				
8	Observations	25				
9						
10	ANOVA					
11		*df*	*SS*	*MS*	*F*	*Significance F*
12	Regression	3	3398.7	1132.9	41.83	0.0000
13	Residual	21	568.8	27.08		
14	Total	24	3967.4			
15						
16		*Coefficients*	*Standard Error*	*t Stat*	*P-value*	
17	Intercept	260.7	162.3	1.61	0.1230	
18	Temperature	-3.32	2.09	-1.59	0.1270	
19	Currency	-164.3	667.1	-0.25	0.8078	
20	Temp-Curr	3.64	8.54	0.43	0.6741	

b.

	A	B	C	D	E	F
1	SUMMARY OUTPUT					
2						
3	*Regression Statistics*					
4	Multiple R	0.9312				
5	R Square	0.8671				
6	Adjusted R Square	0.8322				
7	Standard Error	5.27				
8	Observations	25				
9						
10	ANOVA					
11		*df*	*SS*	*MS*	*F*	*Significance F*
12	Regression	5	3440.3	688.1	24.80	0.0000
13	Residual	19	527.1	27.74		
14	Total	24	3967.4			
15						
16		*Coefficients*	*Standard Error*	*t Stat*	*P-value*	
17	Intercept	274.8	283.8	0.97	0.3449	
18	Temperature	-1.72	6.88	-0.25	0.8053	
19	Currency	-828.6	888.5	-0.93	0.3627	
20	Temp-sq	-0.0024	0.0475	-0.05	0.9608	
21	Curr-sq	2054.0	1718.5	1.20	0.2467	
22	Temp-Curr	-0.870	10.57	-0.08	0.9353	

c.   Both models fit equally well. The standard errors of estimate and coefficients of determination are quite similar.

18.10 a.   Yield = $\beta_0 + \beta_1$ Pressure + β_2 Temperature + β_3 Pressure^2 + β_4 Temperature^2 + β_5 Pressure Temperature + ε

b.

	A	B	C	D	E	F
1	SUMMARY OUTPUT					
2						
3	*Regression Statistics*					
4	Multiple R	0.8290				
5	R Square	0.6872				
6	Adjusted R Square	0.6661				
7	Standard Error	512				
8	Observations	80				
9						
10	ANOVA					
11		*df*	*SS*	*MS*	*F*	*Significance F*
12	Regression	5	42,657,846	8,531,569	32.52	0.0000
13	Residual	74	19,413,277	262,342		
14	Total	79	62,071,123			
15						
16		*Coefficients*	*Standard Error*	*t Stat*	*P-value*	
17	Intercept	74462	7526	9.89	0.0000	
18	Pressure	14.40	5.92	2.43	0.0174	
19	Temperature	-613.3	59.95	-10.23	0.0000	
20	Press-sq	-0.0159	0.0032	-5.04	0.0000	
21	Temp-sq	1.23	0.12	9.86	0.0000	
22	Press-temp	0.0381	0.0174	2.19	0.0316	

c. $s_\varepsilon = 512$ and $R^2 = .6872$. The model's fit is good.

18.12 a. $I_1 = 1$ if Catholic

$I_1 = 0$ otherwise

$I_2 = 1$ if Protestant

$I_2 = 0$ otherwise

b. $I_1 = 1$ if 8:00 A.M. to 4:00 P.M.

$I_1 = 0$ otherwise

$I_2 = 1$ if 4:00 P.M. to midnight

$I_2 = 0$ otherwise

c. $I_1 = 1$ if Jack Jones

$I_1 = 0$ otherwise

$I_2 = 1$ if Mary Brown

$I_2 = 0$ otherwise

$I_3 = 1$ if George Fosse

$I_3 = 0$ otherwise

18.14 a.

	A	B	C	D
1	**Prediction Interval**			
2				
3			MBA GPA	
4				
5	Predicted value		10.11	
6				
7	Prediction Interval			
8	Lower limit		8.55	
9	Upper limit		11.67	
10				
11	Interval Estimate of Expected Value			
12	Lower limit		9.53	
13	Upper limit		10.68	

Prediction: MBA GPA will lie between 8.55 and 11.67

b.

	A	B	C	D
1	**Prediction Interval**			
2				
3			MBA GPA	
4				
5	Predicted value		9.73	
6				
7	Prediction Interval			
8	Lower limit		8.15	
9	Upper limit		11.31	
10				
11	Interval Estimate of Expected Value			
12	Lower limit		9.10	
13	Upper limit		10.36	

Prediction: MBA GPA will lie between 8.15 and 11.31

18.16   a.

	A	B	C	D	E	F
1	SUMMARY OUTPUT					
2						
3	*Regression Statistics*					
4	Multiple R	0.8368				
5	R Square	0.7002				
6	Adjusted R Square	0.6659				
7	Standard Error	810.8				
8	Observations	40				
9						
10	ANOVA					
11		*df*	*SS*	*MS*	*F*	*Significance F*
12	Regression	4	53,729,535	13,432,384	20.43	0.0000
13	Residual	35	23,007,438	657,355		
14	Total	39	76,736,973			
15						
16		*Coefficients*	*Standard Error*	*t Stat*	*P-value*	
17	Intercept	3490	469.2	7.44	0.0000	
18	Yest Att	0.369	0.078	4.73	0.0000	
19	I1	1623	492.5	3.30	0.0023	
20	I2	733.5	394.4	1.86	0.0713	
21	I3	-765.5	484.7	-1.58	0.1232	

b. $H_0 : \beta_1 = \beta_2 = \beta_3 = \beta_4 = 0$

H_1 : At least on β_i is not equal to 0

$F = 20.43$, p-value = 0. There is enough evidence to infer that the model is valid.

c. $H_0 : \beta_i = 0$

$H_1 : \beta_i \neq 0$

I_2 : t = 1.86, p-value = .0713

I_3 : t = −1.58, p-value = .1232

Weather is not a factor in attendance.

d. $H_0 : \beta_2 = 0$

$H_1 : \beta_2 > 0$

t = 3.30, p-value = .0023/2 = .0012. There is sufficient evidence to infer that weekend attendance is larger than weekday attendance.

18.18 a.

	A	B	C	D	E	F
1	SUMMARY OUTPUT					
2						
3	*Regression Statistics*					
4	Multiple R	0.5602				
5	R Square	0.3138				
6	Adjusted R Square	0.2897				
7	Standard Error	5.84				
8	Observations	60				
9						
10	ANOVA					
11		*df*	*SS*	*MS*	*F*	*Significance F*
12	Regression	2	887.9	443.95	13.03	0.0000
13	Residual	57	1941.7	34.06		
14	Total	59	2829.6			
15						
16		*Coefficients*	*Standard Error*	*t Stat*	*P-value*	
17	Intercept	7.02	3.24	2.17	0.0344	
18	Length	0.250	0.056	4.46	0.0000	
19	Type	-1.35	0.947	-1.43	0.1589	

b. $H_0 : \beta_2 = 0$

$H_1 : \beta_2 \neq 0$

t = −1.43, p-value = .1589. There is not enough evidence to infer that the type of commercial affects memory test scores.

c.   Let

$I_1 = 1$ if humorous

$I_1 = 0$ otherwise

$I_2 = 1$ if musical

$I_2 = 0$ otherwise

	A	B	C	D	E	F
1	SUMMARY OUTPUT					
2						
3	*Regression Statistics*					
4	Multiple R	0.6231				
5	R Square	0.3882				
6	Adjusted R Square	0.3554				
7	Standard Error	5.56				
8	Observations	60				
9						
10	ANOVA					
11		*df*	*SS*	*MS*	*F*	*Significance F*
12	Regression	3	1099	366.17	11.85	0.0000
13	Residual	56	1731	30.91		
14	Total	59	2830			
15						
16		*Coefficients*	*Standard Error*	*t Stat*	*P-value*	
17	Intercept	2.53	2.15	1.18	0.2445	
18	Length	0.223	0.054	4.10	0.0001	
19	I1	2.91	1.81	1.61	0.1130	
20	I2	5.50	1.83	3.01	0.0039	

d. $H_0 : \beta_i = 0$

$H_1 : \beta_i \neq 0$

I1: t = 1.61, p-value = .1130

I2: t = 3.01, p-value = .0039

There is enough evidence to infer that there is a difference in memory test scores between watchers of humorous and serious commercials.

e. The variable type of commercial in parts (a) and (b) is nominal. It is usually meaningless to conduct a regression analysis with such variables without converting them to indicator variables.

18.20 a. Let

$I_1 = 1$ if no scorecard

$I_1 = 0$ otherwise

$I_2 = 1$ if scorecard overturned more than 10% of the time

$I_2 = 0$ otherwise

b.

	A	B	C	D	E	F
1	SUMMARY OUTPUT					
2						
3	*Regression Statistics*					
4	Multiple R	0.7299				
5	R Square	0.5327				
6	Adjusted R Square	0.5181				
7	Standard Error	4.20				
8	Observations	100				
9						
10	ANOVA					
11		*df*	*SS*	*MS*	*F*	*Significance F*
12	Regression	3	1933	644.46	36.48	0.0000
13	Residual	96	1696	17.67		
14	Total	99	3629			
15						
16		*Coefficients*	*Standard Error*	*t Stat*	*P-value*	
17	Intercept	4.65	2.06	2.26	0.0260	
18	Loan Size	0.00012	0.00015	0.83	0.4084	
19	I1	4.08	1.14	3.57	0.0006	
20	I2	10.18	1.01	10.08	0.0000	

c. $s_\varepsilon = 4.20$ and $R^2 = .5327$. The model's fit is mediocre.

d.

	A	B	C	D	E
1		*Pct Bad*	*Loan Size*	*I1*	*I2*
2	Pct Bad	1			
3	Loan Size	0.1099	1		
4	I1	-0.1653	-0.0346	1	
5	I2	0.6835	0.0737	-0.5471	1

There is a high correlation between I_1 and I_2 that may distort the t–tests.

e. $b_1 = .00012$; in this sample for each additional dollar lent the default rate increases by .00012 provided the other variables remain the same.

$b_2 = 4.08$; In this sample banks that don't use scorecards on average have default rates 4.08 percentage points higher than banks that overturn their scorecards less than 10% of the time.

$b_3 = 10.18$; In this sample banks that overturn their scorecards more than 10% of the time on average have default rates 10.18 percentage points higher than banks that overturn their scorecards less than 10% of the time.

f.

	A	B	C	D
1	**Prediction Interval**			
2				
3			Pct Bad	
4				
5	Predicted value		9.94	
6				
7	Prediction Interval			
8	Lower limit		1.39	
9	Upper limit		18.49	
10				
11	Interval Estimate of Expected Value			
12	Lower limit		8.08	
13	Upper limit		11.81	

We predict that the bank's default rate will fall between 1.39 and 18.49%.

18.22   a.

	A	B	C	D	E	F
1	SUMMARY OUTPUT					
2						
3	*Regression Statistics*					
4	Multiple R	0.7296				
5	R Square	0.5323				
6	Adjusted R Square	0.5075				
7	Standard Error	2.36				
8	Observations	100				
9						
10	ANOVA					
11		*df*	*SS*	*MS*	*F*	*Significance F*
12	Regression	5	593.9	118.78	21.40	3.08E-14
13	Residual	94	521.7	5.55		
14	Total	99	1115.6			
15						
16		*Coefficients*	*Standard Error*	*t Stat*	*P-value*	
17	Intercept	10.26	1.17	8.76	8.12E-14	
18	Wage	-0.00020	0.000036	-5.69	1.43E-07	
19	Pct PT	-0.107	0.029	-3.62	0.0005	
20	Pct U	0.060	0.012	4.83	5.38E-06	
21	Av Shift	1.56	0.50	3.11	0.0025	
22	UM Rel	-2.64	0.492	-5.36	5.99E-07	

b. $H_0 : \beta_4 = 0$

$H_1 : \beta_4 \neq 0$

t = 3.11, p-value = .0025. There is enough evidence to infer that the availability of shiftwork affects absenteeism.

c. $H_0 : \beta_5 = 0$

$H_1 : \beta_5 < 0$

t = –5.36, p-value = (5.99E-07) /2 = 3.00×10^{-7} = virtually 0. There is enough evidence to infer that in organizations where the union–management relationship is good absenteeism is lower.

18.24

	A	B	C	D	E	F
1	SUMMARY OUTPUT					
2						
3	Regression Statistics					
4	Multiple R	0.8311				
5	R Square	0.6907				
6	Adjusted R Square	0.5670				
7	Standard Error	1.86				
8	Observations	8				
9						
10	ANOVA					
11		df	SS	MS	F	Significance F
12	Regression	2	38.47	19.24	5.58	0.0532
13	Residual	5	17.23	3.45		
14	Total	7	55.70			
15						
16		Coefficients	Standard Error	t Stat	P-value	
17	Intercept	2.01	4.02	0.50	0.6385	
18	Score	3.25	1.00	3.25	0.0227	
19	Gender	-0.039	1.35	-0.03	0.9782	

In this case male–dominated jobs are paid on average $.039 (3.9 cents) *less* than female–dominated jobs after adjusting for the value of each job.

18.26 The strength of this approach lies in regression analysis. This statistical technique allows us to determine whether gender is a factor in determining salaries. However, the conclusion is very much dependent upon the subjective assignment of weights. Change the value of the weights and a totally different conclusion is achieved.

18.28 $\ln(\hat{y}) = -2.15 + .00847x_1 + .00214x_2 + .00539x_3 + .00989x_4 - .0288x_5$

$= -2.15 + .00847(0) + .00214(200) + .00539(25) + .00989(50) - .0288(0) = -1.0928$

$\hat{y} = e^{\ln(\hat{y})} = e^{-1.0928} = .3353$

Probability of heart attack $= \dfrac{\hat{y}}{\hat{y}+1} = \dfrac{.3353}{.3353+1} = .2511$

18.30 $\ln(\hat{y}) = -2.15 + .00847x_1 + .00214x_2 + .00539x_3 + .00989x_4 - .0288x_5$

$= -2.15 + .00847(20) + .00214(200) + .00539(0) + .00989(50) - .0288(0) = -1.0581$

$\hat{y} = e^{\ln(\hat{y})} = e^{-1.0581} = .3471$

Probability of heart attack $= \dfrac{\hat{y}}{\hat{y}+1} = \dfrac{.3471}{.3471+1} = .2577$

18.32 $\ln(\hat{y}) = .1524 + .0281x_1 + .0223x_2 + .0152x_3 + .0114x_4$

Applicant 1: $\ln(\hat{y}) = .1524 + .0281(37) + .0223(55) + .0152(6) + .0114(5) = 2.5668$

$\hat{y} = e^{\ln(\hat{y})} = e^{2.5668} = 13.0241$

Probability of repaying loan $= \dfrac{\hat{y}}{\hat{y}+1} = \dfrac{13.0241}{13.0241+1} = .9287$

Applicant 2: $\ln(\hat{y}) = .1524 + .0281(58) + .0223(78) + .0152(3) + .0114(12) = 3.7040$

$\hat{y} = e^{\ln(\hat{y})} = e^{3.7040} = 40.6094$

Probability of repaying loan $= \dfrac{\hat{y}}{\hat{y}+1} = \dfrac{40.6094}{40.6094+1} = .9760$

Applicant 3: $\ln(\hat{y}) = .1524 + .0281(47) + .0223(39) + .0152(12) + .0114(10) = 2.6392$

$\hat{y} = e^{\ln(\hat{y})} = e^{2.6392} = 14.0020$

Probability of repaying loan $= \dfrac{\hat{y}}{\hat{y}+1} = \dfrac{14.0020}{14.0020+1} = .9333$

For each applicant the probability of repaying the loan increased.

18.34 $\ln(\hat{y}) = 5.8687 - 5.1546x_1 - .3725x_2 - .3213x_3$

$= 5.8687 - 5.1546(.25) - .3725(3) - .3213(1) = 3.1413$

$\hat{y} = e^{\ln(\hat{y})} = e^{3.1413} = 23.1328$

Probability of repaying the loan $= \dfrac{\hat{y}}{\hat{y}+1} = \dfrac{23.1328}{23.1328+1} = .9586$

18.36 $\ln(\hat{y}) = 6.1889 - .6462x_1 - .0009254x_2 - .8721x_3$

$= 6.1889 - .6462(4) - .0009254(1,855) - .8721(1) = 1.0154$

$\hat{y} = e^{\ln(\hat{y})} = e^{1.0154} = 2.7604$

Probability of repaying loan $= \dfrac{\hat{y}}{\hat{y}+1} = \dfrac{2.7604}{2.7604+1} = .7341$

18.38   a.

	I	J	K	L	M	N	O
1	Results of stepwise regression						
2							
3	Step 1 - Entering variable: GMAT						
4							
5	Summary measures						
6		Multiple R	0.6365				
7		R-Square	0.4052				
8		Adj R-Square	0.3984				
9		StErr of Est	0.8201				
10							
11	ANOVA Table						
12		Source	df	SS	MS	F	p-value
13		Explained	1	39.8580	39.8580	59.2645	0.0000
14		Unexplained	87	58.5113	0.6725		
15							
16	Regression coefficients						
17			Coefficient	Std Err	t-value	p-value	
18		Constant	1.7991	0.8304	2.1667	0.0330	
19		GMAT	0.0111	0.0014	7.6983	0.0000	
20							
21	Step 2 - Entering variable: I_2						
22							
23	Summary measures			Change	% Change		
24		Multiple R	0.6837	0.0471	%7.4		
25		R-Square	0.4674	0.0622	%15.4		
26		Adj R-Square	0.4550	0.0567	%14.2		
27		StErr of Est	0.7805	-0.0396	-%4.8		
28							
29	ANOVA Table						
30		Source	df	SS	MS	F	p-value
31		Explained	2	45.9787	22.9894	37.7375	0.0000
32		Unexplained	86	52.3905	0.6092		
33							
34	Regression coefficients						
35			Coefficient	Std Err	t-value	p-value	
36		Constant	0.8175	0.8488	0.9630	0.3382	
37		GMAT	0.0125	0.0014	8.6786	0.0000	
38		I_2	0.7046	0.2223	3.1698	0.0021	
39							
40	Step 3 - Entering variable: Work						
41							
42	Summary measures			Change	% Change		
43		Multiple R	0.7341	0.0504	%7.4		
44		R-Square	0.5389	0.0715	%15.3		
45		Adj R-Square	0.5226	0.0676	%14.8		
46		StErr of Est	0.7305	-0.0500	-%6.4		
47							
48	ANOVA Table						
49		Source	df	SS	MS	F	p-value
50		Explained	3	53.0079	17.6693	33.1095	0.0000
51		Unexplained	85	45.3613	0.5337		
52							
53	Regression coefficients						
54			Coefficient	Std Err	t-value	p-value	
55		Constant	-0.0629	0.8307	-0.0757	0.9398	
56		GMAT	0.0129	0.0014	9.5336	0.0000	
57		I_2	0.7891	0.2094	3.7690	0.0003	
58		Work	0.1047	0.0288	3.6293	0.0005	

b.   The stepwise regression equation includes the independent variables that are significantly related to the dependent variable. It does not include the variables undergraduate GPA, I_1, and I_3.

18.39   a.

	F	G	H	I	J	K	L
16	Regression coefficients						
17			Coefficient	Std Err	t-value	p-value	
18		Constant	4.4847	1.3333	3.3635	0.0010	
19		Minor_HR	0.6582	0.0889	7.4045	0.0000	
20							
21	**Step 2 - Entering variable: Years_Pro**						
22							
23	Summary measures			Change	% Change		
24		Multiple R	0.5923	0.0386	%7.0		
25		R-Square	0.3508	0.0442	%14.4		
26		Adj R-Square	0.3402	0.0392	%13.0		
27		StErr of Est	6.9655	-0.2040	-%2.8		
28							
29	ANOVA Table						
30		Source	df	SS	MS	F	p-value
31		Explained	2	3224.3332	1612.1666	33.2277	0.0000
32		Unexplained	123	5967.8018	48.5187		
33							
34	Regression coefficients						
35			Coefficient	Std Err	t-value	p-value	
36		Constant	0.4525	1.9028	0.2378	0.8124	
37		Minor_HR	0.6680	0.0864	7.7289	0.0000	
38		Years_Pro	1.3045	0.4509	2.8930	0.0045	

b.   In the stepwise regression equation both the number of minor league home runs and the number of years as a profession are significant. In Exercise 17.4 only the number of minor league home runs was significant.

c.   The difference is that by eliminating age as an independent variable allowed the stepwise regression to reveal that the number of years as a profession is significant.

18.42   a.   Mileage $= \beta_0 + \beta_1$ Speed $+ \beta_2$ Speed$^2 + \varepsilon$

       b.

	A	B	C	D	E	F
1	SUMMARY OUTPUT					
2						
3	*Regression Statistics*					
4	Multiple R	0.8428				
5	R Square	0.7102				
6	Adjusted R Square	0.6979				
7	Standard Error	3.86				
8	Observations	50				
9						
10	ANOVA					
11		*df*	*SS*	*MS*	*F*	*Significance F*
12	Regression	2	1719.9	859.94	57.60	0.0000
13	Residual	47	701.64	14.93		
14	Total	49	2421.5			
15						
16		*Coefficients*	*Standard Error*	*t Stat*	*P-value*	
17	Intercept	9.34	1.71	5.47	0.0000	
18	Speed	0.802	0.077	10.39	0.0000	
19	Speed-sq	-0.0079	0.00073	-10.73	0.0000	

       c. $s_\varepsilon = 3.86$ and $R^2 = .7102$. The model fits moderately well.

18.44   a.

	A	B	C	D	E	F
1	SUMMARY OUTPUT					
2						
3	*Regression Statistics*					
4	Multiple R	0.8668				
5	R Square	0.7514				
6	Adjusted R Square	0.7284				
7	Standard Error	1.27				
8	Observations	60				
9						
10	ANOVA					
11		*df*	*SS*	*MS*	*F*	*Significance F*
12	Regression	5	262.95	52.59	32.65	0.0000
13	Residual	54	86.99	1.61		
14	Total	59	349.93			
15						
16		*Coefficients*	*Standard Error*	*t Stat*	*P-value*	
17	Intercept	404.5	327.0	1.24	0.2214	
18	Cars	-66.57	6.54	-10.19	0.0000	
19	Speed	-2.35	10.54	-0.22	0.8246	
20	Cars-sq	0.107	0.097	1.10	0.2741	
21	Speed-sq	-0.070	0.085	-0.82	0.4180	
22	Cars-Speed	1.08	0.096	11.21	0.0000	

       b. $F = 32.65$, p-value = 0. There is enough evidence to infer that the model is valid.

18.46 a.

	A	B	C	D	E	F
1	SUMMARY OUTPUT					
2						
3	*Regression Statistics*					
4	Multiple R	0.9347				
5	R Square	0.8736				
6	Adjusted R Square	0.8654				
7	Standard Error	0.0183				
8	Observations	50				
9						
10	ANOVA					
11		*df*	*SS*	*MS*	*F*	*Significance F*
12	Regression	3	0.107	0.0355	106.01	0.0000
13	Residual	46	0.0154	0.00034		
14	Total	49	0.122			
15						
16		*Coefficients*	*Standard Error*	*t Stat*	*P-value*	
17	Intercept	0.357	0.0592	6.03	0.0000	
18	BA	-0.401	0.236	-1.70	0.0964	
19	ERA	0.0764	0.00478	15.98	0.0000	
20	Fired	-0.0509	0.00591	-8.61	0.0000	

b. $H_0 : \beta_3 = 0$

$H_1 : \beta_3 < 0$

t = −8.61, p-value = 0. There is enough evidence to infer that a team that fires its manager within 12 months wins less frequently than other teams.

18.48 a.   Depletion $= \beta_0 + \beta_1 \text{Temperature} + \beta_2 \text{PH–level} + \beta_3 \text{PH–level}^2 + \beta_4 I_4 + \beta_5 I_5 + \varepsilon$

where

$I_1 = 1$ if mainly cloudy

$I_1 = 0$ otherwise

$I_2 = 1$ if sunny

$I_2 = 0$ otherwise

b.

	A	B	C	D	E	F
1	SUMMARY OUTPUT					
2						
3	*Regression Statistics*					
4	Multiple R	0.8085				
5	R Square	0.6537				
6	Adjusted R Square	0.6452				
7	Standard Error	4.14				
8	Observations	210				
9						
10	ANOVA					
11		*df*	*SS*	*MS*	*F*	*Significance F*
12	Regression	5	6596	1319	77.00	0.0000
13	Residual	204	3495	17.13		
14	Total	209	10091			
15						
16		*Coefficients*	*Standard Error*	*t Stat*	*P-value*	
17	Intercept	1003	55.12	18.19	0.0000	
18	Temperature	0.194	0.029	6.78	0.0000	
19	PH Level	-265.6	14.75	-18.01	0.0000	
20	PH-sq	17.76	0.983	18.07	0.0000	
21	I1	-1.07	0.700	-1.53	0.1282	
22	I2	1.16	0.700	1.65	0.0997	

c. $H_0 : \beta_1 = \beta_2 = \beta_3 = \beta_4 = \beta_5 = 0$

H_1 : At least on β_i is not equal to 0

F = 77.00, p-value = 0. There is enough evidence to infer that the model is valid.

d. $H_0 : \beta_1 = 0$

$H_1 : \beta_1 > 0$

t = 6.78, p-value = 0. There is enough evidence to infer that higher temperatures deplete chlorine more quickly.

e. $H_0 : \beta_3 = 0$

$H_1 : \beta_3 > 0$

t = 18.07, p-value = 0. There is enough evidence to infer that there is a quadratic relationship between chlorine depletion and PH level.

f. $H_0 : \beta_i = 0$

$H_1 : \beta_i \neq 0$

$I_1 : t = -1.53$, p-value = .1282. There is not enough evidence to infer that chlorine depletion differs between mainly cloudy days and partly sunny days.

$I_2 : t = 1.65$, p-value = .0997. There is not enough evidence to infer that chlorine depletion differs between sunny days and partly sunny days.

Weather is not a factor in chlorine depletion.

Chapter 19

19.2 H_0 : The two population locations are the same

H_1 : The location of population 1 is to the right of the location of population 2

Rejection region: $z > z_\alpha = z_{.05} = 1.645$

$$E(T) = \frac{n_1(n_1 + n_2 + 1)}{2} = \frac{30(30 + 40 + 1)}{2} = 1,065$$

$$\sigma_T = \sqrt{\frac{n_1 n_2 (n_1 + n_2 + 1)}{12}} = \sqrt{\frac{(30)(40)(30 + 40 + 1)}{12}} = 84.26$$

a. $z = \dfrac{T - E(T)}{\sigma_T} = \dfrac{1,205 - 1,065}{84.26} = 1.66$, p-value $P(Z > 1.66) = 1 - .9515 = .0485$. There is

enough evidence to infer that the location of population 1 is to the right of the location of population 2.

b. $z = \dfrac{T - E(T)}{\sigma_T} = \dfrac{1,065 - 1,065}{84.26} = 0$, p-value $= P(Z > 0) = .5$. There is not enough evidence to

infer that the location of population 1 is to the right of the location of population 2.

c.   The value of the test statistic decreases and the p-value increases.

19.4 H_0 : The two population locations are the same

H_1 : The location of population 1 is different from the location of population 2

Rejection region: $T \geq T_U = 127$ or $T \leq T_L = 83$

Sample 1	Rank	Sample 2	Rank
15	4.0	8	2.0
7	1.0	27	18.0
22	14.0	17	7.0
20	.5	25	16.0
32	20.0	20	11.5
18	9.5	16	5.0
26	17.0	21	13.0
17	7.0	17	7.0
23	15.0	10	3.0
30	19.0	18	9.5
	$T_1 = 118$		$T_2 = 92$

There is not enough evidence to infer that the location of population 1 is different from the location of population 2.

19.6　H_0 : The two population locations are the same

　　　H_1 : The location of population 1 is different from the location of population 2

	A	B	C	D	E
1	**Wilcoxon Rank Sum Test**				
2					
3			Rank Sum	Observations	
4	*Business*		4004	40	
5	*Economy*		8086	115	
6	z Stat		3.6149		
7	P(Z<=z) one-tail		0.0002		
8	z Critical one-tail		1.6449		
9	P(Z<=z) two-tail		0.0004		
10	z Critical two-tail		1.96		

　　a.　　z = 3.61, p-value = .0004. There is enough evidence to infer that the business and economy

　　　　　class differ in their degree of satisfaction.

　　b.　　The printout is identical to that of part a.

　　c.　　All codes that preserve the order produce the same results.

19.8　　H_0 : The two population locations are the same

　　　　H_1 : The location of population 1 is to the right of the location of population 2

　　　　Rejection region: $z > z_\alpha = z_{.05} = 1.645$

$$E(T) = \frac{n_1(n_1 + n_2 + 1)}{2} = \frac{82(82 + 75 + 1)}{2} = 6478$$

$$\sigma_T = \sqrt{\frac{n_1 n_2(n_1 + n_2 + 1)}{12}} = \sqrt{\frac{(82)(75)(82 + 75 + 1)}{12}} = 284.6$$

$$z = \frac{T - E(T)}{\sigma_T} = \frac{6,807 - 6,478}{284.6} = 1.16,$$ p-value P(Z > 1.16) = 1 − .8770 = .1230. There is not enough

evidence to infer that members of the Mathematics department rate nonparametric techniques as
more important than do members of other departments.

19.10　　H_0 : The two population locations are the same

　　　　　H_1 : The location of population 1 is to the left of the location of population 2

　　　　　Rejection region: $z < -z_\alpha = -z_{.05} = -1.645$

$$E(T) = \frac{n_1(n_1 + n_2 + 1)}{2} = \frac{125(125 + 125 + 1)}{2} = 15,687.5$$

$$\sigma_T = \sqrt{\frac{n_1 n_2(n_1 + n_2 + 1)}{12}} = \sqrt{\frac{(125)(125)(125 + 125 + 1)}{12}} = 571.7$$

$$z = \frac{T - E(T)}{\sigma_T} = \frac{14,873 - 15,687.5}{571.7} = -1.42,$$ p-value P(Z < − 1.42) =.0778. There is not enough

evidence to infer that women are doing less housework today than last year.

19.12 H_0 : The two population locations are the same

     H_1 : The location of population 1 is different from the location of population 2

     Rejection region: $z < -z_{\alpha/2} = -z_{.025} = -1.96$ or $z > z_{\alpha/2} = z_{.025} = 1.96$

$$E(T) = \frac{n_1(n_1 + n_2 + 1)}{2} = \frac{50(50 + 50 + 1)}{2} = 2525$$

$$\sigma_T = \sqrt{\frac{n_1 n_2(n_1 + n_2 + 1)}{12}} = \sqrt{\frac{(50)(50)(50 + 50 + 1)}{12}} = 145.1$$

$$z = \frac{T - E(T)}{\sigma_T} = \frac{2810 - 2525}{145.1} = 1.964, \text{ p-value} = 2P(Z > 1.964), \text{ which is slightly less than } 2P(Z >$$

1.96)
= 2(1 − .9750) = .05. There is enough evidence to infer that men and women experience different levels of stomach upset.

19.14 H_0 : The two population locations are the same

     H_1 : The location of population 1 is to the right of the location of population 2

     Rejection region: $z > z_{\alpha} = z_{.05} = 1.645$

$$E(T) = \frac{n_1(n_1 + n_2 + 1)}{2} = \frac{20(20 + 20 + 1)}{2} = 410,$$

$$\sigma_T = \sqrt{\frac{n_1 n_2(n_1 + n_2 + 1)}{12}} = \sqrt{\frac{(20)(20)(20 + 20 + 1)}{12}} = 37.0$$

$$z = \frac{T - E(T)}{\sigma_T} = \frac{439.5 - 410}{37.0} = .80, \text{ p-value} = P(Z > .80) = 1 - .7881 = .2119. \text{ There is not enough}$$

evidence to infer that women perceive another woman wearing a size 6 dress as more professional than one wearing a size 14 dress.

19.16 H_0 : The two population locations are the same

     H_1 : The location of population 1 is different from the location of population 2

     Rejection region: $z < -z_{\alpha/2} = -z_{.025} = -1.96$ or $z > z_{\alpha/2} = z_{.025} = 1.96$

$$E(T) = \frac{n_1(n_1 + n_2 + 1)}{2} = \frac{182(182 + 163 + 1)}{2} = 31,486$$

$$\sigma_T = \sqrt{\frac{n_1 n_2(n_1 + n_2 + 1)}{12}} = \sqrt{\frac{(182)(163)(182 + 163 + 1)}{12}} = 924.9$$

$$z = \frac{T - E(T)}{\sigma_T} = \frac{32,225.5 - 31,486}{924.9} = .80, \text{ p-value} = 2P(Z > .80) = 2(1 - .7881) = .4238. \text{ There is not}$$

enough evidence to infer that the night and day shifts rate the service differently.

19.18 H_0 : The two population locations are the same

     H_1 : The location of population 1 is to the left of the location of population 2

     Rejection region: $z < -z_{\alpha} = -z_{.10} = -1.28$

$$z = \frac{x - .5n}{.5\sqrt{n}} = \frac{28 - .5(69)}{.5\sqrt{69}} = -1.57, \text{ p-value} = P(Z < -1.57) = .0582. \text{ There is enough evidence to}$$

infer that the location of population 1 is to the left of the location of population 2.

19.20 H_0 : The two population locations are the same

H_1 : The location of population 1 is to the right of the location of population 2

Pair	A	B	Sign of Difference
1	5	3	+
2	3	2	+
3	4	4	0
4	2	3	−
5	3	3	0
6	4	1	+
7	3	3	0
8	5	4	+
9	4	2	+
10	3	5	−
11	4	1	+
12	5	2	+
13	4	2	+
14	5	3	+
15	3	2	+
16	2	2	0

Rejection region: $z > z_\alpha = z_{.05} = 1.645$

$x = 10$, $n = 12$, $z = \dfrac{x - .5n}{.5\sqrt{n}} = \dfrac{10 - .5(12)}{.5\sqrt{12}} = 2.31$, p-value = $P(Z > 2.31) = 1 - .9896 = .0104$

There is enough evidence to infer that the population 1 is located to the right of population 2.

19.22 H_0 : The two population locations are the same

H_1 : The location of population 1 is to the right of the location of population 2

Rejection region: $z > z_\alpha = z_{.01} = 2.33$

$E(T) = \dfrac{n(n+1)}{4} = \dfrac{108(109)}{4} = 2943$; $\sigma_T = \sqrt{\dfrac{n(n+1)(2n+1)}{24}} = \sqrt{\dfrac{108(109)(217)}{24}} = 326.25$

$z = \dfrac{T - E(T)}{\sigma_T} = \dfrac{3457 - 2943}{326.25} = 1.58$, p-value = $P(Z > 1.58) = 1 - .9429 = .0571$. There is not

enough evidence to conclude that population 1 is located to the right of the location of population 2.

19.24 H_0 : The two population locations are the same

   H_1 : The location of population 1 is different from the location of population 2

   Rejection region: $T \geq T_U = 39$ or $T \leq T_L = 6$

Pair	Sample 1	Sample 2	Difference	|Difference|	Ranks	
1	18.2	18.2	0	0		
2	14.1	14.1	0	0		
3	24.5	23.6	.9	.9	6.5	
4	11.9	12.1	−.2	.2		2
5	9.5	9.5	0	0		
6	12.1	11.3	.8	.8	5	
7	10.9	9.7	1.2	1.2	8	
8	16.7	17.6	−.9	.9		6.5
9	19.6	19.4	.2	.2	2	
10	8.4	8.1	.3	.3	4	
11	21.7	21.9	−.2	.2		2
12	23.4	21.6	1.8	1.8	9	

$$T^+ = 34.5 \quad T^- = 10.5$$

   $T = 34.5$. There is not enough evidence to conclude that the population locations differ.

19.26 H_0 : H_0 : The two population locations are the same

   H_1 : The location of population 1 is to the right of the location of population 2

	A	B	C	D	E
1	Sign Test				
2					
3	Difference			Brand A - Brand B	
4					
5	Positive Differences			21	
6	Negative Differences			15	
7	Zero Differences			14	
8	z Stat			1.00	
9	P(Z<=z) one-tail			0.1587	
10	z Critical one-tail			1.6449	
11	P(Z<=z) two-tail			0.3174	
12	z Critical two-tail			1.96	

a. $z = 1.00$, p-value $= .1587$. There is no evidence to infer that Brand A is preferred.

b.   The printout is identical to that of part a.

c.   All codes that preserve the order produce the same results.

19.28 H_0 : The two population locations are the same

H_1 : The location of population 1 is different from the location of population 2

	A	B	C	D	E
1	**Sign Test**				
2					
3	Difference			*Sample 1 - Sample 2*	
4					
5	Positive Differences			51	
6	Negative Differences			74	
7	Zero Differences			0	
8	z Stat			-2.06	
9	P(Z<=z) one-tail			0.0198	
10	z Critical one-tail			1.6449	
11	P(Z<=z) two-tail			0.0396	
12	z Critical two-tail			1.96	

a. $z = -2.06$, p-value = .0396. There is enough evidence to infer that the population locations differ.

b.

	A	B	C	D	E
1	**Wilcoxon Signed Rank Sum Test**				
2					
3	Difference		*Sample 1 - Sample 2*		
4					
5	T+		3726.5		
6	T-		4148.5		
7	Observations (for test)		125		
8	z Stat		-0.52		
9	P(Z<=z) one-tail		0.3016		
10	z Critical one-tail		1.6449		
11	P(Z<=z) two-tail		0.6032		
12	z Critical two-tail		1.96		

$z = -.52$, p-value = .6032. There is not enough evidence to infer that the population locations differ.

c.   The sign test ignores the magnitudes of the paired differences whereas the Wilcoxon signed rank sum test does not.

19.30 H_0 : The two population locations are the same

H_1 : The location of population 1 is to the left of the location of population 2

Rejection region: $z < -z_\alpha = -z_{.05} = -1.645$

$$E(T) = \frac{n(n+1)}{4} = \frac{72(72+1)}{4} = 1314 \; ; \; \sigma_T = \sqrt{\frac{n(n+1)(2n+1)}{24}} = \sqrt{\frac{72(72+1)(2[72]+1)}{24}} = 178.2$$

$$z = \frac{T - E(T)}{\sigma_T} = \frac{378.5 - 1314}{178.2} = -5.25, \text{ p-value} = P(Z < -5.25) = 0.$$ There is enough evidence to infer that the drug is effective.

19.32　H_0 : The two population locations are the same

H_1 : The location of population 1 is to the right of the location of population 2

Rejection region: $z > z_\alpha = z_{.05} = 1.645$

$z = \dfrac{x - .5n}{.5\sqrt{n}} = \dfrac{60 - .5(98)}{.5\sqrt{98}} = 2.22$, p-value = $P(Z > 2.22) = 1 - .9868 = .0132$. There is enough

evidence to conclude that concern about a gasoline shortage exceeded concern about an electricity shortage.

19.34　H_0 : The two population locations are the same

H_1 : The location of population 1 is to the left of the location of population 2

Rejection region: $T \leq T_L = 110$

$T = 111$. There is not enough evidence to infer that the swimming department has higher gross sales.

19.36　H_0 : The two population locations are the same

H_1 : The location of population 1 is to the left of the location of population 2

Rejection region: $z < -z_\alpha = -z_{.01} = -2.33$

$z = \dfrac{x - .5n}{.5\sqrt{n}} = \dfrac{5 - .5(20)}{.5\sqrt{20}} = -2.24$, p-value = $P(Z < -2.24) = .0125$. There is not enough evidence to

conclude that children feel less pain.

19.38　H_0 : The two population locations are the same

H_1 : The location of population 1 is to the right of the location of population 2

Rejection region: $z > z_\alpha = z_{.05} = 1.645$

$z = \dfrac{x - .5n}{.5\sqrt{n}} = \dfrac{32 - .5(53)}{.5\sqrt{53}} = 1.51$, p-value = $P(Z > 1.51) = 1 - .9345 = .0655$. There is not enough

evidence to infer that preference should be given to students for high school 1.

19.40　H_0 : The locations of all 3 populations are the same.

H_1 : At least two population locations differ.

Rejection region: $H > \chi^2_{\alpha, k-1} = \chi^2_{.05, 2} = 5.99$

$H = \left[\dfrac{12}{n(n+1)} \sum \dfrac{T_j^2}{n_j} \right] - 3(n+1) = \left[\dfrac{12}{88(88+1)} \left(\dfrac{984^2}{23} + \dfrac{1502^2}{36} + \dfrac{1430^2}{29} \right) \right] - 3(88+1) = 1.56$. There is

not enough evidence to conclude that the population locations differ.

19.42　H_0 : The locations of all 3 populations are the same.

H_1 : At least two population locations differ.

Rejection region: $H > \chi^2_{\alpha, k-1} = \chi^2_{.10, 2} = 4.61$

$H = \left[\dfrac{12}{n(n+1)} \sum \dfrac{T_j^2}{n_j} \right] - 3(n+1) = \left[\dfrac{12}{143(143+1)} \left(\dfrac{3741^2}{47} + \dfrac{1610^2}{29} + \dfrac{4945^2}{67} \right) \right] - 3(143+1) = 6.30.$

There is enough evidence to conclude that the population locations differ.

19.44 H_0 : The locations of all 3 populations are the same.

       H_1 : At least two population locations differ.

       Rejection region: $H > \chi^2_{\alpha,k-1} = \chi^2_{.05,2} = 5.99$

1	Rank	2	Rank	3	Rank
25	10.5	19	2	27	12
15	1	21	4	25	10.5
20	3	23	8.5	22	6
22	6	22	6	29	15
23	8.5	28	13.5	28	13.5
$T_1 = 29$		$T_2 = 34$		$T_3 = 57$	

$$H = \left[\frac{12}{n(n+1)}\sum\frac{T_j^2}{n_j}\right] - 3(n+1) = \left[\frac{12}{15(15+1)}\left(\frac{29^2}{5}+\frac{34^2}{5}+\frac{57^2}{5}\right)\right] - 3(15+1) = 4.46, \text{ p-value} = .1075.$$

There is not enough evidence to conclude that at least two population locations differ.

19.46 H_0 : The locations of all 4 populations are the same.

       H_1 : At least two population locations differ.

	A	B	C	D
1	**Kruskal-Wallis Test**			
2				
3	Group	Rank Sum	Observations	
4	*Printer 1*	4889.5	50	
5	*Printer 2*	5350	50	
6	*Printer 3*	4864.5	50	
7	*Printer 4*	4996	50	
8				
9	H Stat		0.899	
10	df		3	
11	p-value		0.8257	
12	chi-squared Critical		7.8147	

a   H = .899, p-value = .8257. There is not enough evidence to conclude that differences exist between the ratings of the four printings.

b.   The printout is identical to that of part a.

c.   All codes that preserve the order produce the same results.

19.48 H_0 : The locations of all 3 populations are the same.

    H_1 : At least two population locations differ.

    Rejection region: $H > \chi^2_{\alpha,k-1} = \chi^2_{.05,2} = 5.99$

$$H = \left[\frac{12}{n(n+1)} \sum_{j=1}^{k} \frac{T_j^2}{n_j} \right] - 3(n+1) = \frac{12}{75(75+1)} \left(\frac{767.5^2}{25} + \frac{917^2}{25} + \frac{1165^2}{25} \right) - 3(75+1) = 6.81, \text{p-}$$

value = .0333. There is enough evidence to infer that there are differences in student satisfaction between the teaching methods.

19.50 H_0 : The locations of all 4 populations are the same.

    H_1 : At least two population locations differ.

    Rejection region: $H > \chi^2_{\alpha,k-1} = \chi^2_{.05,3} = 7.81$

$$H = \left[\frac{12}{n(n+1)} \sum_{j=1}^{k} \frac{T_j^2}{n_j} \right] - 3(n+1)$$

$$= \frac{12}{132(132+1)} \left(\frac{2195^2}{33} + \frac{1650.5^2}{34} + \frac{2830^2}{34} + \frac{2102.5^2}{31} \right) - 3(132+1)$$

= 14.04, p-value = .0029. There is enough evidence to conclude that there are differences in grading standards between the four high schools.

19.52 H_0 : The locations of all 3 populations are the same.

    H_1 : At least two population locations differ.

    Rejection region: $H > \chi^2_{\alpha,k-1} = \chi^2_{.05,2} = 5.99$

$$H = \left[\frac{12}{n(n+1)} \sum_{j=1}^{k} \frac{T_j^2}{n_j} \right] - 3(n+1) = \frac{12}{90(90+1)} \left(\frac{1565^2}{30} + \frac{1358.5^2}{30} + \frac{1171.5^2}{30} \right) - 3(90+1) = 3.78, \text{p-}$$

value = .1507. There is not enough evidence to infer that Democrat's ratings of their chances changed over the 3–month period.

19.54 H_0 : The locations of all 4 populations are the same.

    H_1 : At least two population locations differ.

    Rejection region: $H > \chi^2_{\alpha,k-1} = \chi^2_{.05,3} = 7.81$

$$H = \left[\frac{12}{n(n+1)} \sum_{j=1}^{k} \frac{T_j^2}{n_j} \right] - 3(n+1)$$

$$= \frac{12}{428(428+1)} \left(\frac{28,304^2}{123} + \frac{21,285^2}{109} + \frac{21,796^2}{102} + \frac{20,421^2}{94} \right) - 3(428+1) = 4.64, \text{p-value} = .1999.$$

There is not enough evidence to infer that there are differences in support between the four levels of students.

19.56 H_0 : The locations of all 4 populations are the same.

        H_1 : At least two population locations differ.

        Rejection region: $F_r > \chi^2_{\alpha,k-1} = \chi^2_{.10,3} = 6.25$

		Treatment						
Block	1	Rank	2	Rank	3	Rank	4	Rank
1	10	2	12	3	15	4	9	1
2	8	2	10	3	11	4	6	1
3	13	2	14	3	16	4	11	1
4	9	1.5	9	1.5	12	3	13	4
5	7	1	8	2	14	4	10	3
		$T_1 = 8.5$		$T_2 = 12.5$		$T_3 = 19$		$T_4 = 10$

$$F_r = \left[\frac{12}{b(k)(k+1)}\sum_{j=1}^{k}T_j^2\right] - 3b(k+1) = \left[\frac{12}{(5)(4)(5)}(8.5^2 + 12.5^2 + 19^2 + 10^2)\right] - 3(5)(5) = 7.74, \text{ p-}$$

value = .0517. There is enough evidence to infer that at least two population locations differ.

19.58 H_0 : The locations of all 4 populations are the same.

        H_1 : At least two population locations differ.

        Rejection region: $F_r > \chi^2_{\alpha,k-1} = \chi^2_{.05,3} = 7.81$

		Orange Juice Brand						
Judge	1	Rank	2	Rank	3	Rank	4	Rank
1	3	1.5	5	4	4	3	3	1.5
2	2	1	3	2	5	4	4	3
3	4	3	4	3	3	1	4	3
4	3	2	4	3	5	4	2	1
5	2	1	4	3.5	4	3.5	3	2
6	4	2	5	3.5	5	3.5	3	1
7	3	1.5	3	1.5	4	3.5	4	3.5
8	2	1	3	3	3	3	3	3
9	4	2.5	3	1	5	4	4	2.5
10	2	1	4	3	5	4	3	2
		$T_1 = 16.5$		$T_2 = 27.5$		$T_3 = 33.5$		$T_4 = 22.5$

$$F_r = \left[\frac{12}{b(k)(k+1)}\sum_{j=1}^{k}T_j^2\right] - 3b(k+1) = \left[\frac{12}{(10)(4)(5)}(16.5^2 + 27.5^2 + 33.5^2 + 22.5^2)\right] - 3(10)(5) =$$

9.42,

p-value = .0242. There is enough evidence to infer that differences in sensory perception exist between the four brands of orange juice.

19.60 H_0 : The locations of all 4 populations are the same.

   H_1 : At least two population locations differ.

	A	B	C
1	**Friedman Test**		
2			
3	Group		Rank Sum
4	*Brand A*		65
5	*Brand B*		65
6	*Brand C*		85
7	*Brand D*		85
8			
9	Fr Stat		8.00
10	df		3
11	p-value		0.0460
12	chi-squared Critical		7.8147

a. $F_r = 8.00$, p-value $= .0460$. There is enough evidence to infer that differences exist between the ratings of the four brands of coffee.

b.   Printout is identical to that of part a.

c.   Different codes produce identical results provided the codes are in order.

19.62 H_0 : The locations of all 3 populations are the same.

   H_1 : At least two population locations differ.

   Rejection region: $F_r > \chi^2_{\alpha,k-1} = \chi^2_{.05,2} = 5.99$

$$F_r = \left[\frac{12}{b(k)(k+1)} \sum_{j=1}^{k} T_j^2 \right] - 3b(k+1) = \left[\frac{12}{(20)(3)(4)} (33^2 + 39.5^2 + 47.5^2) \right] - 3(20)(4) = 5.28, \text{ p-value}$$

$= .0715$. There is not enough evidence to infer that there are differences in the ratings of the three recipes.

19.64 H_0 : The locations of all 3 populations are the same.

   H_1 : At least two population locations differ.

   Rejection region: $F_r > \chi^2_{\alpha,k-1} = \chi^2_{.05,2} = 5.99$

$$F_r = \left[\frac{12}{b(k)(k+1)} \sum_{j=1}^{k} T_j^2 \right] - 3b(k+1) = \left[\frac{12}{(12)(3)(4)} (28.5^2 + 22.5^2 + 21^2) \right] - 3(12)(4) = 2.63, \text{ p-value}$$

$= .2691$. There is not enough evidence to infer that there are differences in delivery times between the three couriers.

19.66   Rejection region: $z < -z_{\alpha/2} = -z_{.025} = -1.96$ or $z > z_{\alpha/2} = z_{.025} = 1.96$

   $z = r_s \sqrt{n-1} = (.23)\sqrt{50-1} = 1.61$, p-value $= 2P(Z > 1.61) = 2(1 - .9463) = .1074$ There is not enough evidence to reject the null hypothesis.

19.68 $H_0 : \rho_S = 0$

$H_1 : \rho_S \neq 0$

Mathematics	a	Economics	b	a^2	b^2	ab
4	5.5	5	6.5	30.25	42.25	35.75
2	3	2	1.5	9	2.25	4.5
5	7	3	4	49	16	28
4	5.5	5	6.5	30.25	42.25	35.75
2	3	3	4	9	16	12
2	3	3	4	9	16	12
1	1	2	1.5	1	2.25	1.5
Totals	28		28	137.5	137.0	129.5

$$\sum_{i=1}^{n} a_i = 28 \quad \sum_{i=1}^{n} b_i = 28 \quad \sum_{i=1}^{n} a_i^2 = 137.5 \quad \sum_{i=1}^{n} b_i^2 = 137.0 \quad \sum_{i=1}^{n} a_i b_i = 129.5$$

$$s_{ab} = \frac{1}{n-1}\left[\sum_{i=1}^{n} a_i b_i - \frac{\sum_{i=1}^{n} a_i \sum_{i=1}^{n} b_i}{n}\right] = \frac{1}{7-1}\left[129.5 - \frac{(28)(28)}{7}\right] = 2.917$$

$$s_a^2 = \frac{1}{n-1}\left[\sum_{i=1}^{n} a_i^2 - \frac{\left(\sum_{i=1}^{n} a_i\right)^2}{n}\right] = \frac{1}{7-1}\left[137.5 - \frac{(28)^2}{7}\right] = 4.250, \; s_a = \sqrt{s_a^2} = \sqrt{4.250} = 2.062$$

$$s_b^2 = \frac{1}{n-1}\left[\sum_{i=1}^{n} b_i^2 - \frac{\left(\sum_{i=1}^{n} b_i\right)^2}{n}\right] = \frac{1}{7-1}\left[137.0 - \frac{(28)^2}{7}\right] = 4.167, \; s_b = \sqrt{s_b^2} = \sqrt{4.167} = 2.041$$

$$r_S = \frac{s_{ab}}{s_b s_b} = \frac{2.917}{(2.062)(2.041)} = .6931$$

$H_0 : \rho_S = 0$

$H_1 : \rho_S \neq 0$

Rejection region: $r_S > .786$ or $r_S < -.786$

There is not enough evidence to infer a relationship between the grades in the two courses.

19.70 $H_0 : \rho_S = 0$

$H_1 : \rho_S \neq 0$

Stock 1	a	Stock 2	b	a^2	b^2	ab
−7	4.5	6	8.5	20.25	72.25	38.25
−4	6.5	6	8.5	42.25	72.25	55.25
−7	4.5	−4	2	20.25	4	9
−3	8	9	12.5	64	156.25	100
2	10.5	3	5	110.25	25	52.5
−10	2.5	−3	3.5	6.25	12.25	8.75
−10	2.5	7	10.5	6.25	110.25	26.25
5	12	−3	3.5	144	12.25	42
1	9	4	6	81	36	54
−4	6.5	7	10.5	42.25	110.25	68.25
2	10.5	9	12.5	110.25	156.25	131.25
6	13	5	7	169	49	91
−13	1	−7	1	1	1	1
Totals	91		91	817	817	677.5

$$\sum_{i=1}^{n} a_i = 91 \quad \sum_{i=1}^{n} b_i = 91 \quad \sum_{i=1}^{n} a_i^2 = 817 \quad \sum_{i=1}^{n} b_i^2 = 817 \quad \sum_{i=1}^{n} a_i b_i = 677.5$$

$$s_{ab} = \frac{1}{n-1}\left[\sum_{i=1}^{n} a_i b_i - \frac{\sum_{i=1}^{n} a_i \sum_{i=1}^{n} b_i}{n} \right] = \frac{1}{13-1}\left[677.5 - \frac{(91)(91)}{13} \right] = 3.375$$

$$s_a^2 = \frac{1}{n-1}\left[\sum_{i=1}^{n} a_i^2 - \frac{\left(\sum_{i=1}^{n} a_i\right)^2}{n} \right] = \frac{1}{13-1}\left[817 - \frac{(91)^2}{13} \right] = 15.00, \; s_a = \sqrt{s_a^2} = \sqrt{15.00} = 3.873$$

$$s_b^2 = \frac{1}{n-1}\left[\sum_{i=1}^{n} b_i^2 - \frac{\left(\sum_{i=1}^{n} b_i\right)^2}{n} \right] = \frac{1}{13-1}\left[817 - \frac{(91)^2}{13} \right] = 15.00, \; s_b = \sqrt{s_b^2} = \sqrt{15.00} = 3.873$$

$$r_S = \frac{s_{ab}}{s_b s_b} = \frac{3.375}{(3.873)(3.873)} = .2250$$

$H_0 : \rho_S = 0$

$H_1 : \rho_S \neq 0$

Rejection region: $r_S > .566$ or $r_S < -.566$

There is not enough evidence to infer a relationship between the two stock returns.

19.72 $H_0 : \rho_S = 0$
$H_1 : \rho_S \ne 0$

	A	B	C	D
1	**Spearman Rank Correlation**			
2				
3	*Price and Odometer*			
4	Spearman Rank Correlation			-0.0201
5	z Stat			-0.20
6	P(Z<=z) one tail			0.4206
7	z Critical one tail			1.6449
8	P(Z<=z) two tail			0.8412
9	z Critical two tail			1.96

$z = -.20$, p-value $= .8412$. There is not enough evidence to infer that odometer reading and price are related.

19.74 $H_0 : \rho_S = 0$
$H_1 : \rho_S > 0$

	A	B	C	D
1	**Spearman Rank Correlation**			
2				
3	*Age and Heartburn*			
4	Spearman Rank Correlation			0.0302
5	z Stat			0.54
6	P(Z<=z) one tail			0.2931
7	z Critical one tail			1.6449
8	P(Z<=z) two tail			0.5862
9	z Critical two tail			1.96

$z = .54$, p-value $= .2931$. There is not enough evidence to conclude that age and severity of heartburn are positively related.

19.76 $H_0 : \rho_S = 0$
$H_1 : \rho_S > 0$

	A	B	C	D
1	**Spearman Rank Correlation**			
2				
3	*Floor and Price*			
4	Spearman Rank Correlation			0.553
5	z Stat			3.87
6	P(Z<=z) one tail			0.0001
7	z Critical one tail			1.6449
8	P(Z<=z) two tail			0.0002
9	z Critical two tail			1.96

$z = 3.87$, p-value $= .0001$. There is sufficient evidence to conclude that price and floor number are positively related.

19.78 $H_0 : \rho_S = 0$

$H_1 : \rho_S > 0$

	A	B	C	D
1	**Spearman Rank Correlation**			
2				
3	*Wager and Enjoyment*			
4	Spearman Rank Correlation			0.3912
5	z Stat			5.52
6	P(Z<=z) one tail			0
7	z Critical one tail			1.6449
8	P(Z<=z) two tail			0
9	z Critical two tail			1.96

z = 5.52, p-value = 0. There is enough evidence to infer that the greater the wager the more enjoyable the game is.

19.80 H_0 : The two population locations are the same

H_1 : The location of population 1 is different from the location of population 2

	A	B	C	D	E
1	**Wilcoxon Rank Sum Test**				
2					
3			Rank Sum	Observations	
4	*Section 1*		15297.5	113	
5	*Section 2*		14592.5	131	
6	z Stat		2.65		
7	P(Z<=z) one-tail		0.0041		
8	z Critical one-tail		1.6449		
9	P(Z<=z) two-tail		0.0082		
10	z Critical two-tail		1.96		

z = 2.65, p-value = .0082. There is enough evidence to infer that the two teaching methods differ

19.82 H_0 : The locations of all 4 populations are the same.

H_1 : At least two population locations differ.

	A	B	C
1	**Friedman Test**		
2			
3	Group		Rank Sum
4	*Typeface 1*		50.5
5	*Typeface 2*		38
6	*Typeface 3*		66
7	*Typeface 4*		45.5
8			
9	Fr Stat		12.615
10	df		3
11	p-value		0.0055
12	chi-squared Critical		7.8147

$F_r = 12.615$, p-value = .0055. There is enough evidence to conclude that there are differences between typefaces.

19.84 H_0 : The two population locations are the same

H_1 : The location of population 1 is to the left of the location of population 2

	A	B	C	D
1	**Wilcoxon Signed Rank Sum Test**			
2				
3	Difference		*Drug A - Drug B*	
4				
5	T+		36	
6	T-		342	
7	Observations (for test)		27	
8	z Stat		-3.68	
9	P(Z<=z) one-tail		0.0001	
10	z Critical one-tail		1.6449	
11	P(Z<=z) two-tail		0.0002	
12	z Critical two-tail		1.96	

Note that the number of non-zero observations is less than 30, invalidating the use of z statistic. T = 36, rejection region: $T \leq 120$. There is enough evidence to conclude that drug B is more effective.

19.86 H_0 : The two population locations are the same

H_1 : The location of population 1 is to the right of the location of population 2

	A	B	C	D	E
1	**Wilcoxon Rank Sum Test**				
2					
3			Rank Sum	Observations	
4	*New Material*		2747	50	
5	*Old Material*		2303	50	
6	z Stat		1.53		
7	P(Z<=z) one-tail		0.063		
8	z Critical one-tail		1.6449		
9	P(Z<=z) two-tail		0.126		
10	z Critical two-tail		1.96		

z = 1.53, p-value = .0630. There is not enough evidence to conclude that the new material takes longer to burst into flames.

19.88 H_0 : The two population locations are the same

H_1 : The location of population 1 is different from the location of population 2

	A	B	C	D	E	F
1	**Sign Test**					
2						
3	Difference			*Commercial 1 - Commercial 2*		
4						
5	Positive Differences			15		
6	Negative Differences			21		
7	Zero Differences			24		
8	z Stat			-1.00		
9	P(Z<=z) one-tail			0.1587		
10	z Critical one-tail			1.6449		
11	P(Z<=z) two-tail			0.3174		
12	z Critical two-tail			1.96		

z = −1.00, p-value = .3174. There is not enough evidence to infer differences in believability between the two commercials.

19.90 H_0 : The two population locations are the same

H_1 : The location of population 1 is to the left of the location of population 2

	A	B	C	D	E
1	**Wilcoxon Rank Sum Test**				
2					
3			Rank Sum	Observations	
4	*This Year*		37525.5	200	
5	*10 Years Ago*		42674.5	200	
6	z Stat		-2.23		
7	P(Z<=z) one-tail		0.013		
8	z Critical one-tail		1.6449		
9	P(Z<=z) two-tail		0.026		
10	z Critical two-tail		1.96		

z = −2.23, p-value = .0130. There is enough evidence to infer that people perceive newspapers as doing a better job 10 years ago than today.

19.92 H_0 : The two population locations are the same

   H_1 : The location of population 1 is different from the location of population 2

	A	B	C	D	E
1	**Wilcoxon Rank Sum Test**				
2					
3			Rank Sum	Observations	
4	*Males*		10336.5	100	
5	*Females*		9763.5	100	
6	z Stat		0.70		
7	P(Z<=z) one-tail		0.24		
8	z Critical one-tail		1.6449		
9	P(Z<=z) two-tail		0.484		
10	z Critical two-tail		1.96		

z = .70, p-value = .4840. There is not enough evidence to conclude that businesswomen and business men differ in the number of business trips taken per year.

19.94 H_0 : The two population locations are the same

   H_1 : The location of population 1 is to the right of the location of population 2

	A	B	C	D	E
1	**Wilcoxon Rank Sum Test**				
2					
3			Rank Sum	Observations	
4	*2 Years Ago*		10786.5	100	
5	*ThisYear*		9313.5	100	
6	z Stat		1.80		
7	P(Z<=z) one-tail		0.036		
8	z Critical one-tail		1.6449		
9	P(Z<=z) two-tail		0.072		
10	z Critical two-tail		1.96		

z = 1.80, p-value = .0360. There is enough evidence to indicate that the citizens of Stratford should be concerned.

19.96   a. H_0 : The two population locations are the same

   H_1 : The location of population 1 is to the right of the location of population 2

	A	B	C	D	E	F	G
1	**Sign Test**						
2							
3	Difference			*Female Professor - Male Professor*			
4							
5	Positive Differences			45			
6	Negative Differences			7			
7	Zero Differences			48			
8	z Stat			5.27			
9	P(Z<=z) one-tail			0			
10	z Critical one-tail			1.6449			
11	P(Z<=z) two-tail			0			
12	z Critical two-tail			1.96			

$z = 5.27$, p-value = 0. There is enough evidence to infer that female students rate female professors higher than they rate male professors.

b. H_0 : The two population locations are the same

H_1 : The location of population 1 is to the left of the location of population 2

	A	B	C	D	E	F	G
1	**Sign Test**						
2							
3	Difference			*Female Professor - Male Professor*			
4							
5	Positive Differences			21			
6	Negative Differences			31			
7	Zero Differences			48			
8	z Stat			-1.39			
9	P(Z<=z) one-tail			0.0828			
10	z Critical one-tail			1.6449			
11	P(Z<=z) two-tail			0.1656			
12	z Critical two-tail			1.96			

$z = -1.39$, p-value = .0828. There is not enough evidence to infer that male students rate male professors higher than they rate female professors.

19.98 H_0 : The two population locations are the same

H_1 : The location of population 1 is to the right of the location of population 2

	A	B	C	D	E
1	**Wilcoxon Rank Sum Test**				
2					
3			Rank Sum	Observations	
4	*Telecommuters*		10934.5	100	
5	*Office*		9165.5	100	
6	z Stat		2.16		
7	P(Z<=z) one-tail		0.0153		
8	z Critical one-tail		1.6449		
9	P(Z<=z) two-tail		0.0306		
10	z Critical two-tail		1.96		

z = 2.16, p-value = .0153. There is enough evidence to conclude that telecommuters are more satisfied with their jobs.

19.100 H_0 : The two population locations are the same

H_1 : The location of population 1 is to the left of the location of population 2

	A	B	C	D	E
1	**Wilcoxon Rank Sum Test**				
2					
3			Rank Sum	Observations	
4	*3 Hours Before*		22553.5	180	
5	*Closing*		42426.5	180	
6	z Stat		-10.06		
7	P(Z<=z) one-tail		0		
8	z Critical one-tail		1.6449		
9	P(Z<=z) two-tail		0		
10	z Critical two-tail		1.96		

z = −10.06, p-value = 0. There is enough evidence to conclude that alcohol impairs judgment.

Appendix 19

A19.2   Spearman rank correlation coefficient test

H_0: $\rho_S = 0$

H_1: $\rho_S > 0$

$z = r_S \sqrt{n-1}$

	A	B	C	D
1	**Spearman Rank Correlation**			
2				
3	*Satisfaction and Time*			
4	Spearman Rank Correlation			0.541
5	z Stat			8.984
6	P(Z<=z) one tail			0
7	z Critical one tail			1.6449
8	P(Z<=z) two tail			0
9	z Critical two tail			1.96

$z = 8.98$; p-value = 0. There is enough evidence to infer that those who do more research are more satisfied with their choice.

A19.4   Histograms (not shown) are approximately bell shaped

Unequal-variances t-test of $\mu_1 - \mu_2$

$H_0 : (\mu_1 - \mu_2) = 0$

$H_1 : (\mu_1 - \mu_2) < 0$

$$t = \frac{(\bar{x}_1 - \bar{x}_2) - (\mu_1 - \mu_2)}{\sqrt{\left(\dfrac{s_1^2}{n_1} + \dfrac{s_2^2}{n_2}\right)}}$$

	A	B	C
1	t-Test: Two-Sample Assuming Unequal Variances		
2			
3		*British*	*American*
4	Mean	7137	9304
5	Variance	38051	110151
6	Observations	28	33
7	Hypothesized Mean Difference	0	
8	df	53	
9	t Stat	-31.61	
10	P(T<=t) one-tail	2.26E-36	
11	t Critical one-tail	1.6741	
12	P(T<=t) two-tail	4.51E-36	
13	t Critical two-tail	2.0057	

$t = -31.61$; p-value = 0. There is overwhelming evidence to conclude that the total distance of American golf courses is greater than that of British courses.

A19.6   t-test of ρ or β_1

$H_0 : \rho = 0$

$H_1 : \rho > 0$

$$t = r\sqrt{\frac{n-2}{1-r^2}}$$

	A	B
1	**Correlation**	
2		
3	*Visits and Income*	
4	Pearson Coefficient of Correlation	0.1747
5	t Stat	2.48
6	df	195
7	P(T<=t) one tail	0.0071
8	t Critical one tail	1.6527
9	P(T<=t) two tail	0.0142
10	t Critical two tail	1.9722

t = 2.48; p-value = .0071. There is enough evidence to infer that more affluent people shop more downtown than poorer people.

A19.8   All histograms (not shown) are somewhat bell shaped.

One-way analysis of variance

$H_0 : \mu_1 = \mu_2 = \mu_3$

H_1: At least two means differ

Miami-Dade

	A	B	C	D	E	F	G
10	ANOVA						
11	*Source of Variation*	*SS*	*df*	*MS*	*F*	*P-value*	*F crit*
12	Between Groups	6,409,467,776	2	3,204,733,888	231.37	1.1E-57	3.03
13	Within Groups	3,476,645,492	251	13,851,177			
14							
15	Total	9,886,113,268	253				

F = 231.37; p-value – 0. There is overwhelming evidence to infer that there are differences between the three groups of Americans residing in Miami-Dade.

Florida

	A	B	C	D	E	F	G
10	ANOVA						
11	*Source of Variation*	*SS*	*df*	*MS*	*F*	*P-value*	*F crit*
12	Between Groups	4,160,159,751	2	2,080,079,875	99.21	7.62E-34	3.03
13	Within Groups	6,331,923,528	302	20,966,634			
14							
15	Total	10,492,083,279	304				

F = 99.21; p-value – 0. There is overwhelming evidence to infer that there are differences between the three groups of Americans residing in the state of Florida.

United States

	A	B	C	D	E	F	G
10	ANOVA						
11	*Source of Variation*	*SS*	*df*	*MS*	*F*	*P-value*	*F crit*
12	Between Groups	5,742,495,149	2	2,871,247,574	110.48	9.27E-41	3.01
13	Within Groups	13,618,559,386	524	25,989,617			
14							
15	Total	19,361,054,535	526				

F = 110.48; p-value – 0. There is overwhelming evidence to infer that there are differences between the three groups of Americans residing in the United States.

A19.10 All three histograms (not shown) are bell shaped.

One-way analysis of variance

$H_0 : \mu_1 = \mu_2 = \mu_3$

H_1: At least two means differ

	A	B	C	D	E	F	G
10	ANOVA						
11	*Source of Variation*	*SS*	*df*	*MS*	*F*	*P-value*	*F crit*
12	Between Groups	1116.46	2	558.23	73.45	3.90E-29	3.01
13	Within Groups	4369.92	575	7.60			
14							
15	Total	5486.38	577				

F = 73.45; p-value = 0. There is overwhelming evidence to infer that there are differences in distance driven between cars, buses, and vans, pickups, and SUV's.

A19.12 Both histograms (not shown) are positively skewed but not sufficiently so to violate the normality requirement of the t-test of $\mu_1 - \mu_2$.

Equal-variances t-test of $\mu_1 - \mu_2$

$H_0: \mu_1 - \mu_2 = 0$

$H_1: \mu_1 - \mu_2 < 0$

$$t = \frac{(\bar{x}_1 - \bar{x}_2) - (\mu_1 - \mu_2)}{\sqrt{s_p^2 \left(\dfrac{1}{n_1} + \dfrac{1}{n_2} \right)}}$$

	A	B	C
1	t-Test: Two-Sample Assuming Equal Variances		
2			
3		*5 years ago*	*This year*
4	Mean	7.14	7.81
5	Variance	12.87	18.64
6	Observations	84	91
7	Pooled Variance	15.87	
8	Hypothesized Mean Difference	0	
9	df	173	
10	t Stat	-1.11	
11	P(T<=t) one-tail	0.1338	
12	t Critical one-tail	1.6537	
13	P(T<=t) two-tail	0.2677	
14	t Critical two-tail	1.9738	

t = − 1.11; p-value = .1338. There is not enough evidence to allow us to infer that investors' portfolios are becoming more diverse.

A19.14 Chi-squared test of a contingency table

H_0 : The two variables are independent

H_1 : The two variables are dependent

$$\chi^2 = \sum_{i=1}^{15} \frac{(f_i - e_i)^2}{e_i}$$

	A	B	C	D	E	F	G	H
1	**Contingency Table**							
2								
3		Group						
4	Side Effect		1	2	3	4	5	TOTAL
5		1	11	10	10	30	106	167
6		2	126	61	54	101	440	782
7		3	111	55	41	78	473	758
8		TOTAL	248	126	105	209	1019	1707
9								
10								
11		chi-squared Stat			20.6415			
12		df			8			
13		p-value			0.0082			
14		chi-squared Critical			15.5073			

$\chi^2 = 20.64$; p-value = .0082. There is not enough evidence to conclude that there are differences in side effects between the three groups.

A19.16 a.   t-test of μ

$H_0 : \mu = 0$

$H_1 : \mu > 0$

$$t = \frac{\bar{x} - \mu}{s / \sqrt{n}}$$

	A	B	C	D
1	**t-Test: Mean**			
2				
3				*Decrease*
4	Mean			24.73
5	Standard Deviation			17.92
6	Hypothesized Mean			0
7	df			222
8	t Stat			20.61
9	P(T<=t) one-tail			0
10	t Critical one-tail			1.6517
11	P(T<=t) two-tail			0
12	t Critical two-tail			1.9707

$t = 20.61$; p-value = 0. There is overwhelming evidence to infer that there is a decrease in metabolism when children watch television.

b. Both histograms (not shown) are roughly bell shaped.

Unequal-variances t-test of $\mu_1 - \mu_2$

$H_0 : (\mu_1 - \mu_2) = 0$

$H_1 : (\mu_1 - \mu_2) > 0$

$$t = \frac{(\overline{x}_1 - \overline{x}_2) - (\mu_1 - \mu_2)}{\sqrt{\left(\dfrac{s_1^2}{n_1} + \dfrac{s_2^2}{n_2}\right)}}$$

	A	B	C
1	t-Test: Two-Sample Assuming Unequal Variances		
2			
3		*Obese*	*Nonobese*
4	Mean	30.86	23.35
5	Variance	112.85	358.58
6	Observations	41	182
7	Hypothesized Mean Difference	0	
8	df	106	
9	t Stat	3.46	
10	P(T<=t) one-tail	0.0004	
11	t Critical one-tail	1.6594	
12	P(T<=t) two-tail	0.0008	
13	t Critical two-tail	1.9826	

t = 3.46; p-value = .0004. There is enough evidence to conclude that the decrease in metabolism is greater among obese children.

A19.18 a. Histograms (not shown) are bell shaped.

Equal-variances t-test of $\mu_1 - \mu_2$

$H_0 : (\mu_1 - \mu_2) = 0$

$H_1 : (\mu_1 - \mu_2) < 0$

$$t = \frac{(\overline{x}_1 - \overline{x}_2) - (\mu_1 - \mu_2)}{\sqrt{s_p^2 \left(\dfrac{1}{n_1} + \dfrac{1}{n_2}\right)}}$$

	A	B	C
1	t-Test: Two-Sample Assuming Equal Variances		
2			
3		4 or more	Less
4	Mean	6.00	7.40
5	Variance	5.62	8.61
6	Observations	100	100
7	Pooled Variance	7.11	
8	Hypothesized Mean Difference	0	
9	df	198	
10	t Stat	-3.71	
11	P(T<=t) one-tail	0.0001	
12	t Critical one-tail	1.6526	
13	P(T<=t) two-tail	0.0003	
14	t Critical two-tail	1.9720	

$t = -3.71$; p-value = .0001. There is enough evidence to infer that children who wash their hands four or more times per day have less sick days due to cold and flu.

b.   Histograms (not shown) are bell shaped.

Unequal-variances t-test of $\mu_1 - \mu_2$

$H_0 : (\mu_1 - \mu_2) = 0$

$H_1 : (\mu_1 - \mu_2) < 0$

$$t = \frac{(\bar{x}_1 - \bar{x}_2) - (\mu_1 - \mu_2)}{\sqrt{\left(\dfrac{s_1^2}{n_1} + \dfrac{s_2^2}{n_2}\right)}}$$

	A	B	C
1	t-Test: Two-Sample Assuming Unequal Variances		
2			
3		Four or more	Less
4	Mean	1.76	3.17
5	Variance	1.48	3.19
6	Observations	100	100
7	Hypothesized Mean Difference	0	
8	df	174	
9	t Stat	-6.52	
10	P(T<=t) one-tail	0.0000	
11	t Critical one-tail	1.6537	
12	P(T<=t) two-tail	0.0000	
13	t Critical two-tail	1.9737	

$t = -6.52$; p-value = 0. There is enough evidence to infer that children who wash their hands four or more times per day have less sick days due to stomach illness.

A19.20 a.　Histograms (not shown) of sick days are bell shaped.

Unequal-variances t-test of $\mu_1 - \mu_2$

$$H_0 : (\mu_1 - \mu_2) = 0$$

$$H_1 : (\mu_1 - \mu_2) < 0$$

$$t = \frac{(\bar{x}_1 - \bar{x}_2) - (\mu_1 - \mu_2)}{\sqrt{\left(\dfrac{s_1^2}{n_1} + \dfrac{s_2^2}{n_2}\right)}}$$

	A	B	C
1	t-Test: Two-Sample Assuming Unequal Variances		
2			
3		Days flu shot	Days placebo
4	Mean	2.82	3.22
5	Variance	1.25	2.07
6	Observations	150	150
7	Hypothesized Mean Difference	0	
8	df	281	
9	t Stat	-2.69	
10	P(T<=t) one-tail	0.0038	
11	t Critical one-tail	1.6503	
12	P(T<=t) two-tail	0.0076	
13	t Critical two-tail	1.9684	

$t = -2.69$; p-value $= .0038$. There is overwhelming evidence to indicate that the number of sick days is less for those who take the flu shots.

b.　Histograms of number of visits

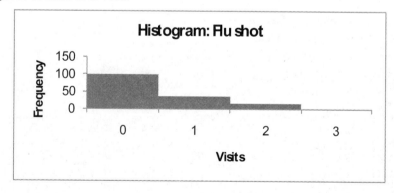

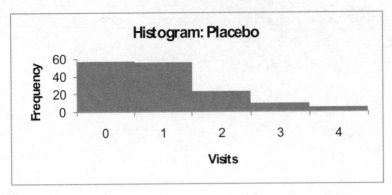

The number of visits is extremely nonnormal.

Wilcoxon rank sum test

H_0: The two population locations are the same

H_1: The location of population 1 is to the left of the location of population 2

	A	B	C	D
1	**Wilcoxon Rank Sum Test**			
2				
3			Rank Sum	Observations
4	*Visits flu shot*		19152	150
5	*Visits placebo*		25998	150
6	z Stat		-4.56	
7	P(Z<=z) one-tail		0	
8	z Critical one-tail		1.6449	
9	P(Z<=z) two-tail		0	
10	z Critical two-tail		1.9600	

z = –4.56; p-value = 0. There is overwhelming evidence to indicate that those who take the flu shots visit their doctors less frequently

A19.22 Chi-squared test of a contingency table

H_0 : The two variables are independent

H_1 : The two variables are dependent

$$\chi^2 = \sum_{i=1}^{6} \frac{(f_i - e_i)^2}{e_i}$$

	A	B	C	D	E
1	**Contingency Table**				
2					
3		*City*			
4	*Outcome*		1	2	TOTAL
5		1	503	201	704
6		2	536	215	751
7		3	308	83	391
8		TOTAL	1347	499	1846
9					
10					
11		chi-squared Stat			8.47
12		df			2
13		p-value			0.0145
14		chi-squared Critical			5.9915

$\chi^2 = 8.47$; p-value $= .0145$. There is enough evidence to conclude that there are differences in the death rate between the three cities. Recommendation: Spend less time at accident scene and get patient to the hospital as soon as possible.

A19.24 Chi-squared test of a contingency table

H_0 : The two variables are independent

H_1 : The two variables are dependent

$$\chi^2 = \sum_{i=1}^{6} \frac{(f_i - e_i)^2}{e_i}$$

	A	B	C	D	E
1	**Contingency Table**				
2					
3		*Income*			
4	*University?*		1	2	TOTAL
5		1	101	29	130
6		2	261	87	348
7		3	40	25	65
8		TOTAL	402	141	543
9					
10					
11		chi-squared Stat			6.35
12		df			2
13		p-value			0.0417
14		chi-squared Critical			5.9915

$\chi^2 = 6.35$; p-value $= .0417$. There is enough evidence to conclude that family income affects whether children attend university.

A19.26 Case 13.1: Wilcoxon rank sum test

H_0 : The two population locations are the same.

H_1 : The location of population 1 is to the right of the location of population 2.

	A	B	C	D
1	**Wilcoxon Rank Sum Test**			
2				
3			Rank Sum	Observations
4	W Rate		64365.5	101
5	M Rate		490565.5	952
6	z Stat		3.83	
7	P(Z<=z) one-tail		0.0001	
8	z Critical one-tail		1.6449	
9	P(Z<=z) two-tail		0.0002	
10	z Critical two-tail		1.9600	

$z = 3.83$, p-value $= .0001$. There is enough evidence to conclude that women pay higher rates of interest than men.

Case A16.1 Relationship between interest rates and sales: Spearman rank correlation coefficient test

$H_0 : \rho_S = 0$

$H_1 : \rho_S \neq 0$

$z = r_S \sqrt{n-1}$

	A	B	C	D
1	**Spearman Rank Correlation**			
2				
3	Rates and Sales			
4	Spearman Rank Correlation			-0.2629
5	z Stat			-8.53
6	P(Z<=z) one tail			0
7	z Critical one tail			1.6449
8	P(Z<=z) two tail			0
9	z Critical two tail			1.9600

$z = -8.53$, p-value $= 0$. There is overwhelming evidence to infer that interest rates and sales are linearly related.

Relationship between interest rates and ages: Spearman rank correlation coefficient test

$H_0 : \rho_S = 0$

$H_1 : \rho_S \neq 0$

$z = r_S \sqrt{n-2}$

	A	B	C	D
1	**Spearman Rank Correlation**			
2				
3	Rates and Age			
4	Spearman Rank Correlation			-0.1853
5	z Stat			-6.01
6	P(Z<=z) one tail			0
7	z Critical one tail			1.6449
8	P(Z<=z) two tail			0
9	z Critical two tail			1.9600

z = –6.01, p-value = 0. There is overwhelming evidence to infer that interest rates and age of business are linearly related.

Difference between sales: Wilcoxon rank sum test

H_0 : The two population locations are the same.

H_1 : The location of population 1 is to the left of the location of population 2.

	A	B	C	D
1	**Wilcoxon Rank Sum Test**			
2				
3			Rank Sum	Observations
4	*W Sales*		12285	101
5	*M Sales*		542646	952
6	z Stat		-14.09	
7	P(Z<=z) one-tail		0	
8	z Critical one-tail		1.6449	
9	P(Z<=z) two-tail		0	
10	z Critical two-tail		1.9600	

z = –14.09, p-value = 0. There is sufficient evidence to conclude that businesses owned by women have lower sales than businesses owned by men.

Difference between ages: Wilcoxon rank sum test

H_0 : The two population locations are the same.

H_1 : The location of population 1 is to the left of the location of population 2.

	A	B	C	D
1	**Wilcoxon Rank Sum Test**			
2				
3			Rank Sum	Observations
4	*W Age*		35034.5	101
5	*M Age*		519896.5	952
6	z Stat		-6.26	
7	P(Z<=z) one-tail		0	
8	z Critical one-tail		1.6449	
9	P(Z<=z) two-tail		0	
10	z Critical two-tail		1.9600	

z = –6.26, p-value = 0. There is sufficient evidence to conclude that businesses owned by men are older than businesses owned by women.

Interest rates among the 3 types of businesses: Kruskal Wallis test

H_0 : The locations of all 3 populations are the same

H_1 : At least two population locations differ

$$H = \left[\frac{12}{n(n+1)} \sum \frac{T_j^2}{n_j} \right] - 3(n+1)$$

	A	B	C
1	**Kruskal-Wallis Test**		
2			
3	Group	Rank Sum	Observations
4	*Bus 1*	111554	193
5	*Bus 2*	42305.5	86
6	*Bus 3*	401071.5	774
7			
8	H Stat		7.22
9	df		2
10	p-value		0.0270
11	chi-squared Critical		5.9915

H = 7.22, p-value = .0270. There is enough evidence to conclude that there are differences in interest rates among the three types of business.

Chapter 20

20.2

Time series	Moving average
48	
41	
37	(48 +41+37+32+36)/5 = 38.8
32	(41+37+32+36+31)/5 = 35.4
36	(37+32+36+31+43)/5 = 35.8
31	(32+36+31+43+52)/5 = 38.8
43	(36+31+43+52+60)/5 = 44.4
52	(31+43+52+60+48)/5 = 46.8
60	(43+52+60+48+41)/5 = 48.8
48	(52+60+48+41+30)/5 = 46.2
41	
30	

20.4

Time series	Moving average
16	
22	(16+22+19)/3 = 19.00
19	(22+19+24)/3 = 21.67
24	(19+24+30)/3 = 24.33
30	(24+30+26)/3 = 26.67
26	(30+26+24)/3 = 26.67
24	(26+24+29)/3 = 26.33
29	(24+29+21)/3 = 24.67
21	(29+21+23)/3 = 24.33
23	(21+23+19)/3 = 21.00
19	(23+19+15)/3 = 19.00
15	

20.6

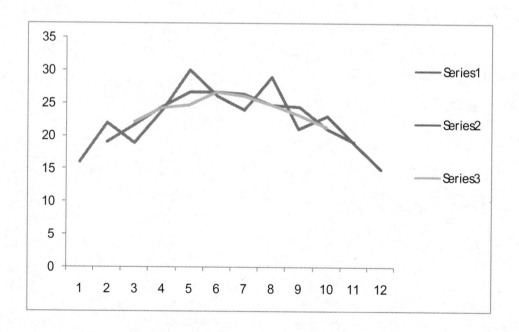

20.8   Time series   Exponentially smoothed time series
           12   12
           18   .8(18) +. 2(12) = 16.80
           16   .8(16) +. 2(16.80) = 16.16
           24   .8(24) +. 2(16.16) = 22.43
           17   .8(17) +. 2(22.43) = 18.09
           16   .8(16) +. 2(18.09) = 16.42
           25   .8(25) +. 2(16.42) = 23.28
           21   .8(21) +. 2(23.28) = 21.46
           23   .8(23) + .2(21.46) = 22.69
           14   .8(14) + .2(22.69) = 15.74

20.10   Time series   Exponentially smoothed time series
           38   38
           43   .1(43) +. 9(38) = 38.50
           42   .1(42) +. 9(38.50) = 38.85
           45   .1(45) +. 9(38.85) = 39.47
           46   .1(46) +. 9(39.47) = 40.12
           48   .1(48) +. 9(40.12) = 40.91
           50   .1(50) +. 9(40.91) = 41.82
           49   .1(49) +. 9(41.82) = 42.53
           46   .1(46) + .9(42.53) = 42.88
           45   .1(45) + .9(42.88) = 43.09

20.12

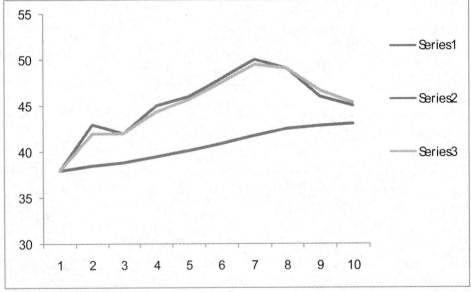

There is a trend component.

20.13 & 20.14

Sales	3-Day moving average	5-Day moving average
43		
45	(43+45+22)/3 = 36.67	
22	(45+22+25)/3 = 30.67	(43+45+22+25+31)/5 = 33.2
25	(22+25+31)/3 = 26.00	(45+22+25+31+51)/5 = 34.8
31	(25+31+51)/3 = 35.67	(22+25+31+51+41)/5 = 34.0
51	(31+51+41)/3 = 41.00	(25+31+51+41+37)/5 = 37.0
41	(51+41+37)/3 = 43.00	(31+51+41+37+22)/5 = 36.4
37	(41+37+22)/3 = 33.33	(51+41+37+22+25)/5 = 35.2
22	(37+22+25)/3 = 28.00	(41+37+22+25+40)/5 = 33.0
25	(22+25+40)/3 = 29.00	(37+22+25+40+57)/5 = 36.2
40	(25+40+57)/3 = 40.67	(22+25+40+57+30)/5 = 34.8
57	(40+57+30)/3 = 42.33	(25+40+57+30+33)/5 = 37.0
30	(57+30+33)/3 = 40.00	(40+57+30+33+37)/5 = 39.4
33	(30+33+37)/3 = 33.33	(57+30+33+37+64)/5 = 44.2
37	(33+37+64)/3 = 44.67	(30+33+37+64+58)/5 = 44.4
64	(37+64+58)/3 = 53.00	(33+37+64+58+33)/5 = 45.0
58	(64+58+33)/3 = 51.67	(37+64+58+33+38)/5 = 46.0
33	(58+33+38)/3 = 43.00	(64+58+33+38+25)/5 = 43.6
38	(33+38+25)/3 = 32.00	
25		

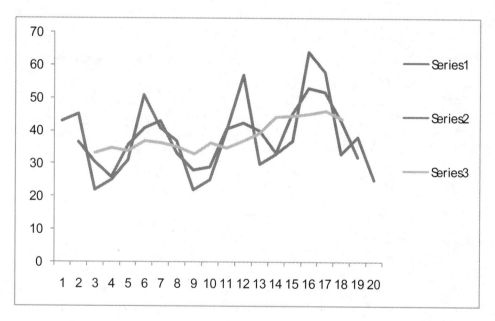

c.   There appears to be a seasonal (weekly) pattern.

329

20.16 & 20.17

Sales	Exponentially smoothed w = .4	Exponentially smoothed w = .8
18	18	18
22	.4(22)+.6(18) = 19.60	.8(22)+.2(18) = 21.20
27	.4(27)+.6(19.6) = 22.56	.8(27)+.2(21.2) = 25.84
31	.4(31)+.6(22.56) = 25.94	.8(31)+.2(25.84) = 29.97
33	.4(33)+.6(25.94) = 28.76	.8(33)+.2(29.97) = 32.39
20	.4(20)+.6(28.76) = 25.26	.8(20)+.2(32.39) = 22.48
38	.4(38)+.6(25.26) = 30.35	.8(38)+.2(22.48) = 34.90
26	.4(26)+.6(30.35) = 28.61	.8(26)+.2(34.90) = 27.78
25	.4(25)+.6(28.61) = 27.17	.8(25)+.2(27.78) = 25.56
36	.4(36)+.6(27.17) = 30.70	.8(36)+.2(25.56) = 33.91
44	.4(44)+.6(30.70) = 36.02	.8(44)+.2(33.91) = 41.98
29	.4(29)+.6(36.02) = 33.21	.8(29)+.2(41.98) = 31.60
41	.4(41)+.6(33.21) = 36.33	.8(41)+.2(31.60) = 39.12
33	.4(33)+.6(36.33) = 35.00	.8(33)+.2(39.12) = 34.22
52	.4(52)+.6(35.00) = 41.80	.8(52)+.2(34.22) = 48.44
45	.4(45)+.6(41.80) = 43.08	.8(45)+.2(48.44) = 45.69

20.16   b.

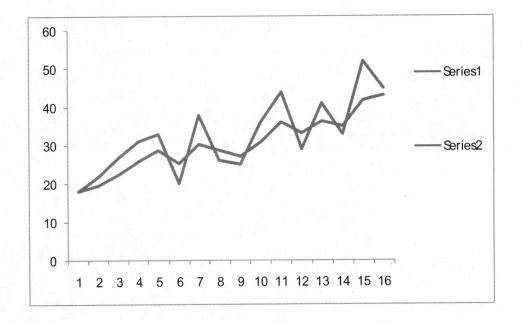

20.18

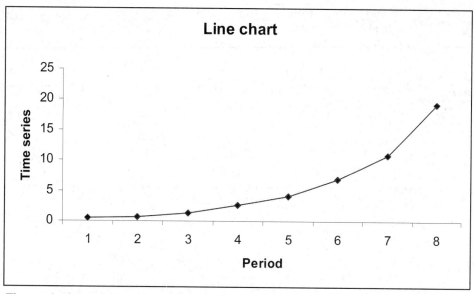

The quadratic model would appear to be the best model.

20.20

$\hat{y} = -4.96 + 2.38t$ $(R^2 = .81)$

$\hat{y} = 3.14 - 2.48t + .54t^2$ $(R^2 = .98)$

The quadratic trend line fits better.

20.22

Week	Day	Period t	y	$\hat{y}$	$y / \hat{y}$
1	1	1	12	17.2	0.699
	2	2	18	17.5	1.027
	3	3	16	17.9	0.894
	4	4	25	18.3	1.369
	5	5	31	18.6	1.664
2	1	6	11	19.0	0.579
	2	7	17	19.4	0.878
	3	8	19	19.7	0.963
	4	9	24	20.1	1.194
	5	10	27	20.5	1.320
3	1	11	14	20.8	0.672
	2	12	16	21.2	0.755
	3	13	16	21.6	0.742
	4	14	28	21.9	1.277
	5	15	25	22.3	1.122
4	1	16	17	22.7	0.750
	2	17	21	23.0	0.912
	3	18	20	23.4	0.855
	4	19	24	23.8	1.010
	5	20	32	24.1	1.327

Week	Day					Total
	Monday	Tuesday	Wednesday	Thursday	Friday	
1	.699	1.027	.894	1.369	1.664	
2	.579	.878	.963	1.194	1.320	
3	.672	.755	.742	1.277	1.122	
4	.750	.912	.855	1.010	1.327	
Average	.675	.893	.864	1.213	1.358	5.003
Seasonal Index	.675	.892	.864	1.212	1.357	5.000

20.24

Year	Quarter	Period t	y	$\hat{y}$	$y/\hat{y}$
2001	1	1	52	62.9	0.827
	2	2	67	64.1	1.045
	3	3	85	65.3	1.302
	4	4	54	66.5	0.812
2002	1	5	57	67.7	0.842
	2	6	75	68.8	1.090
	3	7	90	70.0	1.286
	4	8	61	71.2	0.857
2003	1	9	60	72.4	0.829
	2	10	77	73.6	1.046
	3	11	94	74.7	1.258
	4	12	63	75.9	0.830
2004	1	13	66	77.1	0.856
	2	14	82	78.3	1.047
	3	15	98	79.5	1.233
	4	16	67	80.6	0.831

Year	Quarter				Total
	1	2	3	4	
2001	.827	1.045	1.302	.812	
2002	.842	1.090	1.286	.857	
2003	.829	1.046	1.258	.830	
2004	.856	1.047	1.233	.831	
Average	.838	1.057	1.270	.833	3.998
Seasonal Index	.839	1.058	1.270	.833	4.000

20.26   a.

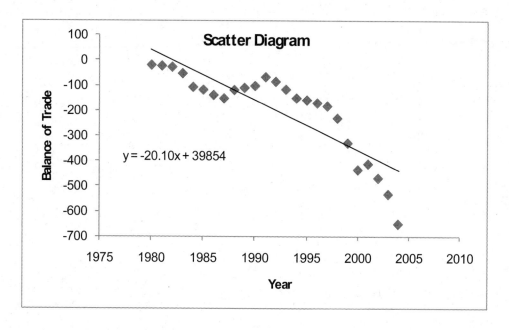

b. $\hat{y} = 39,854 - 20.10\text{Year}$

20.28   Regression line: $\hat{y} = 145 + 1.66\,t$

Week	Day	Period t	y	$\hat{y} = 145 + 1.66t$	$y / \hat{y}$
1	1	1	240	146.66	1.636
	2	2	85	148.32	0.573
	3	3	93	149.98	0.620
	4	4	106	151.64	0.699
	5	5	125	153.3	0.815
	6	6	188	154.96	1.213
	7	7	314	156.62	2.005
2	1	8	221	158.28	1.396
	2	9	80	159.94	0.500
	3	10	75	161.6	0.464
	4	11	121	163.26	0.741
	5	12	110	164.92	0.667
	6	13	202	166.58	1.213
	7	14	386	168.24	2.294
3	1	15	235	169.9	1.383
	2	16	86	171.56	0.501
	3	17	74	173.22	0.427
	4	18	100	174.88	0.572
	5	19	117	176.54	0.663
	6	20	205	178.2	1.150
	7	21	402	179.86	2.235
4	1	22	219	181.52	1.206
	2	23	91	183.18	0.497

333

3	24	102	184.84	0.552
4	25	89	186.5	0.477
5	26	105	188.16	0.558
6	27	192	189.82	1.011
7	28	377	191.48	1.969

				Day				
Week	Sunday	Monday	Tuesday	Wednesday	Thursday	Friday	Saturday	Total
1	1.636	.573	.620	.699	.815	1.213	2.005	
2	1.396	.500	.464	.741	.667	1.213	2.294	
3	1.383	.501	.427	.572	.663	1.150	2.235	
4	1.206	.497	.552	.477	.558	1.011	1.969	
Average	1.405	.518	.516	.657	.676	1.187	2.126	7.085
Seasonal Index	1.404	.517	.515	.621	.675	1.145	2.123	7.000

20.30

$$MAD = \frac{|166 - 173| + |179 - 186| + |195 - 192| + |214 - 211| + |220 - 223|}{5}$$

$$= \frac{7 + 7 + 3 + 3 + 3}{5} = \frac{23}{5} = 4.60$$

$$= (166 - 173)^2 + (179 - 186)^2 + (195 - 192)^2 + (214 - 211)^2 + (220 - 223)^2$$

$$= 49 + 49 + 9 + 9 + 9 = 125$$

20.32

$$MAD = \frac{|57 - 63| + |60 - 72| + |70 - 86| + |75 - 71| + |70 - 60|}{5}$$

$$= \frac{6 + 12 + 16 + 4 + 10}{5} = \frac{48}{5} = 9.6$$

$$SSE = (57 - 63)^2 + (60 - 72)^2 + (70 - 86)^2 + (75 - 71)^2 + (70 - 60)^2$$
$$= 36 + 144 + 256 + 16 + 100 = 552$$

20.34

Quarter	t	$\hat{y} = 150 + 3t$	SI	Forecast
1	41	273	.7	191.1
2	42	276	1.2	331.2
3	43	279	1.5	418.5
4	44	282	.6	169.2

20.36 $\hat{y}_t = 625 - 1.3_{y_{t-1}} = 625 - 1.3(65) = 540.5$

20.38 $F_{17} = F_{18} = F_{19} = F_{20} = S_{16} = 43.08$

334

20.40

Quarter	t	$\hat{y} = 47.7 - 1.06t$	SI	Forecast
1	21	25.44	1.207	30.71
2	22	24.38	.959	23.38
3	23	23.32	.972	22.67
4	24	22.26	.863	19.21

20.42 a. $\hat{y}_{2004} = 4{,}881 + .698y_{2003} = 4{,}881 + .698(16{,}638) = 16{,}494$

b. $F_{2004} = S_{2003} = 16{,}340$

20.44

Quarter	t	$\hat{y} = 143 + 7.42t$	SI	Forecast
1	25	328.50	1.063	349.20
2	26	335.92	.962	323.16
3	27	343.34	.927	318.28
4	28	350.76	1.048	367.60

20.46

Day	t	$\hat{y} = 90.4 + 2.02t$	SI	Forecast
1	17	124.74	1.094	136.47
2	18	126.76	0.958	121.44
3	19	128.78	0.688	88.60
4	20	130.80	1.260	164.81

20.48   There is a small upward trend and seasonality.

20.50

	A	B
1	**Seasonal Indexes**	
2		
3	**Season**	**Index**
4	1	0.646
5	2	1.045
6	3	1.405
7	4	0.904

Chapter 21

21.4   a.   Chance variation represents the variation in student achievement caused by differences in preparation, motivation, and ability.

b.   Special variation represents variation due to specific event or factors that can be corrected.

21.6 $ARL = \dfrac{1}{.0124} = 81$

21.8 $ARL = \dfrac{1}{.0456} = 22$

21.10   a.   From Beta-mean spreadsheet, $\beta = .6603$

b.   Probability $= .6603^8 = .0361$

21.12   Number of units = Production $\times$ ARL $= 50(385) = 19{,}250$

21.14 $P = 1 - \beta = 1 - .8133 = .1867$; $ARL = \dfrac{1}{P} = \dfrac{1}{.1867} = 5.36$

21.16   Number of units = Production $\times$ ARL $= 2000(385) = 770{,}000$

21.18 $P = 1 - \beta = 1 - .7388 = .2612$; $ARL = \dfrac{1}{P} = \dfrac{1}{.2612} = 3.83$

21.20   a.   From Beta-mean spreadsheet, $\beta = .3659$

b.   Probability $= .3659^4 = .0179$

21.22   Sampling 10 units per half hour means that on average we will produce 770,000 units before erroneously concluding that the process is out of control when it isn't. Sampling 20 units per hour doubles this figure. Sampling 10 units per half hour means that when the process goes out of control, the probability of not detecting a shift of .75 standard deviations is .7388 and we will produce on average $3.83 \times 2000 = 7660$ units until the chart indicates a problem. Sampling 20 units per hour decreases the probability of not detecting the shift to .3659 and decreases the average number of units produced when the process is out of control to $4000 \times 1.58 = 6320$.

21.24   Centerline = $\bar{\bar{x}}$ = 181.1

Lower control limit = $\bar{x} - \dfrac{3S}{\sqrt{n}} = 181.1 - 3\left(\dfrac{11.0}{\sqrt{9}}\right) = 170.1$

Upper control limit = $\bar{x} + \dfrac{3S}{\sqrt{n}} = 181.1 + 3\left(\dfrac{11.0}{\sqrt{9}}\right) = 192.1$

Zone boundaries: 170.10, 173.77, 177.44, 181.10, 184.77, 188.43, 192.10

21.26   a.   S Chart

	A	B	C	D
1	**Statistical Process Control**			
2				
3			*Data*	
4	Upper control limit		10.0885	
5	Centerline		4.452	
6	Lower control limit		0	

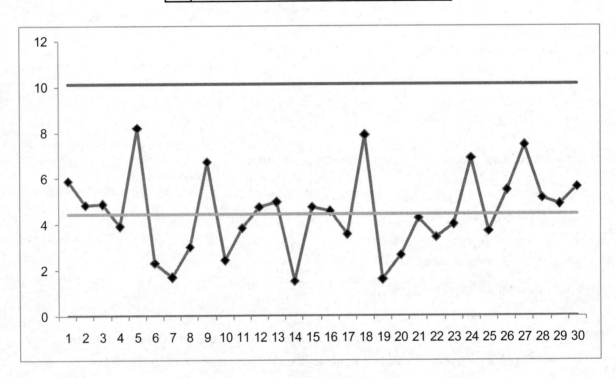

338

$\bar{x}$ Chart

	A	B	C	D
1	**Statistical Process Control**			
2				
3			*Data*	
4	Upper control limit		19.9668	
5	Centerline		12.7386	
6	Lower control limit		5.5103	
7	Pattern Test #2 Failed at Points: 29			
8	Pattern Test #6 Failed at Points: 29, 30			

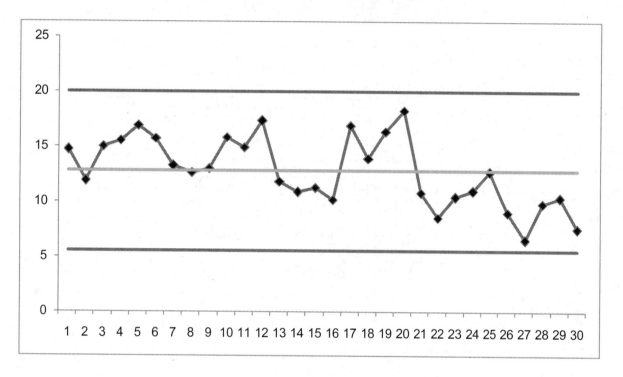

c.   The process is out of control at samples 29 and 30.

d.   A level shift occurred.

21.28

	A	B	C
1	**Statistical Process Control**		
2			
3			*AEU*
4	Upper control limit		0.0031
5	Centerline		0.0015
6	Lower control limit		0

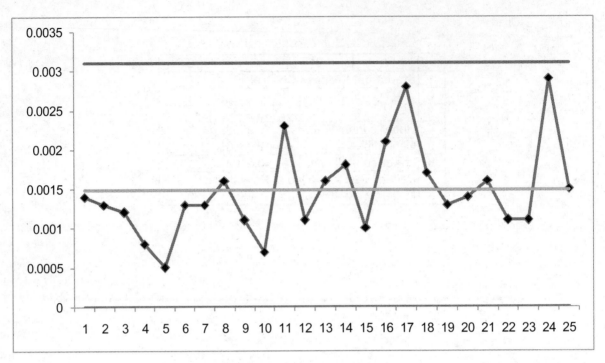

	A	B	C
1	**Statistical Process Control**		
2			
3			*AEU*
4	Upper control limit		0.4408
5	Centerline		0.4387
6	Lower control limit		0.4366

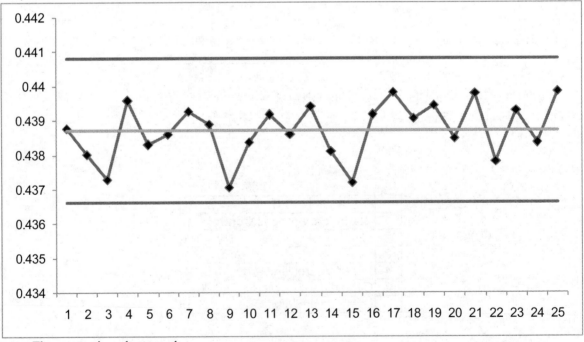

The process is under control.

21.30

	A	B	C
1	**Statistical Process Control**		
2			
3			*Volume*
4	Upper control limit		1.8995
5	Centerline		0.9093
6	Lower control limit		0

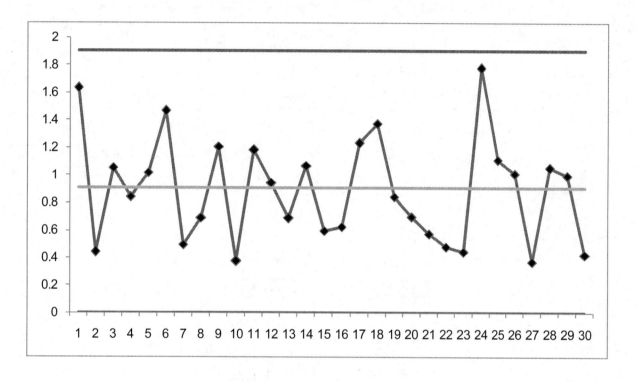

	A	B	C
1	**Statistical Process Control**		
2			
3			*Volume*
4	Upper control limit		1.3871
5	Centerline		0.092
6	Lower control limit		-1.2031

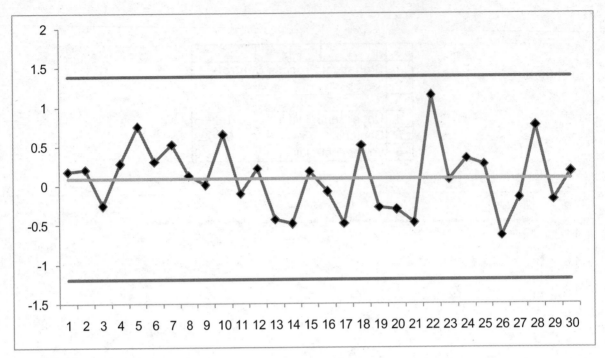

The process is under control.

21.32

	A	B	C
1	**Statistical Process Control**		
2			
3			*Headrest*
4	Upper control limit		2.3313
5	Centerline		0.9078
6	Lower control limit		0

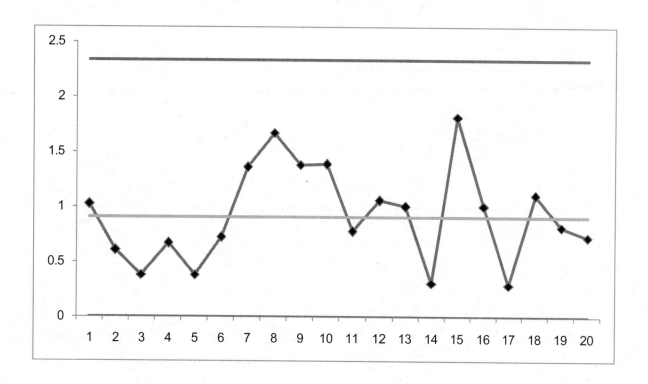

	A	B	C	D
1	**Statistical Process Control**			
2				
3			*Headrest*	
4	Upper control limit		241.3248	
5	Centerline		239.5617	
6	Lower control limit		237.7986	
7	Pattern Test #1 Failed at Points: 19, 20			
8	Pattern Test #5 Failed at Points: 20			

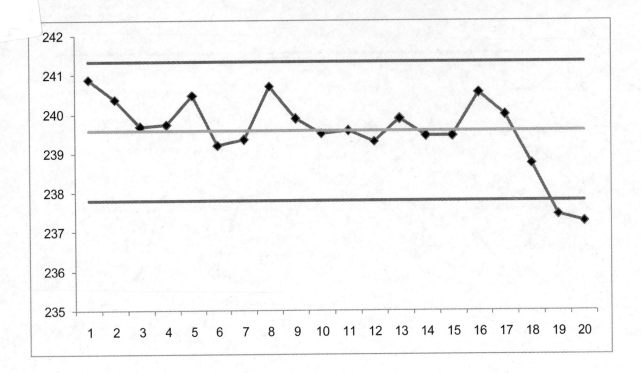

a. The process is out of control.

b. The process is out of control at sample 19.

c. The width became too small.

21.34

	A	B	C	D
1	**Statistical Process Control**			
2				
3			*Seats*	
4	Upper control limit		11.1809	
5	Centerline		5.3523	
6	Lower control limit		0	
7	Pattern Test #1 Failed at Points: 23, 24			

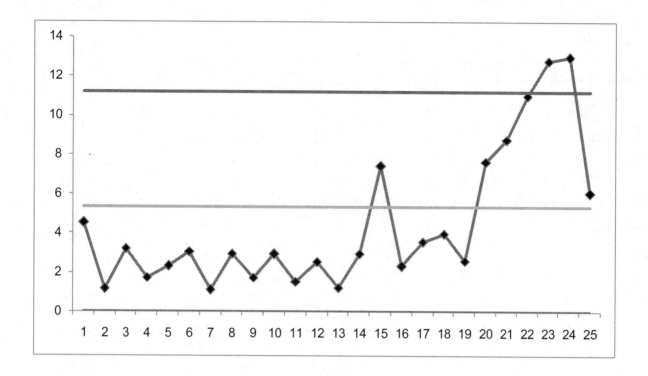

The process is out of control at sample 23. It is not necessary to draw the $\bar{x}$ chart.

21.36 $\quad \dfrac{S}{\sqrt{n}} = \dfrac{\text{Upper control limit} - \text{Centerline}}{3} = \dfrac{4.9873 - 4.9841}{3} = .00107$

$\dfrac{S}{\sqrt{4}} = .00107;\ S = .00214$

$CPL = \dfrac{\bar{\bar{x}} - LSL}{3S} = \dfrac{4.9841 - 4.978}{3(.00214)} = .95$

$CPU = \dfrac{USL - \bar{\bar{x}}}{3S} = \dfrac{4.990 - 4.9841}{3(.00214)} = .92$

$C_{pk} = Min(CPL, CPU) = .92$

21.38

	A	B	C
1	**Statistical Process Control**		
2			
3			*Bottles*
4	Upper control limit		69.6821
5	Centerline		33.3567
6	Lower control limit		0

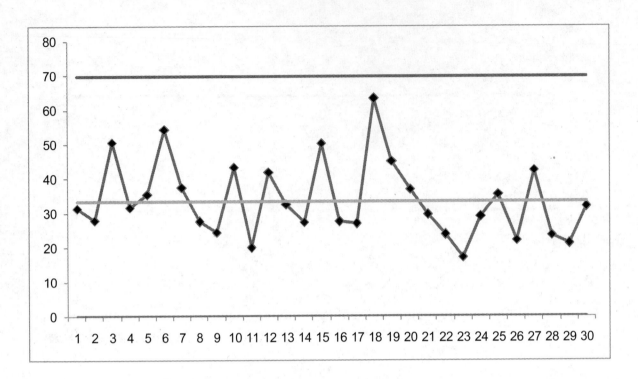

	A	B	C	D
1	**Statistical Process Control**			
2				
3			*Bottles*	
4	Upper control limit		803.9376	
5	Centerline		756.4267	
6	Lower control limit		708.9157	
7	Pattern Test #1 Failed at Points:		30	
8	Pattern Test #5 Failed at Points:		29, 30	
9	Pattern Test #6 Failed at Points:		30	

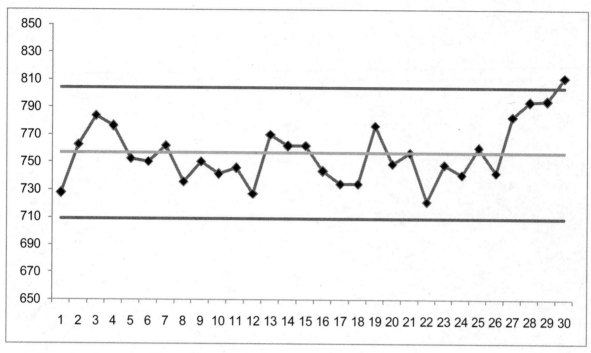

The process went out of control at sample 29.

21.40

	A	B	C
1	**Statistical Process Control**		
2			
3			*Pipes*
4	Upper control limit		0.0956
5	Centerline		0.0372
6	Lower control limit		0

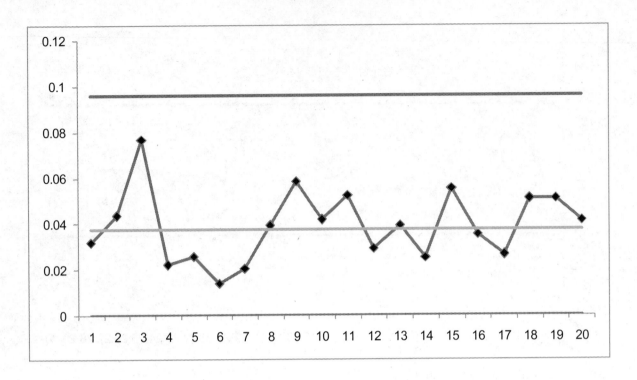

	A	B	C
1	**Statistical Process Control**		
2			
3			*Pipes*
4	Upper control limit		3.0615
5	Centerline		2.9892
6	Lower control limit		2.9168

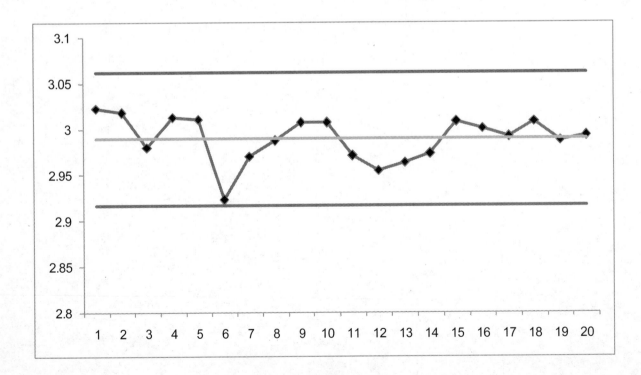

The process is under control.

21.42 $\dfrac{S}{\sqrt{n}} = \dfrac{\text{Upper control limit} - \text{Centerline}}{3} = \dfrac{1504.572 - 1496.952}{3} = 2.54$

$\dfrac{S}{\sqrt{5}} = 2.54;\ S = 5.68$

$CPL = \dfrac{\overline{\overline{x}} - LSL}{3S} = \dfrac{1496.952 - 1486}{3(5.68)} = .64$

$CPU = \dfrac{USL - \overline{\overline{x}}}{3S} = \dfrac{1506 - 1496.952}{3(5.68)} = .53$

$C_{pk} = Min(CPL, CPU) = .53$

The value of the index is low because the statistics used to calculate the control limits and centerline were taken when the process was out of control.

21.44 Centerline $= \overline{p} = .0324$

Lower control limit $= \overline{p} - 3\sqrt{\dfrac{\overline{p}(1-\overline{p})}{n}} = .0324 - 3\sqrt{\dfrac{(.0324)(1-.0324)}{200}} = -.00516\ (= 0)$

Upper control limit $= \overline{p} + 3\sqrt{\dfrac{\overline{p}(1-\overline{p})}{n}} = .0324 + 3\sqrt{\dfrac{(.0324)(1-.0324)}{200}} = .06996$

	A	B	C	D
1	**Statistical Process Control**			
2				
3			*Copiers*	
4	Upper control limit		0.07	
5	Centerline		0.0324	
6	Lower control limit		0	
7	Pattern Test #1 Failed at Points: 25			

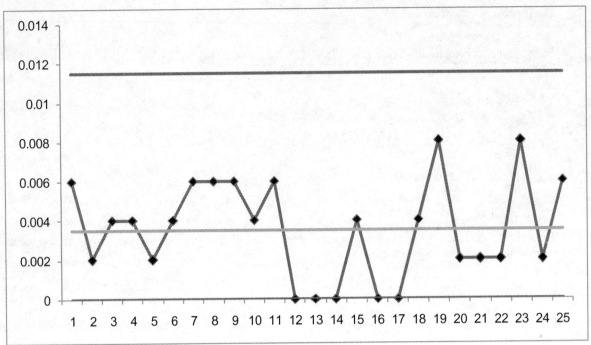

The process is out of control at sample 25.

21.46   Centerline = $\bar{p}$ = .0383

Lower control limit = $\bar{p} - 3\sqrt{\dfrac{\bar{p}(1-\bar{p})}{n}} = .0383 - 3\sqrt{\dfrac{(.0383)(1-.0383)}{100}} = -.0193 \; (= 0)$

Upper control limit = $\bar{p} + 3\sqrt{\dfrac{\bar{p}(1-\bar{p})}{n}} = .0383 + 3\sqrt{\dfrac{(.0383)(1-.0383)}{100}} = .0959$

	A	B	C	D
1	**Statistical Process Control**			
2				
3			*Telephones*	
4	Upper control limit		0.0959	
5	Centerline		0.0383	
6	Lower control limit		0	
7	Pattern Test #1 Failed at Points: 25, 30			
8				

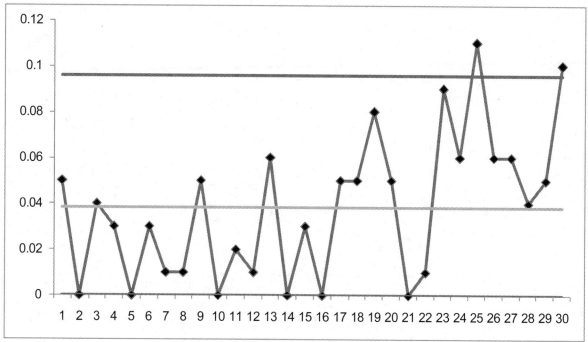

The process is out of control at samples 25 and 30.

21.48

	A	B	C	D	E
1	**Statistical Process Control**				
2					
3			*Batteries*		
4	Upper control limit		0.047		
5	Centerline		0.0257		
6	Lower control limit		0.0045		
7	Pattern Test #1 Failed at Points: 28, 29, 30				

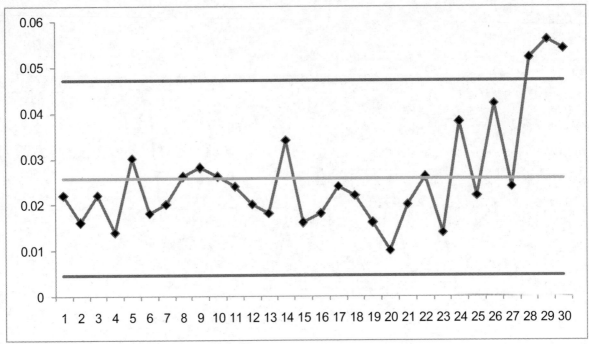

The process is out of control at sample 28.

21.50

	A	B	C	D
1	**Statistical Process Control**			
2				
3			*Scanners*	
4	Upper control limit		0.0275	
5	Centerline		0.0126	
6	Lower control limit		0	
7	Pattern Test #1 Failed at Points: 24			

352

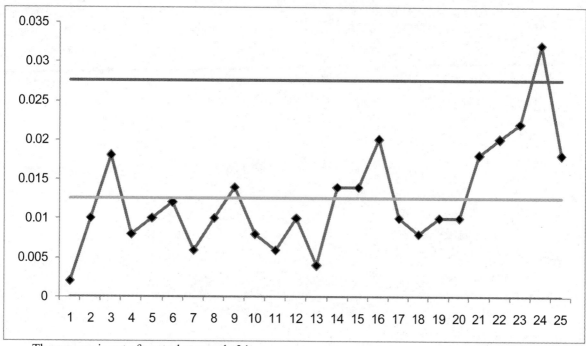

The process is out of control at sample 24.

Chapter 22

22.2

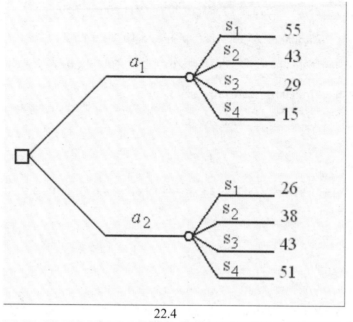

22.4

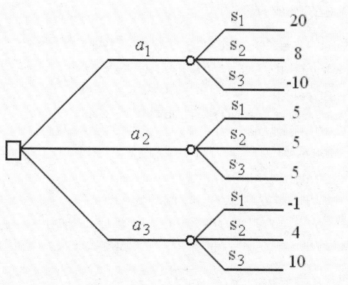

22.6 $EOL(a_1) = .2(0) + .6(0) + .2(20) = 4.0$

$EOL(a_2) = .2(15) + .6(3) + .2(5) = 5.8$

$EOL(a_3) = .2(21) + .6(4) + .2(0) = 6.6$

The EOL decision is a_1.

22.8   a. $EMV(a_0) = 0$

$EMV(a_1) = .25(-3.00) + .25(5.00) + .25(5.00) + .25(5.00) = 3.00$

$EMV(a_2) = .25(-6.00) + .25(2.00) + .25(10.00) + .25(10.00) = 4.00$

$EMV(a_3) = .25(-9.00) + .25(-1.00) + .25(7.00) + .25(15.00) = 3.00$

EMV decision is $\qquad a_2$ (bake 2 cakes)

b $\quad EOL(a_0) = .25(0) + .25(5.00) + .25(10.00) + .25(15.00) = 7.50$

$EOL(a_1) = .25(3.00) + .25(0) + .25(5.00) + .25(10.00) = 4.50$

$EOL(a_2) = .25(6.00) + .25(3.00) + .25(0) + .25(5.00) = 3.50$

$EOL(a_2) = .25(9.00) + .25(6.00) + .25(3.00) + .25(0) = 4.50$

EOL decision is $\qquad a_2$ (bake 2 cakes)

22.10 $\quad EMV(a_1) = -40,000$

$EMV(a_2) = .05(0) + .15(-18,000) + .30(-36,000) + .40(-54,000) + .10(-72,000) = -42,300$

EMV decision is a_1

22.12

$EMV(a_{100}) = 200$

$EMV(a_{200}) = .20(0) + .25(300) + .40(600) + .15(600) = 405$

$EMV(a_{300}) = .20(-150) + .25(150) + .40(450) + .15(750) = 300$

EMV decision is order 200 shirts.

22.14 a. $\quad$ EMV(Small) = .15(-220) + .55(-330) + .30(-440) = -346.5

EMV(Medium) = .15(-300) + .55(-320) + .30(-390) = -338.0

EMV(Large) = .15(-350) + .55(-350) + .30(-350) = -350.0

EMV decision: build a medium size plant; EMV*= -338.0

b $\quad$ Opportunity Loss Table

	Small	Medium	Large
Low	0	80	130
Moderate	10	0	30
High	90	40	0

c. $\quad$ EOL(Small) = .15(0) + .55(10) + .30(90) = 32.5

EOL(Medium) = .15(80) + .55(0) + .30(40) = 24.0

EOL(Large) = .15(130) + .55(30) + .30(0) = 36.0

EOL decision: build a medium size plant

22.16   Payoff Table
        Decision

        Produce   Don't produce

        Market share

        5%   -28 million   0

        10%   2 million   0

        15%   8 million   0

        EMV(produce) = .15(-28 million) + .45(2 million) + .40 (8 million) = -.1 million

        EMV (don't produce) = 0

        EMV decision: don't produce

22.18   Opportunity Loss Table

	a_1	a_2	a_3
s_1	50	0	35
s_2	110	40	0
s_3	0	100	135
s_4	0	130	120

$EOL(a_1) = .10(50) + .25(110) + .50(0) + .15(0) = 32.5$

$EOL(a_2) = .10(0) + .25(40) + .50(100) + .15(130) = 79.5$

$EOL(a_3) = .10(35) + .25(0) + .50(135) + .15(120) = 89$

$EOL* = 32.5$

22.20   a. $EPPI = .75(65) + .25(110) = 76.25$

             $EMV(a_1) = .75(65) + .25(70) = 66.25$

             $EMV(a_2) = .75(20) + .25(110) = 42.5$

             $EMV(a_3) = .75(45) + .25(80) = 53.75$

             $EMV(a_4) = .75(30) + .25(95) = 46.25$

             $EVPI = EPPI - EMV* = 76.25 - 66.25 = 10$

        b. $EPPI = .95(65) + .05(110) = 67.25$

             $EMV(a_1) = .95(65) + .05(70) = 65.25$

             $EMV(a_2) = .95(20) + .05(110) = 24.5$

             $EMV(a_3) = .95(45) + .05(80) = 46.75$

             $EMV(a_4) = .95(30) + .05(95) = 33.25$

             $EVPI = EPPI - EMV* = 67.25 - 65.25 = 2$

22.22   Posterior Probabilities for I_1

s_j	$P(s_j)$	$P(I_1|s_j)$	$P(s_j$ and $I_1)$	$P(s_j|I_1)$
s_1	.25	.40	$(.25)(.40) = .10$	$.12/.20 = .500$
s_2	.40	.25	$(.40)(.25) = .10$	$.10/.20 = .500$
s_3	.35	0	$(.35)(0) = .0$	$0/.20 = 0$

$$P(I_1) = .20$$

Posterior Probabilities for I_2

s_j	$P(s_j)$	$P(I_2|s_j)$	$P(s_j$ and $I_2)$	$P(s_j|I_2)$
s_1	.25	.30	$(.25)(.30) = .075$	$.075/.28 = .268$
s_2	.40	.25	$(.40)(.25) = .10$	$.10/.28 = .357$
s_3	.35	30	$(.35)(.30) = .105$	$.105/.28 = .375$

$$P(I_2) = .28$$

Posterior Probabilities for I_3

s_j	$P(s_j)$	$P(I_3|s_j)$	$P(s_j$ and $I_3)$	$P(s_j|I_3)$
s_1	.25	.20	$(.25)(.20) = .05$	$.05/.29 = .172$
s_2	.40	.25	$(.40)(.25) = .10$	$.10/.29 = .345$
s_3	.35	.40	$(.35)(.40) = .14$	$.14/.29 = .483$

$$P(I_3) = .29$$

Posterior Probabilities for I_4

s_j	$P(s_j)$	$P(I_4|s_j)$	$P(s_j$ and $I_4)$	$P(s_j|I_4)$
s_1	.25	.10	$(.25)(.10) = .025$	$.025/.23 = .109$
s_2	.40	.25	$(.40)(.25) = .10$	$.10/.23 = .435$
s_3	.35	.30	$(.35)(.30) = .105$	$.105/.23 = .456$

$$P(I_4) = .23$$

22.24   a.   Prior probabilities: $EMV(a_1) = .5(10) + .5(22) = 16$

$EMV(a_2) = .5(18) + .5(19) = 18.5$

$EMV(a_3) = .5(23) + .5(15) = 19$

$EMV^* = 19$

I_1: $EMV(a_1) = .951(10) + .049(22) = 10.588$

$EMV(a_2) = .951(18) + .049(19) = 18.049$

$EMV(a_3) = .951(23) + .049(15) = 22.608$

Optimal act: a_3

I_2 : $EMV(a_1) = .021(10) + .979(22) = 21.748$

$EMV(a_2) = .021(18) + .979(19) = 18.979$

$EMV(a_3) = .021(23) + .979(15) = 15.168$

Optimal act: a_1

b. $EMV` = .515(22.608) + .485(21.748) = 22.191$

$EVSI = EMV` - EMV* = 22.191 - 19 = 3.191$

22.26   Prior probabilities: $EMV(a_1) = .5(60) + .4(90) + .1(150) = 81$
$EMV(a_2) = 90$
$EMV* = 90$

Posterior Probabilities for I_1

s_j	$P(s_j)$	$P(I_1 \mid s_j)$	$P(s_j \text{ and } I_1)$	$P(s_j \mid I_1)$
s_1	.5	.7	$(.5)(.7) = .35$	$.35/.57 = .614$
s_2	.4	.5	$(.4)(.5) = .20$	$.20/.57 = .351$
s_3	.1	.2	$(.1)(.2) = .02$	$.02/.57 = .035$
			$P(I_1) = .57$	

Posterior Probabilities for I_2

s_j	$P(s_j)$	$P(I_2 \mid s_j)$	$P(s_j \text{ and } I_2)$	$P(s_j \mid I_2)$
s_1	.5	.3	$(.5)(.3) = .15$	$.15/.43 = .349$
s_2	.4	.5	$(.4)(.5) = .20$	$.20/.43 = .465$
s_3	.1	.8	$(.1)(.8) = .08$	$.08/.43 = .186$
			$P(I_1) = .43$	

I_1 : $EMV(a_1) = .614(60) + .351(90) + .035(150) = 73.68$

$EMV(a_2) = 90$

I_1 : $EMV(a_1) = .349(60) + .465(90) + .186(150) = 90.69$
$EMV(a_2) = 90$
$EMV` = .57(90) + .43(90.69) = 90.30$
$EVSI = EMV` - EMV* = 90.30 - 90 = .30$

22.28   As the prior probabilities become more diverse EVSI decreases.

22.30 $EMV* = 0$
$EPPI = .15(0) + .45(2 \text{ million}) + .40(8 \text{ million}) = 4.1 \text{ million}$
$EVPI = EPPI - EMV* = 4.1 \text{ million} - 0 = 4.1 \text{ million}$

22.32   a   Payoff Table
          Market share   Switch   Don't switch
          5%   5(100,000) – 700,000 = -200,000   285,000
          10%   10(100,000) – 700,000 = 300,000   285,000
          20%   20(100,000)-700,000 = 1,300,000   285,000

   b.   EMV(switch) = .4(-200,000) + .4(300,000) + .2(1,300,000) = 300,000
        EMV(don't switch) = 285,000
        Optimal act: switch (EMV* = 300,000)

   c.   EPPI = .4(285,000) + .4(300,000) + .2(1,300,000) = 494,000
        EVPI = EPPI – EMV* = 494,000 – 300,000= 194,000

22.34   Likelihood probabilities (binomial probabilities)
        $P(I \mid s_1) = P(x = 12, n= 100 \mid p = .05) = .0028$
        $P(I \mid s_2) = P(x = 12, n= 100 \mid p = .10) = .0988$
        $P(I \mid s_3) = P(x = 12, n= 100 \mid p = .20) = .0128$
        $P(I \mid s_4) = P(x = 12, n= 100 \mid p = .30) = .000013$

Posterior Probabilities

s_j	$P(s_j)$	$P(I \mid s_j)$	$P(s_j \text{ and } I)$	$P(s_j \mid I)$
s_1	.5	.0028	(.5)(.0028) = .0014	.0014/.0323 = .0433
s_2	.3	.0988	(.3)(.0988) = .0296	.0296/.0323 = .9164
s_3	.1	.0128	(.1)(.0128) = .0013	.0013/.0323 = .0402
s_4	.1	.000013	(.1)(.000013) = .000001	.000001/.0323 = .000031
			P(I) = .0323	

EMV(proceed) = .0433(-30,000) + .9164(-5,000) + .0402(45,000) + .000031(95,000) = -4,069
EMV (don't proceed = 0
EMV decision: don't proceed

22.36

I_0 = neither person supports format change

I_1 = one person supports format change

I_2 = both people support format change

Likelihood probabilities $P(I_i \mid s_j)$

	I_0	I_1	I_2
5%	.9025	.0950	.0025
10%	.81	.18	.01
20%	.64	.32	.04

Posterior Probabilities for I_0

s_j	$P(s_j)$	$P(I_0|s_j)$	$P(s_j$ and $I_0)$	$P(s_j|I_0)$
s_1	.4	.9025	$(.4)(.9025) = .361$	$.361/.813 = .444$
s_2	.4	.81	$(.4)(.81) = .324$	$.324/.813 = .399$
s_3	.2	.64	$(.2)(.64) = .128$	$.128/.813 = .157$

$$P(I_0) = .813$$

Posterior Probabilities for I_1

s_j	$P(s_j)$	$P(I_1|s_j)$	$P(s_j$ and $I_1)$	$P(s_j|I_1)$
s_1	.4	.0950	$(.4)(.0950) = .038$	$.038/.174 = .218$
s_2	.4	.18	$(.4)(.18) = .072$	$.072/.174 = .414$
s_3	.2	.32	$(.2)(.32) = .064$	$.064/.174 = .368$

$$P(I_1) = .174$$

Posterior Probabilities for I_3

s_j	$P(s_j)$	$P(I_2|s_j)$	$P(s_j$ and $I_2)$	$P(s_j|I_2)$
s_1	.4	.0025	$(.4)(.0025) = .001$	$.001/.013 = .077$
s_2	.4	.01	$(.4)(.01) = .004$	$.004/.013 = .308$
s_3	.2	.04	$(.2)(.04) = .008$	$.008/.013 = .615$

$$P(I_2) = .013$$

I_1: EMV(switch) = .444(-200,000) + .399(300,000) + .157(1,300,000) = 235,000
EMV(don't switch) = 285,000
Optimal act: don't switch
I_2: EMV(switch) = .218(-200,000) + .414(300,000) + .368(1,300,000) = 559,000
EMV(don't switch) = 285,000
Optimal act: switch
I_3: EMV(switch) = .077(-200,000) + .308(300,000) + .615(1,300,000) = 876,500
EMV(don't switch) = 285,000
Optimal act: switch
EMV` = .813(285,000) + .174(546,000) + .013(876,500) = 338,104
EVSI = EMV` - EMV* = 338,104 – 300,000 = 38,104

22.38   a.   Payoff Table

Demand	Battery 1	Battery 2	Battery 3
50,000	20(50,000)-900,000 = 100,000	23(50,000)-1,150,000 0	25(50,000)-1,400,000 -150,000
100,000	20(100,000)-900,000 =1,100,000	23(100,000)-1,150,000 1,150,000	25(100,000)-1,400,000 1,100,000
150,000	20(150,000)-900,000 =2,100,000	23(150,000)-1,150,000 2,300,000	25(150,000)-1,400,000 2,350,000

b.   Opportunity Loss table

Demand	Battery 1	Battery 2	Batter3
50,000	0	100,000	250,000
100,000	50,000	0	50,000
150,000	250,000	50,000	9

c.   EMV(Battery 1) = .3(100,000) + .3(1,100,000) + .4(2,100,000) = 1,200,000

EMV(Battery 2) = .3(0) + .3(1,150,000) + .4(2,300,000) = 1,265,000

EMV(Battery 3) = .3(-150,000) + .3(1,100,000) + .4(2,350,000) = 1,225,000

EMV decision: Battery 2

d.   EOL(Battery 2) = .3(100,000) + .3(0) + .4(50,000) = 50,000

EVP = EOL* = 50,000

22.40

I_0 = person does not believe the ad

I_1 = person believes the ad

Likelihood probabilities $P(I_i \mid s_j)$

	I_0	I_1
30%	.70	.30
31%	.69	.31
32%	.68	.32
33%	.67	.33
34%	.66	.34

Posterior Probabilities for I_0

s_j	$P(s_j)$	$P(I_0|s_j)$	$P(s_j \text{ and } I_0)$	$P(s_j|I_0)$
s_1	.1	.70	$(.1)(.70) = .070$	$.070/.674 = .104$
s_2	.1	.69	$(.1)(.69) = .069$	$.069/.674 = .102$
s_3	.2	.68	$(.2)(.68) = .136$	$.136/.674 = .202$
s_4	.3	.67	$(.3)(.67) = .201$	$.201/.674 = .298$
s_5	.3	.66	$\underline{(.3)(.66) = .198}$	$.198/.674 = .294$

$$P(I_0) = .674$$

Posterior Probabilities for I_1

s_j	$P(s_j)$	$P(I_1|s_j)$	$P(s_j \text{ and } I_1)$	$P(s_j|I_1)$
s_1	.1	.30	$(.1)(.30) = .030$	$.030/.326 = .092$
s_2	.1	.31	$(.1)(.31) = .031$	$.031/.326 = .095$
s_3	.2	.32	$(.2)(.32) = .064$	$.064/.326 = .196$
s_4	.3	.33	$(.3)(.33) = .099$	$.099/.326 = .304$
s_5	.3	.34	$\underline{(.3)(.34) = .102}$	$.102/.326 = .313$

$$P(I_1) = .326$$

I_0: EMV(Change ad) = .104(-258,000) + .102(-158,000) + .202(-58,000) + .298(42,000) + .294(142,000) = -400
EMV (don't change) = 0.
Optimal decision: don't change ad

I_1: EMV(Change ad) = .092(-258,000) + .095(-158,000) + .196(-58,000) + .304(42,000) + .313(142,000) = 7,100
EMV (don't change) = 0.
Optimal decision: change ad

EMV` = .674(0) + .326(7,100) = 2,315
EVSI = EMV` - EMV* = 2,315 – 2,000 = 315

22.42

EMV(25 telephones) = 50,000
EMV(50 telephones) = .50(30,000) + .25(60,000) + .25(60,000) = 45,000
EMV(100 telephones) = .50(20,000) + .25(40,000) + .25(80,000) = 40,000
Optimal decision: 25 telephones (EMV* = 50,000)
I_1 = small number of calls

I_2 = medium number of calls

I_3 = large number of calls

Likelihood probabilities (Poisson distribution)

	I_1	I_2	I_3
$\mu = 5$	$P(X < 8 \mid \mu = 5)$	$P(8 \leq X < 17 \mid \mu = 5)$	$P(X \geq 17 \mid \mu = 5)$
	$= .8667$	$= .1334$	$= 0$
$\mu = 10$	$P(X < 8 \mid \mu = 10)$	$P(8 \leq X < 17 \mid \mu = 10)$	$P(X \geq 17 \mid \mu = 10)$
	$= .2202$	$= .7527$	$= .0270$
$\mu = 15$	$P(X < 8 \mid \mu = 15)$	$P(8 \leq X < 17 \mid \mu = 15)$	$P(X \geq 17 \mid \mu = 15)$
	$= .0180$	$= .6461$	$= .3359$

Posterior Probabilities for I_1

s_j	$P(s_j)$	$P(I_1 \mid s_j)$	$P(s_j \text{ and } I_1)$	$P(s_j \mid I_1)$
s_1	.50	.8667	$(.50)(.8667) = .4333$	$.4333/.4929 = .8792$
s_2	.25	.2202	$(.25)(.2202) = .0551$	$.0551/.4929 = .1117$
s_3	.25	.0180	$(.25)(.0180) = .0045$	$.0045/.4929 = .0091$
			$P(I_1) = .4929$	

Posterior Probabilities for I_2

s_j	$P(s_j)$	$P(I_2 \mid s_j)$	$P(s_j \text{ and } I_2)$	$P(s_j \mid I_2)$
s_1	.50	.1334	$(.50)(.1334) = .0667$	$.0667/.4164 = .1601$
s_2	.25	.7527	$(.25)(.7527) = .1882$	$.1882/.4164 = .4519$
s_3	.25	.6461	$(.25)(.6461) = .1615$	$.1615/.4164 = .3879$
			$P(I_2) = .4164$	

Posterior Probabilities for I_3

s_j	$P(s_j)$	$P(I_3 \mid s_j)$	$P(s_j \text{ and } I_3)$	$P(s_j \mid I_3)$
s_1	.50	.0	$(.50)(0) = 0$	$0/.0907 = 0$
s_2	.25	.0270	$(.25)(.0270) = .0068$	$.0068/.0907 = .0745$
s_3	.25	.3359	$(.25)(.3359) = .0840$	$.0840/.0907 = .9254$
			$P(I_3) = .0907$	

I_1: EMV(25 telephones) = 50,000
EMV(50 telephones) = .8792(30,000) + .1117(60,000) + .0091(60,000) = 33,624
EMV(100 telephones) = .8792(20,000) + .1117(40,000) + .0091(80,000) = 22,780
Optimal act: 25 telephones

I_2: EMV(25 telephones) = 50,000

EMV(50 telephones) = .1601(30,000) + .4519(60,000) + .3879(60,000) = 55,191
EMV(100 telephones) = .1601(20,000) + .4519(40,000) + .38791(80,000) = 52,310
Optimal act: 50 telephones

I_3: EMV(25 telephones) = 50,000

EMV(50 telephones) = 0(30,000) + .0745(60,000) + .9254(60,000) = 60,000
EMV(100 telephones) = 0(20,000) + .0745(40,000) + .9254(80,000) = 77,012
Optimal act: 100 telephones
EMV` = .4929(50,000) + .4164(55,191) + .0907(77,012) = 54,612
EVSI = EMV` - EMV* = 54,612 – 50,000 = 4,612

Because the value is greater than the cost ($4,000) Max should not sample. If he sees a small number of calls install 25 telephones. If there is a medium number install 50 telephones. If there is a large number of calls, install 100 telephones.

22.44   EMV(Release in North America) = .5(33 million) + .3(12 million) + .2(-15 million) = 17.1 million
EMV(European distributor) = 12 million
Optimal decision: Release in North America

Posterior Probabilities for I_1 (Rave review)

s_j	$P(s_j)$	$P(I_1\|s_j)$	$P(s_j$ and $I_1)$	$P(s_j\|I_1)$
s_1	.5	.8	(.5)(.8) = .40	.40/.63 = .635
s_2	.3	.5	(.3)(.5) = .15	.15/.63 = .238
s_3	.2	.4	(.2)(.4) = .08	.08/.63 = .127
			$P(I_1) = .63$	

EMV(Release in North America) = .635(33 million) + .238(12 million) + .127(-15 million) =21.9 million
EMV(European distributor) = 12 million
Optimal decision: Release in North America

Posterior Probabilities for I_2 (lukewarm response)

s_j	$P(s_j)$	$P(I_2\|s_j)$	$P(s_j$ and $I_2)$	$P(s_j\|I_2)$
s_1	.5	.1	(.5)(.1) = .05	.05/.20 = .25
s_2	.3	.3	(.3)(.3) = .09	.09/.20 = .45
s_3	.2	.3	(.2)(.3) = .06	.06/.20 = .30
			$P(I_2) = .20$	

EMV(Release in North America) = .25(33 million) + .45(12 million) + .30(-15 million) = 9.2 million
EMV(European distributor) = 12 million
Optimal decision: Sell to European distributor

Posterior Probabilities for I_3 (poor response)

s_j	$P(s_j)$	$P(I_3|s_j)$	$P(s_j$ and $I_3)$	$P(s_j|I_3)$
s_1	.5	.1	$(.5)(.1) = .05$	$.05/.17 = .294$
s_2	.3	.2	$(.3)(.2) = .06$	$.06/.17 = .353$
s_3	.2	.3	$\underline{(.2)(.3) = .06}$	$.06/.17 = .353$
			$(I_3) = .17$	

EMV(Release in North America) = .294(33 million) + .353(12 million) + .353(-15 million) = 8.6 million
EMV(European distributor) = 12 million
Optimal decision: Sell to European distributor.
EMV` = .63(21.9 million) + .20(12 million) + .17(12 million) = 18.2 million
EVSI = EMV` - EMV* = 18.2 million – 17.1 million = 1.1 million

Because EVSI is greater than the sampling cost (100,000) the studio executives should show the movie to a random sample of North Americans. If the response is a rave review release the movie in North America. If not sell it to Europe.